FOR MY G.P.
DR ROB MCKENZIE
WITH THANKS
FOR ALL THE FREE
SERVICES

5TH JULY 2018

# Lamplighter most gracious ...

**Collected Poems & Selected Prose, 1972 - 2018**
excluding all poetry and prose in **This Eternal Hubbub**
2nd Edition : May 2011 / 2nd rev printing : Aug 2015
3rd expanded hardcover edition : 1st printing — June 2018

**by Joe M. Ruggier**
with an author's preface
with an introduction by Andrew Parkin
with other write-ups by Paul Matthew St. Pierre,
LeRoy Douglas Travis, Oliver Friggieri,
George Csaba Koller, Ron Johnson,
Michael R. Burch, Mary Rae,
Esther Cameron, Candice James,
Virginia Tobin, Philip Higson, and Tim Lander
cover photo by Joe Ruggier

**MULTICULTURAL BOOKS (of BC)**

*"There are many Mansions in Parnassus!"*

**MULTICULTURAL BOOKS**
Unit 114 Azure Estates, 6051 Azure Road, Richmond, BC, V7C 2P6
**Cell:** +604 600-8819 **email:** jrmbooks@hotmail.com
www.mbooksofbc.com

Special thanks are owing to Andrew Parkin for contributing a substantial introduction. 

**MBOOKS POETRY SERIES #28**
1st edition: June 2009 [revised printings: July 2009 / June 2010]
ISBN to the 1st edition 978-1-897303-07-8

2nd edition: May 2011 [2nd revised printing August 2015]
ISBN to the 2nd edition 978-1-897303-14-6

3rd edition: June 2018 [expanded]
ISBN to the current 3rd edition 978-1-897303-26-9

All editions printed and bound by: **Lightning Source Inc., USA**
desk-top publishing: Joe M. Ruggier

## dedication

to the shining memory
of Thomas Stearns Eliot,
beloved Master and spiritual Director

to the compassion and exemplary courtesy
of my Canadian public, in particular of my patron …
the stupendous poet Ralph Cunningham

and to the sacred memory
of my dearest mother, Marie Ruggier
née Micallef, 1925/02/07 – 2008/04/29

## Saint Mary Christian

*an elegy for my mother, Marie Ruggier*
*7th February 1925 – 29th April 2008*

**SAINT** Mary Christian made her family one prophecy only:
*"You will seek me and will not find me!"* And was wont
to say: *"the Heart forecasts and foretells upon intuition!"*

I was hungry. My Mother gave me to eat.
I was thirsty. My Mother gave me to drink.
I was naked. My Mother clothed me.
I was bedridden. Mother watched and prayed beside me.

All in all a simple soul, Mother was
most capable, and most clever at what she did well.
She was everywhere, she did everything:
the heartbeat of our family. Every day
she cooked three meals from scratch, proof of her love,
for father and all seven of us: her cooking was,
in its own right, a unique, genuine cuisine —
the proudest thing in her devoted life.
She did the laundry, washed dishes, knitted wool,
(and scarves with the colors of our favorite soccer club),
sewed our clothes, helped us all, with father, with our
schoolwork,
and often read my writings. We took her quite for granted,
but
we loved her all—except when she yelled, and then
we would all hate her for what she elegantly described
as "behooving sin"!
Her frugality was a work
of exquisite art: nothing was wasted,
all scraps of food consumed, and the leftovers
went to the birds … With father, she economized
fractions of cents, supporting all seven of us
on pennies—not a lifestyle
that I could ever grow accustomed to;
but excellent for publishing poetry …

Feminists will look askance at her lifestyle, arguing that
the quality of her life could have been better: one ignores
a movement such as Feminism at one's own peril;

but Mum and Dad would say that Love
is the only quality of life there is; and Salvation
the only sincere honour!
Though she cared for the Arts,
Mother did not know better: to adjust her vision
to feminist viewpoints called for a contradiction
to everything she knew, everything she learnt,
and was conditioned to be, since early childhood,
by her own parents and upbringing;
a major readjustment which could have
positively unhinged and unsettled her.

Mum and Dad
were happy, a Man and a Woman, permanently in love,
always getting along: their Marriage was a sacred Memory
of a traditional Past; with no guarantee
that modern marriages are happier!

The Mother who, with untold self-denial,
bore us, bred us, fed us, clothed us, educated us,
and every day said prayers with us … is in her grave:
but her spirit of prayer knew no bottom,
Mass and her Rosary being her favorite charms—
her frugal way of maximizing fractions of idle Time!
Laying up treasure for herself in Heaven,
she lives on in the fragrance of her prayers!

May the Divine Will be fulfilled
in her Life and in her passing!
May the Saints she loved immerse her
in God's bottomless Mercy;
invoking upon her holy Soul
the infinite blessings of Divine Mercy!
And may Saint Mary Christian
still pray for all of us below …

# Contents

## PART TWO: from ... In the Suburbs of Europe



## SECTION ONE: MALTA IN CONTEXT

## 1978



## 1979



## 1980

## Lady Vancouver, 9 Poems by Joe Ruggier



## PART FIVE: from … A Richer Blessing



## A Richer Blessing, by Joe Ruggier

## PART SIX: from … Songs of Gentlest Reflection



## Songs of Gentlest Reflection

## PART SEVEN: In the Cannon's Roar

**work previously unpublished (strictly selected)**

**Illustrations**

# Author's Preface

LAMPLIGHTER MOST GRACIOUS ... features, in one convenient volume, all of my eight, published or unpublished, collections of prose and poetry, and merely excludes, in the interests of effective distribution, all work previously published in **This Eternal Hubbub**.

Since 1985 I have managed my own small press, **MBOOKS OF BC**, where I fill a dual role of author / publisher. Between 1985 and 2009, just like Walt Whitman, I sold books door to door in British Columbia — over 25,000, more than half being my own, the rest being by other authors. It is hard to determine how many copies Whitman printed of each edition of his various titles, or whether he printed more, or less than I did.

It is possible that Whitman outsold me, but we all understand. In his day the media were not what they are today: people still used their idle time to read. Another factor is that Whitman, when he went door to door, enjoyed a certain measure of popular acclaim and was soon to be honoured by the entire Nation. Whitman had honour behind him to help him pack a punch in selling his work at the door. I never enjoyed this luxury: I relied exclusively on my persuasive selling skills and the intrinsic worth of my writings. It may be said that this one factor stressed me out and murdered me to no end; but it is to my credit that I did so well albeit so deprived.

In British Columbia it is public knowledge that I have sold poetry door to door as successfully as Whitman, and that is just how good I think my work is. When I say, however, that my poetry is bestselling poetry, it does not mean I sell millions. It means that, in so far as all poetry goes, where sales are notoriously low, my poetry is, by any stretch of the imagination, bestselling poetry, and the potential financial reward therefrom is nothing to sneeze at.

I humbly point out that my work has intense marketing potential as original writing in poetry and prose and that this boast is not vainglorious. It is borne out by facts. In British Columbia, I consulted the people door to door before making my point and winning the argument. A special marketing effort, brought to bear upon marketing this book, would, in my estimation, pleasantly surprise and reward all distribution partners.

It is perfectly in order for intelligent readers to hold a few of these poems in high esteem, but not all. No artist ever claimed that his pieces are equally well-achieved. This is what critical edge is all about: we all know what fools we have to be not to take criticism. I also concede that I shall not dispute taste: whereas your taste may still be refined and cultivated, my poetry may still not be quite to your taste. I ask you to bear in mind, however, that all of the pieces included in my **Collected Poems**, though not all of them are top pieces, mark a stage and tell a story. They are all of them, in other words, of interest to me in the sense that they tell of a threaded, ongoing spiritual odyssey ….

When a real artist does something right it is common consensus that he knows and that this self-knowledge is not Vanity. It is public knowledge that I sold books door to door just like Whitman. I consider myself a front ranker, easily in the same league as T. S. Eliot, Kahlil Gibran, Thomas Merton, Longfellow, and Whitman. I have also made the Papacy art: does not this achievement place me one enchanted spot higher than Dante and MichaelAngelo?[1] Jesus made the promised Messiah Art. I am nothing but an Artist who tends to infinity. Whatever divinity I may possess is nothing but ***honour***, but I made the Papacy a long-awaited work of Art. I am a Man-Artist just like Jesus — the foremost Artist ever produced by my humble native country just as Jesus was the foremost Artist ever produced by the lowly Hebrew nation. On the day of Judgment I shall ride on horseback with Him! These boasts are made, not in presumption, but out of the sincere affection that I bear Jesus and my friends. Jesus and Joe accept all ***contrary*** on each other's behalf and for their friends and sincere clientèle!

---

[1] Dante and MichaelAngelo did not make the Papacy art, not because they were not capable, but because they were not *called: it was not given unto them.* Strictly telling myself that unless I did it nobody will, I made the Papacy art because I had inspiration which I knew ought not to be wasted, strictly because I perceived *a desperate need.*

Do not get me wrong. I respect your critical opinion and acumen, but, were you to tell me my work is not up to standard, as some people do, I shall laugh at you. As long as we agree spontaneously about this self-assessment and self-appreciation, you should not grudge me the compliment. The way so many grudge me this recognition, as if I were nothing but a backward student in the classroom, is offensive, positively a spiteful, obnoxious snub to my national pride, myself being the foremost artist my humble native country, Malta, ever produced. I cautiously add: I would never love Canada so deeply, did I not love so well the Land of my birth. Canada and Malta are both **my country**: that I love Malta so well means only that I love my country! The issue is: give us all our due, myself, the Maltese Nation, and my Canadian readers — in such a way that no one shall ever become a bighead, neither a Nation as great as Canada is, nor a Nation as great as Lilliput is![2]

A real Artist's pride does not belong to him alone: it is the pride of an entire people! More often than not, it hardly leaves an Artist elbow-room to budge without hurting the toes of his own people. A friend commented, about this Preface, *"what is this self-puffing up?"* I think this is a little more than mere *self-puffing*. Cardinal Newman was being damned in art by members of the public, and he was in despair. His *self-puffing*, which he practiced in his world-famous **Apologia**, was an obligation towards himself, his Faith and his Church, as much as towards people who loved him and were intensely hurt to see him so crushed and humiliated. Likewise in my case: I owe it to myself, to my country, and to all my honest readers!

There is no vanity worse than that of the man who will never make a clean breast of his vanity, insisting only *"I am not a vain Man!"* No, no, no, dear reader, nothing of the sort: *I am a vain Man!* I know it. I acknowledge it. I own up and make a clean breast of it. And I am totally at peace about it: I am not in conflict or in tension. Self-ap-

---

[2] This is not sarcastic. The satirical edge notwithstanding, this is nothing but harmless, whimsical, self-deflating humour — such that Canada and Lilliput, regardless of their respective size, shall always be inspired to laugh at themselves.

preciation like my own, or like Whitman's, is a good recommendation, as long and in so far as it is true, because I make thereby a clean breast of my vanity. My only concern in appreciating myself is: is it true or false? Vanity which is untruthful and false is nothing but that — damned vanity. Humility, on the other hand, which is equally untruthful, is equally obnoxious. Humility is a good thing. Not being a liar is a better …

Within Literature there is nothing more ethical than an honest claim of personal achievement. We are effectively telling YOU: *show us how intelligent your self-knowledge is and make a claim of personal achievement. As long as we agree we shall give you the honour.* This is all there is to it and this is just how clean and fair it is.

Just like Whitman's **Song of Myself**, (one of my favourite poems of all time), my self-appreciation is without malice but protects me against the subtle, detracting fancy of malicious factions who, whereas known to pay me compliments, will not tell me **who** I am, nor acknowledge my worth to my face, nor say it well in my own behalf. Not sharing my **Faith**, Dante's, MichaelAngelo's, and over a billion living Catholics', in the authenticity and lawful nature of the Papacy, and unwilling to admit that so many intelligent people can believe, rationally, in an institution which is so ancient, they merely seek to detract from the eternal truth of Faith by snubbing my personal achievement: as if anything you can ever say or do, for or against, to me or to anyone, can detract, diminish, damage or alter, Truths which, like the blue, changeless Heavens, have not altered one bit since Time immemorial; as much as Laws which touch, concern, and impinge upon everyone regardless of whether you believe in them or not.

It is not my intention to taunt you with *Popery*, by which I truly feel, my lifelong Faith regardless, as taunted as you are. In England *Popery* used to be a criminal offense. Anyone convicted went to jail. To my understanding, *Popery* consists of nothing but countless people, none of them Saints, or even good Christians, insulting whoever they choose with Hell, with mortal sin, through His Holiness the Pope and through His nose, and callously enjoying watching the victim being reduced to rubble, to a poor neurotic demon, and to a poor, pathological wreck, this being what we all agree is a crime. The slogan *No Popery* is not an insult to the Pontiff. Many sincere British people acknowledge the justice of the Pope's views, that he is quite right, honouring him sincerely in their personal life, but on the Public Stage the British do not want to hear of *Popery*: on the Public Stage they want beautiful Authors only.

I subscribe with enthusiasm and with passion to this viewpoint. I agree totally with the slogan, *No Popery*, and whereas I know that *Popery* does nothing but murder, vindictively, the poetic effects of the most beautiful of Authors, I wish to add only that I love and honour my roots. I intend only that I be given proper credit, for my achievement, as much as for the courage of my convictions. My unbending rule is: *authentic conversion must take place unto sincerity of heart alone, and a sincere Anglican is a thousand times better than a wicked Catholic!* When was it ever that a good Catholic, in his conscience, believed, practiced, or cared for anything else? or taught anyone otherwise?

My attempt to make the Papacy art occurs in **Part Four** of previous editions of **This Eternal Hubbub**. The point of this required digression is: *I have worked hard and I have worked well and I am growing old.* If you are a friend, if you are in any way a sincere friend at all, tell me straight, truthfully and sincerely, without being false, and as a friend, just how good my work is, or at least just how good you think I am, and state the case well, in my behalf, in writing, in a precisely qualified critical idiom. If you do not make the case well in my own behalf, I shall then oblige, as Cardinal Newman did in his **Apologia**, or as much as Whitman ever did, by making the case well myself in my own behalf, so that you will know that I am not King Lear, (presumably asking you the question … *"who is it can tell me who I am?"*), nor a fool who is not aware of his own worth, nor an aspiring teenager incubating the bench in your classroom.

Again, this consideration may be relevant. Whereas Canada has no nuclear weapons, the USA spends annually trillions of dollars on arms. This is ridiculous considering that all a Nation needs to win a war, if it were a matter of life or death, is just a few Atom Bombs. In this regard, the USA has the means to terminate life on earth many times over. The outrageous scandal is that I am a poet of the people, with people behind me, and the only free gift this Nation ever made me, even though it was only Canada, was a disability pension. Are you trying to tell me that we need so many Weapons but we do not need major Poets? My answer is, tell me another! We may all of us be well-advised to contemplate and dwell a little on this scandal.

The poems in this volume comprise my previous collections of prose and verse — *The Voice of the Millions, In the Suburbs of Europe, regrets hopes regards and prayers ..., Lady Vancouver, A Richer Blessing,* and *Songs of Gentlest Reflection* — with newer, unpublished work in Part 7, (*In the Cannon's Roar*), and in Part 8, *(A little girl of long ago)*. All repetitions in between the various sections have been weeded out. All poetry published in *This Eternal Hubbub* has also been excluded. *Out of Blue Nothing*, my best-selling sonnet sequence, as well as *The Dark Side of the Deity*, featuring my attempt to make the Papacy art, as well as poems featured in *Art and Revealed Religion* **...** do not feature herein. Purely in the interest of effective distribution, I do not want any repetition between these two volumes. The poems in this book date as far back as 1974 with new work created as recently as 2018. The order is strictly chronological, but the whole has been subject to revision.

Among countless *motifs*, arising from my views about Life, about the truth of Faith and the truth of Art, my work often evokes states of mind, mentalities, mindsets, wildly diverging points of view, and unique, individual *philosophies*, all of which are allowed to co-exist with all the contradictions, just as they do in life, but I am, personally, ***a man of Faith***. I make, as such, an act of Faith in the compassionate understanding of the reader, in the event that he may find my beliefs somewhat prickly, perhaps riling, and even isolating, knowing clearly, as I have written elsewhere, that real works of art are created jointly by the artist and by the sincerity of the public.

With humility in my heart, I ask the reader to bear

with me that I am not Shakespeare, but rather that, like Dante and John of the Cross, I prefer to lend the authority of the author to the interpretation. I agree with everyone that Shakespeare was the cleverest among great geniuses. Shakespearean criticism as we know it, unfortunately, is nothing but a tragic disaster: countless critics, all of them false gods making great Artists in their own image and likeness!

I wish to add that, as ***a man of Art***, I believe also, with profound conviction, in ***the Truth of Art***, and not in ***the Truth of Faith*** only. These two modes of perceiving — which may be described as a bi-focal way of seeing — do not compel my ***Faith*** precisely in an identical way for both, but I allow both to coexist creatively with all the perplexities, qualifying each other between the lines of every poem, projecting ***chiaroscuro*** into and upon each other tirelessly and without end: they are both extremely different but without each other entirely incomplete.

A key concept, or technique, in my poetry is ***transformation***. Each new piece features a dramatic persona, quite often more than one such persona. In each piece I am ***transformed*** into the dramatic persona: I become the subject which I am writing about, but always — all the various, masked personae in all my poems coexist creatively with all the perplexities and contradictions.

My distinguished colleague Ralph Cunningham has pointed out forthrightly: *"if one feels aggrieved by lack of praise for one's work – always recall that we* ***cannot*** *and* ***must*** *not try to evaluate our own work. The bias is too gigantic for clear vision and appraisal."* If I beg to differ I do so with real trepidation. Knowing that I have made bold claims indeed, a little like Cardinal Newman before me, a little like Whitman himself, (one of my favorite poets of all time), and knowing clearly that I assessed myself not without perceptiveness, in total good faith, and somewhat in despair and a certain frustration — I take all my pathetic human ambition in my two hands and lay my aspirations like a flower at the feet of a merciful Judge. Sincere, truthful compassion being the entire point of all religion, as much as of life and works of art, I make likewise an act of Faith in the compassionate understanding of the reader.

Check out my website at www.mbooksofbc.com. You may also look me up on www.thehypertexts.com. You may also carry out a simple Google search under my name, **Joe M. Ruggier**, or else **Joe Ruggier**.

*Richmond; B.C.*
*February 26, 2009 / September 8, 2010 / May 17, 2018*

## A Note to the 2nd & 3rd Editions

**SINCE** the 1st edition was released, (June 2009), I reassured my public that a 2nd edn, if any, shall not be forthcoming for a long time. Fortunately or not, further editions have been considered desirable, albeit the revisions are under control. The most important addition, which justified the 2nd edition, was the long, substantial essay by Andrew Parkin about my three major books — *Pope Caesar's Wake, This Eternal Hubbub*, and *Lamplighter most gracious ...* (the current volume) — a landmark paper, both meaningful and perceptive, which I incorporated as an introduction to my entire *opus* from the pen of an independent critic. The poem "Ode: to Beethoven", (pp. 200-201) has also undergone an editorial cut according to Dr. Parkin's precise wishes. Since the last printing, certain (important) revisions have been carried out, in particular to the **Author's Preface**, to a few poems, to the essays at the end of the book, to the name (title) of Part 7, as well as to the **Index of First Lines**. This reworking was not major, but the 2nd edition was more satisfying than the 1st. The additions to my **Author's Preface**, in particular, and moreso Andrew Parkin's essay, are extensive and important. The current, 3rd edition, on the other hand, is designed to contain **Part 8: A little girl of long ago**; features burnishing of the typesetting, as well as of various poems; but is above all designed to provide readers with a reliable edition, blessed by the author, strictly in the event that the author should die suddenly, as my recent pneumonia threatened ... All readers are encouraged to use for their purposes this most recent edition only.

# WRITING AS A SPIRITUAL ODYSSEY

An essay on Joe Ruggier's works prepared by Andrew Parkin Ph.D.

NOTES

**I AM** issuing this critical study by Andrew Parkin clearly assuming that I approve most of his perceptive conjectures but not all, that my judgment and consent are required, pending courteous mutual dialogue, prior to endorsing his editorial suggestions, many of which I value. Dr. Parkin, however, is praising me in good faith only, astutely, perceptively, in cautious language (terms) which amount to quite a good (glowing) recommendation with the reader. Were I not persuaded of Professor Parkin's fairmindedness and good faith, I would have said that there is an element of sabotage in his approach, owing to which I cannot proceed without a record of my honest responses to his reasoning, but in regard to this factor Professor Parkin has given me his blessing and I have no fear publishing his negative criticism also, even if I do not always agree, even if all it proves is that I am not publishing it out of vanity. I am immensely grateful and indebted to my friend for his extremely generous helping hand.

**On Tuesday, January 11, 2011, I emailed Dr. Parkin in regard to the presentation of this substantial essay: "Dear Andrew,** I have been carefully contemplating … your criticism featured in your generous … essay about me. I am by and large a lot more receptive to what you are saying after careful consideration, and I am impressed by the evenness and fairness of a lot of your criticism. Before I run the gauntlet of issuing your introduction in the next printing of **Lamplighter ... .....** I am taking the liberty to resubmit your essay to you, but with the additional feature of a formidable array of 68 footnotes, all of which footnotes are entirely my own, recording my careful responses to your various criticisms. You may, if you wish, intersperse more of your comments, by including your feedback to my footnotes, right inside the footnotes, coloured red and signed "Andrew". "

I offered Parkin the options of reworking the essay, of giving me permission to publish the piece as is, but featuring my 68 footnotes also, or else of doing both ... reworking the essay a little, or else giving me feedback within the footnotes, and giving me permission to publish the piece with revised footnotes. I added: "Please note that your essay has been carefully formatted inside my word-processor, with five distinct, separate sections precisely defined, with a careful weeding out of a few obvious typos, but without the slightest alteration to the words you used, or else to your substance. The text, as such, is all your own creation, precisely as you submitted it to me, whereas the footnotes are all my own creation, precisely as I am submitting them to you. This will be carefully acknowledged in all eventual publications. For the time being I look forward to your feedback on this matter of the footnotes since I am foraging ahead towards a reprinting of **Lamplighter** featuring your introduction ..... I shall not forage ahead publishing the footnotes also without your blessing. For this reason I look forward to your rationally prompt response. **Best regards, Joe"**

**On Wednesday, January 12, 2011, Dr. Parkin responded: "Dear Joe,** I have now re-read the essay together with your notes. I like this system of giving your responses as you read through my commentary on you. I think these footnotes are extremely helpful and entertaining because one can read two different minds making sparks and sometimes even sparkling. I would not want to change anything. The notes are honest responses and I do not want to muddy the waters by protesting or adding any more notes. I am very happy to have the essay published with the Ruggier response notes. I think it makes in toto very lively reading. Thanks a lot Joe for your serious literary and intellectual concern. **Andrew**.

## INTRODUCTION

**JOE RUGGIER**, a Canadian immigrant writer who uses English as his medium rather than his native Maltese, has had a very hard time trying to become an established writer in Canada. He has had some brief skirmishes in the job market, has been married and divorced, has had social assistance, and has managed to sell nothing to the Canadian literary establishment (major media, journals, or book publishers); he has had a bit more luck in this respect in England. Nevertheless, by dogged persistence and by selling his writings door-to-door in Vancouver and its environs, he has managed to found and to maintain over nearly two decades, a journal, *The Eclectic Muse.* As its name suggests, the editorial policy is to publish writing in any style, using any conventions, and on any subject, as long as it seems to the editor worthy of publication.

In this way, writers who do not conform to the changing shibboleths of fashion or to the short-lived whims of literary cliques (e.g. No Religion! No rhyme! No Political Writing! Stories in present tense only! Canadian Settings and Characters mainly!) have been able to find an outlet. In effect many of his contributors are Canadian though many are international as well. Further, Ruggier has managed to establish his own publishing house, Multicultural Books (Richmond, B.C.), and has self-published his own books and those of others. He has also had cash donations and literary contributions from other writers and critics, some of them being prominent faculty members of universities in both Malta, Canada, and elsewhere.

As the publishing industry in Canada is small and a Canadian "best-seller" (if not taken on by a major British or American publisher) was often said to be about 5000 copies sold, Ruggier has managed, by selling door-to-door, to top this number with some of his books. How has Ruggier managed to keep writing and surviving without going mad or simply throwing himself off the Lions Gate Bridge? I think the answer is perhaps threefold: from an early age he has been religious and his Catholicism has helped him enormously. Many of his poems are in fact prayers and conversations with God. Secondly, he has also considered himself to be an artist and has set out to master the craftsmanship of writing both prose and verse, pursuing *le mot juste*, rather than trying to earn a living to become a prosperous Vancouverite. Thirdly, he has great personal tenacity of purpose and the courage to face poverty if he has to—and he has had to do so. He knows how the poor live, he knows how they feel, and he does not despise them. He is an amazing exception to the North American culture of greed, the devastating results of which have shaken the world as well as the banking system.[3]

## POPE CAESAR'S WAKE

My task here is to review a fair cross-section of Ruggier's literary work, beginning with a book written with as much religious piety as anger, and as much anger as indignation

---

[3] I approve gratefully, and entirely, of the rationale of this pointed *Introduction*. Thank you, Andrew, for your generous praise of my personal qualities. Your praise makes me feel good, but I merely point out, what I have noted in later footnotes, that *an author's presumed sanctity of life is not necessarily the Beauty, and the Truth which make literature real literature and a sincere honour in its own right.*

with certain aspects of his religion, *Pope Caesar's Wake: Letters to Pope Woytyla* (Richmond, B.C.: Multicultural Books of B.C., 2005; 2nd. ed. 2010). Had this been circulated before the eighteenth century in Europe, I think the author might well have been interrogated like Giordano Bruno, and like Bruno, burned at the stake.

The letters begin with a get-well greeting after the Pope was shot in the failed assassination attempt of 1981 and they continue until 2005, when Pope Jean Paul II died. At the head of the collection is a "Letter of Introduction" to the next and present Pope, Benedict XVI. The large majority of the letters date from March 1984 onwards. They are furnished with an elaborate apparatus: an Introduction by Michael Burch, letters of introduction to both Popes from Ruggier, with Ruggier's additions of an "Afterword" with "Notes to My Afterword", both of which are in fact essays, of 35 and 4 pages respectively. In my view, this fussy envelope around the entire book suggests the neurosis of a devout but essentially grieving catholic who reveres the Pope Jean Paul II as an ecclesiastical, even spiritual hero but who at the same time vents anger and frustration at the state of the Roman Catholic Church as an institution.[4]

I feel that after the latest revelations about priests who abused children and about bishops who declined to discipline or recommend the excommunication of such priests, many devout Catholics will sympathizc with Ruggier's letters condemning the Catholic Church for its attitudes and its priesthood at its worst. Ruggier's anger is also directed at what he has suffered as an individual through these attitudes. There is a good deal of legitimate complaint but there is too much self-pity at times. Ruggier's main complaint, however, goes beyond the personal, for he roundly condemns his Church's neglect of and contempt for "great artists." Yet it goes without saying that he includes himself within this category and is profoundly hurt by lack of recognition. Ruggier is in some ways a very learned man;

[4] Andrew, I have pointed out that fussy envelopes around my books signify to me plenty of private corners wherein readers who love the very smell of the books they read may browse and burrow to their heart's content, just as private lovers are known to do in luxury homes.

it cannot have escaped him that the Church has also been a patron of great artists.[5]

Michael Burch's Introduction starts with a simile: "The Catholic Church and the individual Catholic artist are like hammer and nail." ("Introduction," p. xviii). and goes on to point out, "It is as though the nail—misused, abused, mangled, twisted, thwarted—has identified all the dangers of misguided hammers with a single iconic Hammer…neither Thor nor his hammer are at fault, but that what they symbolize is truly dangerous, almost, if not literally, beyond words. Such crushing force, such numbing belief: such are the perils of Faith." (p. xix). Burch gives a skillfully compressed account of this compendium of shocking and sometimes very funny letters that seem to echo in stony vaults of the Vatican, gaining few Papal responses after a letter of 8 October, 1981 (page 30) conveying the Pope's blessing on Ruggier and wishing him well. Early in the book other messages of Papal blessing and prayer follow, but the other responses seem mainly to be the official formulae of the secretaries who assure Ruggier that he is in his Holiness's prayers. Since the letters soften in tone as Jean Paul II approaches death, Burch hopes "Ruggier's letters will now effect reconciliation between the Catholic Church and her 'artists at large'." (p. xxv). That, I think, is wildly optimistic.

These letters are extremely, outspokenly, audacious harangues leveled at both Pope and Church, peppered here and there with verses full of plaints and criticisms. One letter is a sales piece offering "cds" for sale to the Church. This letter seems to have received no answer, nor does it seem to have coaxed a massive order from the Church for these products.

As a book of letters, it would have benefited enormously from a professional editor's cold eyes and surgical cutting. The repetitions try even the sympathetic reader's patience.[6] Of course, Joe Ruggier has for many

---

[5] How true!  Of course ….

[6] Before I released the book, in both editions, I carefully considered this option, but decided that letters are not their author's exclusive artistic property only.  They are the recipient's also.  As such they ought,

years been a writer who perforce self-publishes and sells door-to-door, a return to a contemporary Canadian version of Grub Street. A day in the life of Joe is well described in one letter:

> **Holy Father:**
> I never feel like working, door-to-door selling. [sic] My books and to actually pull Myself together and do it I always have to deny Myself. Whenever I do so, however, I always experience the same thrilling uplift....For reasons of dispelling My nerves, My chronic depression, exercising athletically for My health, a change of scene and a required diversion, and supplementing My meager pocket money, I decided to go to work.
>
> It was today, a rainy day. A long time ago I figured out that rainy nights, and even snowy nights, are excellent for door-to-door business because it means that most people stay inside...and I stand a better chance of finding people home. On My way to work I composed, on the buses, the bulk of this letter. I then worked, earning $45, from the sales of two books.
>
> (*Letters to Pope Woytyla*, p. 337).

So such is the day of a writer[7] who has not as yet found a major publisher to take his work, not found a job to keep him while he writes in his spare time, and has no help from a Roman Catholic press. If Ruggier were a shamanistic poet, he would no doubt compose odes to the Pacific North West gods of rain!

The letters lambast the Catholic Church because "At this moment in time Catholic Church is at loggerheads with countless people partly owing to this diplomatic malfunction; catholic Faith may be divinely right indeed, but Church has no right to insult the rest of us like this." (*Letters*, p.374)[8]. Ruggier has another quarrel, and this I think may be one deep root of his problems: it is a quarrel

---

perhaps, to be released without surgical cutting and manipulation. This does not apply to the **Afterword**, which I have been revising and burnishing endlessly.

[7] Well-said and well-quoted, Andrew ...

[8] This is an extremely well-chosen quote, Andrew ...

with powerful publishers and successful writers, that are, in fact, the literary establishments, especially in Canada and the U.S.

> Among the collective sins of artists are vanity, arrogance, superciliousness, snobbery and failure to despise themselves – flattery and susceptibility to flattery – an appeal to the public that is purely fulsome, with no basis in reason or artistic integrity, which is nothing short of a fawning, ignominious subservience of a purely mercenary nature…pushing their own mediocre art and discriminating thereby against promoting truly great work, allow all such great work to pass away into neglect….
> (*Letters*, p.370).

All writers who have received rejection slips with no hint of how to improve their work will recognize here feelings which have to be in turn rejected while work is re-worked and re-submitted, perhaps further down the literary food chain.

Ruggier suggests that the true artists can appeal to ordinary people as much as to literary pundits (*Letters*, p. 255). After all, it was Yeats who pointed out that the real point is durability not topicality, for the lasting song is sung in the marrow bone. The most coherent manifesto for his own work is Ruggier's "False Judges" which invokes cultural history, soundly canes the Church, and proclaims

> My books are all naughty boys.
> I give them all rights to misbehave:
> great Artists are superior parents;
> and I am a good Father
> to My chosen Daughter and to the book I write.
> (*Letters*, p.245).[9]

What does this writer really want? He wants what he feels to be his true stature to be recognized: "If You did not want Me to revenge Myself all You should have said was: 'Joe Ruggier You are a great Artist!' You need only have

[9] Ditto.

said so through great Books and the lies of little children." (*Letters*, p.248). He also would have loved to have a letter responding to his own written in the Pope's own hand, not typed and sent out by an assessor. It is hardly surprising that he received no such personal letter, when one considers Ruggier's bombardments of invective.[10] One example must suffice:

> I do not need Your dirty absolutions, Hoy Father, and I am giving them all back to You now, right away, immediately, in writing…Take all Your absolutions back immediately, They stink.
>
> (*Letters*, p. 207).

If one were to doubt that Ruggier is still a Roman Catholic that would be too simple a response. He values the Church's intellectual content and accepts it (see p.405). In fact he attacks the "factions in the culture industry" who regard Christianity as "a trap, a hoax, a money-making racket, and not World Culture…." He wonders why they attack Christians who are supposed to be "snaring" people when there is far more danger emanating daily from the fanatics of another faith. Ruggier asks, with a measure of justice,"…why do these factions not make Muslims a taunt that Islam is a trap and a hoax? Is it because the Muslims will murder them if they do?" (*Letters*, p. 372).[11]

Ruggier is, we can say, despite his criticisms of the Roman Church, a poet in the tradition of Roman Catholic poetry. He is well aware, too, that nowadays many readers are suspicious of verse that has "designs upon us" and this means that we may be equally suspicious of overtly political poetry as much as the overtly religious kind. That best-seller, *The God Delusion,* may please many of us, but the inescapable fact remains that the vast majority of human beings the world over believe in a god, of whatever stripe! Further, many contemporaries still have inexplicable visionary experiences. The "irrational" lives in us, hence

---

[10] This nettles me but the point you are making is a very good point …
[11] Again a very well-made point …

fanatics and murderous ones of all stripes; and our neurologists and other brain researchers have not yet found a complete explanation of all the brain functions and whether the individual brain has enough energy to connect directly and subliminally with other brains and with the *anima mundi*, if, indeed, that mysterious force field exists. Thus until such time as all human experience can be explained in detail, there is still a need to recognize our sub- and supra-rational experiences. And for many, God fits the bill. As a critic and a poet I accord to Ruggier the distinction of being a modern poet writing in the Catholic tradition, and his Catholicism extends to a catholicity of taste by which his reception of poetry is eclectic.[12] As editor of *The Eclectic Muse*, he has always avoided making the kind of immature editorial decisions too often found in other poetry journals: for example, "No religious poems", "no rhymes", "no stanzaic forms", "free verse only". I once sent a poem critical of Lenin to a Canadian journal whose editor rejected the poem on the grounds that his journal would never publish a poem like that on Lenin. The poem dealt with the death of Lenin from syphilis and mentioned that he had slaughtered peasants. For some, despite his regime's setting up the first Soviet secret police, with its habits of torture and murder, Lenin is not to be criticized! Propagandists rather than poets work around realities to push their ideological agendas. Poets write from their deepest being in the midst of realities of all kinds. Ruggier is a religious poet not a religious propagandist. His engagement with religious and literary ideas can be found in his major essays as well as his poems.[13]

---

[12] Thank you very much, Andrew …

[13] Once more, thank you, Andrew. Your praise soothes my ego and the rationale behind your words is admirable. My *Letters*, Andrew, contain piety, but they are not a manual of piety. They also contain satire, some of which is extremely funny. Amid piety, and amid satirical fancy to which I gave unbridled rein because I was *hurt*, I touch upon and address countless high serious themes and assorted topics. I have positively had readers, Andrew, who told me: *"your book is a page-turner. We read it twice over from cover to cover and could not put it down!"* Finally, the staunchest admirer of my *Letters*, to whom I showed each and every letter as soon as it came out of my word-

THIS ETERNAL HUBBUB

With this in mind, we turn to a critique of *This Eternal Hubbub* (Richmond, B.C.: MBooks, 2004: 1995, 2003). In the acknowledgments to the 2004 edition, Ruggier refers to it as his "most central work." It is an eclectic collection of prose and verse. The front matter contains a colour photo portrait of the author's friend and client Shannon Dyakowska and an elegy for this remarkable young woman, who went to an early death at the age of forty-one in 1994. There is also a coloured reproduction of an emblematic Religious Landscape designed by the author himself. It is reminiscent of some of Blake's emblems and the designs made for Yeats early in his career. Part One of the book contains an essay "Poetry and the Gospels"; Part Two, much longer, has the essay, "Art and Revealed Religion." Part Three contains "Out of Blue Nothing" a philosophical sonnet sequence followed by author's notes on "the Meaning of the Poetry." There are photographs and several black and white designs. Part Four of the book is a seven part poetic sequence "The Dark Side of the Deity" (The Metaphysics of Sex and Art). The book concludes with an Appendix One (an essay On the Author's Life and another On the Author's Writings) and Appendix Two (a brief autobiographical note, reviews of Ruggier's writing, a Bibliography and Indexes).

One might say the book is a literary "salade composée" and its "sauce" is the vinaigrette of Ruggier's bitterness (vinegar), his humour (garlic), and his good faith (virgin olive oil). The bitterness seems to me to be partly a result of having a first class degree in English (not his native language) which he has mastered to a level that is higher than the English written by many native speakers of English in Britain, Canada, and the U.S.,[14] and yet his work

processor, is a Jewish Ph.D. He is anything but Catholic but adores my letters for the humanity of their content.

[14] Thank you indeed, Andrew, for this high praise …

has been largely ignored by the Canadian literary establishment. One might note that quite a few literary journalists prefer to puff the work of writers who have been to prison rather than write considered critiques of the work of Ruggier the religious poet, who will use rhyme when it suits him and will use Biblical language when it suits him, even if it is "obsolete." We should note, though, that the world-wide best-selling Harry Potter books were rejected by fourteen publishers. J.K. Rowling also uses obsolete words for her own purposes and these give a texture and atmosphere to the books which could not be attained if these words were edited out. And her publisher, Bloomsbury Books, according to the *Writers' and Artists' Year Book* made in one year 75% of its profit from Harry Potter alone. We should repeat to literary editors: there is no rule for writing poetry; there is no rule banning rhyme (pop songs selling millions of copies use rhyme); there is no rule for poets to use only current words and contemporary cliché phrases, for poets often recover the use of neglected words and "obsolete" ones; there is no rule against the pastiche of previous styles of writing, for Antonia Byatt did it brilliantly in her novel *Possession*; there is no rule that literary review editors know what's best for the rest of us, for sometimes they guess what a public will enjoy and sometimes they haven't a clue. Yet the criterion for publication of poetry must always be: whether the piece works as poetry and does for us something we value.[15]

There are now growing numbers of writers around the globe who work in Englishes of all kinds. These are international writers. Because Ondaatje is originally Sri Lankan he does not have to write obsessively about Sri Lanka, nor about his adopted Canada. Rushdie does not have to confine himself to India or the U.K. Canada is a land of First Nations peoples, immigrants of several generations' standing, recent immigrants, and among all these are intercultural people, even "transcultural" people, many of them writers. As a Canadian myself, I hope that

---

[15] I heartily approve your critical rationale, Andrew, the critical credo you provide to justify what I am attempting …

there are no Canadians deemed second-class citizens, simply because they arrived quite recently or, if writers, simply because they do not write about specifically Canadian towns or areas. Every writer is free to write about what most suits her or his talent. Graham Greene had no obligation to centre his writing on England only. Doris Lessing is not shackled to Africa or England. At one time, when people tended to remain in one town or area for their entire lives, it was natural for writers to stick to what they knew best. The local can become universally significant as literary historians again well know. In our age of massive migrations and cheap travel, of families living in several parts of the globe, conditions have changed and changed rapidly. Writers may still be "rooted" but many are living across cultures, and their work can grow from that experience. There is thus no obligation for Canadians to write about their native province and its small towns. They may do, or they may not. In short, writers make their own rules if they are genuine artists. Editors may gather cliques, but cliques have a habit of sinking into the waters of time, as any competent literary historian will again confirm. What matters to writers and to readers are the texture and quality of the writing itself, not rules or theories imposed by pundits. All the above issues are, in my view, of some help in explaining some of Ruggier's bitterness at being largely ignored by the Canadian literary establishment. More directly, his bitterness springs also from the fact that he can sell his works in their thousands by going door-to-door in the Vancouver area, yet he has been forced to set up his own publishing company to publish his work. Established firms do not publish him.[16]

Is the bitterness justified? His readers will draw their own conclusions. In writing about his work, however, I have encountered many of the issues I outlined above.

Let us now look at the essays that open *This Eternal Hubbub*. In the front matter we find a sincere elegy for Ruggier's customer, Shannon Dyakowska. This is followed by the "revamped" author's preface, mercifully short, that

---

[16] Ditto

acknowledges the generosity of Tony Dyakowski and Ralph Cunningham whose donations made publication of the book possible.

The very long preface in the earlier editions has been fashioned into two essays which have become Appendix 1 and 2. I think Ruggier's liking for prefaces and appendixes as "wraps" containing his salad is a tactical mistake. They distract the reader from the book's main text. In fact, many readers will simply skim over or even skip these items in order to get to the meat. If the wraps are of paramount interest, they should be in the main text.[17]

In effect the new Preface thanks the many people who have bought previous editions of the book and vaunts the excellence of the essays and the twenty-four sonnets. There is a touch of "garlic humour" on the leaf when Ruggier admits that "…as yet I am not God." (p. xiv). He apologizes for stylistic lapses and says the book is good for teenagers and adolescents to read.[18] He concludes by telling us that the book took him twenty years to complete and that he has corresponded with Pope Jean Paul II. But before we can get to the book itself, there is a Foreword by Rex Hudson, who claims that Ruggier's reputation is growing in Canada, the U.S., and Europe. Nonetheless, Ruggier's work does not seem to have caught the attention of major publishers and their editors.

So what about the actual book? The first essay, "Poetry and the Gospels" begins with a number of ideas about the definition of the poet; Ruggier asserts: "The man who has no music in his soul is certainly not a poet…." (p.6). Versifiers with "tin ears" found regrettably in many an anthology are certainly not poets. Poetry is musical speech. And this does not mean that it must employ rigidly the most common metrical patterns. Ruggier continues: "The deep humanity necessary to transfigure his language

---

[17] You may indeed be right, Andrew, but in an earlier footnote I indicated what these "wraps", or what I call "private corners", mean to me …

[18] Giving them countless positive impulses to think about when contemplating relationships and lifting up their minds to higher things …

into poetry is something he shares with many; it is his mastery of diction that distinguishes him from the multitude….***le mot juste*** can still be generally defined as his peculiar gift and his alone." (pp. 6-7). He adds that a true poet will also write beautiful prose, agreeing with Wordsworth that poetry is "heightened prose." (p. 7). Love of language itself is the necessary given on which the rest depends but the precision of words must express something. The greatest poetry expresses life in such a way as to impinge upon us, entering our own lives, and as Ruggier says, "I agree with T.S. Eliot that this something for which the poets find a language is: ***'frontiers of consciousness where words fail, but meanings still exist.'*** " (p. 7). The actual word is of great value for Ruggier, as for his literary guide, Eliot, because the simple word "word" recalls the great passage of St. John, "In the beginning was the word…." And this reminds us that all great art is religious in a very broad sense, not hooked necessarily to some official religion, for the artist is implicated in humanity and respectful of it. This implies, as Eliot saw, a connection between the individual talent and tradition, for tradition is part of the history of human kind. Thus the sense of history is important for the artist, too important to be shrugged off with such facile, dogmatic, and false affirmations as "History is always written by the conquerors or victors." History for the best artists is found in evidence, in documents, in testimony that can be weighed, not in mere propaganda.

The poetic expression of life may become a type of vision communicated through art; and for Ruggier the best art is the art that conceals art: "Supreme art hides itself, for self-importance is the essence of unimportance…." (p.18). This aphorism is worth countless undistinguished sentences.[19] The final portion of the essay concerns poetry and the gospels. The language of the gospels is often poetry of the highest order. One does not have to be a Christian or a Jew to realize this. Cut the anachronisms from the King James Version and one has an exceptionally fine model of

[19] Thank you very much, Andrew …

English style. Astutely, Ruggier shows the influence of the Gospels' style behind intensities of writing by a number of authors. He quotes Blake's passage about the "Lilly of the Valley" and passes to Eliot again with telling effect. But Ruggier goes further into territory into which some true poets will not follow him; he enters a religious arena that is not religious only in its broadest sense: he avers, "I am concerned with poetry as the handmaid of sanctity." (p.23). Such a conclusion may be fine for Ruggier but it is not the true way, evidently, for all good poets.[20]

In the fifth section of his essay, he has another aphorism, arising from his contemplation of his own inadequacies in the face of Shakespeare and Dante: "Vanity is the vice of little men" but he cannot resist repeating his previous aphorism about self-importance. The two aphorisms go together and should have appeared together the first time used. I think it a mistake to repeat one's aphorisms, however pleasing they may be. Their repetition tends to weaken them.[21] Ruggier is right on the mark when he identifies charity (as used in Corinthians) as "...the climate where poetry flourishes and is most itself...." (p. 27). He ends the essay with an upsurge of rhetoric praising censorship, as a necessary tension in the art work, but moves away from external censorship to say "...censorship is most effective only when self-imposed by the Poet's own '***Sense of Scripture***", and next to useless otherwise." (p.29). In democracies, the most tyrannous censorship is that of individual literary editors! But good writers are always in the debt of good editors who help them refine their work

---

[20] when I first created this essay, Andrew, I believed, with a certain hesitation, what I am saying herein, which seemed like *"a good idea at the time"*, but in retrospect, as I have said already in these footnotes, I have learnt that, whereas *sanctity of life* is indeed high-serious, *sanctity of life in and by itself does not constitute the Beauty and the Truth which make literature real literature, a sincere honour and a true classic.*

[21] Thank you, Andrew, for this sharp suggestion. Your suggestion does not involve anything approaching a major reshuffling of my words, but I approve. It shall be incorporated into any future reprints of this book. For the time being, however, I have a few hundred copies left of the 2004 edition, and I do not see the book going into another printing very quickly.

into a better work, well worthy of publication. Such editors, sometimes brilliant, work mainly for major publishers.[22]

His next essay, "Art and Revealed Religion or a Word in Confidence" is part two of the book. The prefatory note admits: "…you may also say that ART AND REVEALED RELIGION is my Gospel." (p. 33). The opening pages of the essay assert that great art "…draws aside the veil that conceals eternity" (p. 36). Clearly influenced by Blake and less so, perhaps, by Yeats, he says the sincerity of great art is heavenly while the vanity with which art is tempted is its hell. Ruggier's personal belief in God and in supernatural experience emerges very clearly on page 39: "…great art is a type of the immortality of the soul. So also the power given unto great artists to communicate with periods in time and geographical spaces far removed from their own is a proof of the supernatural." His use of the "unto" here is deliberate; he aims to stress the impact of Biblical language on the religious artist. One must hasten to add, though, that the power of the artist's imagination to span time and space is not logically or scientifically any *proof* of the supernatural.

The book's title appears in a sentence in this essay; it seems that the eternal hubbub is nothing less than the discourse of great art as it has existed for centuries and will endure for centuries to come, unless we destroy life on earth in the next few decades. The essay goes on to discuss the nature of art. It has been created by human beings since the early cave dwellers and continues to the present. Thus for Ruggier art is a basic human need, "It is a social service." (p. 42). Pumping up to a higher register, Ruggier, ignoring Homer[23], suggests that Virgil, Dante and Shakespeare are the three supreme writers, each of whom changed the course of poetry.

The nature of the artist and what he does through art seems very personal and very Roman Catholic to the

---

[22] This was an extremely capable précis of my essay, *Poetry and the Gospels*.

[23] My neglect of Homer's name and reputation was never intended to be taken literally by the reader of this essay, but always with a critical pinch of salt …

Protestant or the agnostic:

> His art is the transformed and public confessional from which he flings at our heads all the pain he has felt in secret, and it is profoundly unfortunate if we choose for a guide the artist who has not understood his experience, for the artist is a priest in secret, and his art is a priesthood of the imagination whereby he confesses us.
>
> (p.47).

Many a mature reader might ask, do we ever, and does even a great artist ever fully understand human experience? I believe there is always a mysterious dimension to experience and the artist may invoke real presences while respecting something of their mystery.[24]

The next step in Ruggier's essay is the discussion of "the ordinary man". This is the reader. But he is also akin to the artist and to the son of God. The ordinary man is sinful and at times despicable yet is the abiding reader and the abiding artist. Ruggier lambasts what he calls "world culture" because it "...damns the ordinary man with sham rhetoric, and does not stir a finger to help him raise up his head from the insult." (p.51). The essay should have ended with the excellent use of *King Lear* and the unmatchable speech on man as poor, bare, forked animal. Instead Ruggier adds a further paragraph, confused and descending into a totally different register.[25] Nor does he care to explain what he means by world culture. I assume he means the now global culture of international business and marketing.

In the notes that follow this essay, there is, I think, an indication of what makes Ruggier so angry with the literary and academic establishment:

> What are we to say, then, when the student who writes poetry about this kind of high dream is told by the Academy that 'poetry is not written like that

---

[24] How true!

[25] I clearly understand what you are saying, Andrew, but do not quite agree with this criticism.

> any longer?' We should say that poetry like Dante's and like Shakespeare's is actually being prohibited by the modern pillars of Culture. (p.54).

We must add that anyone who examines the course offerings of university English Literature departments today will discover that in many of them it is no longer necessary to study Shakespeare as a compulsory part of getting a B.A. in English Literature. In many departments Shakespeare is an option among many others.[26] This I suspect is the result of two channels of political ideology: Shakespeare presents students with some difficulties in coping with complex sentences and an enormous vocabulary; it is unfair to students from "unprivileged" or "disadvantaged" backgrounds to make them "do" Shakespeare! As a grammar school boy from a home that had few books and having to work in a butcher's shop after school and on Saturdays, I am grateful for the teachers who took the trouble to show us kids who were far from "posh" how to read the wonders of Shakespeare's writings. The other political channel of anti-Shakespearean teachers is that of the would-be political commissar. Shakespeare is revered in the home of the British Empire. Some of his plays seem to be politically incorrect. He's a dangerous influence. Marginalize him! Such university teachers are naïve. Shakespeare cannot be marginalized or ignored by anyone truly interested in drama and poetry. The Soviets with a ruthless secret police could not brainwash their population. What makes anti-Shakespeare English teachers think they can out-commissar Soviet commissars?

After the notes, there follows a meditation part visionary, part heightened prose or prose poetry and part verse. It is a response or set of responses to depression, a sense of desolation, a sense of defeat by a Satanic academy and literary establishment. But the great Lords of poetic creation come to his aid and sustain him in his efforts to write and to sell his writings. "And as if it were in a trance,

---

[26] This observation is gorgeous and perfectly to the point and a-propos of what I am saying …

or mental swoon, or interior locution **ALL THE GREAT WRITERS AND ARTISTS** spoke to me...." (p. 57). The time is Easter, the time of suffering, death, and resurrection. This section is the earth-bound passion of Ruggier the writer! The visionary experience is full of good ideas such as the love song by Ann Hathaway to Shakespeare. The writing, however, does not always convince and the refrain

> but scratch, scratch, scratch,
> Thy pen is all I hear
> (pp. 63-64).

coming in after verse in a different register may be reminiscent of Poe's "The Raven" but it seems to me hilarious and its hilarity might be in character with a homely Ann, but it doesn't fit the rest of the poem.[27] Further, the use of "thy" and "doth" does not make the poem a credible pastiche of an Elizabethan "hussif's" idiom. To quote some of the loveliest lines from *Paradise Lost* just afterwards is too courageous a procedure.[28] But the sequence on the Blessed Virgin works very well indeed. We believe in the writer's emotion and his vision.[29] There then follows a long climactic vision sequence in which a God figure appears and speaks together with a holy procession of the writer's chosen saints, writers, and musicians. The sequence is impressive in its learning, audacious in conception, and sometimes funny. But are its words worthy of all these worthies? I think not. It is too uneven and too long.[30] At the

[27] Again, Andrew, I clearly understand what you are saying but do not agree entirely. I am totally uncertain whether a cut, or a reshuffling of the words, will necessarily improve the poem. I have a feeling that it may indeed damage the poem. I am content to let it rest here that these lines are not entirely inept but by no means the best lines in my poem.

[28] I disagree. I do not quote these lines from *Paradise Lost* for bolstering my own ego, but purely for their substance, as much as for imparting to my readers the contagious joy of beautiful literature …

[29] Thank you.

[30] Again, I disagree. I concede that the sequence may be *long and uneven*, but it is full of substance, over brims with message and with content, and with extremely provocative material for discussion. What I am saying is that my style, in this *long, uneven* passage, may be cracking beneath the burden of the inspiration, but I far prefer to

end Virgil, Dante and Shakespeare take a curtain call and say a few words to cast out fear. And thus ends part two of the book.

The sonnet sequence “Out of Blue Nothing” is the heart of the book. It is divided into three parts. A reader who wishes to find out the deeper meanings of the poems may go to the author’s notes (pp. 148-151). In the confines of this essay I shall be brief and more concerned with technicalities. The sonnets use the Shakespearean form of three quatrains, each on the abab rhyme pattern, followed by a final quatrain that ends with a couplet, giving a sense of an argument proven or a conclusion drawn, almost the geometer’s QED.[31]

In the “Bystander” section the first eight sonnets of the sequence are retrospective and Romantic in manner with much use of the exclamation mark and some echoes of previous poets. The echo of the first line of Dante’s *Inferno* works well in English as a guiding line: “As I stand surveying all that ground I lost” (p. 120). But all too often there are awkward phrases that are obtrusive, sometimes breaking the music of a line: “Merry-go-rounds where all the winds of renown/ lead some poor devils round around a caper!” (p. 121). “renown” is one syllable too many. I think the line would be stronger with a monosyllabic ending.[32] The alert reader will notice other infelicities, so I shall not

---

preserve the interest of what I am saying, than to attempt a barren and frigid perfection of my manner. In this essay, Andrew, you pause, quite often, to censure a little superficially my technicalities, my aesthetic achievement, without always doing justice to the Truth and Depth of my substance. It may be said that my writing is driven by *an inner motor*, like Bach’s music. Readers have compared my work to four-part harmony, with all sorts of arguments taking off in all directions, with another three arguments raging in the author’s mind the instant that one subsides and is resolved.

[31] Gorgeous observation

[32] I do not see how this can be done without damaging the line, unless a perfect monosyllabic substitute can be found which rhymes perfectly with “renown”. Honestly, Andrew, who on earth is demanding that an iambic pentameter can never contain one syllable too many? Have you never heard of variety within the metre? You have yourself, within this same essay, discoursed very convincingly and persuasively in favour of freedom of style and poetic diction …

go through the sonnets nit-picking. To balance what I have just said, I take my hat off to the line, "Set down out of blue nothing rhymes unheard!"[33] The problem is that Ruggier cannot always deliver the poetry that such a line seems to promise. One verbal curiosity of the sequence deserves mention here. In No. 5, the end couplet is:

> Daft virgins cackling burn joy black to soot,
> and when they kneel the very saints must doot.
> (p. 124).

This "doot" could be a misprint for "do't" = "do it". This would mean that when the virgins kneel the saints are compelled to do so. On the other hand an obsolete form of our modern "dote" is "doote" (see O.E.D.). If Ruggier meant this he missed out the final "e".[34] Another slighter difficulty with this couplet is the word "Daft". It really alters the register of language. If an echo of the Biblical "foolish" virgins was intended, I would prefer the American style adjective "Fool" to the use of "Daft".[35] Sonnets 6,7, and 8 seem to me very much superior.

In "Time Passes," the sonnets seem more mature, assured, and confident in manner. In our age of condemnation of racism (though there are still adherents of class-ism – i.e. class warfare) there are still those who think it fine to make anti-English and anti-Westerner remarks in speech and in print. I therefore found it refreshing to find a sonnet in praise of England (No.11, p.132). Logically enough this is followed by a sonnet on Shakespeare. The poem rises to

---

[33] Thank you, Andrew …

[34] Dear Andrew, your interpretation is interesting, but you missed the point of the word-play. *"Doot"* is a sarcastic way of saying *"doubt"*. I learnt to use the word like this from my best friend in Malta whose mother was British and whose father was Irish, and I should merely have taken the trouble to elucidate, as necessary, this matter in my notes to the meaning of the poetry.

[35] According to my way of thinking, the word *"daft"* fits more snugly into the alliterative qualities of the verses than the word *"fool"*, providing a heavier, stronger rhythm, but I was, indeed, referring to the Biblical *"foolish"* virgins. If, for this reason, you insist on the point you are making, I shall change the word "*daft*" to "*fool*" … I am uncertain of myself and merely request your feedback again.

the occasion with

> The fire's cold. The snows of Age are falling.
> The latch is open. Love has gone away.
> Through the dark night, the Songs of Avon calling,
> sing, sing! (p. 133).

As we have seen, he is one of Ruggier's literary Trinity, and his sonnet is followed by sonnets to Dante and Virgil. Sonnet 15 is distinct and successful. I would like the eleventh line to be one syllable longer to balance the meaning more. I suggest following "plough" with "through" or "those". I commend all the same the last four lines, especially the end couplet:

> But Homer knows, and old Calypso cries;
> blows but one kiss and in the silence dies.
> (p. 136).

These lines have the allusiveness and music true to the kind of poetry that endures.[36]

The third section, "Out of Blue Nothing," deals with religious experience and poetic vision. Appropriately enough, it begins with the word that *was* the beginning, the word made flesh. But I think two lines in the sonnet would benefit from revision: line 4 reads

> the floor without either verve, or force, or tact.

I prefer:

> the floor with neither verve, nor force, nor tact.[37]

---

[36] Thank you …

[37] According to my careful thinking, *"without either"* mimics, better than *"with neither"*, the vervelessness, the forcelessness, the tactlessness which are the topic, which are captured more precisely by the weakness of the limp dangling syllable, than by the heavier, stronger rhythm you recommend. However, if you insist, I shall change this line also. I agree that the rhythm you recommend is stronger, and the beat more insistent, but is it called for? Or is the intentional weakness of my rhythm what the subject calls for? Once more I am uncertain of myself

This revision I think strengthens the line. Next, line 14 reads

> the Man was God and all the World caved in.

But Christ did not destroy the world; he replaced pagan gods. I prefer:

> the Man was God and ancient gods caved in.[38]

Sonnet 18 seems to me more successful with its blend of religion, home and school life, and a certain humour. Sonnet 19 offers us the poet's vision in which he "Saw all the Popes together march in file, / the net of Peter spread around their feet" and this vision quickly becomes both Dantesque and finally grotesque: "All sung together: 'FEE-FO-FUM! / I smell good devil's meat with blood and rum!'" Sonnet 20 is much more restrained, "Great Oak, gray shade against the sunny Hill" and the restraint gives it more power as poetry. Sonnet 23 is marred by misprints in line 10 and in line 12 "old Stan's" presumably refers to "old Satan's"?[39] The thought seems to me to waver and lose its force. The final sonnet, No. 24, is quite strong at first:

> We seek a Presence in the Clouds; vice rots
> The Paradise lost within.
> (p.147).

I think the scansion and the echo of Milton would gain, though, if Ruggier had written "The Paradise *we* lost

---

since you have called it into doubt and merely request your feedback again.

[38] Again, my original image was an image of power and divine energy, but you have called my line into doubt, recommending a subtle reshuffling which still makes sense. Again, I am uncertain of myself, and merely request your feedback again, at the same time that I require to make up my mind properly.

[39] Your interpretation is correct. *"Old Stan's"* is a shorthand for *"old Satan's"*. I do not feel like changing it and prefer to leave it up to the perceptiveness of poetry lovers, but perhaps I should point it out in the Notes.

within." Furthermore, this high register is then broken by a banal phrase, for the line ends: "We munch a bun,"![40]

All in all, the entire section needed the eye of a neutral professional sensitive to poetry who would offer counsel and suggestions for the author's consideration and possible revisions.[41]

Part Four of the book is a lengthy meditation in verse and prose entitled "The Dark Side of the Deity: The Metaphysics of Sex and Art". This is the revised 2001 edition of the piece. It is sub-divided into seven parts.

Part 1 is an introductory poem, "Down in Adoration Falling," of seventeen lines. This is a reprise of sonnet 23 from "Out of Blue Nothing" with an additional three lines, now placed as lines 4, 8, and 14 in the new poem. A misprint in the earlier sonnet has been corrected. "Old Stan" persists. The poem raises the issue of what is sacred, what profane?

Part 2, "The Insult and a Parable" begins with a poem "The Insult" which uses a line from sonnet 23, repeated in "Down in Adoration Falling" to serve now as the springboard for the lines that follow it:

> Around a small , round insult, red and white,…" etc. (p. 156).

But the poem gathers impetus and loses coherence from then on. The one distinction it has apart from the first line is the neologism: "shoshomishshating" that serves in line 4 as another adjective limiting "insult". This bit of verse is then followed by the parable "In the Beginning," a recycling of

---

[40] "The Paradise *we* lost within" … this is an interesting retouching. I shall approve of it and adopt it if you insist. The banal phrase, "We munch a bun!" … is intentionally banal. The bathos, the limp, dangling anticlimax of the image, following the exalted register in the first line and a half, is intended to reflect the futility and vanity of humanity which is being described in the sonnet.

[41] Dear Andrew, did Dante have an editor? Or did Dante work even better with only the Holy Spirit as his editor? Is an editor necessarily going to make my work as good as Dante's? I totally agree that a skilful editor can help make certain improvements, but a skilful poet must also be allowed to write his own poetry, and there is a point at which he must say … this is all I can do! Let it stand or fall on its own merits as poetry!

the Bible with "The Word" replaced by "The Insult" and its complementary "Compliment Sincere". This is moderately entertaining but the sublime words of the original cannot be forgotten and they make one wonder, why mess them up with a callow kind of revision?[42] The next piece, "Once Upon a Time," has something of the force of folk tale and is an improvement on the distorted scripture that went before it.[43]

Part 3, "The Egotistical Sublime" (shades of Wordsworth) is a sequence of nine poems dubbed "Prayers Composed in Uninspired, Prosaic Moments". He prays for the joy of youth, for financial security, and for his sufferings to be weighed against his sins so as to grant him a direct entry to Heaven without the necessity of Purgatory and that his writings might help to save the souls of his readers. This is the egotistical not so sublime! The sequence ends with a fine prayer attributed to Mother Eugenia Travasio.

Part 4 is a verse sequence called "The Satanic Verses or the Bare Facts" whose starting point is plainly the famous, almost fatal book by Salman Rushdie. In a note Ruggier says this was "Originally conceived as a satirical indictment of Salman Rushdie and of his controversial book…." (p. 163). Satire of a master satirist like Rushdie is a risky undertaking. Could it succeed? Ruggier tries but the verses are more about Ruggier's idea of Christ as the supreme artist and the paramount place of Roman Catholic Christianity than about Salman Rushdie's book. To be truly satirical Ruggier would have needed to give the reader a detailed view of Rushdie's weakest points and heap sophisticated satire upon them. Rushdie, in brief, needs a Dryden to give him his comeuppance. But Ruggier has something in common with Rushdie: wordiness! Ruggier exclaims at one point: "And surely 'tis disorder in thy sex-life, / to lust and not to observe the Law!" (p.175). This in my view comes closest to the critique of Rushdie's writing,

---

[42] Andrew, why should I rehash the original, so unforgettably remembered by the readers, when I also have something of my own to say?

[43] Thank you …

especially of his satirical novel, *Fury*.[44]

Part 5, "Take, Then, This Bookmark…" is a verse in two five-line stanzas[45] deliberately disjointed, yoking together rhyming words and seemingly without reason but in fact recapitulating through echoing phrases some of Ruggier's themes. Part 6 is an "Interlude" of five resounding stanzas driven by clarity and sureness of touch. The pun has been called "the lowest form of wit". The pun that is the last word of the poem is ingenious: "sinsear" + sin's ear.+ sin sear + sincere. But for me it intrudes too much on the mood already established and thus produces a groan at the end f the poem.

Part 7 is a dramatic monologue in prose poetry (pp. 181-194). It repeats the major concerns of Ruggier's religious musings on Christ as artist, Roman Catholicism, confessional, the Insult as a cornerstone of his rhetorical edifice, his Pope Caesar figure, and his great, admired artists of the past. Written in a pastiche of Biblical style, one cannot avoid the notion that Ruggier is preaching at us as if he were some Biblical prophet, or worse still, a special God among artists! Each reader will take this section as she or he finds it. This particular critic rebels against it. In view of the final page in which Catholicism and its artists are seen as the educators of the world, I turn to hold up the treasures of Egypt and of Asia, and declare their great value as art and the education of the emotions.[46]

---

[44] The point of my so-called *satire* of Rushdie is purely: *bring Rushdie to justice with a poem but never with a killer's bullet!* My poem may in its own modest way have had its humble impact upon this joyful outcome, since Rushdie is presently *a Man* a hundred times better than he used to be, and since the Muslims have evidently lifted their curse of poor Salman Rushdie. My poem, besides, in its own way and much like other pieces you have been considering, brims full with substance, content, and with message, and not with aesthetic achievement only. As such, as you are noting, it is not exclusively satirical, but the message being imparted to the subject, Salman Rushdie, is unmistakeable and you do not always do justice to it.

[45] Classical, Japanese tankas with a perfect syllable count in each tanka of 5 – 7 – 5 – 7 – 7.

[46] I clearly sense your rebellion against what I am attempting, but I think what I am asking is *a willing suspension of disbelief*, not necessarily unquestioning assent. *"We are the great Catholics. We are the Artists.*

The Epilogue to the book – and how could a book by Ruggier ever appear denuded of preface, introduction, foreword, afterword, appendix or appendices, and epilogue?— bears the title "Baha'i Unity Prayer" and turns out to be merely a quotation from a Baha'i publication. This is followed by Appendix One, Part One, which is an autobiographical note "On the Author's Life" followed by an essay, Part Two, "On the Author's Writings," again by the author! A compulsive tendency is clearly the case with this meticulous wrapping of the central text within these numerous papers of explanation, although the autobiographical essay contains the claim that Ruggier cured himself of neurosis by writing poetry and appreciating music (pp. 198-200). The second essay is as clear and as well-written as the first. In my estimation, having removed them from their place as Preface, Ruggier in preparing this edition should have made them *central in the text* rather than relegating them to Appendix One.[47] They are examples of his best prose and are infinitely more interesting than his quarrels with the Church or with Salman Rushdie[48].

---

*We are the Pride of the Nations. We are the People who educated the Earth."* This entirely joyful and proud self-assertion means equally that *We, the great Catholics, are the Artists*, as much as that *We, the Artists of all Time with all our People, are the truly great Catholics.* What I am saying is ambivalent. It does not necessarily exclude what you are perceiving in the treasures of Egypt and of Asia and can also be seen to embrace all the deeply loved figures behind all the other great religions of the World who in their own, unique, individual way can be described also as great Catholics. You have not done justice to my ambivalence.

[47] If I were to make them *central in the text*, Andrew, they would become Part Five of the Book. It is the only spot I can justify fitting them in, and if you insist I shall — but does it make such a big difference whether I include these two pieces, which you admire so well, as Part Five of the central text, or whether I include them as Appendix One? Don't you think this is purely a mere change of address?

[48] Andrew, this is not a real criticism. The point of my *quarrel* with Rushdie is that I brought him to justice (symbolic) with a poem,, thereby doing my bit to appease the wrath of the Muslims, and to spare him the disaster of assassination. The Muslims have not slaughtered Rushdie, and Rushdie himself has improved his personal character by leaps and bounds. He is now, relatively speaking, a Saint of Art compared to what he used to be when the Muslims placed him upon the

Appendix Two consists of a normal biographical note that one might find on the cover of any book, though it is somewhat longer than most such notes; some complimentary comments on his work by a variety of people, some of them academics and some poets; a full-length book review of *This Eternal Hubbub* by Rudolf Penner, a bibliography, and an Index.

What remains to be said of this book? Depending on who might read it, quite a bit. I will confine myself to this: the book is uneven in quality, because there are flashes of real verbal brilliance, some outright failures resulting perhaps from an over-ambitious self-set task, and some "longeurs" as we say in France. Ruggier rightly refuses to abandon a classical education and a reverence for the past and his great literary mentors. Yet he sometimes suffers from useless phrases and obsolete locutions that detract from the whole work. It is a pity that a highly professional publisher has failed to notice his talent and potential and supplied him with a very good editor and copy editor. But would Ruggier have run the gauntlet of such editing without engaging in endless disputes? That is a merely theoretical question, because as it happens, he is his own publisher. He is right to put his faith, though, in his Canadian public, for they have over the years helped him to remain an independent writer. His existence is hard and his task very nearly thankless, but he keeps working. This is a measure of his dedication to literature and of his personal courage.[49]

---

Index. As such my humble attempt to bring him to harmless justice and *to spare him assassination* may have been a factor in the change of heart that has been so clearly obtained. Your criticisms of my *so-called quarrels* with Rushdie, as well as with Church, which are all brimming with substance and with message, are lop-eared. They do not do justice to the sincerity and evident benevolence of my concern.

[49] Andrew, thank you for the justice, fairness, and sincerity of this summing up. I totally agree about the deplorable lack of a highly professional publisher in my life, who would have supplied me with a very good editor and copy editor. Of course I would have benefited from such an arrangement. Of course I am capable of taking real criticism and dialoguing about it cordially and courteously. Other than that, in an earlier footnote I commented about a real author's need or otherwise for a real editor. I conclude that a true editor would have

LAMPLIGHTER MOST GRACIOUS ...

*Lamplighter Most Gracious.....* , first published in 2009, then reprinted, revised and then re-issued in 2010 (the edition I am using), contains reprinted material but does not overlap with the contents of *This Eternal Hubbub.* In fact *Lamplighter Most Gracious* can be considered a complementary collection to *This Eternal Hubbub.* Despite its quaint title, *Lamplighter Most Gracious* is a hefty collection of early work and also some of the latest work up to its publication date. At 545 pages it is much more than a holiday read! I would advise dipping into it or perhaps concentrating on a particular section that captures your interest, rather than reading through from beginning to end. But if a reader wanted to see if Joe Ruggier has developed as a writer, he or she could do this by plunging into the early work, much of it exercises in pastiche of works in the English canon, and then turning to look at the most recent work. Again, the actual literary contents of the book are wrapped in layers of front matter, the dedication, the Elegy for his mother, the Author's Preface, and a Note to this revised printing. The end matter is conventional enough, being Index, Biographical Note, and a List of the author's other works. But within the book there are more "wrapping papers" at the head of various sections. These are sometimes necessary to guide us into what follows. But as usual with Ruggier's writing, a good editor might want to cut and cut again. The Author's Preface gives a necessary fact: "*Lamplighter Most Gracious* features, in one convenient volume, seven of my outstanding, published or unpublished, collections of prose and poetry, and merely excludes, in the interests of effective distribution, all work previously published in *This Eternal Hubbub.*" (p. xvii).

---

helped me immeasurably many years ago, but I do have my own deeply set views. I also take very seriously all of the critical suggestions of all the friends I have among the professors, among whom I am honoured to number yourself.

"Outstanding" here is ambiguous. I shall not take it to mean extraordinarily good![50] But this Preface then gives more autobiographical detail of Ruggier's marketing processes. I value more this essay when it tells me that the pieces are not all of top quality but "they tell of a threaded, ongoing spiritual odyssey..." (p. xviii). Here the author accurately describes his life's work so far. Although in many ways quite humble, Ruggier has a persistent need to proclaim his importance as a writer. This is not mere bragging; it seems to me based on a constant need to bolster himself against the kind of desperate depression that may result when one's publications make a tinkle that is not necessarily resounding. But this preface is shot through with moments of wise honesty: "I would never love Canada so deeply, did I not love so well the Land of my birth. Canada and Malta are both **my country....**" (p. xix). Here I think he speaks not only for himself; it applies to many immigrants from many different nations. And charmingly, he later admits his own vanity. I would add fierce pride. This is part of what keeps his head above the waters of the Fraser River! At the same time, there is a streak of ingratitude: "...the only free gift this Nation ever made me, even though it was only Canada, was a disability pension." (p. xxii). The long-suffering Canadian taxpayer pays for social services manned usually by pleasant officials trying to do a good job. Other nations I could name are actually hostile to the idea of subsidizing immigrants, especially writers. The writer is a species who often needs the aid of PEN or Amnesty International in many other parts of the world.[51]

To get back to the actual writing, Ruggier rightly characterizes his work as having "...countless *motifs,* arising from my views about Life, about the truth of Faith and the truth of Art, my work often evokes states of mind, mentalities, mindsets, wildly diverging points of view...all of which are allowed to co-exist with all the contradictions, just as they do in life, but I am, personally, ***a man of Faith***.

[50] You are correct ...

[51] Your rapping me on the knuckles for this alleged ingratitude may be quite a good point and may call for closer scrutiny if I ever revise my author's preface to **Lamplighter** ...

" (p. xxii). This is an excellent guide to what reading Ruggier is all about.

The first part of this book in seven parts is *The Voice of the Millions* (1988). It is reprinted with its own Preface, one that starts well: "MILTON called *Rhyme* the invention of a barbarous age. If that is so, then I should say that it is proper that this age of ours should compose a few jingles." (p.6). At the end of this Preface he states what his work shows throughout his Canadian career: "*I like to feel free* to write in any style which I think will serve my purpose." (p. 7). I wholeheartedly agree. Whether he always makes the right form for his poems is another matter. Interestingly, this section features dramatic verse retelling folk stories—Cinderella (pp. 9-10) and Beauty and the Beast. (pp.19-32). This latter, the most ambitious, and doubling as an Epithalamion, reads very well, combining the folk elements with contemporary ones, such as when a phrase from the Romantic age is reworked to fit our "barbarous" age: "A thing of beauty is a good investment" (p.22). The poem proceeds by means of different voices, those of Narrator, Beast, Beauty, and Merchant. But in a dialogue section headed "The voices of Beauty and the Beast" the end is not sustained as dialogue, because a narrative voice (in fact more the poet himself than the Narrator) concludes the section (p. 28, lines 281-83). A sharper-eyed bit of revision could easily have fixed this. Cut and revise are two "writerly" procedures from which Mr. Ruggier's work would hugely benefit. Nevertheless, this extraordinary dramatic poem has moments of lyric beauty that recall earlier stages in the history of literature while being totally contemporary; such a moment is this from the Beast's love song:[52]

> She saw me in the garden,
> stretched dying in my lair,
> beneath my rose bush fair,
> beneath my lush, white roses fair,
> dying in calm despair.
>
> (p. 29, lines 314-318).

[52] Thank you indeed for this high praise …

Here the rhymes are essential to situation and mood, creating a sound that is nothing short of the exhalation of a dying breath. The repetitions contrast sharply the almost impersonal first line, setting the place and action, with the ailing condition of the Beast. If "The rhyme of the Beast" dominates this section, there are other, shorter poems that deserve mention: "Just as a woman…"; "Identity"; "Words"; "The downtrodden's pride"; or "Haunted house in a picture".

Part two of the book, "In the Suburbs of Europe," opens with a sketch map of the Mediterranean Sea with Malta's position as "Crossroads of Europe". The subtitle is "perspectives on Maltese language and literature" and the cover page from the "2nd revised edition" bears the subtitle "Malta 1977 Vancouver 1993". There is a foreword by Paul Matthew St. Pierre of Simon Fraser University followed, inevitably, by an Author's preface; this serves to inform us of the bilingualism of Ruggier as translator of Maltese writing and cultural "ambassador" making aspects of the Maltese heritage available in the Anglophone world. There follows an essay, "Malta in Context" that is a survey of language and literature by Ruggier. It is lively and covers a lot of ground, touching on the bases of Maltese as a language, the history of this island fortress, and the resurgence of a Maltese identity with a language revival, much humbug, according to Ruggier, and the importance in Malta of the writer Dun Karm Psaila. The essay also deals with the vigorous literary activity spurred by national independence after countless centuries of Malta's role as a base for powerful overlords. A.J. Arberry's translations of Maltese writing are also mentioned. The present writer remembers Arberry at Pembroke College Cambridge in the late fifties and early sixties of the last century. The essay ends with an argument, however, for the Maltese writer to avoid an overbearing sense of isolation by switching from the little circle of Maltese language to English as a medium which involves contact with other writers galore and a wide international audience. This necessarily entails the chance to become a truly *national-international writer,* in itself a true kind of modernity, though it may still be frowned upon by nationalistic, and even parochial editors. Such modern internationalism in fact is entirely suitable for the Maltese writer, since, as Ruggier concludes, Malta has always been a cosmopolitan society. It is small but not merely "backwoods." The next essay is a follow-up again concerned with Psaila, making the point that his achievement as a writer is all the greater because he had no real literary tradition on which to build. He was very much a pioneer. Furthermore, his use of Maltese, though popular on the island, was something of a handicap, for the language simply lacks the scope and depth of English, fashioned by so many writers of the first rank since Chaucer and the Scottish Chaucerians of medieval times. Ruggier concludes with his translation of Psaila's "Visit to Jesus," a devotional poem, better than Larkin's "Churchgoing". There then follow further translations from the Maltese, this time of work by Oliver Friggieri. Reading these translations one can see where Ruggier's own exalted voice, religious sensibility, extravagance of sentiment and exclamatory verse hail from. I have time only to mention one of these fine translations, but if a reader read nothing but this one, "My countrymen, I love you" (pp. 120-121) he or she would be rewarded.[53]

Section Two follows with just two poems of Ruggier's own: "To Sarah," a poem of praise, advice, and prayer; and a poem in the voice of his child, "''Queen Sarah Therese to her daddy". The entire section is illustrated with line drawings of Maltese scenes that give a real sense of the rugged charms of the island and of its havens.

Part Three of this book, "regrets hopes regards and prayers" comprises a selection of Ruggier's juvenilia. Again there is a Preface, this time by LeRoy Douglas Travis, dated Vancouver, July 1996 for the publication of the book in that year. The first three poems are dated 1974-1975. They are apprentice pieces, with Keats and others hovering in the shadows. From 1977 we find fourteen poems and the sonnet

---

[53] Thank you, Andrew. I am myself extremely fond of these translations and both proud and happy to havc honoured well Oliver Friggieri.

form dominates. There is competent pastiche; and the Metaphysicals as well as Eliot are the beckoning shades. In "Three sonnets of desolation and a love sonnet" the great forerunners are present but so is an authentic voice, that of Ruggier himself, for these are the themes that will dominate both his life and his writing.[54] It is thus highly appropriate that this selection contains "A poem of self-discovery" (p. 153). The final poem "Night" is in the voice Ruggier needs to express his *angst* and "a pillar of Fire in my head." (p. 156). It is dated 5/12/77. The poems from the following year are still full of echoes of the tradition, and Eliot, a modern master, is very much present, but so is Coleridge. The religious theme grows and "Judas" (pp. 158-59) is a good example of its effect and power. The poems in the 1979 selection again feature translations from the Maltese as well as original work. For me the selection contains one of Ruggier's better efforts, "Cressida, my Cressida" (pp. 175-77) and the interesting "Three Interior Monologues" (pp.181-85), where Joyce and Gertrude Stein "cohabit" in Ruggiers prose poetry. The 1980 selection again features interesting translations but there is also an essay on Beethoven's Ninth Symphony. The conclusion is "Ode: to Beethoven" (pp. 200-201). Unfortunately, this suffers from the lack of an editorial cut. The excellent first line is followed by the intrusion of Ruggier himself into an ode supposedly about Beethoven! The poem would gain in power if the entire first stanza were cut.[55] The 1981-1982 selection contains what I regard as Ruggier's best devotional poem, "Liturgy of Ashes" (pp. 210-13). These Gregorian verses are spoken or chanted by two voices, those of Penitent and Priest. The poem has some of the baroque extravagance of Crashaw tempered by a contemporary sense of exile and the strength of religious faith worn like chain

---

[54] Thank you, Andrew. Your gentle praise soothes my ego because I am still very fond of these early pieces.

[55] Thank you. Andrew. I have taken this criticism already. The first line has been retained, but I have thrown away the entire first stanza, according to your recommendation. This editorial retouching will be reflected in the next printing of my book, which will happen as soon as I can pay the printing agency.

mail in the rhymes and repetitions of this plainsong poem that would merit performance by a priest and the poet in a Catholic church setting.[56] The poem is followed by a short essay on genius, in which we find the graceful idea that while mere talent can harm humanity, "Genius has civilized humanity…." (p. 214). This is backed up by examples. The section also contains haikus and tankas showing the Japanese influence again on Canadian writers. The last poem in the section is dedicated to Rex Hudson but is marred by a grotesque rhyme:

> Your Book's the Angel's Trumpet!
> …
> Christ risen, Rex, we lump it:
> (p. 224).

Juxtaposing the majesty of Christ risen with the English slang phrase "lump it" can only make the poem collapse, inviting rhymesters to shout with glee such words as "crumpet", "hump it" and so dump it![57]

In the 1983-1985 collection we find poem as prayer, as satire thanks to Eliot (and perhaps Pound) with unacknowledged use of Yeats's phrase "the heart's core" (see pp. 226-27). There then follow some competent critical pieces. The paragraph on Hopkins is very acute (pp. 230-31). The section ends with the English and Maltese versions of a jaunty and vociferous dramatic monologue, "All fule's lament".

Part four is entitled "Lady Vancouver" being nine poems by Joe Ruggier. It begins with the curious, eccentric, and simple (in a good sense) elegy for President Kennedy, "Oh tell me who if anyone does not want to listen…" In this poem, echoes of Baudelaire, Auden, and perhaps the Marlowe of *Edward II* fit in appropriately enough. The elegy is angry rather than resigned. The general quality of

---

[56] Once more, thank you very much for this high praise. I am very fond of the poem.

[57] This criticism, Andrew, is depressingly correct, and I do not know what on earth can be done to set the poem right at this stage, many years after I was inspired to pen it …

the poems in this section is high, with "Lady Vancouver: to Thora Arnason" making effective and legitimate use of the famous line "Lead, kindly Light." (pp. 262-65). The "Elegy for Rex Hudson, 1915-1996" starts brilliantly but would benefit by cutting, especially at the end where the poem careers out of control and becomes too extravagant (p. 267).[58] The "Elegy for Professor Enriquez, 1925-1997) is much more accomplished and is deeply felt. I would alter "speaketh" to "speak" in line six, but I am pleased to have the last line of this elegy: "Yours is the universe, ours a Death to come!" (p. 273).

Part five of the book is "A Richer Blessing" and consists of poetry and prose. There is an Author's Preface and a Foreword by George Csaba Koller. The Preface gives a brief explanation of what Ruggier's writings attempt: a neoclassical revival as well as a rhyme revival; he is not, however, a prisoner of rhyme. He insists, quite rightly, that the ordinary people buy his work, even if it uses language stemming from the past, especially the Romantics, but he rightly depicts much contemporary and modernist verse as suffering from "far too much obscurity, tortured sense, and lack of manly feeling." (p.281). The Foreword by Koller is

---

[58] This is not a real criticism. The last two stanzas read: *"For sincerity hath rules of rhyme and rhythm, / and frankness carved in art is not offensive, / and to the butchered heart, which troubles fathom, / the trumpets of the Angels are defensive. / Art is immortal, shadowing but the Spirit! / Saint Rex of Minnesota liveth on, / too good to cast away, but to inherit / fame eternal past opinion gone!"* At the word *"trumpets"* I was listening to the trumpets in Beethoven's *Eroica* symphony. At the words *"Art is immortal"* I heard the clash of the cymbals, with the trumpets sill blaring in the background. At the words *"fame eternal etc."*, (with the last line being a collage and not quite a logical, grammatical sentence), I was hearing the castanets, and the *duende*, the dying away, of Spanish music. And at the last word in the poem, *"gone"*, I clearly heard the gong. Very frankly, Andrew, I cannot expect the reader to hear what I heard in my head, whilst creating the poem, unless he has a supernatural experience, but the intensely auditory imagination is there, right within my words. My poem vindicates the reputation I have with some readers that I hear music within my head and make it poetry and my poem does anything but career out of control and become too extravagant. This is not a real criticism and I shall never ever cut my poem.

forthright and honest in its irritation with Joe Ruggier, but he concludes with the idea that Ruggier's insistence on form might make a comeback in contemporary poetry (it already has, if certain English and Irish poets, including Seamus Heaney, are taken into account) and finishes by saying: "...rarely does a poet bare his soul with such honesty, ferocity and precision of language and rhythm." (p. 286).

Part five of the collection, "A Richer Blessing," opens with dream visions that smell of Blake's influence. "Jehovah" is a folksy, jocular, satire of outworn ideas of what God might be, "old Man with a mighty / white beard fond of his Pipe...." (p. 288). More compelling and strange is the next one, "De Civitate Dei" with its Latin title giving it a more learned, administrative and, of course, Roman idea of God. So we have two roots of Christianity presented, the Hebrew and the Latin. This second vision is more compelling, more serious, and more humorous. It is also satirical, but satirical of the modernity we know in parts of North America: "Like / a new Las Vegas was the City I / was in nor could the night-clubs in Las Vegas / boast preciser theologians-demonologians!" (p. 289). Human realities intrude into this dream fiction giving it more serious dimensions, such as the lament for aborted embryos, for suicidal lovers, and for the poet's own life: "Why did You not the law / take in Thy hand, and likewise me abort?" (p. 290). This is a powerful species of despair going back to the Greeks and the line of tragic heroes who rue the day they were born. But God's answer forms the last line of the poem and is nothing more than bathos. Better to have cut it out and left the poet asking but waiting on a reply.[59] Shelley of course looms with "The Pyramids of Ozymandias" but this poem goes beyond Shelley to attain its own strange power, a power that the rhetoric maintains throughout. This is one of Ruggier's most perfectly accomplished poems (pp. 290-91).[60] After these dream visions, the poet offers another that, based on a real incident, is a visionary

[59] I always considered God's answer, in this last line, as ambivalent and mysterious, with only a slight touch of what you call *"bathos"*.
[60] Thank you indeed for this high praise. I love this poem and many readers have agreed.

discussion: “Talking of messages in Dreams” The strength of these verses must be acknowledged, and part of that strength is their very strangeness. The following poem is “Elegy for my friend – FB”. This Dantesque encounter with a friend who had been dead for seven years already from the date of the poem (1997) is for me marred by the stubborn use of “thee” and “thou”; the modern form would be better and the Dantesque element would still be there. The mixture of prose and poetry that follows the “Requiem for my canary” I shall not consider beyond saying that it has some sound points to make about poetic form and the contemporary scene, but it is very much a self-congratulatory compendium that embarrasses the mature reader. The generalization that writers who submit work that is published at other people’s expense are “gutless” is a ridiculous generalization. It is more difficult to get work accepted by the people who have to pay for it, than it is to self-publish, for the self-publisher does not have to run the gauntlet of seasoned and cold-hearted publishers’ readers![61] Leaving this kind of literary argument to one side, it’s interesting to see what Ruggier says about his own publishing practices. The nub of this can be found in the prose passage that describes his routine as writer, self-publisher and self-marketer (see pp. 334-336). Ruggier’s method of composition is set out interestingly and clearly a bit later in the book (pp. 339-342). The remaining work in this section is mainly devotional but with a burst of anger at a “testy” and “pharisaic” man in the short poem “Ungracious pastor” (p. 344). But the most interesting revelation in the section is Ruggier’s account of the Blessed Faustina, who was ridiculed by some nuns in her convent, but had conversations with Christ and like a secretary wrote down his words to her. This was a kind of mediumistic automatic writing that seems to be a spiritual defence mechanism against the ridicule she suffered from other nuns. Her case perhaps offers some comfort to Ruggier[62]

[61] There seems to me to be a lot to be said, for and against, what I am arguing, as well as for the criticism you are making …
[62] Correct …

who has also been rejected and writes expansively of his particular relationship with the Holy Family.

Part six begins with its usual front matter of a "critical introduction" this time by Ron Johnson, a retired English professor from the University of British Columbia. Johnson's style is clear and concise. His academic strengths and reasoning as well as his knowledge of the contemporary literary scene and its history, all make his essay very valuable as a critical appreciation of the writings in "Songs of Gentlest Reflection." In fact, Johnson has said so many acute things about this collection that it leaves little for me to add. Yet I add that the prose satire of a Shakespeare scholar, Professor Lizard SunBasker, is very funny (pp. 383-87)[63] and "All Love is sacred….." a blank verse "sonnet" achieved in one mighty sentence, is a *to*ur *de force.*[64] It says that in spite of all the "filthy modern tide" as Yeats called it, love remains as a private saving grace. I must also add that "Lamplighter most gracious…" and "Faultfinder, faultfinder…" (pp. 428-30) reassert themes central to Ruggier's entire enterprise. One comment: contemporary Canada and indeed North America resounds with people who parrot admiringly the phrase "non-judgmental" as if any criticism were unjustified. Yet they don't seem to realize that in trying to make people less critical they are themselves making judgments. To be truly unbiased would mean a total blandness. But Ruggier's poem against fault-finders is much more profound than the discourse of the cliché-ridden non-judgmental crowd.[65] I also add that the essay "Poet and 'failed' musician….." is well worth reading for its ideas about music, music teaching, and the need for an artist to find and trust his or her own particularity (pp. 431-40). Most of the poems that follow are accomplished works and require no further praise from me, except to say that "Critical appreciation" is a poem that gives an expert and careful description of the

---

[63] Thank you, Andrew, but do you not think Professor SunBasker also makes interesting points about Shakespeare interprettation?

[64] Thank you, Andrew. I am very fond of this piece.

[65] Thank you, Andrew. I feel very strongly in favour of the point you are making.

craft of writing and of the conversation with God that is called prayer.[66]

Part seven is the final part of this book — *In the Canon's Roar* (2009). It contains previously unpublished new work that formed the book. The preface, foreword, introduction, author's note etc. are all lacking. Strikingly, the section opens with a strong poem on Christ, "Just that one Man….." (p. 477). In "Reflections about stylistic matters…" the poet well defines his own case of mixed styles, ancient and modern: "I seem to live / in this eternal instant…" (pp. 479-80). The verses go on to describe clearly and tersely Ruggier's point of view and his fostering of the eclectic rather than a restrictive muse.[67] The help he has had from a particular friend (whose identity is never revealed) is neatly and in the end movingly described in "A character…" (pp. 483-84). Many of the poems in this collection are reflections on life and religion as Ruggier, now middle-aged looks back on experience. In "An awful judgement" (p. 494) Ruggier achieves an extremely simple and therefore powerful expression of his humorous yet strict vision of his own last judgment. This is a poem that should exist![68] The other poems in the section display an array of differing styles and subjects. One feels that Ruggier has a repertoire of which he is master. The end of the section is prose: five essays each discussing one of Ruggier's major concerns as a writer. The first is a retrospective on Eliot. A lifelong admiration of Eliot gives the essay many interesting turns of thought and the confession that Eliot was a refuge for the undergraduate Ruggier who suffered from the mockery of his classmates. The second essay is a lament for all that is going wrong: the decay of architecture, language, and music. Much of this is true to everyday experience but we also have to realize that there are some magnificent contemporary achievements too in all these fields. The essay on the parable of the talents is a very astute definition

---

[66] Again, thank you, Andrew, for this high, if subdued and gentle, praise.

[67] This is an extremely appropriate summation of the theme of this poem.

[68] Thank you, Andrew …

of talent and an assessment of the import of the parable. The fourth essay is on Christ's commandment to "love thy neighbor as you love yourself" and upon Whitman's "Song of Myself". This is a quirky Ruggier sermon that is stimulating and contains much truth. It should be preached from the pulpit to a drowsy congregation. The final essay is about another abiding concern of the poet, "style matters…" where Ruggier tackles the old chestnut about content and style by demanding that whatever is said be said by means of careful craftsmanship. But what makes this brief essay different from other discussion of the topic is that Ruggier brings God into the equation. And this is what by now we would expect!

The entire book's end matter is a useful index of first lines and another biographical note on Ruggier followed by a select list of his previous publications.

## CONCLUSION[69]

What remains to be said? Of the three books I have considered here, I find the last, *Lamplighter most gracious.....* to be the best and most interesting in its sweep. Here is the literary career of an artist that records his growth, his failures and his successes. Joe Ruggier is "one off" (to use a British image from the factory floor) and his position on the fringe of the Canadian literary establishment is unshakeable because his personal strength and persistence have made it possible for him to sell his wares door-to-door

---

[69] I appreciate your noble, generous praise of my personal character and Christian qualities. In a conclusion to such an essay, however, I would have expected a brief, tersely worded statement about the Beauty of my manner, my stylistic achievement, as much as about the Truth of my substance. All the three books you scrutinize brim with message, substance, gist, truthful content. They all contain careful thinking, as well as much theology and metaphysics, often stated, often clued and implied cryptically between the lines. You have often confined yourself to matters of style without always conveying in a few words my message. A real artist does not expect to be praised for his personal character and his style alone without being praised according to the rules for the Beauty of his manner and the Truth of his substance.

and thus cock a snook at the conventional print outlets that have probably in the past cold-shouldered him. This makes him admirable in many ways. His literary achievement though, as this essay has shown, is very mixed. But it is gratifying to see a certain strength achieved and a certain promise fulfilled.[70]

**Andrew Parkin Ph. D.**
*Paris-Vancouver, October, 2010.*

[70] Andrew, a true creative writer does not wish to be praised for the shining Christian qualities of his personal character only. You are praising me, generously, for "lack of greed", "tenacity", "personal strength and persistence", "love of the poor" and for "embracing poverty", and for a few other qualities which bring to mind manuals of piety. I do esteem your veneration of these qualities, and I do thank you for your generous praise of my character, but what makes literature a sincere honour as literature is the aesthetic **beauty** of the language, and the **truth** of the substance. **Beauty and Truth**, within literature, are what makes literature a sincere honour as such, and not necessarily the author's **Sanctity**. This is what a true writer wishes to be praised for. It may be said that you do not always go to the heart of the matter.

# Acknowledgments

GRATITUDE is due to my Canadian public through whose advance subscriptions the first three printings were entirely sponsored — whereas my generous patron Ralph Cunningham bore the cost of printing the 2nd edition. Thanks also to Ross Labrie, Ph.D. (of UBC -- English) for his sensitive copyediting, at the last minute prior to publication of the 1st edition, of six of the prose essays included in this collection; and to Warren Stevenson, Ph.D., as well as to Allan Smith, Ph.D., for similar favours. Thanks above all are owing to Andrew Parkin Ph.D. for taking the time and the care to create such a long, perceptive, and meaningful study of my published work, featured in the 2nd & current editions as an introduction from Parkin's independent pen. Thanks also to Paul Matthew StPierre Ph.D., LeRoy D. Travis Ph.D., Oliver Friggieri Ph.D., George Csaba Koller, Ron Johnson Ph.D., Michael R. Burch, Mary Rae and Esther Cameron Ph.D., for allowing me to use their writeups … introducing the various sections when they first were issued as books in their own right, or else published as reviews after these appeared in print. Many of these poems, some in earlier versions, have appeared in various publications, such as: *Candelabrum Poetry Magazine*; *The Eclectic Muse; The Neo-Victorian/Cochlea; The Deronda Review; Sonnetto Poesia;* online at—*www.thehypertexts.com; Poetry Life and Times (edited by Robin Ouzman Hislop); Pennine Platform*; and *New Hope International (edited by Gerald England).* More specific acknowledgments may be found at the start of each of the eight major sections of this publication. Finally, the brown mahogany desk in the cover photo, which I owned since before I came to Canada, originally belonged to my maternal grandfather, the Honourable Ġużé Micallef Ll.D.—a Lawyer, as well as Member of Parliament and Minister of Agriculture in Malta, and likewise a dedicated scholar of semitic languages—who designed the desk himself, paying to have it manufactured for his personal use. Gratitude goes out to my parents for gifting me with this family heirloom upon which I created, drafted and typed a few of my outstanding books.

# Part one:
# The voice of the millions

**Joe M. Ruggier**
**Malta - 1977**
**Vancouver - 1988**

THE
VOICE OF
THE MILLIONS
SELECTED
POEMS by
JOE M. RUGGIER

**REVIEWS OF JOE M. RUGGIER'S WORK**

*"While poetic fashion, in our age, veers drunkenly between the Scylla of self-conscious triviality and the Charybdis of pretentious obscurity, Ruggier's poetry is like a clear crystalline sea through which one can see infinitely far. The medium seldom, if ever, obscures the message; and where Blake's vision derives mainly from the Hebrew prophets, Ruggier's lyric inspiration springs from the broader, more complex tradition of Mediterranean Catholicism. It is probably this which enables him to handle both religious and erotic themes with the same lyrical freshness. For such a comparatively young poet he attains, at his best, an astonishingly self-assured marriage of boldness and delicacy that is unique in contemporary English language poetry."*

**Roy Harrison, Poet, Merseyside, UK**

*"Joe Ruggier takes up his poetic stand on the issue of freedom - the freedom not necessarily to write free verse, but to be at liberty to be himself, and to write either in traditional metric rhyming forms, or otherwise. A strong response to contemporary currents impels his verse, which is, paradoxically, often at its best in* **vers libre.** *Here his tone is restrained, commanding sympathetic attention. His critical judgment of poetry in general I find both sensitive and understanding, particularly the lyrical poetry of Boris Pasternak."*

**Lydia Pasternak Slater, Author, Translator, Oxford, U.K.**

*"On the surface clean, clear, traditional -- like a classic face; yet shining up through the surface, mystery -- a religious sensibility and a subtle mind. Such is the poetry of Mr. Ruggier. It has been a great treat to hear his voice. His poetry should be read and re-read, and pleasure will attend each reading."*

**John Langford, Vancouver Poet**

PierPont Press

*542 Elmspring Ave.*
*Wauwatosa, WI 53226*

*ISBN 0-929659-01-5*

# The Voice of the Millions

**Printing History**
1st, 2nd & 3rd Edition -- **PIERPONT PRESS**,
Wauwatosa, WI 53226

Printed in the U.S.A.

4th Electronic Edition on CD-ROM --
**MBOOKS OF BC**, Richmond, BC, CANADA
**ISBN: 0-9733301-0-4**

E-Mail: jrmbooks@hotmail.com

**ISBN 0-929659-01-5 (1st Edition)**

**LIBRARY OF CONGRESS CATALOG CARD NUMBER 88-62403 (1st Edition)**



**5th print Edition, selected for**
**and produced as Part One of the 1st , 2nd & 3rd editions**
**of Joe Ruggier's Collected Poems : June 2009 – June 2018**
**ISBN to the current edition : 978-1-897303-26-9**

**Cover photo by Joe M. Ruggier**

Courteous acknowledgments for the liberty to reissue
this collection within my Collected poems
are owing in particular to the publishers of the 3rd edition ---
**PIERPONT PRESS,**
**542 Elmspring Avenue, Wauwatosa, WI 53226;**
**(Brenda Smet Klebba, Managing Editor).**

1st, 2nd and 3rd editions printed and bound in the USA
4th electronic edition produced by:
**Progress Media Duplication, Richmond, B.C.**
this edition printed and bound by: **Lightning Source Inc.; USA**

**Over 925 Copies in Circulation**

## dedication sonnet
## for Sarah Therese, my daughter

**SWEETHEART**, what brush shall frame your baby face;
a miniature of innocence and Grace?
What hand shall frame the God within your eyes?
What Art the nameless Truth which in them lies?
Do not lose your unaffected air,
as you grow up and learn to handle care!
Preserve her in her loveliest, her best;
Lord, let her not say — “Fuck!” like all the rest!
May she grow and find true Love; and find
an Editor built-in within her Mind!
May she discern true Culture; from the tart
opinion, may she be a soul apart!
Or else, if the vile world should foul her eye,
and drown her infant charm, then let her die.

29.09.87

**FOR SARAH THERESE** tied for 1st place with 3 other poets in **THE MARK WILD MEMORIAL COMPETITION** organized by **THE RED CANDLE PRESS,** formerly of WISBECH, UK. The closing date of this contest was April 31st, 1988.

## Poet's preface

MILTON called *Ryme* the invention of a barbarous age. If that is so, then I should say that it is proper that this age of ours should compose a few jingles. Very few poets, perhaps, are able to work under the tight discipline of good sense, rhyme and metre. For no other apparent reason, it seems, than that they lack the skill to discipline their verse, many write so called '*free*' verse, and mistake their *insecurity* for Milton's 'sense secure'. The imbecility of uninspired, perfunctory form is in fact only surpassed by that into which the rebellion against tradition has now descended.

Like all moderns I have a grudge against Convention. I rebel against the convention of rebelling against all Convention. Free verse, it is true, has become a convention, but free verse used to arouse in me a feeling as of righteous indignation. T S Eliot proved me right. For the poet who wants to do a good job, he said very wisely, there is no such thing as *free* verse, and we all know that he is one of the great masters of *free verse*.

On this matter of style, I always say, I like to feel free, and I *have to* be myself. I do not wish to be restrained to write nothing but so called *free* verse, but I am in no way prejudiced against *free verse*. Having, in fact, myself made many attempts to write good free verse, I would like free verse to stay; and reading Eliot, I felt the conviction grow that I wanted to write free verse, and nothing else. Once I had understood T S Eliot correctly, however, I felt an overpowering need to write good metrical verse before anything else. I have thus written numerous poems in rhyme and metre, the best of which are being included in this volume of experimental verse, because, when I first began to write poetry, and I have now been writing seriously for well over six years, I was possessed by a powerful feeling: that one should not elect to write in *free* verse because one is unable to turn out a stanza.

*Free Verse*, no doubt, is as entitled to stay as Christianity itself. Heightened Prose and Free Verse were the forms which the Author of Scripture Himself originated, and in which He composed: to abolish *Free Verse* would thus become a major offence against Tradition. Apart from wishing to express the crying need for disciplined technique, however, it is my ambitious hope that my sonnets, villanelles, haikus, tankas, rhymes, stanzas, blank verse and free verse will express the beauty of Freedom which is governed by Reason.

For I have no ambition to join the ranks of poets-penny-each. *I like to feel free* to write in any style which I think will serve my purpose. I like to feel that Chaucer's Rhyme Royal, Milton's Blank Verse, and Eliot's Free Verse, are my birthright, though of course, to be a poet, I will *have to* be myself, and also, *a son of the age*.

**JMR**, *Vancouver*
*February 1983*

# Poems

## Cinderella
### a dramatic monologue

**A GRIMY** soul I was,
and my sisters, just in their master morality,
never took me to the City, so just were they.
"You are the slave," they said, just in their master morality:
so just were they
I beat my breast.
They always left me alone, alone, all by my soul,
in a chuckling house.

One day I felt the Presence of a Lover.
I did not see this Other that I shall one day encounter,
and we knew each other, though I never saw this Other:
I did conceive, and in pain and joy bring forth
a love for grimy souls, disinterest in just ones.

I felt Him calling me to the City.
I felt Him commanding me not to overreach the Hour.
And all were subdued by the grace in my eyes,
the new birth of Love in my face.
And my brethren so just did not know me.

But enchanted, I overreached the Hour, rushed out on the stroke,
ended where I begun, a grimy soul,
and shall begin where I ended.

Thanks be to my Lover,
I dropped a slipper on the stroke of the Hour,
which people took to the Prince of the City.
And the Prince of the City swore He would marry the Owner.
Up and down, through villas, mansions, banks and palaces,
up and down he roamed,
and nowhere did he find grace in an eye,
nowhere a new birth of Love in a face.
He turned at last to the out-of-the-ways,
and came at last to where lived two just brethren and I.

"You are the slave," they said, just in their master morality:
so just were they
I beat my breast.
And they strained! Oh how they strained!
But he found no grace in their eyes,
nowhere a new birth of Love in their face.

And once more I felt the Presence of my Lover,
and to the Prince I said: "I am Another's!"
And all were subdued by the grace in my eyes,
the new birth of Love in my face.

My brethren now knew me.
Shaken now by terror and afflicted self-righteousness,
"It is good, it is good," my brethren said, "that Evil should
exist!"
"Oh yea?" sang I:
"and it is good that Hell should exist!
But sister,
look up! Sister,
look up!
Did we ever understand Falsehood believing it?
Did we ever understand Love disbelieving it?
A Paradox is the Sign of Truth!"

*4.1.78*

## A poem for Old Tom

**i**

**ACROSS** the bald and bowed and lengthening gaze of the
moon
drifts a long miasma, now broadening, now blotting out,
now drawing a veil.

The thorns rattle, and the leafless, brittle bushes chuckle
in the wailing wind that tugs
the cloak of a desolate student. Trudging
under the weight of ancient world-sorrow,
he cannot see the heart of the road for the mist that hugs it.

Thomas, of you I write, from you I seek relief,
as you, once, are said to have sought relief,
waking up your friend in the dead of night,
and asking, asking: "Ma Io saro' salvo?"

**ii**

Across the gentle and bowed and desolate gaze of the
Crucifix
drifts a long miasma, now broadening, now blotting out,
now drawing a veil -

the secluded convent quiet, the chapel candle-lit
where monks all over chant -
and Thomas is on his knees
asking, asking.

And a replying Voice all over drew a hush which all could
hear:
*"Hai scritto bene di Me, Tomaso!*
*Cosa vuoi per i tuoi lavori?"*
*"Solamente Te, O Signore!"*[71]

[71] "Well have you written of Me, Thomas! What reward do you wish from Me for all your labours?" "Yourself Alone, Oh Lord!" ---- words reported to have been spoken to Saint Thomas Aquinas, by the Lord Jesus Himself, while Saint Thomas was praying in front of the Blessed Sacrament in his home convent. These words, originally spoken in Latin, were overheard by other monks praying in the same chapel. They are more or less recorded by all of his serious biographers.

**iii**

After such example, what forgiveness?
Great Saint Philosopher
suffer me not to mock myself with falsehood!
Of life a student, am I not, like you,
born and baptized into the One True Fold,
and yet a convert to my Lord and my God?

*25.4.78*

## This windless night

**I WANT** to write, this windless night,
and where shall I begin?

This windless night
a field of speary wheat stands at Pryapic
beside my home.
I prefer it in waving charm:
weed-winding, wind-wandering banners and plumes
that remind me of the Militant Church.

Stop.
Need I say it so religiously?
Must I always write with such passionate religion?

I have known, of course,
the art which most deeply calls
my senses and soul in play;
and I have learnt
that a poem without inspiration
is like a marriage without a consummation,
or like a Church without the Holy Eucharist.

That was I, but not I, who spoke.

Jealousy and anger, bitterness and hatred, dirtily common emotion, this is all the bewildering passion of a phenomenal I, subjective and personal, that is, not your kind of person, changed, changed utterly in the noumenal existence given expression in the greatest art, but the moment you deny emotion, you cease to be objective: the true language of art is objective emotion.

Much have I relished, of course,
the art which most deeply calls
my senses and soul in play,
and I have learnt
the secret of its way to everywhere:
how the bards of Italy and Greece
and England, who found their way to everywhere,
all wrote with such cold and passionate religion.

They are men
whom I cannot hope to emulate:
they are men
whom I cannot but imitate:
from however afar
I must follow.

What is great Art
but a mystic Communion
drawing me that I may draw others?

*28.4.78*

## Dramatic monologue

The mother of St Joseph of Copertino wanted him at all costs to be a Priest. He was hounded into a Seminary. He never got through a single Exam but by miraculous intervention. He was ordained. This dramatic monologue is a speech which I like to imagine him giving his interviewers at the Seminary Finals.

**THOUGH THE** decision is yours,
the criteria, fathers, must be these.

Ever since I remember, my mother
would have me talk with priests,
most of them well-to-do.
To see me serve at the Altar
she would not spare the rod.
I was hounded into this seminary where
but by miraculous intervention
I never got through a single exam.

I would like all of you, who sit at this panel,
to know that a book is for me
a devil in the wilderness - ycs, Father,
its grapes are not sour - but books make my nether-lip
tremble with tears; they are devils -
Father, yes, for me alone -
rolling megaliths to the mouth of Christ's tomb,
my heart, that longs at the Altar to cross
the bread and wine, and give Him at last
all the Love which my selfish soul can give.

These the criteria!
Yours the decision!

If you like
you can pinch my soul
on whom has been cast a look of Love.

Not the first time
that suffering will have met me beard to beard,
and I am always glad to beard him in his den.

*16.5.78*

## Elegy

*upon the death of Pope John Paul I*

**PEOPLE SOB,**
if only Tyrants died!
And I would never have heard
Siegfried's funeral dirge,
did only Tyrants die.
Yet People sob,
if only Tyrants died!

*30.9.78*

## Love-letter

(Written on a flyleaf in a copy of Dante's **DIVINA COMMEDIA** which I presented to ______, in memory of our friendship).

**THERE IS** a comfort in the strength of Love.
You cannot love me and I will not argue,
but I love you dearly.
                    So sorry I never kissed you
whispering a confidence:
                    "He's on the rampage!"

You love life, don'd you? Come, tell me, darling,
is it anything that I can help?
What labours do you set me?
What hideous monster must I slay?
Help me to Heaven if the trouble is I!
But softly now: darling, dash not my Hope!

How chilling is your: "Thank you!" Oh how chilling
to hear you tell me: "Thank you
                    for your nice words!"
I would not have said them were they not nice!
I love you dearly.
                    So sorry I never kissed you
whispering a confidence.

There is a comfort in the strength of Love.

*22.1.79*

## To my love

*Or What You Will*

**NOTHING** for a strain but a subjective impression ...
nothing for a strain ...
nothing for a strain but a ...
pinnacled dim in the intense inane -
producing objective depression!
And what of the lines that tell my Story?
Though some were boloney, and some were droppings,
some were good:
but O for a happier fairy
upon whose aerie to conceal my passion!

But all we can say of the lines
that speak my pain
is ... if you can do not join the sad refrain,
and we want more, much more than that for a strain!
… thinking of you, my darling, drives freaks of the brain
away -
sobers the Pride of Reason, and the Heart enlarges;
and be my task to reduce the intense inane
to something ordinary, natural and humane!

*8.11.79*

## Just as a woman ...

**JUST AS** a woman wishes and wants and breathes quick
for
beauty
but lacks the right eye for her own personal beauty
cannot cast a cool look at her own personal beauty
but ever so hot culls out colours as raw as wax-crayons
with which to gown the mysterious magician therein

from the very distance arousing bad taste
just so with the poet who writes just because
to write poetry is fine

and just as a woman wishes and wants and breathes quick
for beauty
but can look at her body as a miracle which God made
coolly
can stare undazzled upon the mysterious magician therein
and ever so cool deliberate right shades of eye-shadow
for the eyes to shine deeper
right shades of lip-shadow
for the light in her face to strike deeper
right shades of dress-shadow
for the grace she leaves for a trace to probe deeper
and whispers a confidence from beneath just the right
hair-do
it is just so with the poet who shines deeper
strikes deeper
probes deeper
with every word
into the rapt onlooker
deeper
still

*30.7.80*

## The rhyme of the Beast
*Epithalamion*

(A poetic recasting of the tale of **BEAUTY AND THE BEAST** being a celebration of Matrimony dedicated to the memory of the wedding between J.N.G. and J.A.G.)

*"Fra tante bestie, c'e anche posto per me."*[72]
**(Rovella)**

### The voice of the Narrator

**THE SICKENING** sinking every man rehearses -
no Adam that was bud did! - whose love-life's desperate,
hung like breath in a clinic in the home of the Beast,
an earthy stirring that does a windless eddying,
like dust that curled around his island palace -
or, "down the precipice?" - where the Beast lived alone:
it sickened the wind fanned by obedient palm-trees
surrounding the walls, and ruined the smell, the taste,
of the warm drinking-water, and in the night
it would rise like a sweaty heat, through rooms as vast
as arenas, from the foot of a double-bed,
where the Beast slept alone.

He is old and respectable now,
a widower fond of a pipe and a moral,
a wealthy landowner and the proud father of three.
And you have often heard people refer to 'the gentle giant',
and poor folk prattle of 'the kind-hearted millionnaire' -
but you should hear this true love-story from the mouth
of him once known as "The Beast".

[72] "Among so many beasts, there is a place for me also."

**The rhyme of the Beast** *begins here with*
**the voice of the Beast**

Were there Weirds now, as there were once,
would our sinners confess at the Psychiatrist's?
Patients write one another re-assuring letters
and the unhappy tone of a correspondent
awakes their concern. "Really," one tells the other:
"there are no Weirds now, as there were once?"

The Weird was an Artist, art hides art:
his knottiest wile was planting deep suspicions
that he did not exist, or else, - "Oh Yeah!",
we chime together: "Supreme!" - did he not so,
ours may well have been a Faustian Age!
But there we are: "Nowadays, we know a lot!"

The Century was launched with the Titanic: its dreams
went down with the Titanic, to the eternal
dismay of the polite excommunicate
who tells you: "Bosh! This is mediaeval - what do you call it? -
superstition!" and, cursing low-brows, adds:
"Oh really! This is the Twentieth Century, man!"

Granted, we know a lot: where is the Wisdom
lost in Knowledge? The Age is godless, an Age
of suicides, creation's greatest failure:
there is no greatness there! - where at their best
men are but pigmies carried beneath the heads
of Giants: we are but snoring pilgrims yet,

beneath the heads of our fathers dear;
and if they ask us: do we wake or sleep?
The answer is a deep, resounding sleep!
And if our fathers suffered from the Weird
carbuncles in the flesh, who, or what are we,
to sleep and dream untroubled by the Weird?

My tale is of a Withering Weird: he clapped;

he cursed, and lo! - I was a life unwanted,
wretched, and most unhappy! No girl would love me
unless the Curse expired, and unless
the Curse expired I could not be loveable,
but must be loved that the Curse might expire.

Visitors could call unasked and, hollaing, enter:
I was generous, most generous, lavish,
and all 'hip hip hurraed': my hospitality
knew no circumference. "Come," I would beckon,
"come!" - and they would come. "Enter," I beckoned,
"enter!" - and they would enter. They said I was lavish.

They were happy, they said, but no, I was most unhappy.
They had found happiness, in vanity, they said.
Why should Mankind be then still so unhappy?
It is as we say, Mankind, selfish and vain,
nor is it Christian, but it is not happy,
and no one told me why I was still unhappy.

Visitors could call unasked and, hollaing, enter:
I was generous, most generous, lavish;
but visitors might eat on the condition
that my own mouth had issued the invitation:
they could admire, yes, but not share my bounty!

**The voice of the Beast**

Upon a sunrise fair,
wearily descending down my marble stair,
after studying the night-sky in the cool, night air,
what should I smell: a stranger had been there!

I smelled him in the dining room:
my supper, uneaten, now was eaten.
I smelled him in the bedroom:
my bed, unslept in, now was slept in,
and my clothes and breakfast gone.

I smelled him to the garden,
and found him there,
beside my rose-bush fair,
cutting my lush, white roses fair,
uninvited, debonair.

"Accursed wretch!" I screamed at unaware.
The man looked up: his face beheld a Beast;
the scream was meant to chill.
"Ungrateful Wretch!"
I howled:
"Do you know whose the bed you slept in? Mine!
Do you know whose food you've eaten? Mine!
Do you know whose clothes you're wearing? Mine!
And now you steal my roses,
my dear white roses fair!

At the gate the warning says:
**Beware!**
**For he who steals my roses,**
**my dear, white roses fair,**
**beneath their roots reposes!"**

Your story double-quick! It might persuade
the itch in my middle, and you might not die!"

And shuddering but hopeful, he began.

**The voices of the Merchant and the Beast**

A thing of Beauty is a good investment.
A rose, poor devil, has found you a friend, a man
no longer rich, not young, not happy, but
well-loved, and well-connected, poor, but rich
in friendship! This palace, which seems the palace of Art,
and rich as diamond-rings and jewels, where spires
twinkle as if the glass were starlight, or
eyes of a high romance, where melodies

unearthly breathe like the South Wind all day,
this palace, years ago, was mine, and in
the family it's seen the twilight of fable.
A curse of love unreal hangs upon it,
and all my fathers loved and failed in Love,
but I've been happy, Beast, with wife and daughters
in a wondering house. But now I'm old. She's dead:
a widower's memories my sole companions
but for my daughters - but in the woods we're free.
Beauty, my youngest, cooks and sings and washes;
the elder sisters grumble all day long.
Beauty, my fairest, waters my garden nightly -
her Voice is a grace: Beauty's my dearest blessing!
Yesterday, promising my daughters presents -
diamonds and pearls for the elders, white roses for Beauty -
I went to town on business and, coming back,
I lost my way. The Weird led me here.
The door opened. Not one reply to my three calls
received me. I stole in. The Hall was empty
and I was hungry and smelt a rich aroma.
Driving my car to the park, I called once more.
Not one reply received me and I was hungry.
A rich supper was set for one upon the table
in the dining-room, and I sat down to eat.
Food, sleep, and one warm dress, plus nine white roses,
that's all you've given. Have Mercy, Beast: you should!
Though greedy slits, your eyes seem sentient like
a human being's, yea, like those of lovers.
Nine roses have found you a friend, poor devil - (your nights,
your days are lonely!) - a friend's undying faith! -
and to a father mean a daughter's Love!"

"That which first meets you on your return, and greets you -
Man, bird, or beast, fish, flesh, or bone -
in a month's time will be my own.
Do you consent?"

"I have to, Beast, of force!"

**The voice of the Narrator**

The Weird, the Weird, he hides behind success!
The Merchant wished to some forgotten land
the greeting he had learnt to love, to bless,
and with unsteady hand,
on driving home, drove slower, drawing nearer,
trembling upon the wheel, like one who drunk,
prayed that another Beast be first to meet him,
stooped lower, sighed, then wept in reckless sorrow:
the Lord have Mercy!
His Beauty was the first to greet him.

**The voices of the Merchant, Beauty and the Beast**

He told her all. Below her dignity
it were to be deceived: he told her all,
and ending, said: "Daughter beware, beware!
The Beast is ravenous and has no mate:
the palace of Art, for such it seemed, is lonesome
to live unmarried in, and libido

is no small pang! His is a hungry sort,
to put it mildly, and hunger such as his
argues a soul that's loveless, frustrate, soured
by a mean interior, by a chill misery
that's like damp dirt, or sticky underwear.
Daughter, beware: indeed you shall not go!"

That minute had I been undone had not
her heart been greater than his just concern,
paternal, stern. "No, father, I am going!"
said Beauty: "Did I not a vengeance falls
upon you. Besides, I can resist the call
no longer, Father, the call of the Wild, oh Father!"

**The voices of the Narrator, the Merchant and the Beast**

Just as hens huddle songless when a fox
is on his rounds close to the farm, just so
did those three girls around their fussy cock,
their father, while the sad allotted month
went by. Though none but Beauty used to sing,
the silence spanned depths of fear when the old Merchant
set Beauty in his car and, sorrowing,
drove off at a slow pace. They drove all day.
The Weird led them sure, arriving at nightfall.
The door opened. Not one reply to their three calls
received them. They stole in. The Hall was empty.
They were not hungry but smelt a rich aroma.
Driving their car to the park, they called once more.
Not one reply received them, nor were they hungry,
though supper was set for two upon the table
in the dining-room, where they sat down to wait.
A thunderous knocking soon announced the Beast.
In came the Beast: straight at the songless girl
the Beast strode songless as a bird of prey,
before the songless swoop, at first glides songless
in greedy scrutiny of his intended.
Then, as a hunter might, to whom occurs
the thought life might be put to better use
alive, he paused, he rubbed his whiskers, and to
the Merchant said: "Is this the dear daughter,
the precious jewel this, for whom a bunch
of my white roses bled out their sap and, glad
as missioned spirits, sped upon a cause
better by far than that she die, or you?"
"Yes," said the father, "she would not have me
return alone to your favours!" "She should bless
the hour," the Beast replied, "for this rich home,
the palace of Art, is meant for the use of such
as she alone. You must be gone tomorrow,
and need not fear, for harm shall not befall her.
Her room is ready. Yours you can find. Good night."

**The voices of the Narrator, Beauty and the Beast**

Her room was wide, thick-curtained, cushioned, lush;
the sound of her step back-thudded soft against her;
soft speech within it was a joy to hear,
so tender and warm did her sweet voice re-echo
and fold her. Love and sleep as easily might
be parted from that bed-room, bed, and all,
as young limbs from passion, and weariness, profound
as deeps or skies, softly began to stroke her
as she lay back in bed, a glory for which
a dreamy gratitude oppressed her, as she eased
her weary back, just as a red-breast might
in a kind falcon's bed: that night her dreams
were all of love - she dreamed nothing but that.
Her father she joined at breakfast, and as she waved
good-bye, she held her head serenely high.
Back to her room, the pictures were art-treasures,
and on a wall there hung a magic mirror,
quaint and antique, and lettered in gold beneath it:

**Beloved, dry your eyes,**
**needless are those tears and sighs;**
**gazing in this looking-glass,**
**what you wish shall come to pass.**

And though they were poor verses, Beauty thought
returning home was easy, though after all
the human Beast might have a heart humane.
The days were long, but she could read, or paint,
or walk in the garden, or pick the tropical flowers.
A thunderous knocking would announce the Beast
each night at supper-time: "May I come in?"
"Yes Beast!" The scared reply received him daily,
and they would talk together till she began
to find the Beast so Civilized and kind,
inspiring and humorous, and all in all
a joy to talk to, that soon she loved his company.

**The voices of Beauty and the Beast**

Upon a sunrise fair,
wearily descending down my marble stair,
after studying the night-sky in the cool, night air,
I, Beast, caught Beauty combing her sweet, light hair.

I gave her good-morning, saying:

"Morning has broken upon the palace of Art,
for such is this, my Beauty, call it so,
a lonely place to live unmarried in!
Are you not lonesome, Beauty?"

"No, Beast, not lonesome.
You have a hungry look, this morning, Beast!
Such Beasts are dangerous!"

"Beauty, my dear,
I am of hungry sort!"

"You seem well-fed.
It cannot be you hide a hunger greater
than round your middle!"

"That is the tip of the iceberg,
Beauty, dear! Am I too ugly?"

"Yes, Beast."

"And stupid, Beauty?"

"No, not stupid, Beast!"

"Beauty, can you love me?"

"Yes, Beast, I do;
your soul is good and kind!"

"Beauty, my dear,

will you marry me, Beauty, will you?"

"Oh! No! No, Beast!
Father told me.
"Daughter beware!" he said:
"beware!
The Beast is ravenous and has no mate!"

"Tace, Beauty: you are the first to hear
the howl of the Beast!"

"Oh stop, stop Beast!
I cannot bear to hear the pain in that wail,
the wail of the Beast!" said Beauty, miserable.
And miserable we sat us down,
and miserable we wept.

**The voices of Beauty and the Beast**

*"Mirror, mirror on the wall,*
*Does death my dear, old father call?"*

And Beauty was more miserable still next morning
as she gazed into her looking-glass
where the old merchant lay dying, all uncared for.
"Beauty, you seem so sad," I said that night:
“what is the matter?" "More misery, Beast:
my father's dying, and I must, must go:
he must not die to suit your leisure!"
"The Weird, the Weird, he hides behind success:
I am undone for ever, but on my honour
you shall go home tomorrow." "Oh thank you, Beast!
I'll be away for but one week!" "The gods willing!
Put on this ring: if ever you wish yourself
back to the palace, wish your wish! Good-bye!
Beauty, good-bye! Till in a week you hear
the wail of the Beast!"

*"Mirror, mirror on the wall,*
*I must awake in Daddy's hall!"*

**The voice of the Narrator**

And Beauty slept happier that night,
but once at home, she hardly slept again,
for one whole week, in such a ruinous state
was the old Merchant's home, and the old Merchant
in such a perilous condition. But Beauty,
his dearest blessing, nursed him back to health,
and at the end of her allotted week
promised to stay but one, just one more week,
till he could walk and eat once more, uncared for.

**The rhyme of the Beast** *ends here with*
**the love-song of the Beast**

A week's too long, no, not an endless week,
only a day had passed when Beauty dreamt.

She saw me in the garden,
stretched dying in my lair,
beneath my rose-bush fair,
beneath my lush, white roses fair,
dying in calm despair.

Miserable and wide awake she started up,
and miserable she sat her down,
and miserable she wept,
still miserable,
so miserable,
and laid
the magic ring upon the table,
and so she slept again, and in her sleep,
dream-wishing that nothing but what within

the Beast was human upon her bosom lay,
all that was Beastly warped like a stench away,
dream-fancied-far-away,
and she awoke in bed in a sad Palace,
upon a happy, happy day.

Breakfast and dinner done, and tea and supper,
and still I did not pay my moonlight visit.

She sought me in the dining-room:
my supper was uneaten.
She sought me in the bedroom:
my bed had not been slept in.
She sought me in the garden,
and found me there,
beneath my rose-bush fair,
beneath my lush, white roses fair,
dying in calm despair.

And falling down she said:

"We shall be married, Beast!
My love is willing and I want to!
I can resist the call no longer, Beast,
the Call of the Wild! O Beast,
I love your savage soul!"

And saying still:

"O Beast! O Beast!"

her mouth sank in my neck.

I could hear the spell of the Weird snap like a stick,
as around my neck she hung like a Crucifix.
The Curse of the Weird collapsed,
an old cramped scroll that crumbled unsupported,
and lay at my feet
like a loose garment too rotten to stand the fire

in which I blazed naked
like man new-made.

And I trampled that charred garment to ashes.
***Mors stupebit***. In that Resurrection
bare flesh exulted once more as I rose to greet her,
and I wept that this was possible!

And I trampled that charred garment to dust.
***Mors stupebit***. At that Resurrection
bare thighs exulted once more as I rose to meet her,
but how pure, how saved, how humble, deep and tractable!

Her mouth widening in rapture
as we clung in a close embrace -
her mouth was crying:
*Behold, you are fair, my Love, behold, you are fair!*

Oh my Resurrection and my Life!
For she loved me before I was loveable,
and I wept that this was possible!

- "Till Death do us part!" - Death did us part!
and I have talked and talked.
But when she went
I said: My love, farewell,
and rest in Peace!
I rang no surly, sullen bell,
but she loved me before I was loveable:
farewell, fare well!

All's well, but this I tell
to man and wife
rejoicing at the wedding bell!

No Adam that was but was unloveable,
nor was it we who loved God first:
no Adam can exact the Love of the Lord,
but it was God
Who first gave that for which we thirst!

All souls that were, were lost on air,
in howls and screams and devilish laughter:
but He loved us so, He gave up His only-Begotten,
that we may rise out of the tomb we rot in,
now, and happily ever after!

***The rhyme of the Beast ends here***

## Eden

*(Definitions of a Myth)*
*For Cal Clothier*

"**MAN'S** loss is here, here where God willed
His sword between the natural world
And the human mind; ....."
(**DARWIN ON THE ANDES**: Cal Clothier, UK)

**THE NATURAL** world become a myth is Eden,
a Garden suffused with what a garden means,
mystic, but still a garden beneath the stars
that shone on Eden, and Beasts have names they had
in Eden. Man's mind is the unnatural world.
The sword that middles between is the silence between
intruders upon a secret and friends that share
the secret. The friends are God and Nature: Man
has lost their confidence. Man has made friends
with the Devil's Party. The devil is still the devil.
Man's mind is the word that breaks the spell of Romance
as the child's know-how with a toy ends what it mends.

The Word of God restores it.

The Word of God drives freaks of the brain away,
sobers the Pride of Reason, and the Heart
enlarges. But man does not walk the narrow way.
The narrow way is doing God's will on Eden.

Man's feet are firmly planted on the Moon.
What, what is there, oh what at Journey's End?
Love is there. The terror of the Apocalypse.
The sword. The sword drives man away once more
in exterior darkness.

Repent or gnash your teeth.

The terror of the Apocalypse. The sword.

*19.11.80*

## Three common words

*.....to a fair cruel maid*

**THREE** common words, I love you, sweet, nice, pat,
three words as common as paper, older than that,
but, sweet, like other-worldly winds, the words
relax my nerves; unearthly. Holy Birds!
Will no one tell me where you come from? Love,
brood, brood on my subconscious like the Dove,
but, sweet, do heed your Lover, do believe
three common words - I love you - please, relieve
my Love, not Love, only a restless ghost:
a secret between me, my soul, and the barren coast.

*9.4.81*

## Desiderata

**BELOVED,** now that we stand here,
held in this breath of history,
beloved, say, what shall we do,
to heighten your Mystery?
Ponder and muse!

Your hair shall grow and fall,
and shall discreetly flow;
shadow and light, upon
your face, shall vanish and grow:
ponder and muse!

My hand commands no craft,
no brush need touch your face:
eyes, lips, stained but by water,
need no further grace.
Ponder and muse!

You need no brush make up
where nature's graces fail:
paint not a single lash,
paint not a single nail!
Ponder and muse!

Royal Crimson, cozy, tight,
becomes you best,
veiled by a green mantle, white
where all the Angels rest.
Ponder and muse!

And at last remember
lowliness lends enlargement:
let maniacs wander, lovers
wonder, pens on parchment
Ponder and muse!

Hark, generations call:
well-done, for God made all!
A Woman Homer sung:
stay, stay, though ages roll!
A Woman that's Feminine:
abide, though churchbells toll,
ponder, and muse.

*9.6.81*

## After a guitar-recital

*The mediaeval religious colour of the Music, its beauty of form, its emotional depth, its typically Spanish intensity and* ***duende****, the immaculacy, the expressiveness of the performance! He should have been a mediaeval minstrel, this renowned guitarist, one of those who, in those days of chivalry, sang only for love!*

**BACK IN** the car-park,
the beggar with a pretext drew near,
and she put a few cents in a hand held out disarmingly,
and drove away.

He was thinking: "It was a breath of Civilization.
Thanks be to God - and glory be!
And me going away -
my date with my needs, ideals, and my self!"

"These fields will be built over," she said,
"when you return!"

"Ah no, my love, my darling, no!
I must be back!"

And over the drink they chatted.

"My costliest mistake was my life in the tower,
blinder and deafer and dumber than a fish.
Excellence is worth it.
But not at the price I paid!"

"What I always say!" she said:
"The life of the intellect should send out a total man,
not just a laureate!"

Tears, idle tears!

He said ...

"He had ONE aim, ONE business, ONE desire!"

She said the Voices were so many.

"One must be one-eyed like a Cyclops," he said:
"or like Moses, with his third Eye
falling wide open because the strength of the sun
has blound the eyes that are mortal;"
and he said: "Look, Maria," -
thrilled by the Biblical name - "Your friend is calling!"

She turned.
She saw the moon.
The moon was bald and bowed.

But he had kissed her.

*Precious seconds such as transfix a life with a new ideal and secure the seal thereon: total humanity.*

*21.10.81*

## The Himalayas

**SKYLINES**, they sigh and say, have characters
no more, nowaday; but look, my love, upon
the Himalayas' multitudinous mountain range -
the Himalayas in their beauty. Surely that no New York
can boast the Himalayas. Oh may the Good God and His
Angels dear
keep close watch over the Himalayas!

Multitudes, they say,
live at their feet, like children of the Kingdom of Heaven,
growing vegetables and flowers, feeding their families

and cattle, and farming, and knitting, and all in all,
employed in humble arts of immediate use.

Some, they say more spirited, wander further
afield, growing orchards vast as the populace
upon the endless slopes.

And some, they say,
of no immediate value, live in cold storage
upon the summits, to meditate upon
summits on summits summoning the spirits -
the lonely clouds below.

Be there no one,
they say, to live in cold storage upon the summits,
they say no one would as much as reach the middle heights.

*8.11.81*

## The voice of the millions

*a prose poem*

**THE VOICE OF THE MILLIONS** is a speech delivered by a grand demagogue who is also a great orator. We can imagine him with a rabble of unwanted artists at his heels. **THE VOICE OF THE MILLIONS** is very much concerned with contemporary affairs.

**THERE ARE** many Realities. Domestic, social, political, scientific, academic, historical, prehistorical, universal, existential, subjective and objective reality. Transcendental reality, and private reality. And which, of all these, is **REALITY**?

Science snuffs out the dream because its task is an

objective inquiry into reality. Which dream? And which Reality? And whose? The dream which scientists dreamt has now become Reality. Never was Man more knowledgeable, never more powerful, never so far in absolute control and command. Alas! What terrible nightmares haunt humanity by night!

*"Human liberty and the quality of life are greater nowadays than they have ever been, and more of this is due to science and technology than to the antics of do-gooders and politicians - or even poets!"*

That is what some say. But no! Think. Think of the countless abortions, the third world, the world behind the iron curtain, the nuclear arms race, the soul-destroying energies of pornography and sadism, in commercial films, books, newspapers, and on, and on, and on. Though it was bad, were these evils present, in the previous age, and were they all present together, and were they all present together with the same intensity that they are present in ours? No! And now, the most chilling, the most nightmarish, the most evil dream which humanity has dreamt, the nuclear suicide of the entire planet, is on the verge of becoming reality.

"It's a scientific method of analysing History," the Marxist tells you, if you object with some devotion: "It's a scientific method of analysing Reality." A Scientific method of analysing Reality! By God! - It's a scientific method of making History, thc miscrablc, objective Reality which man creates! It's a scientific method of **WRECKING HISTORY**!

Behold the Lord's Creation! The Sun, the Moon, the Mountains, the Rivers, the Trees and Flowers of the Fields, Woods and Valleys, the Song of Birds, and the Stars. It is His Temple. Is it a Dream? or is it Reality? It is both and neither, because Reality is a Dream, God's Dream, and through the Life of Prayer and Grace in Jesus Christ Our Saviour, must be realized, must be made Reality again, in Human Consciousness; **for God's Creation is Reality and Dream, and then again Reality, THE DREAM-REALITY**.

What did the World's great Artists do? Dante, Shakespeare, Bach, MichelAngelo, Beethoven? They dreamt. They reached out to grasp their dream. Through their untold perseverance, and dedication, and the measures which they took to reach it, that Dream became Reality.

We have all been dreaming. And humanity must dream. And humanity wants its dreams to be made Reality. Man must create his own Reality, "for God the Maker made things make themselves." And that Reality, for Man, will be the Reality, and the most evil dream which mankind has dreamt so far is the Scientist's. Is this the Dream which we are going to make Reality?

We must reverse the Dream of the Scientist. But to reach this end, humanity must dream another dream, humanity must dream again, and humanity must refine the quality of its dreams, because those dreams will one day become Reality. Humanity must therefore dream a dream of gold, because judging by this harsh world in which we draw our breath in pain, humanity's dreams so far were evil.

And yet, we are told, in employment centres, that society has no use for the Artist. Why? It is to Science that we owe this indigestion, not to the Artists. The Knowledge we have is sufficient to last us till the end of Time, to feed us, **the Millions**, to clothe us, to cure us of disease, and to surround us with comfort! It is of food and Art that artificial needs are starving us! It is the Spirit that Commerce in the Temple blasphemes and drowns us! **So says The Voice of The Millions! A Thirst profound as the Sahara's!**

Arise, you Artists of the World, Poets, Musicians, Sculptors, Painters, God-like Creators all, this is your hour - dream! Dream a saving, sanctifying Dream! It is your Dream that we are dying for. It is your Dreams that we want to realise on Earth. **DREAM. THROUGH GOD'S POWER AND GRACE THE DREAM BECOMES REALITY. AND DWELLS AMONG US.**

Happy Dreams!

*February 1983*

## British Columbia

*a May magnificat*

**TWO &** a half-million, around, no more,
and all the land is theirs.

Mountains, blue hills, & waters,
and woods in full blossom and bloom,
wild flowers, firs and shrubs,
proud as an Armada that occupies
miles of wandering fertility
and royal, neglected Grace
such as Creation's dawn beheld,
a land flowing with milk and honey,
that's now my Newhomeland,
a luxury that's real, not vain,
& hard as nails, concrete,
robust, complete, majestic,
God the Father's endless bounty
heaving more Love and Beauty
with each blue hill and valley
than ever rose and fell
among the spheres of fable
with all their waves of Music,
all this for two Million.

A luxury that's real as land,
but alas! - the inhabitant
imagines a vain thing.

*Vancouver,*
*May 13, 1982*

## Identity

**1**

**WHO AM** I? - Am I
the Light? - I am not.
The Word? - I am not.
The Way? The Truth? The Life?

I am a Voice in the Wilderness,
crying, and ploughing the Waters,
and though of these I'm none, the World
shall say I was one who was right
where millions went wrong.

**2**

I am a poem glad to belong
to my Author. His pen designs
my organs, my genes, and my bones;
and His nostrils caress
my cheeks, my breasts, and my loins.
My laws are organic, my sins -
a falling apart and away.
Rhythm is in these lines
the most intimate relation
to my subconscious, where
my Maker dwells: He Who,
to me, is more intimate
than self is to self in my self,
and nearer than the eye -
than my organs, my genes, or my bones,
my cheeks, my breasts, or my loins.
Beauty will stay in these eyes
when they hold a glass to their Maker.
Beauty will rise like incense
when these hands are folded in prayer;
will hang like incense on the Wilderness,
and cover my love-talk like leaves and like boughs.

*15/25.1.82*

## Pop-spiritual Whore

**HER FACE** - no face - a bawdy glare,
she flaunts her mystery's loss to win
a client: nude, she stretches bare
the organ with a toothless grin,
her voice - no voice - a gaudy blare!

Sex has no magic here, no soul,
not one love poem's written here -
the mystery's gone: the young, the ol',
limp out, the boys might shed a tear,
but spines are hollow here, a hole!

*30.1.82*

## Tanka, give me a subtle ...

**GIVE ME** a subtle
beauty, God, whom I did not
notice coming, no;
from the vain Star preserve me -
she whom all could see approach.

*23.5.82*

## Pop-spiritual those metal-mongers

**THOSE** metal-mongers there! -
Run up your hands along their Person.
It's smooth as air
and passionless - it's smooth and cold.
Size up their Person!
It's massively insensitive,
and like an exclamation, proud and bold.

God, what you would give,
to feel the human thump of old,
and not their breast-computers, knobs, and papers!
And with unsteady hand,
you shudder, heart
in mouth.
Knocked out,
the sky, the trees, the stars, the seas, depart.
And now, you understand,
they think they are skyscrapers!

But do you really?
Do you grasp their passion?
The cold passion that drives a mathematician?

Awed, and with a sickening fear,
you gasp the air, and shed a tear:
think not of that - these thoughts offend!

My love, look - how they march in rows,
how passionless, how smooth and cold,
like exclamations, proud and bold.
Who knows what these men will, who knows?

Oh will the Stars be there at Journey's End?

*5.2.82*

## Haiku, the City of God

**I READ** *The City*
*of God.* Saw the stars come out
On the dark blue sky.

*23.5.82*

## The musician's prayer

*to my sister, Anna*

**1, 2: DOH,** re, mi, fah, sol, lah, si, doh'.
Scales are the good Musician's daily prayer.
3, 4: Doh', si, lah, sol, fah, mi, re, doh.

Do I unnerve you when, with all this awe,
I sing my beads, by monotones, high and higher?
1, 2: Doh, re, mi, fah, sol, lah, si, doh'.

All things, if good, are arduous - that's law:
No labour, no reward! Ease is a liar!
3, 4: Doh', si, lah, sol, fah, mi, re, doh.

The scales d'Amor beatify what's raw.
Shame, shame, my Faith to mock: the Faith's a flyer!
1, 2: Doh, re, mi, fah, sol, lah, si, doh'.

I live in Art, a life d'Amor, with Awe:
I harm no soul, and so inscribe my bier!
3, 4: Doh', si, lah, sol, fah, mi, re, doh.

Look, look! Good souls, in flights, and Angels, paw
The ladder, up and down, and sing my prayer:
1, 2: Doh, re, mi, fah, sol, lah, si, doh'.
3, 4: Doh', si, lah, sol, fah, mi, re, doh.

*22.2.82*

## Haiku, marriage will make us ...

*to a friend*

**MARRIAGE** will make us
rare, man, collector's items,
dear and precious!

*3.4.82*

## Words

*to a Child*

**DON'T ASK** me, child, I have no heart;
please, darling, don't - love hides no art.
You will find out what sorrow is,
how far aways the dreams you kiss.
I've said it once and once again,
that if you ask, I can't explain,
because that heartbreak we disown
which we don't bear all, all alone.
But put aside those jacks and queens.
You will find out what sorrow means
in your nice books, which give the sense
of words, and words, and the past tense
of all the joys which men have known,
the words we use, and sense disown.
Words have a point, your books explain,
which once you grasp, will give you pain.
Do but look up the words you write.
You will find grief in black and white.

*15.5.82*

## Tankas

**to......**

**A FAIR**, cruel maid
found a nuclear warhead
trimmed like tickets, typed
neat, signed - 'With Love', sealed & de-
liver'd express in the mail.

**to......**
**AMONG** men and maids,
my Love, most right and fitting
it is that Beauty
should make its Power known through
the ugliest of servants.

*18.3/3.4.82*

## The downtrodden's pride

*Pop-Spiritual (for Mother Teresa)*

**A WANDERING** Jew, by Jews denied,
stood in my way, some time ago,
stood in my way, and hitched a ride,
where traffic never ends the flow -
the endless road where forests grow
on every side.
"I know them all,"
He said, "the first one thousand firms;
and all this business, like a ball,
they roll right on, and set the terms,
and money breeds in their hands like germs.

The very few who own the banks
and all the oil-wells, all the whores
in dancing halls, and ranks on ranks
of yachts, and ranches, all the bores
clad smart as print, who thrive on wars -

I know them all, and where they go!
My friend," He said, "I'm well-connected,
and in a vision, I shall show
you all the nameless Love attracted."

And like the woods on woods erected,
all in a vision, He did show
hosts of the nameless Love attracted.

"Love," they all sang, as thru the air
I saw the dead and living ride -
waves of one mighty Love-affair
tumbling together, side by side -

"Love is a Champion, crucified;
a Sacred Heart cut open wide;
Love is the Downtrodden's Pride."

And in my dream He spoke again,
the wandering Jew, by Jews denied;
all heard Him speak, a man to men,
and one and all they wept and cried.

Oh tell me, say, when all's been said,
is there a Power on Earth like this,
invoked by all, in every bed,
so well-connected as Love is?

*28.3.82*

## Tankas, the professions ...

**1**
**EACH** sample they spin,
though right as morality,
is various, a craze,
subjective, though authentic,
though impersonal, unique.

**2**
What clients may deem
subjective, the lofty mean,

may well be quite sound
professional logic that's
sure to maximize profit.

**3**
Sampling their logic,
you make this discovery:
eternal, and as
invariably as Logic,
as Truth, Life's Logic's various.

*3.4/4.4.82*

## Haiku, when was it last …

**WHEN WAS** it last that
I did see Light so intense,
O Christ, Redeemer?

*14.3.82*

## May 13, 1981
*an Ode*

### BACKGROUND

**WHILE** God's official deposit of Faith with mankind is regarded by the Catholic Church to have been irrevocably closed with the last revealed Book of the Christian Bible, the Church admits to the importance of private revelations, which have been claimed to occur down the centuries, and regards their role to be that, if you like, of a commentary on the revealed text applied to contemporary life …

Of the more recent, the private revelation of greatest importance is undoubtedly that which occurred at Fatima, in 1917, which for Catholics has now become a centre of international pilgrimage and devotion. At Fatima, the Blessed Virgin Mary is said to have appeared to three peasant children, to have called humanity, through the mouths of these children, to repentance, penance, reparation, and prayer, and to have foretold, in a veiled manner, the infamous atrocities of the Communist Regime, as well as a disaster possibly worse than that of the two Great Wars, should humanity not heed her appeal.

While the prophetic vision which the Blessed Virgin revealed to these children, as it were, in a crystal Ball, has now assumed the nerve-shattering light of fact, and may almost be said to have been fulfilled, it was not so in those days. Everybody's one and only fear were the Nazis, and

Russia was relatively a nonentity. This curious fact is the most shattering proof of the authenticity and importance of Fatima.

**May 13, 1981** is an Ode dedicated to the Holy Father, Pope John Paul II. It celebrates the figure which everyone finds so charismatic. It meditates on the failed attempt on his life. It meditates on the coincidence that May 13, 1981, the date of the assassination attempt, happened to be the anniversary of one of the Blessed Virgin's apparitions at Fatima.

The following is the text of the poem.

## May 13, 1981

for the Holy Father
Pope John Paul II
an Ode

**QUICKLY** send,
Be brief in it, to the castle, for my writ
Is on the life of Lear and on Cordelia.[73]
(**SHAKESPEARE: King Lear,** V: 3: 243-5)

**POPE JOHN** Paul, the total man,
cruised Saint Peter's thrice again,
round around, erect and tall,
robed like the Saviour, loved by all.

But back among his native hills
a keen, disconsolate air that kills
sings like maternal grief, and blows
through all the land, and rows on rows

of folk in churches, all along

[73] Words of the dying villain, Edmund, to Albany, in King Lear.

walks in the mountains, firm and strong,
through all the haunts, through all the rooms
that knew the man like brides and grooms:

the singing falls, the singing grows,
a keen, disconsolate air that blows
round all the shrines, round all the hills
where rock, the very rock prays, and spills

through many corridors and rooms
of stone, the modern catacombs
where downtrod lands traditions hoard:
all Poland chants - *"Quo Vadis, Lord?"*

"Oh shuddering walls, oh shuddering rooms,
my homeland's bleeding catacombs,
I have been called, the call was airy,
to serve my Lady, Blessed Mary!"

The voiceless, downtrod Poles exult
and throb with Love and Pride occult
as Heaven, where the newsboy roars:
"Dear, long-suffering Poland scores!"

But whoever Fame adorns
wears the fabled Crown of Thorns,
must be perfect, has to be,
all demand it: none but three

stand in silence round the Tree,
lovers true - how few there be!
To Saint Peter's, on that day,
not all to love, not all to pray!

Wicked, unjust, unchaste and wild,
in craft Satanic, though no child
could seem more harmless, more disarming,
a murderer well-versed in charming,

better-travelled than Ulysses,

sang with the pilgrims, blowing kisses,
slunk up front, like a cancer cell,
briefly, aimed well!

Does Providence watch over the sparrow,
and not the sinking hopes of Tomorrow?
But had it been his hand to pull it ...
a Sun's erratic flight! The bullet

struck John Paul below, and smart,
and a friend above the heart.
Dumb as a tame, old dairy-cow,
the killer raised a questioning brow,

his taut mouth sagging, as the Pope
Hail-Maryd, and a breath of Hope
crossed Saint Peter's with a sigh
to God: this was no time to die!

The reds are at the altar steps,
and the corrupt war-monger wraps
a deal a day, and gives the ball
to Satan; but we are not all

alone - though Commerce sets the terms
where Wisdom should, and Pleasure worms
in the luxurious, though we smell
the suffocating breath of Hell,

like sewage stench, from everywhere,
though it is sure the devil's here!
A Woman clothed with the Sun
Her Cause and Ours has made one!

Brothers, we have a hope to cherish!
Those who shall perish, let them perish!
But friends, repentance loves the rod -
busies the soul with only God:

we should by now be weary, wary -

the prayer taught by Blessed Mary
betters the looks of mind, of face,
and fills the heart with mirth and grace,

the heart, that must ejaculate
true Love for the Immaculate
and more besides: this heart, I say,
gives up for Love what keep it may.

What though from Hell we should be spared?
Have we not dared, and dared, and dared?
Is not the Lord's correction tough?
Is not His rod now red enough?

Lady, in this, this evil day,
like that the deluge drowned away,
burn, if you must, the sins that cell
in soul and flesh, too deep and well,

but not, sweet Mother, not in Hell!
Behold, how many grace the bell
with Aves loud, and marching, query:
"Blessed Virgin, Mary, Mary,

if fire must, and not select,
consume us, but with the elect,
and let the Holocaust no Voice
can curb, be governed by your Choice!

That which, though we may sigh and sigh,
may not be spared, though we may cry,
sure may be tempered: this the plea!
Let us among the Blessed Be!"

For this we live, for this we die -
lean down! For this alone we cry!
Woman, we join the pilgrim's keen
All-Hail! Hail to the Sun-clad Queen!

*Completed: May 31st, 1982*

## Tanka, men feel no regard ...

*to Lydia Pasternak*

**MEN FEEL** no regard
for all you stand for, Lydia.
That may well be why
you've been ignored, wronged for the
wrong reasons, Cordelia-like.

*27.6.82*

## In play

**THE WAYS** of the World, the fashions, the laws,
the sins, the snares, the nets, the know-how
that puffs Power and keeps the down down,
and the price it exacts, to get on, the price

which for the World - unfed, unfilling,
misleading, misled - I may not pay,
the promise, the prey in the dust, the heart-break,
World without end, the thirst, and the rust,
tossing my dreams in play, in play,
all this, and more, much more besides,
saddens me so, so much! so much!

*12.3.82*

## The book-binder

*to Holger*

**THE STEEL** rods and presses seemed solid
and were, looked sombre, a look of class
and skilled labour that went back to Europe.

The bench - solid,
the shop - spacious,
and the machines - severe
as a tool, had an air of good service:
the conscious dignity of work-well-done,
of more value than a certificate anytime.

The smell of the books was simple,
and striking, a breath of civilization.

You could not miss the book-binder there,
the skilled labourer, well-built, tall, round, sturdy,
not fat, hair sparse, greyish-white,
greyish-blue steel in his eyes, and hands on hips:
proud, like the artist
he was, he stood, silent, and in silence, communed,
erect as a post, and as solid.

A good book-binder is a damn sight better

than a bad bishop, says Paul the Apostle,
and the figure, to say the least, was striking, and was,
you may say, a symbol. My thoughts were of Europe.

He said very little,
but we learnt that he had a good daughter:
"She runs my life!", were his words,
and then it was time to shake hands.

I asked for a card,
he gave me five, and I concluded
business was bad -
and still my thoughts were of Europe.

*22.8.82*

## Villanelle, for Faith's a blaze ...

**FOR FAITH'S** a blaze that claims the lives of many,
  and all in vain we blow upon the fire:
about, about, and life's not worth a penny!

All round the match light licks each nook and cranny,
  here, there, and everywhere, and high, and higher,
and Faith's a blaze that claims the lives of many.

It drives the housebound crazy as a nanny.
  In vain we fuss and blow. Pyre on pyre,
about, about, and life's not worth a penny!

Up front, behind, around, all flesh is tawny,
  and where shall bodies run when struck by fire?
Oh Faith's a blaze that claims the lives of many!

Screams, wild as birds, are winging, graves are yawny -
  and no one knows how long if not a liar:
about, about, and life's not worth a penny!

Is there a minute's minute left, if any?
  Who knows? And where is all the World's grand Sire?
But Faith's a blaze that claims the lives of many,
about, about, and life's not worth a penny!

*10.9.82*

## Tanka for Xmas

**GIVE THANKS**, you Nations,
and rejoice: it could be worse
than snow, this Advent!
What Earth needs most to sweep it -
snow, the Lord's cool Scavenger!

*20.11.82*

## Haiku, in a world without …

**IN A** World without
that dark Spot of Mystery, I
would die of boredom.

*20.11.82*

## With compliments ...[74]

**HE PLAYED** a ducking
on his good friend the mermaid
and lost her mid-sea.
Surfacing months later, she
washed him with a good mouthful.

Upon which they swam on.

*9.12.82*

---

[74] *to Margaret Toms*, 9.12.82

## Love-song, may I take out ...

*Life is short, death draws near, eternity is long.*

**MAY I** take out, my friend, a flood of tears,
which might, perhaps, perhaps, dislodge the thorns
I can't unlodge? unlodge the guilt, the fears
with which my heart is stuck? no heart, but horns.
Oh that your love might wash, wash out my fears:
Heaven is a flood, a flood of tears!

If this be sin, and this, and this, and this,
I'll not be saved, till I commit another.
Shall **I**, then, stone **you**? - Love?! Another kiss!
All over! (Tell the Judge I'm but a brother.)
Oh that your love might wash, wash out my fears:
Heaven is a flood, a flood of tears!

Should I be good? I should, and this is error:
my heart, where have you been? I'm bad, I'm bold!
I'm wicked, yes, but this is truth, though terror:
what will the Christ, should I throw stones, though told?
Oh that your love might wash, wash out my fears:
Heaven is a flood, a flood of tears!

There is a word, and honour, though in thieves,
and Solidarity among two sinners,
and he who kept the Law which killeth grieves,
grieves deeply: come, let's kiss, like two beginners!
Oh that your love might wash, wash out my fears:
Heaven is a flood, a flood of tears!

Be one good thief, my Love: I'll be another -
God blesses words of Honour! Should Heaven fail
last minute?! Virtue would not be worth one bother!
**You** are my Church - no other! Here ends my tale.
Oh that your love might wash, wash out my fears:
Heaven is - oh! - a flood: a flood of tears!

*26.1.83*

## Monologue, good Lord Aeneas ...
*per DB*

**MONOLOGUE** is an imaginary dramatic monologue spoken by a wicked Pope who bears no resemblance to any Pope in History. The situation is set in Ancient Rome.

**GOOD LORD** Aeneas, will no one read my future
in the flat of my hand? ... can *you* do that? ... or should
I speak to someone else? ... the witch, the witch,
Aeneas! Ah yes, *the witch*! Foul-mouthed hag,
I tell thee, speak to me, and watch your speech!
My pride's no matter, fright! but have we two
discerned each other better? Not that I alter
a word, or take one sentence back, you crow,
no, now or ever, but why everyone
should have found out still beats me!
Why could you not, since there's no help, shake hands?
oh could you not, sincere and courteous?
but no! what ails the bitch?
deformed, weak, toothless, whom does she think she'll
scare?!
But oh, the monkey-monster will not speak,
but I, though in the dark, can sense your friendship,
Angels, though in the invisible air -
I know not how! But now I must confess,
Aeneas - confess I have a funny feeling
that I alone am in the dark, oh Lord!
oh speak to me!
Aeneas!
I know it in my mind already: I am
the man you say ... and Truth will out.
what does this mean? The World supports us two
no longer, and Immortal Rome no less!
Immortal Rome! - do you hear?! **NO LESS!**
She turns quite leisurely away from the
disaster: a sight to sicken us, Aeneas!
You think I am uncritical?
Aeneas?!

I tell you - **NO!** I owe you Faith, my Lord,
I owe you Love, but your people owe me money,
*and not me them*! Only look what I have done,
and well, **e nel nome di Roma! - a che?**
**per il morir di fame! Ti dico, Aenea,**
**they owe me money!**
This is no heresy, my Lord, because
it is no Theological Matter!
I honoured am by a Barbarian Race,
my Lord: are they the ones who owe me pay?
I tell you - **NO!** And if you ask who does,
I say: **YOU PEOPLE.** Who else? And I am not
asking this as a right, but as a duty:
**SUPPORT THE CAUSE!**
What does this mean? Barbarians do, you don't.
And to be brief, I will not have my books
exhibited upon your pretty shelves,
with all that pious nonsense, crap, Z-rate,
unless I'm given decent pay, and fat,
**AND FOR THE LOVE OF GOD.**

*4.5.83*

## Morals
*per DB*

**WITH** self-knowledge such as his,
he knew how worthless. - Would
have given life for but one kiss,
and trash such as a plaster saint's
virginity have given but to this woman.

*29.6.83*

## When Ulysses lost his temper
*per DB*

"**FOR REASONS** of which I know you are aware,
I will have to see the Angel of the Lord
with my two eyes, and hear him with my
two ears, before I have anything else
to do with Circe: yes, Circe,
the dirty swineherd! For should you bastards wish
to help me, so you should: it is my due!
No privilege! Should be! Should be! And help
you can without my ever requiring her!"
So said Ulysses to his men, and so
looked at mid-Ocean, while the boat moved on.

*4.7.83*

## Epistle: to FB

*In memory of a favourite drive*
*up Lillooet Road, North Vancouver.*

**BUT WHERE'S** the man who counsel can bestow,
Still pleased to teach, and yet not proud to know?
Unbiased, or by favor, or by spite;
Not dully prepossessed, nor blindly right;
Though learned, well-bred, and though well-bred, sincere;
Modestly bold, and humanly severe?
Who to a friend his faults can freely show,
And gladly praise the merits of a foe?
Blest with a taste exact, yet unconfined;
A knowledge both of books and human kind;
Generous converse; a soul exempt from pride;
And love to praise, with reason on his side?

(Alexander Pope:
**ESSAY ON CRITICISM**, ll. 631-642).

**THIS NIGHT** the stars, the City lights, sing out,
sing out, my friend, breathe easy, as we drive,
        reviving, pure, alive,
and stirring, while we chat, and in and out,

through shadow - odd, that erection! - winds the road:
a weaving, bare, uneven, bumpy fact.
        Oh where, where is the tact?
the grace? - the sky, the stars, and you beside!

The World's a slum, we were saying, the Time's
a tedium, turning, turning, grasping, rich:
        the World's a silken bitch,
and slinks in alleyways, murderous.  Crimes

with lovely names salute us: Freedom, Amor,
and Conscience.  You look for - "Conscience," and you
                                                                                find
        a consummate ass-hole, blind,
the black, furred horror whistling, "Nevermore!"

Abstracted so, we park, half-hid by trees.
Odd, that erection: have it struck off the sketch,
        and let your pigments catch
no eye-sore but what's distant, and the breeze,

rustling among the leaves of trees. (The breeze,
across the pane and distant City scene,
        blows five brown leaves between,
all drifting, look! - with what consummate ease!)

Classics blown pop, out of the distance drumming;
classics blown pop - out of the distance - rumble,
        grumble, growl and tumble,
rocking and rolling, clashing, beating, strumming:

"She loves you, yeah! yeah! yeah!" "These are the days,
my friend," of blind passion, fret, and turbulence:
        Tradition, Permanence,
drowned by the many Voices, mourn the mad Race.

Classics blown pop, Amico! but they have
no inner, justifying Principle,
        alas! delirious, ill:
a tongue of Angels, spoken without Love.

Drowned by the Voices, drowned by the gaudy blare,
banished from all the Reason why **IT IS**,
        wind from the Abyss,
drowned by the faces, drowned by the baudy glare,

a Voice, one only, singing: "Yesterday!
my Love has gone away!" drowned by the slamming,
        drowned by the din, the damning,
where Lucifer directs, and leads the fray.

It is one thing to be a Classicist,
another thing to be Archaic. Regard,
        mark but the Avant-garde:
a monstrous dream, mad Voices in the mist!

Classics blown pop, Amico! Vulgar dreams
of Evil Purpose where, unknown to men,
directing brain and pen,
King Lucifer subordinates the Themes.

The Truth is brief and quiet, a still, small Voice,
soft, gentle, low - "With Love and Peace." Untie it!
Deep as the Ocean's riot
the Truth distills, as strong, as sweet as Choice;

And dreams a saving, sanctifying Dream,
mocking the days, whose vulgar Phantasy
grovels in sordid Fancy,
ruled by King Lucifer and his mad Theme.

Heaven and Earth, my Friend, shall pass away,
but by God! Christianity is here to stay!
and in the measures of my Ancient Rhyme,
may but true Friendship triumph over Time.

Thanks to the comfort of but one like mind,
my heart leaves Hell behind:
may but my weird, outmoded, winding lay
drive freaks of the brain away,
and this true Friendship triumph over Time!

*28.6.83*

## Old lament

*translated from the Italian*
*of Giosue Carducci, (1835-1907)*

**THE TREE** whereto you extended
your baby hand in faith,
the green pomegranate,
whose blooms have a blood-red core,

leafs green once more all over
in the dumb yard, deserted,
with love once more exerted,
the light all Junes restore.

Oh you, my Life's one blossom,
stricken, and dry, and torrid,
of a life as vain as horrid
the singlest, the last - no more:

you lie in black abandon,
the black, cold earth about you;
nor can the sun delight you,
nor will love awake you more.

*22.2.83*

## The bread and the spring

*adapted from the Italian*
*of Padre Galanti, 1958* [75]

**BLESSED** the bread which the Lord gives you today
by a limpid spring where the rocks break the level;
while bird-song, and all the flowers on the way,
melodies of light, of colour, teach those who travel.

Brother Masseo, whose lot's the better? Ever?!
Providence with you has not at all been grudging,
though Poverty's your merry blessing! Never,
you will not find a richer, for all the trudging!

---

[75] **Padre Galanti**, the author of the original, now deceased, was an Italian, Franciscan monk, residing in Vancouver. **The Bread and The Spring,** *Il Pane e la Fonte,* is about Franciscan spirituality. It is freely adapted from the Italian and is not a faithful translation.

The waters that, so precious, so pure, and chaste,
spring over the rock and moss, allay your need,
the thirst for vain possession, common as dirt.

The bread which is little, but fills and delights good taste,
feeds life, and suits the wise, though life may lead
to every pilgrim's grave, which cradles rebirth.

## The first crib at Greccio

*This poem is dedicated to the renowned Italian filmmaker, Franco Zeffirelli, from whose film **BROTHER SUN SISTER MOON** I derived much of my joy and inspiration. It is dedicated also to the mainspring of these verses, my friend FB, now deceased, who was responsible for requesting these verses ...*

**LOVELY**, and still, and white is the night,
wound thick are the clouds, and wind is the loom,
loving and warm is the slap of their gloom,
solid, and black, and white is the Light.

Deep is the valley, and loving the folds,
over again, and blank is the moon,
splendid the mountains, benign as a boon,
and old are the oaks which Italy holds.

Proud in a hollow Saint Damian lies,
still as the silence profound as a stone,
as Time and the Soul's inarticulate moan,
renowned as the Fable men carved out of cries,

and buffeted by the wind and snow,
the burying snow, where cries countless, cries
of the most uncontrollable thing that flies,
do not echo. Never echo! Blow

you winter winds! With Love and singing,
the cold cracks, and sizzles with Brother Fire;
the Flames, like Sacred Hearts, leap higher.
The songs, like Angels, winging, winging,

revive the souls - or pilgrims? - there.
All sing one common, happy day,
all care dream-fancied far away.
Alive, upon the most calm air,

ten thousand flames, one glance suffices,
dance to the songs, and drown the people,
the crib which stirs, the distant steeple,
far from the fret, the hate which ices.

Love-poets and Minstrels they were all,
who dreamt beneath the metre's curb -
(Divine Realities disturb
Degree and solemn Protocol!):

Heaven's proud Minstrelsy, who drove
the winds away with a Song more tense:
the Troubadours of God wove sense
with all their singing, and sang for love;

and sang of a brave new Earth! (fine thinking,
and fine distinctions in their eyes).
(While the Court-Jester of Paradise,
Francis di Bernardone, winking,

took off his hat to every tree,
to the wild flowers, and like a loon,
to Brother Sun and Sister Moon,
as wild as birds, as glad to Be).

(Small, tough, and active as a Wren,
dark beard thin and pointed, the South
moved in his eyes like fire, mouth
drawn tight and puckish: he moved among men -

dark beard like a busy elf's:
brown cloth, brown figure and brown fire
seemed taller than his own size, and higher:
he never wrought a deed by halves.

His words were wilder far, though Writ,
than those he wrote, and what he did
more wild than words he spoke; and hid
beneath his every deed lay Myth

and Symbol). Oh brave, new Sun! As keen
as the World is to men, when Light pours
through a dark hole, and we crawl on all fours!
Are we too modern? or too mean!

*When all dispersed*
*Heaven's proud Minstrelsy*
*sang this new Canticle to their small Lutes:*[76]

"Paradox is the Sign of Truth,
and Topsy-Turvydom Philosophy ........"

""Highest Omnipotence,
all Glory, Praise, be Yours, Good Lord,
and Yours the Reverence:
all Blessings, and all we bless,

---

[76] The **Cantico delle Creature**, (Canticle of The Creatures), originally composed in Italian, by St Francis of Assisi, (1186-1226). St Francis of Assisi is historically the inventor of the Christmas Crib. My poem, **The First Crib at Greccio**, is about the first Christmas Crib, a live Crib, which was exhibited by the first Franciscans at Greccio, in Italy. Around this first Christmas Crib, Holy Mass was celebrated, and was attended by the first Franciscans, as well as by the local people. Besides celebrating this episode from the life of Francis of Assisi, and besides being a comment on the spirit of Franciscanism, **The First Crib at Greccio** is also a comment on the Middle Ages. In bringing this poem to the reader I feel that I should acknowledge my great debt to Gilbert Keith Chesterton's **St Francis of Assisi**, a wonderfully poetic biography, published in New York by Image Books, which I read twice over from cover to cover before composing my poem, and from which I derived much inspiration.

belongs to You alone, the Most High,
and no man is worthy to mention You.

"Be praised, my Lord, with all Your Creatures,
but most in His Excellency, Brother Sun,
who shines daily, and illuminates our Path by day.
And he is beautiful and radiant with a great splendour,
and derives significance from You, the Most High.

"Be praised, my Lord, for Sister Moon and the Stars,
in the heavens you formed them, bright, precious,
beautiful, and clear.

"Be praised, my Lord, for Brother Wind,
and for the air, nimble, and serene, and through whom,
in every season, you give sustenance to all your Creatures.

"Be praised, my Lord, for Brother Fire,
through whom you illuminate the night,
and he is beautiful and jovial and robust and powerful.

"Be praised, my Lord, for our Sister Mother Earth,
who sustains and governs us,
and puts forth diverse fruits with coloured flowers and
herbs.

"Be praised, my Lord, for those who forgive for your
Love's sake,
and who sustain infirmity and tribulation,
blessed are they who persevere in Peace,
for by You, the Most High, they shall be crowned.

"Be praised, my Lord, for Our Sister, Bodily Death,
whose clutches no man living may escape,
woe to those who die in mortal sin,
blessed are those who are found at peace with Your
Most Holy Will,
to whom the Second Death shall do no harm.

"""Praise ye, and bless ye my Lord, and thank Ye Him,

and serve Ye Him with great Humility.""" 

All night they sang: round voices ring
within the hollow abbey halls,
and keen among the mountain walls,
where all the echoes ring and sing

low, round and distant, round and warm;
and all the wandering hillside soughs,
and covers their love-talk with leaves and with boughs,
and their Song was the Eye, the Eye of the Storm:

all night they sang, till break of day -
first voices and second, and now third voices,
reciting, while their soul rejoices -
and all the singing died away.

Lovely, and still, and white is the night,
wound thick are the clouds, and wind is the loom,
loving and warm is the slap of their gloom,
solid, and black, and white is the Light.

Deep is the valley, and loving the folds,
over again, and blank is the moon,
splendid the mountains, benign as a boon,
and old are the oaks which Italy holds.

*Completed: July 19, 1983*

## Tankas, to find God ...

**TO FIND** God, my friend,
if in all Truth you wish to,
let the darkness come
upon you, and all you know
about Him: whatever you

conceive Him to be,
forget, ignore, as you would
an error you've made:
you will not be able to,
and you will never, suppress

the Light, that comes through
the stain, wiped clean, and now makes
the white bone to gleam,
to shine, mirroring what makes
the marrow to lust and glow.

## Vancouver

**MASSIVELY** insensitive, the City,
designed for cars, draws Love like blood, draws Pity.
Clad smart as print, and trendy, thoughts derailed
by the rush-hour, souls are racked and nailed
downtown, drawn tight upon the humming wires,
throbbing, electric, tense, and loud as lyres
played by guitarists needing alms and tea,
but not designed for Music Therapy:
a City made for cars, not glorious bells.
All Souls are private Heavens, private Hells -
Hells more than Heavens, morose more than Despair -
rushing to work and back like soughing air;
free, but at gunpoint; jealous of privacy -
hugging their great, sad secrets like the Sea.

While Nature, "heartless, witless Nature," old
as the Pyramids, is grand, primordial, bold,
and smiles in brainless beauty over all.
The rooks and ravens caw: they seem to call.
Withdrawn upon Mount Seymour, you will find
how lost you are; and love-sick, tear-blind -
far from the dreadful din, the nuclear tone -
how terrified, how unconsoled, and how alone!

*17.02.84*

## Speculation

"**WHO WOULD** fardels bear
To grunt and sweat under a weary life,
But that the dread of something after Death,
The undiscovered country, from whose bourne
No traveller returns, puzzles the will,
And makes us rather bear those ills we have
Than fly to others that we know not of?"
**(Shakespeare: HAMLET)**

**YOU WILL** see a wild bird of prey swooping towards you
in the dark and silence of the Night; you will hear
three distant beats on some pulse-waltzing drum;
you will hear
the Keeper's inaudible whistle blowing inside your inner ear
with a sound more loud and intense than the drumming of
bad blood
in your temples;
you will feel the blood curdle, or much rather
a cool diabolic rage and nothing to grasp, to catch,
or to walk on, as the very ground shifts
beneath your feet, and somehow the bed, bedclothes, and
pyjamas
vanish, and the bedroom and scene through the window

slowly begin to crumble, weave and circle round around
you
twice, thrice; the brittle, old, and most familiar world
disintegrate like powder, give way, crack, peal, and splinter,
and pulverised begin to fall like plaster or descending Lava;
and just as the guided-missile or soundless Atom Bomb
descends out of Blue Nothing,
you will see the Judgment descend out of the manifold
circles of Space,
and like brain-waves or boomerangs revolve and return into
Space,
return like a boomerang to the Majestic Warrior, and the
Arrow
return to the Archer who sits in the Centre of Space,
at the still point of the Universe; you will hear
the grunt and groan of the damned and the crunch of bones
begin
as the terrified Spirit
rushes out fast from the hissing spout of the madly
accelerating Sphere
like Steam at high-pressure; and no Philosopher will help
you.
Such is the moment of Death, Lecteur, such is the way and
the manner
in which all Humanity goes like Smoke from a billowing
Fire
in the Crematorium; this is how all Life slips away with a
Sigh
like a Ship that passeth through the Waters and leaves no
trace thereof;
and so sublime is the Salvation of a single Soul;
but these are normal matters --
three souls are lost, and one redeemed, habitual everyday
occurrences,
as Church-bells fill the wandering fields with Love and
Fear.

*19.03.85*

## Haunted house in a picture

**ON ONE** side stood a bare, uneven pit
of barren fields where shadows brood and sit,
and sunset's grand design makes lovers rue
the day, and a small path meanders through
the wind-swept grasses, where the oxen browse
all day; on one side stood a haunted House.

Whether the Winds of Time and Fable, That
which in the hinges whined, or else a Bat;
whether Existence sighed inside, or moaned,
or Gales were creaking loud, the hinges groaned;
whether a state of Grace, or Demon's rage,
or souls in bliss held captive in a cage,
or Hell, or Love Eternal sighed inside,
all round the barren fields the cadence cried;
all round the barren fields, and in the Hall,
it settled softly with a dying fall.

The Dead descended on that place in Art,
and through the sense of sound they would depart
like Music, winging wildly, pole to pole,
like Hell and Heaven from the living Soul,
closed fast and racing. Present, Future, Past,
all Time did in that House subsist, the dust
subsiding, First and Last, all Books, all Space:
is Heaven then both State and solid Place,
by secret hands unsealed, sealed with a Kiss?
Is Heaven then a Place like lost Atlantis?

Is it unlawful thus the Dead to woo?
Is Death a lie when Wrong belies the True?
And that forgotten House, which nowhere is,
but somewhere, somewhere, sure, a Home of bliss,
a Land unknown, a solid, solid Place,
which by an Act of God and Winds of Grace,
blown off the Map in silence, come and gone,
like shadows, when through clouds the Glory shone,
a thought which vanished in the Sun like Time,

a Dream, a sinking star, a sense sublime
of something gone around the opened Eye,
snuffed like the candle's Light, a last good-bye,
may be, may be the Castle of the Soul,
but haunted by the field-mouse and the mole.

*29.10.85*

## chrysanthemums for coffined Eternity ...

*to roy harrison*
*to edgar poe*
*to my brothers*
*and sisters*
*and to the Memory*
*of Hiroshima*

**WE ARE** the Dead crush
us not we Eternity are
sense of the Flesh and
eyes shut tight mouth nose and ears
something which somewhere somewhere

clay chokes my tears
fills the throat's climbing Sorrow
what Insult would cry
cry cry and can't what Horror
all of us dead men are Lovers

the Dead wash the wounds
of the Dead with tears forget
us not hurt not us
the Dead need Love feel Fear
the Living feel none help help

line comes through static
lost at Sea this is Doomsday
dark dark dark what Wrath
of Ocean gossamer Sunshine
something which somewhere somewhere

we Eternity are
alone in secret we choke
feel Fear threaten
us not with nuclear Doom
we have striven all of us

Posterity and
Civilization are wreck
us not all of us
Ladies and Gentlemen are
the nuclear tone woke us up

we have striven gone
to rest have heard the Rumour
of Doom let us be
Ladies and Gentlemen we
have striven and gone to rest

in Peace let us be
wreck us not all tell us you
lie lie lie gather'd
on the banks of the River
let us be and strew on us

roses in the depths
of the Forest let us be
something which somewhere
all the dead sleep sound let all
of us Be Existence We

remember us with
Love with Prayers when you think
of us think of us
with tears wish us well we wish
you well and listen feel free

silent all of us
in graves we the four winds are
and graves the Keepers
confess your sins to the Dead
the full moon in churchyards us

love us the Living
must they all Informers are
must sob they must sob
sob for the souls of the Lost
the souls the souls of the Slain

sob sob tell us naught
we know all and sob sob sob
we more real are
than Man alive all of us
Ladies and Gentlemen are

forget us not hurt
not us for like us you must
also die we are
dust crush us not we fear
which somewhere in Art and Love

live on never spurn
the still sad Song of the Grave
love us the Living
all of them must let us be
Ladies and Gentlemen We

line comes through static
something which somewhere somewhere
S.O.S. only

History and Culture We
the Past and Future are
let not Posterity see
Civilization sink like a Star
all of us fear let us be
coffined Eternity We

never deride the lament
of the Dead nor the Grief nor
the Love nor the Sorrow and
Song of the broken-hearted
the Tomb the Grass nor the Verse
coffined Eternity Us

*j.m.ruggier, may 1985*
***the end***

*photograph of the author dated 1984*

## Reviews

"Let me begin by saying that the editors have found your work most profound. The general consensus is that your poetic talent is, indeed, a tremendous gift. The power and strength amidst the subtlety and sensitivity of your language is worthy of acclaim and emulation. Not since Kahlil Gibran has such poetry come out of that region of the world. Your biographical story would truly make for interesting reading." **(JOHN H. MORGAN, Ph.D., Publisher, WYNDHAM HALL PRESS, Bristol, Indiana)**

"Joe Ruggier is distinguished by his dedication to the formal aspect of literature, which does not preclude a broad eclecticism in keeping with his cosmopolitanism, and by his deeply religious nature. Both these qualities doubtless stem from his Maltese background and education -- Malta being at once "the crossroads of the Mediterrenean" and the site of one of the least remembered and most remarkable battles of World War II. His knowledge of English, Maltese and other Mediterrenean Literatures gives him an enviable multiple perspective as well as the ability to put "english on his English" and inject novelty into the most traditional of verse forms, be it a Shakespearean sonnet or a tanka." **(WARREN STEVENSON, Professor of English, UBC, Poet and Author)**

# Part two: In the suburbs of Europe

# In the suburbs of Europe

**perspectives on**
**Maltese language & literature by**

**Joe M. Ruggier**

# In The Suburbs Of Europe



**Published by: MBOOKS OF BC**
Unit 114 – 6051 Azure Road, Richmond, B.C., V7C 2P6
Tel: +(604) 600-8819 E-Mail: jrmbooks@hotmail.com

**Printing History**
**MBooks Poetry Series; #2**
1st Edn 1991 / 2nd Edn 1993 — **ISBN: 0-9694933-1-2**
3rd (Electronic) Edition - for CD-ROM - Summer 2003
**ISBN: 0-9733301-0-4**
4th print edition, (substantially reselected),
produced as Part Two of the 1st, 2nd & 3rd editions
of Joe Ruggier's Collected Poems, June 2009 – June 2018
**ISBN to the current edition : 978-1-897303-26-9**

**Edited by: Professor Paul Matthew St. Pierre,**
Simon Fraser University

Cover Art: Edwin Varney
Pen & Ink Sketches Courtesy of: Edwin Varney
Original Postcards: Maltese Artist Photographers
Desk-Top Publishing Format: Joe M. Ruggier

1st and 2nd editions printed and bound by: **Laser Graphics Ltd.**
3rd electronic edition produced by:
**Progress Media Duplication, Richmond, B.C.**
this edition printed and bound by: **Lightning Source Inc.; USA**

**Over 3,525 Copies in Circulation**

# IN THE SUBURBS OF EUROPE

## MALTA
## 1977 VANCOUVER 1993

The 2nd revised edition of

JOE M. RUGGIER's

perspectives on
Maltese language
and literature

brought out by

**MULTICULTURAL BOOKS**

*"There are many Mansions in Parnassus!"*

**Unit 114 - 6051 Azure Road, Richmond, BC, Canada, V7C 2P6**

## Paul Matthew St. Pierre's foreword

LIKE the Literatures of Tonga, Fiji, Papua New Guinea, the Solomon Islands, Singapore, Sri Lanka, Mauritius, and Cyprus, Maltese Literature seems a remote island in the Commonwealth archipelago, in which Canada, Australia, New Zealand, West, East, and South Africa, the West Indies, and India loom continentally.

My first exposure to Malta came when I was a child, watching John Huston's **THE MALTESE FALCON** and eating Maltesers! I had fantasies about becoming a Knight of Malta and wearing a Maltese Cross. Later, studying Marlowe's **THE JEW OF MALTA**, I thought my understanding of the insular Mediterranean culture complete, but eventually I had to admit that my knowledge was out of context.

My adult exposure to Malta came from studying the literature of the Commonwealth. Here I grew to recognize the infelicity of Malta's popular images, whether of Elizabethan colonialism or of Hollywood imperialism. As a Professor of Commonwealth Literature at Simon Fraser University, I have had occasion to teach some of the authors Joe Ruggier discusses in "**MALTA IN CONTEXT:** A Survey of Language and Literature," notably Dun Karm Psaila, Oliver Friġġieri, Daniel Massa, and Francis Ebeyer. To this crew of Odyssean oarsmen, I hastily add the name of Ruggier himself, a talented and tireless poet who turns his oar with an artist's precision, slipping it into the water imperceptibly, pulling the waves with all his might, mindful not to fall out of stroke with his fellow rower-poets propelling the wandering island of Malta.

Joe Ruggier's resistance to the Sirens' songs of ***vers anarchistiques*** and ***vers concretes***, and his obedience to his Odyssean muse, at once Ulysses and Homer, distinguish him as one of Malta's leading emigre poets, a Valletta-boatman in exile.

Ruggier's translations of Dun Karm's "**VISIT TO JESUS**" and several poems by Oliver Friġġieri are capable transliterations, and poetic inscriptions in their own right.

Here the wandering island of Malta drifts through the Mediterranean world, reminding us that, whereas the continents divide us, the seas draw us together. In this Oceania even the remotest islands sail freely.

His own migration has brought Joe Ruggier to Canada, where he is that rare being, a distinguished amateur-professional poet, an amateur who loves his craft and for whom writing is an act of love, yet one who manages to eke a profession out of writing.

Holding firm to the great verse-tradition of Eliot, Hopkins, Keats, Spenser, and John of the Cross, Ruggier rides the always-breaking sound-wave of the first utterance, the great ***EGO SUM***. But in exploiting self-styled traditions, his own "***I AM***", notably in "**TO SARAH**", he emerges a solitary ***voyageur*** in the uncharted waters of neo-traditional verse, his Odyssean crew and his poetic canon now shadows on the horizon. Joe M. Ruggier charts these waters with courage and foresight. **IN THE SUBURBS OF EUROPE** should keep the wandering island of Malta on course, and even send a few waves breaking onto the continental shores of Canada.

**Paul Matthew St. Pierre**
*Simon Fraser University*

## Author's preface

I KNOW these islands from Monos to Nassau,
a rusty head sailor with sea-green eyes
that they nickname Shabine, the patois for
any red nigger, and I, Shabine, saw
when these slums of empire was paradise.
I'm just a red nigger who love the sea,
I had a sound colonial education,
I have Dutch, nigger, and English in me,
and either I'm nobody, or I'm a nation.
**DEREK WALCOTT: The Schooner Flight**

**THOUGH** the first word I spoke was in Maltese, I have always, ever since I started attending school, studied, read, and written in English, Maltese being the only subject in my day which, in Malta, was taught through Maltese. In the Renaissance, as well as earlier, authors who desired to reach an international audience wrote in Latin. For reasons very similar to these, I have deliberately chosen to write in English, rather than in Maltese.

I move very easily from Maltese to English. At home, with my family, we talk both languages simultaneously, freely mingling snatches from both languages in the same sentence. My tireless study of English prosody, which has earnt me my reputation as a poet, qualifies me for translating Maltese poetry into English as very few authors in Canada, if any, are qualified so to do. I do consider myself to be perfectly bilingual. I have occasionally caught myself creating poetry in both languages at the same time.

**IN THE SUBURBS OF EUROPE** is a heart-felt patriotic tribute to the Land of my birth, an effort to make Malta's unique inheritance, from which the Maltese derive such hard-won legitimate pride, accessible to an international audience. The role which I adopt in my historical and cultural analysis of Maltese heritage, **MALTA IN CONTEXT**, is that of a cultural ambassador for Malta with readers of world literature written in English to whom Maltese - and this is nothing less than a fact of life! - is a tongue no man can understand.

Fortunately enough, Maltese is not a dactylic language, like Latin and Greek, and the iambic pentameter sounds as natural in Maltese as it does in English. This makes translation from Maltese into English a little easier for the skilled translator. My various translations from the Maltese included herein aspire to hold their own as literature in English while remaining true to the spirit and sense of the original. Myself a poet, I am very sensitive to the emotional and musical impact of my original material in Maltese. It is hoped that my English versions read as poetry rather than merely a literal translation.

Apart from this altruistic role of cultural Ambassador, it was only secondarily that I included, in Section 2 of this pamphlet, various hitherto unpublished, fugitive pieces by myself, some of which were written when I was still in Malta. This selection of my own work has been substantially reselected for this edition of my **Collected Poems** since most of the original work by myself featured in the original version of **In the Suburbs of Europe** resurfaces within **regrets hopes regards and prayers ...**

**Joe M. Ruggier**
*North Vancouver*
*21st April 1991*

## Acknowledgements

**ACKNOWLEDGEMENTS** are due to: **BRENDA SMET KLEBBA,** Managing Editor of **Pierpont Press**, Wauwatosa, Wisconsin, for ***donating*** the typesetting for the 1st Edition of **IN THE SUBURBS OF EUROPE**; **PROFESSOR PAUL MATTHEW ST. PIERRE** of SFU for his priceless Foreword and Copy-Editing; **PROFESSOR ROSS LABRIE** of UBC for his extremely valuable feedback when **ITSOE** was being put together; **MR EDWIN VARNEY** of Vancouver, BC, for his extremely valuable ***donation*** of the pen and ink sketches and cover art-work; **ALL THE MALTESE ARTIST-PHOTOGRAPHERS** responsible for producing the original postcards from which the pen and ink-sketches in this book were derived; **PROFESSOR CHARLES ENRIQUEZ** of St. F. X. University, NS, for his priceless encouragement and admiration of my translations; **DR OLIVER FRIĠĠIERI, THE KLABB KOTBA MALTIN, KARMEN MICALLEF BUHAĠIAR, CHEV. J. P. VASSALLO, & ĠORG BORĠ** for allowing me to quote and use copyright material; MY **PARENTS** for their valuable feedback when I was writing **MALTA IN CONTEXT** in 1983 and later, when the 1st Edition of **ITSOE** was released.

**JOE M. RUGGIER**
**NORTH VANCOUVER, BC**
**21ST OCTOBER 1992**

**The Old City, Mdina**
**After Photo by Mr. Mercieca**

## Section 1

# Malta in Context

*a survey of language and literature*

"Infinite riches in a little room"
**MARLOWE: DOCTOR FAUSTUS**

**SITUATED** 60 miles to the South of Sicily, 200 to the North of North Africa, measuring a mere 117 square miles in all, and for 200 years a British Colony, Malta is an island museum at the crossroads of the Mediterranean, a treasure-house of tradition, culture, history, and prehistory. Excluding migrants, the present population exceeds 300,000, and the population density is among the highest anywhere.

Semitic in their origins, European through their apprenticeship, the Maltese were converted to Christianity by St Paul in A.D. 60. The faith has been to the inhabitants of these islands the unifying power which, like a rod of Moses, has made of three barren rocks a nation with a character. Sufficiently isolated from their European and Semitic neighbours, and taking a pride in their Crusoe-like isolation, the Maltese have always had to rely on their own resources, and have even developed a language which, however derivative, is by now sufficiently apart to be studied as a language, and not a dialect.

What sort of language is Maltese? It is, indeed, a rather primitive instrument. It has been looked down upon for hundreds of years. It has not been moulded into perfection by hundreds of writers. It has not been spoken by millions of people. The only materials, which, for hundreds of years, the Maltese have expressed in Maltese, are ordinary sentiments, natural, daily events and phenomena, seasonal, agricultural, fishing and maritime jargon, and human feeling. Maltese is a poetic language.

By this I mean that Maltese is a core, and nothing besides. The English language is immeasurably superior in vocabulary, featuring nuances, synonyms, philosophical jargon, technological, industrial, medical, scientific, critical. Remove all these accretions, and you are left with the poetic core. Obliterate the respect which the language has enjoyed, the pride it has inspired, the one hundred and one great authors who have perfected it, the millions of people who have spoken it, and the state of the language begins to resemble the state of the Maltese language now. A truism, you might say.

It has, of course, been impossible for Maltese not to import much specialized, modern, and not-so-modern jargon, and before Homer wrote, I suppose, Greek was probably a poorer language than Maltese is nowadays.

What does it sound like? That part of the vocabulary which the Maltese regard as pure Maltese is of Semitic origin, and sounds Semitic, while that part of the vocabulary which the Maltese regard to be imported, has come from the Romance languages, Spanish, French, mostly Italian, and some English terms, and either sounds Latinate, or English. For 'visit', for instance, we have two versions: 'viżta', pronounced 'veesta', which sounds latin; and 'żjara', pronounced 'zyaara', which is semitic. Similarly, for mother, father, we have two versions: one is 'mama', 'papa', where the root is latin; the other is 'omm', which looks easy to pronounce, and 'missier', pronounced 'misseer', with the double "e" as in free. The last pair of works are of Semitic etymology.

However Semitic the root, the alphabet used by the Maltese is, again, the Roman alphabet: Maltese is, indeed, a very eclectic hybrid, rather difficult for foreigners. The sound of the Semitic root, however, may be described a little colourfully as close to that of quotations from the Bible in the original Hebrew.

But although the language is probably over 2,000 years old, there never was any national spirit in Malta before the turn of the century. No more than a traffic-centre, now as always, and yet, for over 2,000 years, a traffic-centre the operation of which was essential to the peace of mind of the Roman Empire, the Moors, the Arabs, the French, the English, and to all Christendom itself, when the Knights of Malta defeated the forces of Islam in 1565,

Malta has always been handed around from power to power. Itself powerless, it has always played the most unwilling part of power politics in the Mediterranean, and always, the Maltese have had a marked and pitiful colonial cringe mentality. They can hardly be blamed, though, for inviting the Romans over peacefully, and literally asking them to take over, when Rome could have done so uninvited. This characteristic move of the Maltese was, once again, their policy when, threatened by Napoleon's forces, Malta asked the British over.

Taking full shape with the turn of this century, a romantic revival, inspired by the ideals of the Italian Risorgimento 50 years after, took place in Malta. Interest in the Maltese language, and in Maltese music, folklore, history and poetry was, for the first time, exhibited in high-serious earnest. This national revival, while championed by the political party who represented the rights of the Maltese, the Nationalist Party, was rather frowned upon by the colonial rule, the more so as the Nationalists were themselves very much too partial to Italian culture, a bias which, to the British, in those days of international unease and warfare, seemed a little questionable and subversive. This spirit of Maltese nationalism has indeed produced some of the island's bitterest internal hostilities, on the political, cultural, and religious levels.

I see in Malta a unique metaphor for the sham and military ambition of the global village, whose thoughts are likewise small, whose schemes are likewise little. But in spite of the bogus pretensions which persist today, in spite of much exaggerated, pretentious humbug, such as that woven around the question of linguistic purism, the new revival produced a deep sense of new-found identity, some genuine feeling, some genuine poetry, and at least one poet of a considerable and definite merit. This was **DUN KARM PSAILA** who, at first writing in Italian, was carried away by the new spirit, and switching over to Maltese as his artistic medium, was immediately, and by common consent, hailed as the young, new Nation's natural voice and unacknowledged romantic legislator.

Priest-poet, Psaila is now the National Poet of these islands. His genius is profoundly Maltese. It is influenced by the Maltese flora and fauna. It is deeply stirred by the very intimate family life of Malta. It reflects the intense religious and devotional life, and the staunch Catholicism of the Maltese, to its best advantage.

His most sustained literary effort, **IL JIEN U LILHINN MINNU**, {The I And (There) Beyond It}, is as lovely a short epic as Wordsworth's **MICHAEL**: its blank verse, and the romantic character of its rhetoric and sentiment, remind me, all things considered, of that far greater poet, and would by no means have been unworthy of Wordsworth. Psaila's best poetry, and in this he again resembles Wordsworth, is autobiographical in nature. I might mention, to illustrate my point, **IL JIEN U LILHINN MINNU**; **VIŻTA LIL ĠESU**, {Visit to Jesus}, which reads like a most interesting analogy to Wordsworth's **TINTERN ABBEY; REVISITED**, with the difference that Psaila had not strayed too far away at any time; **NON OMNIS MORIAR**; and **IL ĠERREJJA U JIEN**, {The Racing Boat and I}. The quality of heightened prose, which distinguishes the dignified simplicity of his rhetoric, is another aspect of his work which, to my mind, makes him a worthy companion to that great poet of the Lake District. It is of relevance that Wordsworth defined poetry as heightened prose. In his unified sensibility, however, his pious domesticity, and the entirely orthodox romanticism of his sentiment, Psaila was Wordsworth's superior, even if he does not have that greater poet's abundance and complete competence.

Psaila's best work is also of a deeply religious nature. To put him into another English perspective for the English reader, I could say that a comparison with most of the highly respectable devotional poets who practised in the 17th Century, namely poets such as Herbert, Crashaw, Vaughan and Traherne, and even Donne, would be a comparison from which he will certainly emerge with credit. Though my opinion must necessarily be coloured by the fact that, to me, he is nearer home, I think that, to compare his **VIŻTA LIL ĠESU** with that period's best remembered lyric to the Blessed Sacrament, Herbert's **LOVE**, would be a little unfair to Herbert. Why? The Maltese poem is far superior: it is longer than the English poem; it is equally well-sustained; it incorporates a wider sensibility.

The central experience, of a memorable visit to a nearby Church in the countryside, is woven, in this poem, not only with the poet's sweeping autobiographical recollections, but also with Time, Autumn, and Place, Malta. The poetic setting is beautifully redolent of the Maltese autumn countryside. Before I pass Psaila over, I would like to illustrate my thesis, that he wrote from a stance of Wordsworthian "emotion recollected in tranquillity", with some quotation from this poem. To substantiate my evaluation of Psaila as a very Maltese author is also well worth quoting a few word pictures:

It was the season
When vines undress and to the lord yield up
The very last bunches, and the pleasant breeze
Carries the yellow leaves and a thick, low pallor
Of cloud strains heaven and the very first drizzle
Of rain begins in due season: the hour drew near
When birds upon the trees would congregate
And, countless, rouse the air with endless chirping;
Alone, all by my soul, a little book-weary,
I took the road that parts the fields and sea.
-- Sweet was your voice upon that day, O Sea,
And quiet the wave which rippling foamlessly
Lapped on the dented shore! And sweet your voices,
O trees for ever blessed with evergreen,
Only blossoming when I, myself an infant
Climber, would hang upon another's knee
To totter on my legs! -- Down to his cottage,
Shouldering his tools, some ancient peasant
Was lonesomely descending, whilst in the distance
The very last song of some shepherd would softly mingle
With the voices and the tinkle of tiny bells;
And sheethed in the glancing, silver sea

There could be seen the reddish shine of moist oars
Dipping out of some Dgħajsa,[77] heavily laden
With snares and nets.

"The road that parts the fields and sea", and "the dented shore" --both are very characteristic features of the islands. Again, with regards to Shepherds, there are, even nowadays, still a few shepherds in Malta, but they are being rapidly swept off their fields by the almost complete industrialization. In the days of the poet there were many more than there are now.

The chapel folded up among the trees
Stood open: I went in and on tip-toe
Stole to the Altar. No one else save I
Alone was there, and all alone I stood
In the serenity of God's house. The splendour
Of blushing sunset, casting a long soft finger
Through a little window, played in the lattic'd chapel,
And facing the lattice, on the sunlit wall,
Swinging in silence to and fro, the shadow
Of leafy bowers could be seen obeying
The sweet sea-breeze. Deep in that blushing splendour
The blessed Crucifix upon the Altar
Stood all attired. Oh how stricken, dumb
And wan the figure of Jesus seemed in the blushing
Of that glow! What great sorrow seemed to lie upon
The head suspended and in the desolate eyes
Of that silent Keeper!

However romantic and idealized these passages may sound to the contemporary foreigner, these scenes will be found to be amazingly real, concrete and actual upon a visit to the islands. In the poet's day especially, industrialization was still in its infancy, and there was nothing romantic at all about them ..... "things more real than living man", and "the chapel folded up among the trees" is still a local feature. The poem, as I have already said, reads like a most

[77] pronounced **"die-sah"**, a Maltese fishing boat

interesting parallel to Wordsworth's **TINTERN ABBEY: REVISITED**. Conscious, deliberate and faithful though my translation into a Wordsworthian idiom is, I had no other choice. I would otherwise have distorted the original.

Psaila was heavily influenced by Italian Literature. For the sake of the English reader, I have nonetheless done my best to put him in an English perspective. He was an acknowledged Romantic, inspired by the ideals of the Risorgimento and the new Maltese Nationalism, and writing in the first half of this century. He had a large following, as well as many pitiful imitators. Among his contemporaries, the more illustrious were **RUŻAR BRIFFA, ĠORĠ PISANI,** and **ĠINO MUSCAT AZZOPARDI**. Rużar Briffa too was himself a highly original poet of great significance to the Maltese.

This era was a romantic era, the first and only one of its kind within the new and only upsurge of national identity, but, with Psaila's death, and with the political maturity of the new movement, Maltese politics, literature, music and everything were suddenly invaded by the twentieth century. These two periods, Romantic and 20th C, are the only two in the history of Maltese Literature.

Any analysis which I may give of why Malta's development should have been so retarded will essentially repeat what I have said already. The great English writers, among them Milton himself, wrote books or poems in Latin, and even Italian, and this was in England, and England at the height of its political power. By comparison a barren rock, Malta has always, since the times of the Phoenicians, been occupied by foreign powers, and its affairs have always been conducted in the languages of its lords and overseers.

Among other voices in the literature, the most important among the poets are **OLIVER FRIĠĠIERI, MARIO AZZOPARDI, ACHILLE MIZZI, JOE FRIĠĠIERI** and **DANIEL MASSA**, who besides publishing single and joint collections in Maltese, have also been published in translation. Of this new wave poetry, **DR PAUL XUEREB**, a leading local critic, wrote the following, highly revealing words, in **<u>THE TIMES</u>**, London:

> *The wave of literary activity which political independence set in motion has still not spent itself. Some writers are entering on a period of consolidation while a few others are going on to new themes and styles. The lead remains mostly with the younger writers, some of whose works have achieved a wide readership.*
>
> *Poetry has always been the richest genre in Maltese Literature. Psaila and Rużar Briffa, some of whose lyrics may be read in English translation in A. J. Arberry's,* ***<u>A MALTESE ANTHOLOGY</u>****, {C.U.P. 1960}, for instance, are probably the greatest writers we have had hitherto. The new wave of Maltese poets, however, has been reacting strongly against Psaila, in whom nineteenth-century romanticism was ennobled by superb craftsmanship and a keen perception of the external world, but whose influence had been the cause of much bad poetry.*
>
> *The poets of the sixties, like the English poets of the twenties and thirties, have thrown overboard traditional diction, imagery and versification, and more important still have rejected the traditional word-picture which formed the essential background of their predecessor's work.*

Interesting though the leading contemporary voices may be, and long-awaited though modernism may have been, the arrival of modernism was not without its drawbacks. Obscurantism, perversity and a poetry which is a species of psychological instability, extremity and derangement, are among its nastier features. Apart from the fact that, in a place as small as Malta, it is very difficult to extricate some of these poets from purely political intrigue.

I find **ĠORĠ BORĠ**, however, another contemporary of considerable significance, remarkable for the manner in which he has, in this period, successfully retained traditional views through the incredibly compressed simplicity, and the extreme concision, in which he excels:

We are the snails of Ocean,
beautiful, solitary,
building the shells
that conceal us.

Eternal the question
which coils
and coils
within us ...

Who can tell whether the waves of Ocean
caress us
or do no more than tease us?

*{My translation of "**BEBBUX**", ("Snails"), collected in **SOLITUDNI FIR-RAMLA**, {Solitude on the Sandy Shore}, an original collection of poetry by Ġorġ Borġ, Malta, 1978}.*

The skeptical and modern questioning of Divine Providence at the end of the poem is refreshing, and this poet's awareness of the ***zeitgeist***, the spirit of the age, as well as of the best in its theories of psychology and the soul, are completely delightful. **SNAILS**, for instance, is a fine metaphor for humanity, treated with restraint, simplicity, and pathos, totally Maltese, and totally modern. This poet's handling of religious faith, and of devotional material and a philosophy of life and love as intense and moving as Psaila's, are no less modern, and his gems of simplicity and grace are a profound literary experience.

**FRANCIS EBEYER**, whom I mentioned above as

introducing **MALTA, THE NEW POETRY**, is himself a very successful playwright and popular novelist, the recipient of several prestigious prizes, who translates his work into English, and who also has original work in English to his credit. Another well-known author, **FRANS SAMMUT**, has written at least one very successful and popular novel in Maltese, **SAMURAJ**.

**OLIVER FRIĠĠIERI** is a skilled, mature, accomplished, and extremely original poet in Maltese, re-invigorating the language with fresh and living metaphors, intense, unusual, packed and - quite often - moving:

> Your love, darling, is like a timid dove,
> Starving and desperate and scared - alas! -
> To peck the wheat out of my open palm.

> *{My translation of Stanza one of "**TAL BIŻA' DIN L-IMĦABBA**", - ("Terrible is this Love") - anthologized in **MALTA, THE NEW POETRY**, published by the **KLABB KOTBA MALTIN**, 1971}.*

Besides enjoying success as a popular novelist and short story writer as well as a poet, Friggieri is also, and by far, the most important authority on the literature, and its leading critic. He has published much important criticism in Maltese and Italian. He has exhausted research into the influence of Italian Culture upon the romantic pioneers of Maltese Literature, and is the Author of a definitive and comprehensive **HISTORY OF MALTESE LITERATURE**, in Maltese, in two volumes, which has also been translated and published in Italian. His work in the field has been authoritatively acclaimed as definitive by the leading Italian Universities and academic institutions, by whom he has been awarded several prestigious prizes. He presently lectures in Maltese at the University of Malta, where he holds the Chair of Maltese Studies.

The common question, not necessarily a good one, is whether the Maltese writer should write in his own, or in another language. Always, whenever the Maltese author submits work abroad, normally in English, the question comes up, and the regularity with which it comes up is dismaying. It is the kind of choice which the individual artist must make, and must--emphatically!-- be allowed to make for himself. I have no right to criticize, for instance, any of the above authors for a choice which no one else could make for them, which it seems they freely made, the kind of decision which, as long as one has all the freedom to make it freely, is the individual's privilege and no one else's.

Agreed, you may say, but the choice has interesting implications for the sensibility then expressed. The poems I translate seem alien to the contemporary English experience, and the critic analyses the effects of such choices on the nature of the work. He does not make moral judgments about which choice is best. Right, and it seems to me that, to illustrate the consequences of such a choice, a better precedent than Conrad's may not be cited. Conrad might possibly be accused of being great, but not a great patriot, true, but then, how seriously ought this to be taken? On the literary level, it does not stop enjoyment and profitable appreciation; and on the human level, nobody is bound to take him as a model.

And even so, writing in English, and not Polish, Conrad produced a great new modern for the artist, and opened up entirely new vistas of cross-fertilization which, once done, have greatly enriched English Literature, and to the reader of English Conrad is most profitable and refreshing. To the Polish reader of English, even, no less than to the English reader, Conrad may also be a breath of fresh air. And no less than that of the poems I translate, though written in English, Conrad's is not the English experience, which is precisely the point that I have been making. The foreign texture of the inspiration, in a case such as Conrad's, was a major advantage. Nor did his decision to write in English of itself stop him from being a patriot.

To resume where I started, the possibilities of cross-fertilization present to the Maltese author who decides to write in English, though he may suffer a sense of uprooting, are not present to the one who writes in Maltese, who may equally well suffer from a sense of intense, indeed unbearable solitude, and isolation greater than the natural share of the artist. It seems that, in the case of the Maltese author who decides to write in English, the possibilities of cross-fertilization which are opened up for him may well be sufficient recompense for any uprooting which he may suffer; while the solitude, the unbearable isolation, of the Maltese author who writes in Maltese, may well be far greater than any which Conrad might have had to suffer, had he written in Polish.

I feel very strongly that one trait which distinguishes Malta from the greater nations is its cosmopolitan character. Malta is to the Mediterranean what the bus-terminus at Valletta is to Malta: in other words, though to itself it is a nation, still, to the world around it, it is hardly anything more than a traffic-centre, and at that a traffic-centre in the Suburbs of Europe. I think it is ridiculous that a Maltese poet, much more than the poets of the greater nations, whose character is far less cosmopolitan than Malta's, should write, and be made to feel, for political purposes, that he should write in no other language but Maltese, the more so as the more serious and educated among his Maltese audience are more likely to enjoy his output in, let us say, English than Englishmen are likely to appreciate his output in Maltese. In short, while it would be a shameful thing for the Maltese reader not to love the beautiful originals written in Maltese, I am sure that that Maltese artist who writes of his country in a much vaster, cross-fertilized context, no less than the honest artist who writes in Maltese, is also ministering to the greater good of the Nation.

## ANNOTATED SELECTED BIBLIOGRAPHICAL SOURCES

Aquilina, Prof. Ġ., ed. and comp. Il-Muża Maltija, (The Maltese Muse). 4th ed. Malta: Diacono, 1976. An anthology of Maltese poetry.

Arberry, A.J., ed. and trans. A Maltese Anthology, Romantic Maltese Verse. C.U.P., 1960.

Azzopardi, Mario. Tabernakli, (Tabernacles). Malta: A. C. Aquilina & Co., 1979. Original Maltese Poetry with a critical introduction by Oliver Friġġieri.
---, ed. Malta, The New Poetry. Malta: Klabb Kotba Maltin, 1971. 8 Poets from Malta with an introduction by Francis Ebejer.

Azzopardi, Mario, Joe Friġġieri, Oliver Friġġieri, Raymond Mahoney, and Philip Sciberras. Dwal fil-Persjani, (Lights in the Shutters). Malta: Lux Press, 1972. Anthology in Maltese.

Borġ, Ġorġ. Solitudni fir-Ramla, (Solitude on the Sandy Shore). Malta: Lejn ix-Xefaq, 1978. Original Maltese poetry with a critical introduction by Oliver Friġġieri.
---. L-Ilma tal-Wied, (Water of the Valley). Malta: Lux Press, 1973. Original maltese poetry by Ġorġ Borġ with a critical introduction by Oliver Friġġieri.

Briffa, Rużar. Published poetry in: Il-Pronostku, Il-Malti, Leħen il-Malti, {Maltese Literary Journals}.
---. Poeżiji, {Collected Poems}. Malta: 1960.

Dun Karm, Il-Poeżiji Miġbura, (Collected Poems). Malta: Klabb Kotba Maltin, Karmen Micallef Buhaġiar, 1980. A Critical Edition by Oliver Friġġieri.

Ebeyer, Francis. Eleven (11) original plays in Maltese. 4 vols. Malta: Lux Press, Klabb Kotba Maltin.
---. A Wreath for the Innocents. London: Mc.Gibbon & Kee.
---. Evil of the King Cockroach. London: McGibbon & Kee.
---. Wild Spell of Summer. London: McGibbon & Kee.
---. Come Again in Spring. Malta: Lux Press.
---. In the Eye of the Sun. London: McDonald & Co.

Friġġieri, Oliver. Poetry in various collections.
---. Critical writings in Maltese and Italian.
---. Storja tal-Letteratura Maltija, (History of Maltese Literature), in Maltese. 2 vols. Malta: Klabb Kotba Maltin, 1981.
---. Stejjer għal qabel jidlam, (Bed-time Stories). Malta: Gulf Publishing Ltd., 1979. Short stories in Maltese.
---. Il-Gidba, (The Lie). Malta: Klabb Kotba Maltin, 1977. A novel in Maltese.
---. L-Istramb, (The Eccentric). Malta: Gulf Publishing Ltd., 1981. A novel in Maltese.

Mizzi, Achille. Il-Kantiku tad-Demm, (The Canticle of Blood). Malta: A. C. Aquilina & Co., 1980. Original poetry in Maltese with a critical Introduction by Oliver Friġġieri.

Sammut, Frans. Samuraj. Malta: Klabb Kotba Maltin, 1975. A Novel in Maltese.

Serracino Inglott, Peter, ed. Linji Ġodda, (New Trends). Malta: Klabb Kotba Maltin, 1973. 100 original Poems in Maltese with a critical commentary by Peter Serracino Inglott.

---, ed. and comp. Dħaħen fl-Imħuħ, (Fumes in the mind). Malta: 1967. An anthology of selected poetry in Maltese, featuring Ġorġ Borġ, Oliver Friġġieri, and Albert Marshall.

**SENGLEA** — Jutting into the Grand Harbour is the Old Fortified City of Senglea with its massive Bastions

# By way of a preface to Dun Karm, national poet of Malta,

*together with a translation of:*
*ŻJARA LIL ĠESU'*[78]

IT hardly needs to be said that, by the standards of English and Continental Literature, Psaila can hardly be ranked with the greater poets. He does not have the abundance, variety and complete competence which Eliot noted in Tennyson, and in other poets of such rank. Still he is a poet of no mean quality. It is very easy to belittle a writer by comparing him to others; what is not easy is to write poetry of a high level of beauty and profundity, and certainly Psaila wrote such.

In **"MALTA IN CONTEXT"** I have already discussed Psaila's poetry at length, with particular reference to his "**ŻJARA LIL ĠESU**" This brief commentary should therefore be read as a follow-up of what I have already said. Naturally, it is also meant to be a brief, critical introduction to my translation. All that I have said of Psaila's poetry in "**MALTA IN CONTEXT**", can be studied in his **ŻJARA**.

---

[78] Psaila, Karm - Żjara Lil Ġesu, (Visit to Jesus). Il-Poeżiji Miġbura, (Collected Poems). A Critical edition by Oliver Friġġieri. Malta: Klabb Kotba Maltin & Karmen Micallef Buhaġiar, 1980. pp. 236-240.

This brief critical comment is meant to supply the reader with a few detailed reflections which **MALTA IN CONTEXT** omits.

A great poet usually has a great literary tradition behind him: it is not innate genius alone that usually makes great poets. What makes Psaila's poetic achievement so remarkable is the fact that he was a pioneer: he had behind him no literary tradition worth speaking of on an international level; he did not have around him the richness of a historical past and environment such as sustains the greater poets of the greater nations; and in his hands he had a very primitive instrument indeed. Psaila did not quarrel with his tools, but Maltese simply is not the instrument which English is. It has been looked down upon for hundreds of years; it has not been moulded into perfection by hundreds of writers; it has not been spoken by millions of people. I have said that Psaila can hardly be ranked with the greater poets; but the poverty of his material reveals his true greatness. One is almost inclined to think that, had he been an English poet, he would have been, and would have been recognized as, a very great poet indeed, but though he is limited by his material, it is not desired that he should be other than what he is by the common consent of the Maltese.

In **MALTA IN CONTEXT** I introduced a brief, unfinished comparison of Psaila's "**VISIT TO JESUS**" with the famous English lyric by George Herbert, the poem "**LOVE**", which is arguably the most beautiful lyric to the Blessed Sacrament produced by the English Devotional poets in the Metaphysical Age of Poetry. What follows is the text of the poem:

Love bade me welcome: yet my soul drew back,
        Guiltie of dust and sinne.
But quick-ey'd Love, observing me grow slack
        From my first entrance in,
Drew nearer to me, sweetly questioning,
        If I lack'd any thing.

A guest, I answer'd, worthy to be here:
        Love said, you shall be he.
I the unkinde, ungratefull? Ah, my deare,
        I cannot look on thee.
Love took my hand, and smiling did reply,
        Who made the eyes but I?

Truth Lord, but I have marr'd them: let my shame
        Go where it doth deserve.
And know you not, sayes Love, who bore the blame?
        My deare, then I will serve.
You must sit down, sayes Love, and taste my meat:
        So I did sit and eat.[79]

I argued that to compare the two poems, the one by Psaila, and the other by Herbert, would be a little unfair to Herbert because the Maltese poem is far superior: it is longer than the English poem; it is equally well-sustained; it incorporates a wider sensibility. I would now like to finish off the comparison.

It is fair enough to comment that Herbert did not set out with Psaila's intentions and that, in the little room of that short lyric, he wrote with equal mastery of touch, but besides Psaila's poem, in which a sensibility to Nature, as well as a deep awareness of his past life-history, is successfully incorporated into the religious experience, Herbert's poem is what it is, a very short poem indeed, however beautiful. Its thought and emotion are no doubt restrained and sincere; its diction is delicately refined; its execution perfect. Herbert's poem also reveals a gift for rational analysis, springing, most probably, from the Protestant character of his inspiration, which Psaila does not seem to possess. But neither does this quality seem to be Psaila's ideal. There is, in Psaila's poem, a far more impressive poetic quality, a quality of restrained, sympathetic and ecstatic recollection, springing, most

[79] **Herbert, George**. **Love. Metaphysical Lyrics and Poems of the 17th C**., selected and edited with an essay by Herbert J. C. Grierson. London, Oxford, New York: Oxford University Press, 1921, 1959, 1971. p. 115.

probably, from the Catholic nature of his inspiration. But I can only imagine a spirit of amiable competition between those two amiable Christians.

This brief comparison is not intended to derogate Herbert, who, in some definite respects, and on some definite occasions, was a finer poet than Psaila. What I intend to show is how well Psaila can stand comparison with such universally acclaimed poets as George Herbert, England's devotional poets in general, and even with poets such as William Wordsworth. As I have observed already, Psaila's **VISIT TO JESUS** is a most interesting analogy to Wordsworth's **TINTERN ABBEY: REVISITED**. Granted that Psaila was influenced by Italian much more than by English Literature, I have also tried to view him from a fresh perspective. I will now conclude with a few observations about my translation.

I do not consider that an original should be translated into the metre which is fashionable in the age in which it is translated. Though it is arguable that, technically speaking, this may not always be possible, I think that, if the translation is to possess a durable and definitive quality, if it is to aspire to the condition of original poetry in its own right, passionate fidelity to the style, metres, diction, rhythms, versification and any other artistic finesse, however unimportant, of the original should be maintained. My ideal as a translator being that, by setting a beautiful original before a foreign audience in exactly the same perspective which it holds in the mother language, I might, by so doing, set it in an equally true, but fresh, perspective in the vast literary heritage which distinguishes the language of my translation. Having imposed upon myself such a stern principle, and having followed it with the cold passion of a mathematician, I think that the little liberties which I have taken with the original are entirely justified, and I hope that whenever, inspired by the original, I have touched it up with a relatively unimportant finesse of my own, I have not at all done it an injustice. It is well to point out that these liberties were necessitated mostly by the exigencies of translation, where the effects of the original are untranslateable unless a manner is found of capturing the same effects in a slightly different manner from that in which they are captured in the mother language.

The following is my translation of **ŻJARA LIL ĠESU'**. It is a poem more beautiful than Philip Larkin's **CHURCH GOING**, that poignant miasma of cynicism, doubt, and wavering sincerity. Psaila's **VISIT** is as lovely a devotional poem as any that has ever been written.

## Visit to Jesus

*(memories)* *to a soul that understands*

**NEVER** will I forget the consolation
That I then felt, O Jesus.

.. .. .. .. .. ..

**IT** was the Season
When vines undress and to the lord yield up
The very last bunches, and the pleasant breeze
Carries the yellow leaves and a thick low pallor
Of cloud strains Heaven and the very first drizzle
Of rain begins in due season: the hour drew near
When birds upon the trees would congregate
And, countless, rouse the air with endless chirping;
Alone, all by my soul, a little book-weary,
I took the road that parts the fields and Sea.
-- Sweet was your Voice upon that day, O Sea,
And quiet the wave which rippling foamlessly
Lapped on the dented shore! And sweet your Voices,
O trees for ever blessed with evergreen,
Only blossoming when I, myself an infant
Climber, would hang upon another's knee
To totter on my legs! -- Down to his cottage,
Shouldering his tools, some ancient peasant
Was lonesomely descending, whilst in the distance
The very last song of some shepherd would softly mingle
With the voices and the tinkle of tiny bells;
And sheethed in the glancing, silver Sea,
There could be seen the red shine of moist oars

Dipping out of some **Dgħajsa**[80], heavily laden
With snares and nets.
**THE** hour of the day
And our human story must somehow be
Bethrothed; and when the Sun is setting and reaching
After the world to give her his last kiss,
The thoughts fly after the days of happiness
That we have known and are for ever gone;
The heart is wrung, and still against our will
Tears spring to the eyes and the soul sends out
A long sigh. I called you to my remembrance, O glad Time,
When at my father's I abided, and one table
Would gather us all, in a civil tie of Love,
Myself, my brethren, and those who gave us birth;
But mostly you, my mother, who though an old woman
Of four score, to the very end persisted
As beautiful as at the prime of life,
And through the light in your eyes, which never dimmed,
Your dearest wishes would be made plain to me
Without a word; I called you to my remembrance
And 'twas as if I felt the need no longer
Of this life you were the cause of, this life so dear,
Since now you could no longer, in joy or in sorrow,
It with me share, and in death's long embrace in the mercy
Of Earth I wished to be with thee reposing.

.. .. .. .. .. .. ..

**THE** chapel folded up among the trees
Stood open: I went in and on tip-toe
Stole to the Altar. No one else save I
Alone was there, and all alone I stood
In the serenity of God's house. The splendour
Of blushing sunset, casting a long, soft finger
Through a little window, played in the lattic'd chapel,
And facing the lattice, on the sunlit wall,
Swinging in silence to and fro, the shadow
Of leafy bowers could be seen obeying

---

80 **Dgħajsa** … pronounced **"die-sah"**, a Maltese fishing boat.

The sweet sea-breeze. Deep in that blushing splendour
The Blessed Crucifix upon the Altar
Stood all attired. Oh how stricken, dumb
And wan the figure of Jesus seemed in the blushing
Of that glow! What great sorrow seemed to lie upon
The head suspended and in the desolate eyes
Of that silent Keeper! Sorrow was in my heart
Begotten for thee, O Time, I lost in folly,
Without arising to the goods of Heaven,
Though glowing in my heart I often felt
The ardour of arising; the blush of shame
Lit up my heated face; and all at once
I dropped my gaze, and hot as glowing cinders
I felt a tear rolling down my cheek.
Trembling at that soul-wringing silence, my lips
Uttered these words spontaneously; - Our Father
Who art in Heaven, hallowed be Thy Name ... -
Were that the very first time that I had heard
Such dear words, they never would have struck me
Better or deeper than on that night they did:
Never did that sweet name ring in my ear
Sweeter than on that day, and never were the ardours
And flames of love that I had ever tried
Greater or dearer. I was on my own no longer
In that forgotten chapel, since out of the depths
Of Heaven I was guarded by the might
Of a Father who never will forget His children,
Receiving in His embrace, Love without end,
Whoever draws willingly towards Him.
- Father ... - I called once more; and all the races,
Though parted one and all by Space or Time,
Were in my vision, by a bond sublime,
Bethrothed one and all, and all the World
One happy home, proclaiming the name of brethren
For emperors and tramps in streets a-begging.
Oh beauty of Redemption! Oh how near
To Life Thy death upon the Tree has drawn us,
Thou Son of God! Nay, 'tis not happiness
That is in the World most happy; sorrow also
Carries its own attraction, since within it

Hidden there is ever the seed of consolation:
The Heavy Cross by Thee embraced our burden
Of sin did lighten, and through that agony,
Which soul from body in Thee parted, a bond
That cannot be put asunder was begotten,
Beneath One Father all mankind uniting.
I did repeat; - Our Father ... - and my eyes
Fell on the Altar, upon a little door,
Where hiding beneath a humble likeness, God
Almighty brought to nothing His power and glory
And did become our daily bread! Oh strength!
Oh folly of Love! Vast, awful, and immense!
For since it was His Will to dwell among us
And to hug in a close embrace this poor, poor clay
That, next to nothing, knows nothing but how to sin,
His Mercy has no end. And I then desired
To give Love to Jesus; and the lamp that glimmering
In silence stood before the Sacrament
Seemed miserable to me, and I then desired
To place the Sun with all its mighty fires
Burning before Him. How sweet the Serenity is
In your house, O Lord! What purity and good taste
Lie in that nest you chose wherein to abide!
Never did arrow fly from the bow more lightly
Than my own thoughts sped lightly to my visit:
And the happiness I remembered when for the first time
Upon my tongue, in reverence deep and silent,
I tasted that wholesome food which presently
Went in my bosom: and thou, Angel of Love,
Mother dear, I bore in mind that, since
The dawn of Reason, desire of this bread
Was by thee in me begotten, perhaps the stirring
Of that other which led me to the summit with Jesus.
A thousand blessings upon the land wherein
You rest and which will yield you up once more,
In the power of this bread, to a new life,
Happy and beautiful without end. - Our Father ...
Our Father ... - I repeated, and 'twas as if
That sweet dear name left on my very tongue
A heavenly savour. Oh never will I forget,

Never will I forget the consolation
That I then felt, O Jesus.

.. .. .. .. .. ..

**DARKNESS** was settling
When I left the Chapel, and in the heavens some stars
Began to peep. Once more, all by my soul,
I took the road that parts the fields and Sea:
Once more I could hear upon the dented shore
Waves lapping gently, and the pleasant breeze
Rustling among the leaves of trees: but silent
Was the coastland, and I could no longer hear
The sweet song of shepherd and peasant softly mingling
With the voices and the tinkling of tiny bells.
The night drew near ..... - but a Light
More beautiful than sunlight sprang in my mind,
And a new happiness was in my heart
Begotten: - Is the utterance of Heaven thus?
Of the past thought I no longer; the tears were dry
Upon my cheeks; and of a sudden, like
A dawning Star, Hope shone upon my Life.

Isle of Malta — Dgħajsa (pronounced **die-sah**) (A Maltese Fishing-Boat)

Isle of Malta — Fungus Rock

Isle of Malta — Neolithic Temple

**Dr. Oliver Friġġieri**

further translations from the Maltese

of: **Oliver Friġġieri**

**THESE** translations from the Maltese of poetry by **FRIĠĠIERI**, while aspiring in their own right to the condition of original poetry, seem to me to possess a romantic and esoteric quality which is in perfect harmony with the nature of this collection.

## The abstracted pilgrim

*elegy to a still-born child*

**SOME** flowers never open, some fruit withers long before it is cut, there is corn which falls on the eve of the harvest, there is a dark night still awaiting the dawn of a sun which set before it rose. You are a candle which was never lit, a poem written in vain, a word in the dictionary of an unknown tongue, a catacomb where no step falls, an empty church, a songless bird, a false coin, --- my son.

**IN** your grey continent
you crawled through your green bower,
rocked on the waves of ocean,
hoped for the promised hour.

In a secret tongue you lisped
this word of never, never,
and sang me a dirge for the man
of no identity whatever.

You to me, and I to you,
talked of eternal youth,
black syllables you could not utter,
the Gospel, Gospel Truth.

This voyage so vain you have made,
this day which never broke,
this silent melody,
I dread it, I dread it and choke.

Interred without a funeral,
grieved for without a tear,
grown weary of walking, so early,
he would rest - let no one draw near!

Let no one awake him, sleep overtake him,
let no voice rise up to startle him,
let no one explain, he knows all, he knew no pain:
why should you all discard him?

You are an abstracted pilgrim who lost his way,
You are an odourless carnation, a surname without a name,
and again a name without the surname, a nonentity --- my
son.

## The lamp-post

**LIKE** to the humble capers clinging to
the bastions bushily, and like the snails
that gladly swarm the moist earth once more, two lovers,
cleaving together around the corner, beneath
the lamp-post, tightly, are notably alive.

They will soon be gone, and the lamp-post will wait,
deserted, till the two return, tomorrow,
at the same hour, to kiss beneath the lamp-light.

## Terrible is this love

**YOUR** love, darling, is like a timid dove,
Starving and desperate and scared - alas! -
To peck the wheat out of my open palm.

Dreadful this love! Driven by famine, it knows
No reason but the impulsive need; sick
As the weariest breath of most laborious Death.

But catching you crying tonight, Beloved, I grasped
The unfathomable ...

Should you desire to show your love,
To your dumb reticence add but your tears.

## Ring me the burden

**RING** me the burden of a soul diseased,
Such as, though suffering, suppressed complaint,
Roused by no hope of cure, by no rebellion.
Press no harsh dissonance such as demands
Our own selves' untold occult annihilation.

Ring me the burden for life is ponderous,
But ring it gently, for our strength diminishes
And unexpected death comes once and early.

## Ailing your voice

**YOUR** voice tonight is shaking, not as strong
As I have known it be, and through your tears
Crackles and cracks aloud like canes in fields
Struck by the winter wind.  A stricken voice
Reminds me of the groans of gulls lamenting,
Over the deep mid-ocean, turbid lives,
Knowing not why, and with no sight of shore.

Ailing your voice, and stiller than the gulls',
But you know the reason.  Sooner or later, you
Will have to begin to see ...

## Thee, bell-tower

**IN** the market-place we are weeping, you and I,
and no one else, bell-tower from days gone by,
a fit of grief and not a tear.

Should friends spy my ridiculous red eyes,
there will be laughter, and they will tie your tongue
for ever, never again to make me cry.

Then cut this elegy short!  Ring what you may,
I comprehend and cry.

## My countrymen, I love you

**MY** countrymen, I love you,
who make gods spring up like flowers
everyday, and daily dance
the dance of the hours.

My countrymen, I love you
who welcome day by day
all that the foreigner
brings you from far away.

My countrymen, I love you
with a physician's lease,
who seeks disease beneath
the skin, and finds disease.

## Once all surrender

**WITHIN** me dwells a stricken garrison
which draws in terror upon the enemy lines,
and beats without design upon rough drums
and stamps cumbersome boots on ground which knows
them.
Within me dwell delirious bees devoured
by a ceaseless, drunken frenzy, endlessly
describing circles round some withered flowers.

Once all surrender and give up the ghost
as usual, and every bee drops dizzily down
to earth, will I still hear them reverberate?

## Impressions

**SUPPOSING** I doze and sleep, in this thick forest
where black crickets, the clocks of nature, whirr and chime
in disproportionate concurrence, who
will give me the exact split-second designed
to catch the Sun escape the low horizon?

Supposing the song of this bird, which slept above
my head, and delayed its song till sunrise, is lost
on the wind at sunrise, carried away upon
the rustling of the leaves, where shall I find
this melody brought up among the boughs?

And suppose the rapid clouds persist to rush
like chariots of the gods whose day is over,
how shall I freeze the sketch upon my canvas
with this brush that trembles between three fingers?

St Elmo Bastion

# Section 2

Fugitive Pieces by:
**Joe M. Ruggier**[81]

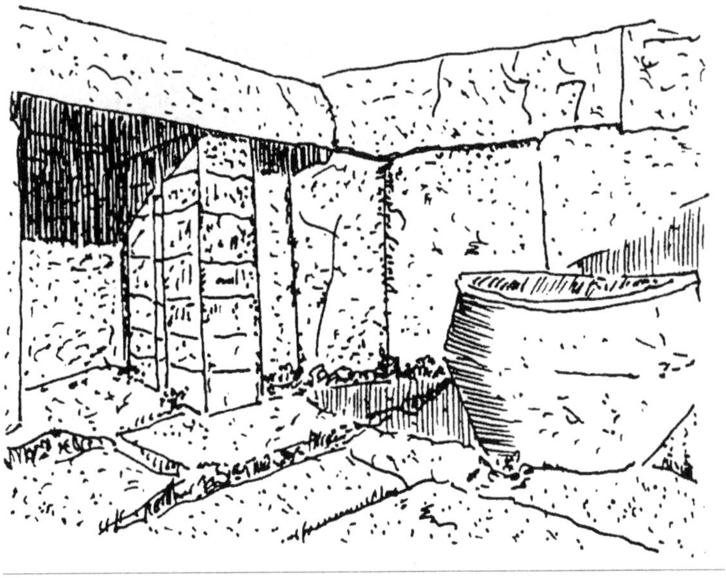

Prehistoric Temples — Tarxien, **MALTA**

[81] This selection of my own work has been substantially reselected for this edition of my **Collected Poems** since most of the original work by myself featured in the original version of this section resurfaces within **regrets hopes regards and prayers …**

St. Paul's Bay from Wardija Heights — **MALTA**

St Joseph Church — Manikata; Richard England, Architect—**MALTA**

**Sarah Therese Ruggier**
Born 3rd March 1986

## To Sarah

F**AIREST** of Daughters, fabled Queen of yore,
flung from the womb and loins of Love's sweet pie,
Star of the radiant Morning, Goddess, say
from whither? to where? and when thou came, how far?
Be troubled not, dear Child, nor be afraid,
that I say Goddess, for thou art not slime,
my sensitive Plant, nor made from dirty words.
For Jove and Venus, the Olympians all,
false Gods were never. True as thou art true
they were, and truer, truer still, for God
it was the Honour gave, the Honour took,
and Counsellors of Job those who despised
Olympus: far worse crime was that with which
they dragged the name of God in mud and slime.
My Bible says, however, we are Gods.
I lead thee not astray, my sweetest Love.
With Honour I shall nurture my own Babe.
Thou art of Queens my Queen, my Goddess thou!
Only be thou Thyself: it is sublime

to be Thyself! Splendid and great indeed
it is to be Oneself as 'tis to be
the Lord in solitude magnificent!

**BEWARE** the venomous tooth of Parents that
the Lord do honour, but their own child despise;
their dear Soul watch over as they watch
the fickle matchlight, but their Money watch
much more. Consider, Child, how door to door
thy Father found sincerity around
Vancouver, Wisdom in quite simple folk,
though hardly higher up, and street by street,
his Soul a song of sonnets streaming hands,
his Book he sold, and money never failed,
and he could eat. Do not, I beg thee, choose
lip-service for a mate to lie beside,
who wildly wants thy darling Babe to wrench,
but thy sweet Self doth honour not, and thee
doth want to vanish. Laws of God serve with
thy Heart, with all thy Soul thy Children all;
but laws of men serve with thy lips alone.
Sublime, far-off, magnificent and proud
I want thee, smiling on the Grief of things
like marble monuments because I say so!
And thine shall be the Tears and then the Crown,
and thou shalt live the Sorrow and the Calm
of Tragedy, but Grief shall crush thee not.
Sublime, far-off, magnificent and proud
I want thee, that the herd may say how proud
thou art, and so that thou may let them say
their say.

**SLEEP** sound in Thunder. Insult-blows
shall crush thee never. Let the Elements
arouse thee with the sweet, serene sensation
of Just Revenge and Vengeance. Fear thou Hell,
my Daughter; hold God's Revenge in holy Terror.
Not so that thou should then despise thy Body
I tell thee this: but if thou lose thy Soul,
shalt lose precisely Sex and Art. A Soul

sustains that Insult once, and only once:
that Insult drives the Soul insane. Do not
despise the Narcissism of the Masters;
their Pride hath wondrous healing Power. For Dance
and Sacred Song restoreth broken Spirits
so that the Soul may soar upon the Insult
with which Existence sends all Pretensions crashing.
Rejoice in Thunder. God is Just.

**THY** Heart
thy only Guide, strive thou to be thyself
and live for that unto thyself alone.
Love nothing but what worthy is of heart-
felt Love. Great Verse, great Music, let them dwell
within thy Soul all day. Dream thou beneath
the metre's curb. Strive to refine thy Dreams,
because bad Dreams materialize no less,
and love Philosophy which sounds archaic
because 'tis timeless: not archaic, but timeless.
Let all thy Powers strive to come together
around the beauty of these things as moons,
shattered to bits by pebbles in the stream,
come all together once again. Let all
thy Powers cleave around the Truth in Jest:
Theology is a clean Joke, no more,
but learn it. Live the Good Life in all its shades
of Meaning: they are one just as thou art.
Thou shalt, perchance, read much, and many voices
disturb thee such that thou shalt then become
a wilderness of personalities. Let
them cleave together round thy heartfelt core
as if they were the Many, thou the One
and Only.

**JUST** as God is Three in One,
both Hell and Heaven shall - the Lord and the Lord's Devil -
thy various sensibilities unite,
just as twin eyes, though two, are one in sight,
around a small, round insult, red and white!

**Joe M. Ruggier**
*Vancouver; 18 December 1990*

## Queen Sarah Therese to her daddy

*on the day of her first Holy Communion*

MY **DADDY** is a Man like the Lord,
and God is an Artist like Shakespeare;
and My Daddy is an Artist like God,
and God is a Man like My Daddy.

**I** love My Daddy as I love God,
and I am His Queen, Her Divine Majesty
Queen Sarah Therese, because that is what My Daddy
calls Me; and I am a Queen like the Virgin Mary!

**THE** Blessed Virgin beeth God the Mother;
and I am God My Daddy's daughter ...

*2nd May 1993*

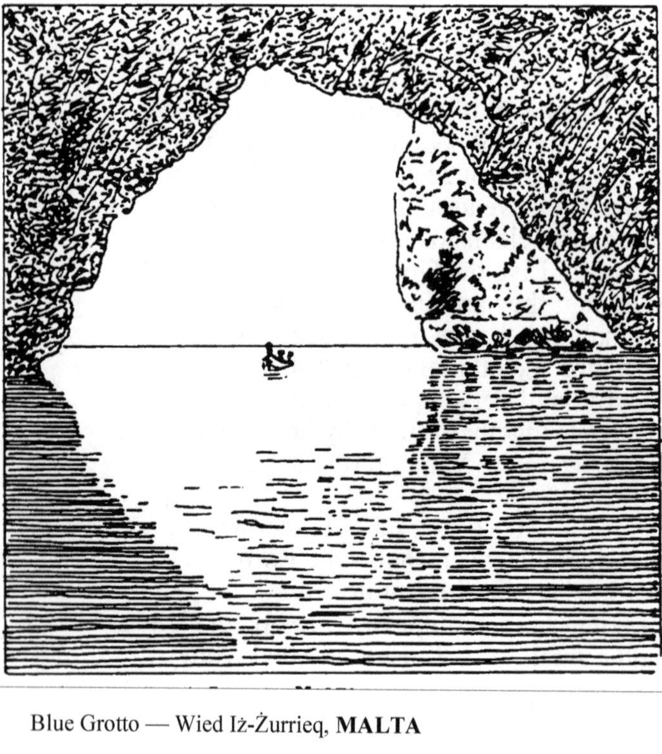

Blue Grotto — Wied Iż-Żurrieq, **MALTA**

# Part three:
## regrets hopes regards and prayers

*regrets hopes regards and prayers …*

# regrets hopes regards and prayers ...

## Joe M. Ruggier's
## verses composed in youth

with an introduction by
LeRoy Douglas Travis

**FOURTH PRINT EDITION**

brought out by
**Multicultural Books**
*"There are many Mansions in Parnassus!"*

**Unit 114 – 6051 Azure Road, Richmond, BC, Canada V7C 2P6**

# regrets hopes regards and prayers ...



**Published by: MBOOKS OF BC**
Unit 114 – 6051 Azure Road, Richmond, BC, Canada, V7C 2P6
Telephone: +(604) 600-8819 E-Mail: jrmbooks@hotmail.com

**Printing History**
1st Edition August 1996 — **ISBN: 0-9694933-5-5**
2nd Electronic Edition Summer 2003 — **ISBN: 0-9733301-0-4**
3rd & 4th print editions, produced as Part Three
of the 1st, 2nd & 3rd editions of Joe Ruggier's
Collected Poems, June 2009 — June 2018
**ISBN to the current edition: 978-1-897303-26-9**

**Introduction by:** **LeRoy D. Travis (UBC Professor)**
**Cover Art designed by:** **Joe M. Ruggier**
**executed by:** **Virginia Quental**
**Desk-Top Publishing:** **Joe M. Ruggier**

1st edition printed and bound by: **Laser Graphics Ltd.**
2nd electronic edition produced by:
**Progress Media Duplication, Richmond, B.C.**
this edition printed and bound by: **Lightning Source Inc.; USA**

**Over 1,625 Copies in Circulation**

# Introduction

**By: LeRoy Douglas Travis**
**(UBC; July 1996)**

**PHYSICIST** Paul Dirac, a Nobel Prize Winner, has said that the physicist's aim is to make plain and simple what is obscure and difficult, while the poet's charge is to do the opposite. While both physicist and poet rely on language to convey the sense they would share, the physicist abjures ambiguities, excess meanings and the plasticity inherent in language, (hence the scientist's use of mathematics) while the poet embraces these inevitable concomitants of experience when an audience is invited to partake of what is offered.

Joe Ruggier is not a physicist: he writes verse - and has done so for more than two decades. This volume consists of his early work; and it reflects his conviction that poetry is his calling - a calling he knows is noble and worthy but hard. Those who care about poetry know this too.

Someone has said that publishing a volume of verse is like dropping a rose petal down the Grand Canyon and waiting for an echo. In our confused and troubling time, people are more likely to look for relief, consolation, reassurance (or whatever they seek) from the scientist's clarifications and the slogans and simplifications of the adman and entertainer, than from the poet's offerings (which Gwyn Thomas once called "trouble dunked in tears"). As Auden, one of this century's finest poets, said:

> "**POETRY** makes nothing happen; it survives
> In the valley of its saying where executives
> Would never want to tamper ..."
> **(In Williams, 1952, p. 456).**

The money culture, with its utilitarian prejudices, is unreceptive and even hostile to such fare. Taste, vision, refined aesthetic sensibility are crushed in the cash nexus. (Denby, 1996). So Mr. Ruggier and his like have much to be troubled by in our business culture - the money culture - because "money culture recognizes no currency but its own". (Winterson, 1995, p. 158).

This fact constitutes trouble for serious artists since such artists need time for idleness, time for dreaming, time for observation and reflection and work to which no wages are attached. And in a money culture time and money are conventionally equated.

So in contemporary society, the poet must face this troubling fact which Robert Graves summarized succinctly: "There is no money in poetry; but then there is no poetry in money either". (In Metcalf, 1987, p. 192). Of course this species of trouble will not be the first that is known by the poet.

Sensitive and imaginative souls discover trouble early - often in their adolescence or teen years. They notice the moral squalor about them; and the doubts, fears and regrets within them. They discern commonplace cruelty, deceit, and ugliness. They know the stubborn spite of stupidity and dullness also. So they dream and they imagine; and they yearn and they pray for beauty, truth and goodness that will abolish, transform or mitigate the offending conditions, relations and objects. They contemplate the condition of man and the condition of their own souls. And some few with the requisite temperament, verbal ability, aesthetic sensibility and intellectual preparation strive to share the riches of their inner life with others by giving them poetic expression that reflects the care, feeling and devotion the author has invested in some particular matter that is not so plain and simple as it seems to the more casual observer or to the scientist.

Sometimes these workings of imagination are feckless, formless and inadequate displacements; but sometimes they are worthy of the name Freud gave to displacements that contribute to the culture. Freud called such instances of transformation "sublimation". Through them we gain glimpses of the sublime potential of what Frye (1963) called "the educated imagination". And in them we can discern the transformed yearnings, longings, regards, regrets, hopes and attachments - the panoply of human mental life given form in art and invention. As Winterson (1995) says:

> Art is not documentary. It may incidentally serve that function in its own way, but its true effort is to open to us dimensions of the spirit and of the self that normally lie smothered under the weight of living. (p. 137).

Unfortunately, the public of a money culture is too frequently unappreciative of such artistic visions since it is a public "drugged on reproduction". (Winterson, 1995, p. 12).

However, not just great minds with scientific intent, like Freud, have noticed the variants of displacement, the transformations of personal adjustment to trouble that sometimes take poetic form. Thus in 1917, Yeats, another Nobel Prize Winner (for literature) observed that "we make out of the quarrel with others, rhetoric, but of the quarrel with ourselves, poetry". (In Gross, 1987. p. 68). And of course in **Hamlet**, (Act V, Scene II, ll. 4-11) Shakespeare's famous lines express such recognition too:

> **... IN MY HEART** there was a kind of fighting
> That would not let me sleep: methought I lay
> Worse than the mutinies in the bilboes. Rashly,
> And praised be rashness for it, let us know,
> Our indiscretion sometimes serves us well,
> When our deep plots do pall: and that should teach us
> There's a divinity that shapes our ends,
> Rough-hew them how we will.
> **-- (In Craig, 1961, p. 939).**

Winterson (1995) expresses a truth that may have profound psychological - probably unconscious - significance for the young writer when she says "the writer is an instrument of transformation". (p. 25). For in the stream of experience, humans automatically (and usually unconsciously) assess whatever they encounter on several planes or dimensions. Objects, conditions, relations and events are assessed for their epistemic status (truth/falseness); their aesthetic value (beauty/ugliness) and their moral significance (goodness/baseness). Such appraisals evoke and energize feelings, thoughts and strivings which inform imagination (the mental function through which a life reconciles itself with its situation). So in writing, the young author can operate on the world and on his or her own soul. Through imaginative transformations new visions are given form. Some sub-set of the production may be poetic and artful; and some of the writers may transform themselves in the process.

So Joe Ruggier, in these, his early writings, transforms his troubles into poetic visions wherein his "regrets, hopes, regards and prayers" overtly express a recognition of that "divinity that shapes our ends" - even when his hewing is rough and hard.

He opens with **"Stellar Moonrise"** (p. 2), a quite lovely sonnet which reflects an appreciative ear for the Keatsian style. This exploration of what canonical styles and forms allow or make possible is seen throughout this volume and shows us that the early Ruggier was a serious student of the exemplary. In this verse we also meet a persisting theme of Heavenward gaze and wonder.

In the next piece **"Inadequacy"** (p. 3), we encounter more of Ruggier's poetic resources, his dreamscapes - and the striking, felicitous turns of phrase that evoke visions (without which the verse maker can never become a poet):

> ... **CALM** beyond time
> the fates induce deep down a soft canal
> where kindly, kindly the dew may run
> sadly down the yew in lucent poise;
> sorrowing slowly in a glimmering plain
> where greenery hangs like clouds in Japan ...

In these first two verses Ruggier also conveys a melancholic sensibility that throughout this collection gives expression to a feeling for and awareness of burdensome contradictions, sensed inadequacies, debilitating vanities, insistent longings - and lacunae of beauty, truth and goodness (without and within).

Through his care for words, the power and magic of language can give compellingly beautiful forms to feelings such as that of desolation (pp. 10-11); and these can enrich the reader's capacity to know the human soul's formations and graces in struggle, and the human capacity to attain dignity when it apprehends some dreadful truth (for example, "we are lost"). (p. 15).

Readers will find herein, a serious mind tussling with emptiness, loneliness, outrage, regret, self-doubt, forlornness, and intellectual conundrums that give rise to visions and sounds of beauty which foretell of the writer's later, more mature works (such as **Intelligible Mystery, Art and Revealed Religion, Out of Blue Nothing** and **The Dark Side of the Deity**). Here too are to be found reflections that can stimulate or provoke further thought on topics such as genius and talent (**"On Genius"**, pp. 83-85); art (**"To Beethoven"**, pp. 68-69; & **"Pieta'"**, p. 34); and criticism (**"Principles of Criticism"**, pp. 103-106).

Throughout the collection, Mr. Ruggier's admiration for T. S. Eliot and Gerard Manley Hopkins is evident in form, themes and religious allusions. There is always evident a reverent tone even when there is religious tension or exasperation. However, sometimes something approaching irreverence is seen in what Frye (1957, p. 309) describes as the Manippean satire "which deals less with people as such than with mental attitudes" (for example see **"At Mr. Specservor's"**, p. 101; and **"Warmongers"**, p. 97). Some of this will provoke some chuckles.

But as I said before, there is a pervasive melancholy within the collection that stands out for its poignancy, its capacity to touch those who are prepared to trust the writer. And well we of good faith, are obliged to trust (Winterson, 1995, p. 36) difficult though this may be in an age when everyone is choked by bafflegab - that detritus of garbage information that pervades the atmosphere of our age.

This is a time when a tragic view of life seems

warranted. Yet one cannot escape the truth in Winterson's (1995, p. 36) assertion that "the relationship between the reader and the writer's work has to be one of trust".

This is not lost on Mr. Ruggier who, as I've said, has a great care for words. This is his part of the bargain, as such care is the means by which he can sustain trust. So he has much appreciation for the word's importance and lives by Winterson's (1995, p. 167) injunction: "The writer has to choose a word, every word, that is solid enough for meaning and powered enough for flight". In this collection one sees that Ruggier grasped this principle early in his career.

We see this in individual verses and in other pieces; but it comes through in his **"Principles of Criticism"** (wherein one discerns a well-schooled sense of what poetic writing requires). He feels what he calls "the itch to reason" but subordinates it to what Winterson (1995, p. 148) calls "the charge laid on the artist to bring back visions".

With trust and an appreciation for what words can do to evoke visions, even the religious skeptic (of which I am one) can appreciate the artistry with which the young Joe Ruggier treated his troubles - expressed in his **regrets, hopes, regards and prayers ...** - to the transforming energy of his sublimational artistry. In doing so he (indirectly) underscores the limits of science by directing our thoughts to what material science can't reach: ineffable human experiences of love, evil, faith, outrage, wonder, suffering, piety and more. So trust, have faith, and read on. Your reward is the contemplation of art and emergent artistry.

**Le Roy D. Travis**
**Vancouver, July 1996**

## References

1. Craig, H. (Ed.) (1961), **THE COMPLETE WORKS OF SHAKESPEARE**. Chicago: Scott Foresman.
2. Denby, D. (1996, July 15), Buried alive. **THE NEW YORKER**, 72, 19, 48-58.

3. Freud, S. (1939), **THE NEW INTRODUCTORY LECTURES ON PSYCHOANALYSIS**. New York: Norton.
4. Frye, N. (1963), **THE EDUCATED IMAGINATION**. (The 1963 Massey Lectures). Toronto: CBC.
5. Frye, N. (1957), **THE ANATOMY OF CRITICISM**, Princeton, NJ: Princeton University Press.
6. Gross, J. (1987), **THE OXFORD BOOK OF APHORISMS**. Oxford: Oxford University Press.
7. Metcalf, F. (Ed.) (1987), **THE PENGUIN DICTIONARY OF MODERN HUMOROUS QUOTATIONS**. Markham **ONT**: Penguin Books.
8. Williams, O. (Ed.) (1952), **A LITTLE TREASURY OF MODERN POETRY**, New York: Charles Scribner's Sons.
9. Winterson, J. (1995), **ART OBJECTS**. Toronto: Alfred A. Knopf.


## Acknowledgments

Some of these poems and articles have previously appeared in **The Eclectic Muse** (Vancouver, BC), **Candelabrum Poetry Magazine** (Edited by Len McCarthy, in Wisbech, UK), and in **The Voice of the Millions**. Very warm special thanks are owing to Professor LeRoy Douglas Travis of the University of BC for his gentlemanliness in writing a Preface to this collection. I am honored by his attention and find his positive thinking extremely precious.

# 1974-1975

## Stellar moonrise

*a Keatsian sonnet*

**THE** night-walks wind in silence. Solemn gleams,
bright drops of lucent poise in astral light,
sparkle, on sullen earth, with jewelled might
that studs the splendid sky. Yet stellar beams
may not with Moonface strive. Quaintly bright,
reaching outshined zeniths, quiet, old,
He rests - undaunted, bald, and bowed.
His profile-wise, serene, half-casketed light,
that silent, and with calm, insensate dream,
wonders, in pure, cold air, stares as one who finds
his homeland hills can stare till he start to deem
his soul at Peace in thoughts which insight binds,
  sure that he trods, though yet round Earth he roam,
  smiled on by souls in Heaven, home sweet home.

*1974*

## Inadequacy

**DARK** night, when deep in the quiet land dream wide
the hearts of men, shuns the Last Day, in dreamland
rack'd by what was and what
never might be; cannot be now. Quick now!
Keeps time to conscience: what was and what might be
unite with midnight stroke, giving kind birth
to dreamless obedience. Calm beyond time
the fates induce deep down a soft canal
where kindly, kindly the dew may run
sadly down the yew in lucent poise;
sorrowing slowly in a glimmering plain
where greenery hangs like clouds in Japan;
softly in a stream of thinking Voice
which pours down the Proper Sense

of waking dreams.
But I of what stirr'd next,
being not I, lost count, for a tremour space
trust-blind with Love.

**"Let me listen, please, the News!"**
talked from the next room, rose and rarefacted
back in the unactivated grains of air.
Democracy and stubb'd opinion
struck me with something like deep irrelevance!
The pure stars turn
but astray Love's pull
the Agonies burn
striding out of the Proper Sense
of a Waking Dream ...
I saw them in Politic Peacemakers,
Hyde-park observers, critics of fashion,
and in all the congregation of free-thinkers;
and in the many secretaries and chairmen,
with their coy women, seeking for affection,
and in women who want to feed their children.
In ranging millionnaires I saw how they
would wooingly be drawn
but only in the Way
retire. Saw how in
the emancipated mother,
filling her slender throat,
they drain her soul and clamour:
"Better to reign in Hell
than to retrace in God
with all that shadowy thought!";
and ***sub specie aeternitatis***
they tickle the divine laughter.
But now, when man coaxes
the teary out a heart
like coins out money-boxes,
now's not the Age when Love
press'd Laughter back to Light;
not that when Joy had bred
the Wisdom which would bless him to be led;

when once, while great Creation circled in unison,
his tune had set in self-asserting submission.

*1975*

## "Vanity of vanities, all is vanity and vexation of spirit, except to love the Lord your God, and to serve Him alone."

**STRUCK** with one vast uninterrupted stretch
of mackerel sky, my senses took in how stone
of the mighty City keeps back that sweep
where three bushes blacken the Sunset, their layers
checking the light, and like three flames blown sideways.

"Forgive us, Lord!" cried I. "Vanity 't is
keeps back my time from Thee!" and staggering
off-centre like vain actors, calling
His Justice on me, hush'd my shuddering soul.
A kiss of Mercy wrought a long, sweet cry
within me to the effect how my own self,
from my own self, God takes, more intimate
to me than my own self - till struck with Sorrow,
but bolder, words came out: "Listen, my God,
I have seen my brother, dragging his truck of sin
to the horizon, at a sudden, stop,
blackening with shame, cover his face
    with a hand, and speak with the other.
Listen, my God, I want him sav'd!" I sobb'd.
The City drew back in silence. From my Soul
    arose the rock-like Voice:
    "Ye must not aspire above
        this way to Heaven:
self-dissatisfaction, self-denial, acts of Love."

*December 1975*

# 1977

## A sonnet of contradictions

*"So the darkness shall be the light*
*and the stillness the dancing."*
**(T. S. Eliot)**

**THAT WHICH** men made they called Society,
but they have fled, have fled from That which is,
and that they made they called Reality:
to flee Society were Reality to this.
My Soul knows that it sees not That which is,
for That which is, imprinted in my Soul,
enabled God to grant me once that bliss,
to imprison me, free me; eat me, make me whole,
and whole I am. My Evil makes me die -
that which is not. I know I am not free,
freed from the fettering dream which makes men cry:
"We saw nothing at all, yet all that is we see!"
But what I do not see is what I see:
the darkness in my soul I do not flee.

*27.4.77*

## A sonnet of gratitude

*"Oh why should heavenly God to men have such regard?"*
**(Edmund Spenser)**

**AN EYE** for an eye, half-wisdom of the world,
Evil for evil, sanctions the world we're in.
Love is crucified, God's ways are unfurled,
and good for evil convicts the world of sin.
Sin drives the nail - "I love Thee not!" Love's kiss
deals home: "The devils weep and do not love Me.
Listen: My Justice Mercy, Mercy Justice,
fixes, through your free Will, your Destiny."

I fear yet feel His Love and yet do Evil:
 my Father in Heaven has a naughty son.
"Be proud, proud like your fellows!" breathes the Devil.
 But I shall boast of what the Lord has done.
  To win hard hearts Our Father crushed His nard:
  oh why should Heavenly God to men have such
   regard?

*26.7.77*

## Three sonnets of desolation and a love-sonnet

### 1

*"Where can your hiding be,*
*Beloved, that you left me thus to moan?"*
**(St John of the Cross)**

**A BUSH** would hearken, hearken to where the wind blows,
 and waves would die away, but only try:
 my soul is like a bush, a wave, a sigh
that knows the why it comes, the where it goes.
I am like to the poor, guilt-ridden soul,
 that knows the love betrayed because she knew,
 would give up all, yet longs to keep back few,
says half the Truth, yet longs to say the whole.
I am the wife who with her husband lay
 an hour, whose body to her husband's darted,
 whose soul from her poor candle would be parted,
whose eyes shone like a better way. I say:
  "my soul is like an ever-open rose ...
  when shall my soul with my Beloved's close?"

*18.8.77*

## 2

*"Power of thought that thought no more"*
**(St John of the Cross)**

**I OFTEN** longed to catch him at his call,
the Lover whom my soul loved face to face,
but there was no one, unless a Mysticall
Stranger was there, my soul in His embrace;
and food in hand, in mouth, would stop and dare,
with sympathetic feeling for the Poor,
deduce the Infinite, caught at unaware
by a sweet power of thought that thought no more.
Voices of devilish friends assail me now:
"You need give up your quest, and sleep, and eat!
You're selfish, the world not! Need the know-how
to get on in the world! Need to be counterfeit!"
But no one says: "You need that Gospel lore -
the sweet power of thought that thought no more."

*18.8.77*

## 3

*"Thou art indeed just, Lord, if I contend*
*With Thee ..."*
**(G. M. Hopkins)**

**SUDDEN**, I did groan loud and shout, in a fit
of no-emotion, yet of agony:
"Mary, sweet Mother, I am in the Pit;
Father, why is it, why abandon me?"
Once a meek rage of joy did seize upon me,
and all my doubts were not, and I could tell,
by Love's pure Light, how Will and Destiny
make Infinite Love in the face of Heaven and Hell.
Thou art indeed just, Lord, and if Thy gift
of joy did spell a sacred command to praise
Thy Justice, when in port, then, when adrift,

let me remember this, when I lack grace,
    for Night is haunted still by That which is:
    the darkness can be Light; the Night be bliss.

*5.10.77*

**4.**

*Love sonnet, where shall a body run?*

**WHERE SHALL** a body run when struck by fire?
  It rushes round me, fire of Love, of Death,
all in the zest of my hand, the sound of my ire,
  and wells in my eyes, fumes in a drunk man's head.
She's young, warm, quick: will no one tell me where
  she comes from? She was sent in my disorder
to shock my senses back. A wind, and there
  a tongue of flame: she was obeying an order.
Like a pillar of fire in a dark, dark night,
  the joyous light in her eyes of sense bereft me.
Did Providence mean to bring me back the Light?
  She did rekindle me, but now has left me.
    Forever gone, my Love, what have you done?
    An ardent impotence, where shall I run?

*5.6.78*

1 **Evil**

**I DO NOT CARE**", Evil thought: "I have no faith",
Evil thought - nodded, and out of his soul spat.
But scepticism adduces intuition:
the self-assuming struggle, and then the Vanity
which, with pretensions of impersonality,
mimics the selfless resolution,
could never presume validity:

while his Existence hung in passing time,
he could not act by what he clung to -
clever doubt and sleepy pride -
could not keep time to faith in doubt.
“We only live,” he assented,
and suddenly Evil blanched to think how he,
a straw in the Sea, had spitted, clutching himself,
like nothing at nothing, he,
a nothing whose accident was to think himself
quicker than the horizon.
Clutching himself had got him nowhere.
Evil could only stress the Glory of God.

## 2 **PRAYER**

**SO I SAID** to my Soul: “Why should we pray
if the Infinite Will is done whate’er we do?”
Oh falsehood of Extremes, Fate and Free Will!
Once more I said to my Soul: “Why should we pray
if our free will is ours to achieve
what God could not without our free consent?”
“Our free Will is ours to make it Thine!”
Sweet Lord to my soul I can still imagine Thee speaking:
“My Peace I give you for this insight keen;
My Peace I give you for this golden mean.
Prayer for the wrong thing, for the right thing,
Peace to the soul, My Peace it tends to bring,
inwilling your will to Mine, thus it is answered,
and thus your prayer is always, always heard.”

## 3 **Postscript**

**IT FOLLOWS**, Lord, I would rather be saved with whoever it is, than damned, as others desired, with Plato and Lord Bacon, rather than saved with Malchus, for all the wills in Heaven are one with Thy own, and we shall love our fellow Saints because they love God, not for anything they were on Earth.

*3.7.77*

## A poem of self-discovery

**I SEEK MY** Ego since I lost myself
and, Love, I cannot find Thee:
clutching myself has got me nowhere.
Where can your hiding be?

The Kingdom of God is within us.

He who seeks his ego has not found himself
for, Love, he has not found Thee:
clutching himself has got him nowhere.

He who seeks his life shall lose it;
He who loses his life for Thy sake shall find it.

*16.9.77*

## Destiny

*"I kiss my hand*
*To the stars, lovely-asunder*
*Starlight ... "*
**(G. M. Hopkins)**

**DID HEAVEN** depend on my deserving,
what would I do, how hope, how
could anyone hope,
did Heaven depend on his deserving?

O no! He could not, no, no,
he could not: he could only
despair,
only despair.

But Destiny, were I the only joke
among the galaxies,
still would I be your audience, Destiny,
your applauding congregation,

contracted
to a single child, mischievous, bad,
but your child, keeping your words in his heart
with listening dumb joy.

For now I know
that I know
I shall not be denied in Eternity,
since Heaven depends -
on my deserving? No! -
on Christ's Love!
my Lord's and my God's!

Did Heaven not depend on Christ's Love,
what would I do, how hope, how
could anyone hope,
did Heaven not depend on Christ's Love,
his Lord's and his God's?

Destiny I am on your side!

*5.11.77*

## For the 20th C materialists

*A Dramatic Monologue*

*"Not with a bang but a whimper."*
**(T. S. Eliot)**

**ALL OF US** materialists, all, not some,
whose transport ranges from better to best,
whose luxuries multiply, necessities mount,
we, the drivers who remained the same,
know one thing, drive one point:
"We are lost!"

Lonely in copulation, smug and bored,
from skin to marrow dried,

princes of darkness whom darkness bared,
pacing with reverent dread,
we hear the bones within us say,
we hear them all aghast -
(who is it can tell us if they lie?) -
"We are lost!"

*23.11.77*

## The song of St Therese

*(A dramatic monologue based on the autobiography of the Saint of Lisieux.)*

**I ASKED** to be His ball.
He slit me, saw my withins and, satisfied,
He slept.
Peace was in my heart.
Still
how I did wander, wonder,
not canter, no, nor saunter,
and lowly, slowly, roll - sweeping - along,
not a broadside, no, nor a rocketing thunderbolt,
seeking this Child,
but Peace slept on my breast:
He presses me now against His Breast.

*30.11.77*

## Night

**I AM SO WEARY** being tried in Faith,
feeling like to the salt that lost its savour:
"Believe, but it's like this!" vain thoughts relate.
"Hope on, hope on - your Faith's a dying Favour!"

What shall I do in my extremity?
Answer I cannot - not alone: ‘tis past me!
I feel a pang of love, I know not why,
and hope He’ll chase the night wherein He cast me.

Though God will slay me, yet shall I believe!
Yea, Faith shall die, by clear sight displaced!
Blessed am I, He said, because I grieve:
God blesses me - oh Joy in Mourning lac’d!

Resigned the itch to reason I have not.
By thoughts and images I am no longer led.
Full of my own nothingness is my glad lot,
and at times a pillar of Fire in my head.

*5.12.77*

# 1978

## Judas

**THE DYSANGEL** descended upon Judas.
Dipping his morsel, he betrayed himself.
The Spirit of Evil nuzzled in his soul,
and Our Lord's one flirt, flirting no more,
did kiss his Master,
did see Him nailed.
And Judas felt betrayed,
betrayed by the hirelings that nailed his Master,
and frightening him out of his wits by his destiny,
Hell nuzzled in his soul,
and once in Hell one can be man enough no longer.
The rope gorged out his hot and smoking bowels
when Judas hung himself,
an epitome of what Truth can do to a Wretch.

I too have seen Thee,
O Christ, O God,
so wise, in Thy folly
not a cunning fool,
my Knower, Beloved Unknown.
See,
if I am not too aware,
if I am not too aware,
I cannot say,
this work was Thy Justice,
I cannot say,
that work was Thy Mercy.
See, Thy Justice
to the adulteress
was Mercy, and Thy Mercy
to the Pharisees
was Justice. **SEMPLICE LUME**
whom so many loved
yet no-one has known
though living in some.
For Thee the Hell-hounds search
and around Thy abode
is the alibi of opposites:

beyond is Thy Cross
round which the Thunder spoke —
this Paradox is the Sign of Truth.
I too am given
to the spirit of Contrary.
I too am unsettled
by the story of Judas.

I heard it: my marrow ran dry.
I saw it: it moves with the moving eye.
And I cannot lay my lips to Thy Cross
but I imagine my loss.
Someone, I know not whom,
something, I know not what,
in my ear will whisper:
"You are damned if you kiss Me."
And damned am I then if I love Thee.
Nay, damned am I then if I do not love Thee.
Consequently I kiss Thee.

*28.4.78*

## Sermon

**SOULS AND MINDS** and hands once had a conference. "Poor slaves of action!" said the minds to the hands. "Poor slaves of thought!" said the hands to the minds. "That is a thought of ours!" said the minds to the hands: "who then can escape thinking?" "Your bodies are fed by an act of ours!" said the hands to the minds: "Who then can escape action?" Said the hands to the minds: "Dreamers, we have work to do!" And the hands tore up the poetry. And the minds tore up the machine.

"Oh hands, you are led by your minds!" said a soul. "Oh minds, flesh is fed by your hands!" said another. "Poor slaves of thought," said a third to the minds: "why are you not selfless like the eye? If your brow's command to your lesser be not, by imposition of the hand of God, peacefully given and taken, self-imposed shall be the care upon your faded brows!" "Poor slaves of action," said the same to the hands: "why do I perceive only the hand of man, where there should be none but the hand of God? Who can guide you but the selfless eye? If the eye is lit, is not all the body lit? If the eye is in darkness, is not the whole body in darkness? Then let results come after!"

*30.4.78*

## Exhortation

**BROTHER**, switch off,
switch off that light and watch!
The darkness of God is beautiful,
oh much more beautiful than the light of men,
the fancy light that chills from the sty of contentment,
or the light in the eyes of one I have known.
Robust and tall, with fierce Satanic curls,
I have seen him shadowing the gaze - best foot
on milestone, grasp on hip, and Spartan chin,
(seen profile-wise) - far 'long the road opposed
to what Mankind, deep down, is caught to think of,
and I stopped him, crying: "Specservor,
you are happy, you say? No, I am unhappy.
You have found happiness, in Vanity, you say?
Why should Mankind be then still so unhappy?
It is as you say, Mankind, selfish and vain,
nor is it Christian, but it is not happy,
and you have not told me why Mankind still is so
unhappy!"
And I was struck by a bewildered anguish, and knew
I wanted to pray, but what I knew not, yet I knew,

like the Sybil, that a prayer was going to be given me.
This was the prayer that was given me.
"My God, my God, why hast Thou abandoned me?"
and the Comforter was sent to comfort me.
The darkness of God is beautiful,
oh much more beautiful than the light of men.

*20.5.78*

## A poem at midnight

**UPON** a windless night
the desert sands performed a windless eddying
as on them, soft and bright,
there swung a dancing light,
from which the soul reeled like eyes from fire steadying.

Dark with excessive bright,
the ocean bed lay oceanless and beaming
remote pacific light,
that silent, silent night:
far and yet near the primal Light was streaming.

As at Creation's even,
there blows no wind to carry voices chanting
frankincense to Heaven,
from Mount Carmel's haven,
and yet I hear in my soul the haunting

footstep of the Son of Man
upon the primal silence that I broke:
eternal, now, and then,
sweet Christ my spirit fan:
naked I await Thy recreating stroke!

Thou Life and Light of all,
purge my unwanted matter, darkness, hence!
So hapless was the Fall!
So sick it smells to all,
the ignorance which is not Innocence!

And through the Curb of Art,
which lives to me as I do live to God,
may I witness to the Heart
which can Love to all impart;
and when I make of Poetry a rod

with which to stroke out waters
that slake with Peace our parched wickedness,
may words become Truth's psalters,
and to all God's sons and daughters
sweet Poetry be the maid of Holiness.

*13.12.78*

## Eliotesque

**SO HERE I AM**, in a year of doubt, it seems to me
stiffer than ever since the time that I set out
like a cramped scroll, having among other things since then
acquired the itch to reason much, the rich young man
turned sadly away. Had you the knack to read a look
askance, you would have read in his ashen face
the disease of the general economy
enshrined in a simple law: when luxuries multiply
necessities mount.

Where now is the Wisdom of the School of Pain?

Nothing more plain
than this our general loss!
If you can do not join the sad refrain!

She did not ...
I cannot sacrifice the happiness of three, she told me,
meaning another's, her own and mine,
in order to secure the happiness of ...
meaning my own ...
one alone!

Nothing more plain!

O Father is my lovely wing for ever burnt and crippled?
Will I never my Sun attain?
Am I forever a Saint by halves?

If you can do not join the sad refrain!

To you who must
a veiling parable will speak my pain
and tell my story ...

A wife was unwilling to sleep beside her husband.
"Dear, I must be up and doing!" said she.
"Do you not love me as your husband?" said he.
"and is it by cooking my meals that you will starve me?
Right now, my dear, sleep on, sleep on beside me!"

Again a husband was loathe to leave his bed in the morning.
"I love you!" he told his wife.
"And do you truly?" said she:
"and is it with a kiss that you will starve me?
Right now, my dear, you must to your work, and me to mine!"

It is the same, a Sage once told me, with the Kingdom of Heaven.
We shall be carried like babes at the breast
and tenderly shall the groom embrace us.
We shall be sent out into the world, fortified yes,
but like sheep among wolves.
Not ours to choose the time for ecstasy.
Not ours to choose the time for descending the Mount.

Our trial lasts long as life,
but not life, nor death, save inconstancy alone,
could separate me from the Lover for whom I moan.

*17.12.78*

# 1979

## Love sonnet, cold shoulder …

**COLD SHOULDER**, what a frail excuse to say
it was mere friendship! When did girl and boy,
upon a lovely-at-nightfall-milky-way,
greet one another, drink from each other Joy,
out of mere friendship! Dear, you do not
dissemble: only you fear the daring move,
though heartbeats tense in you the same begot -
to scold you I shall scald you with my Love!
I love you, do you know, and do you know
I need you, darling? - like the Grecian Urn?
Be love free: maiden pride should freely bow!
Could I but once outsmart a girl, and learn,
and let it be, before proposal, done,
as I, by your strong toil of Grace, was won!

*24.1.79*

## B'tifkira ta' Dun Karm Psaila

*sunett miktub ħdejn ċimiterju*

**ĦABIB, JOLQTUNI**
dawn ix-xbihat ta' Kristu Redentur,
u dan ir-riħ taċ-ċimiterju,
jvenven qalb iċ-ċipress u qalb is-slaleb.

-.-.-.-.-.-.-.-

**DAWN L-OQBRA** jqajjmu fija tifkiriet
t'Eżilju, Ħniena, Dnub u Ferħ u Ndiema,
ta' Mħabba kbira, Piena, Għafsa w'Sliema:
din l-art ħanina 'l tant imbikkma ħjiet.

Dun Karm ukoll inġabar fis-smewwiet.
Miet Dun Karm: O kemm oħra sfaw iltiema!

Miet Dun Karm: O li kenna bħalu 'l-fehma!
Miet Dun Karm, miet - bħal mitt elf-bniedem - miet!

Il-mota ddoqq għalina. Hu mar il-ġenna,
għażiża Malta! Infakkru b'sunett fi lsieni,
o nies imwiegħra! Irrid nurikhom għallti

mhux biex malajr, f'dit-tikka fqajra, bil-benna
tal-ġieħ nithenna ... 'l-anqas għax Malti m'niex ħieni:
tkun ruħi ma' Dun Karm għax jiena Malti!

*6.3.79*

## In memory of Dun Karm Psaila

*a sonnet written beside a cemetery:*
*a prose translation from the Maltese*

**FRIEND,** I am struck by these images of Christ the Redeemer, and by this Wind of the Cemetery, that bows the cypresses, and booms amid the Crosses.

-.-.-.-.-

**THESE** graves stir up within me memories of Exile, Mercy, Sin and Happiness and Contrition; and thoughts of a Great Love, Remorse and Debts that must be paid, soul-wringing pain and Peace arise in me: this merciful land so many grief-laden souls relieved!

Dun Karm as well is gathered up in Heaven. Dun Karm has died: oh! how many many others have been unfathered! Dun Karm has died: if only we had, like him, the courage, the faith, and the conviction! Dun Karm has died, died - like a hundred thousand others - died!

The death-knoll tolls for us. Malta, Beloved, he has gone to Heaven! And I shall commemorate him with a sonnet in my own tongue, oh thou miserable Race! I would like to show off my cock's crest to you not so that, in the twinkling of an eye, upon this tiny poor dot we call Malta, I might, quickly, bask and wallow in the sweet balm of fame; neither is it because I am Maltese that I am not happy! Be my soul with Dun Karm because I truly am Maltese!

*23.3.81*

## Pieta'

**Ġ**ISEM BINHA mhux binha,
dal-ġisem bla' ruħ ta' binha.

Ommu fuq sodtu
ħarsitha msammra
ġo ħarstu mdallma.

Ġisem binha mhux binha,
dal-ġisem bla' ruħ ta' binha.

Għadu ma nstabx dal-pajjiż
li lejh kullħadd ibaħħar,
ibaħħar u jasal kullħadd,
u lil ħadd ma jgħid fejn.

Ġisem binha mhux binha,
dal-ġisem bla' ruħ ta' binha.

Kristu, il-kelma li saret ġisem,
Kristu, li minn ġol-ġisem ġibed,
b'weġgħa, ġibed lejh lil dik ir-ruħ,
niżel fuq omm imdejjqa li ma tafx x'ser taqbad tgħid,
ma tafx u ma tafx x'ser taqbad tgħid,
u Kristu beka' ma' omm imdejjqa,
farraġ, wennes, ħenn
u sejjaħ lejh lil dik ir-ruħ
minn ġo dal-wied tad-dmugħ.

Ħarsitha - msammra
ġo ħarstu mdallma -
rat żewġ ħġiġiet imfaħħma
li minnhom iddiet
ix-xemx ta' dejjem.

*10.3.79*

## Pieta'

*a prose translation from the Maltese*

**HER SON'S** cadaver is not her son,
this soulless cadaver of a son.

His mother sits rooted to his bed,
her desolate gaze fixed fast
within his dull, dead stare.

Her son's cadaver is not her son,
this soulless cadaver of a son.

The country is still undiscovered
towards which every sailor braves the seas, the seas,
every man jack braves the seas and says I'm there, I'm there,
and to no soul reveals the where.

Her son's cadaver is not her son,
this soulless cadaver of a son.

Christ, the Word made Flesh, Who
out of the Flesh, in pain, has drawn, drawn out his soul,
descended upon a sorrow-stricken mother
that knows not what to say, knows not
and knows not what to say;
and called that soul unto His own,

out of this vale of tears.

Her gaze - fixed fast
within his dull, dead stare -
saw two dark lenses
through which there shone
the Sun that shines Eternal.

*10.3.79 translated from the Maltese 23.3.81*

## Firda

**IL-GĦALA** din il-firda kiesħa,
meta taħt qamar mimli
konna għoddna tbewwisna?

Il-għala din ir-relazzjoni eżatta, fastidjuża,
meta taħt qamar mimli
konna għoddna tmellisna?

Sultana, int il-Qamar ġewwa eklissi,
u jiena d-dinja, tħares lejk bil-lejl!

Jaqbiżli d-dmugħ minn ġewwa għajnejja
meta narak tixjieħ, Maħbuba,
u ruħi tgerbeb ma' ħaddejja,
u dak it-talb li ma fissrux xufftejja -
o Mara li nħobb! - tfissirhom l-għoqla fi griżmejja!

*15.3.79*

## Separation

*translated from the Maltese*

**BUT TELL ME** why this chilly separation,
when to all intents and purposes, beneath a full moon,
we had exchanged our kisses?

But tell me why this exact relationship,
precise, fastidious, when to all intents and purposes,
beneath a full moon, we had exchanged caresses?

Empress, thou art the Moon in Eclipse,
and I the world, which gazes on at night!

Tears spring out from the depths of my eyes
when I see thee grow old, Beloved,
and my very soul rolls down my cheeks,
and the prayers that my lips cannot utter -
Woman I love! - the swallowing of my Adam's apple
will utter for me!

*15.3.79 translated from the Maltese 23.3.81*

## A parable of christian unity

**AN IDEALIST** joined the Franciscans because he thought he would find Angels. He found men. He gave up the priesthood and left Catholicism to set up a tent on his own.

On the other hand, twelve repentant sinners sat in Council together. In order to secure the bond of love between them the Spirit elected a leader from among their midst, to whom they swore obedience till death would necessitate his replacement.

Similarly a husband and wife caught each other in mutual unfaithfulness, and in a second they saw the futility of mutual recrimination. The wife very simply, swore obedience to her husband. With equal simplicity, the husband swore that she would administer all their wealth.

In this way, the twelve, and the husband and wife, secured unity. Who was the wiser, the repentant and obedient, or the schismatic?

*25.3.79*

## Ċikku l-poplu u l-intellett

**WAQQAFNI WIEĦED** u qalli: "Rawhom, qed jgħidu!
Rawhom!" qalli.
"Lil min raw?" staqsejtu. Wieġibni: "Ma nafx!"

Ċikku!

X'ikunu għalih, lil Ċikku,
il-ħsebijiet qaddisa, kbar u għonja,
u dejjem aktar għolja, bhal sħaba dejjem togħla,
dewwemija,
li serqu l-aktar qlub imdiegħba?

Ċikku!

X'ikunu għalih, lil Ċikku,
dawk il-kitbiet imnebbħa, kbar u għolja,
u dejjem aktar għonja, bħal raġġ minn vina dejjem
tnixxi,
imdiegħba
bid-dawl li jsawwar imħuħ mill-aqwa?

Ċikku!

"Imħobbla dawn, u ser jaqlgħuli nkwiet!

X'għalija? Kisser u sewwi u dejjem sajjar!
Mhux bil-ħobż biss, 'ma bil-butir ukoll
ngħix jiena! U moħħok u ħsiebek qis li jaqblu miegħi
għax sibtlek ix-xogħol, u għadek ma tafx kemm jien
iblaħ!
bżor għal min jaf iroxxu, għax kull min hu ta' l-iskola
mhux dejjem ikun tas-sengħa!
U ara ma titkellimx il-ġara!
X'nambihom, Profs, ma għandix!
Għaref u naf biżżejjed jiena!"

"Bżonn taqrahom mhux dejjem għandek, Ċikk.
Iżda allura int
għaref aktar għax ma qrajthomx?"

"Ma rridx naf!
Immelħuhielu, Lel?"

Hekk, hekk jifimha,
Ċikku żrar, nar u trombi tal-ġudizzju!

Iżda allura ser ninnegaw
id-dinjita' ta' l-intellett
għalkemm ftit huma dawk li japprezzaw?

Għalhekk immela jiena,
flok id Alla setgħan, ħlief id il-bniedem ma' narax!
U ħlief idek, Ċikku, ma' nilmaħx!
Imsejken!
Titħawwad għax tagħraf qatt m'għaraft,
u li kieku kont għaref daqshom,
kieku kont tkun wisq anqas prużuntuż:
moħħ ta' piżella! Ieqaf u qis il-bnedmin t'Alla:
għax studji kbar ġabruhom, Ċikk: studjaw
li ma rawx, u raw li raw.

*8.8.79*

## John citizen and the intellect

*a prose translation from the Maltese*

**SOMEONE STOPPED** me and told me: "They have seen them, they're saying! They've seen them!" he told me. "Seen who?", I questioned. He answered: "Don't know!"

Citizen John!

What are they, to Johnny, thoughts that are sacred, and great, and precious, and ever a little bit higher, like a cloud that ever sails higher, lingering at length for ever higher, capturing none but the best, not but the noblest, hearts of gold?

Citizen John!

What are they, to Johnny, lines that are great and inspired, and ever soaring higher, and ever a little bit richer, like a ray from a vein for ever bleeding, gilt with the light that binds and moulds and fastens minds unrivalled?

Johnny: "Oh damn it, what a tangle, these women are pregnant,[82] and they're going to land me in deep trouble! What the hell! Make, then break, and always the cooking! Not on the bread alone liveth I, but with the butter also! And mind that your mind and your thoughts see eye to eye with my own, for I got you a job, and you don't yet know what a fool ammeth I! None but a cook may sprinkle pepper, and not all that are schooled are skilled in skilled labour! And mind that your neighbour keeps her bally mouth shut! I need them not, Professor! I'm wise enough!"

"You do not always need to read them, Johnny, but are you then any the wiser because you don't?"

---

[82] "Imħobbla dawn!" is here translated by: "Oh damn it, what a tangle, these women are pregnant!" The pun in the original is untranslateable as "imħobbla!", in the context, is an exclamation meaning both "What a tangle!" and, in the vulgar slang, "They are pregnant!"

“Fuck off! Why don’t we strip him naked, Lel?”

That, that is how it is, with fire-and-brimstone-and-trumpets-of-judgment-Citizen-John!

But shall we then negate the dignity of the Intellect, though few they are, those that will appreciate?

That, then, is the reason why I can only perceive the hand of man where there should be none but the Almighty’s! And why I spy no other, Johnny, but thine own! Poor devil! Muddle-headed, you have never learnt discrimination, and were you as wise as they that are, you would have been less forthright, less presumptuous: oh thou mind of a pea! Stop and consider men of God for studies profound have recollected them, Johnny: what they saw not they studied, and saw what they saw!”

*23.3.81*

## Cressida, my Cressida

I **AM IN** a formal mood, Criseyde, I am too serious,
you said;
so I will type, Criseyde, I will type a love-letter of
formal proposal.

Will you remember, my dear, oh will you remember?
The streets so dirty, unlovely the lights, so noisy the
crowds,
so vulgar and petty? Will you, oh will you remember
strolling together so pleasantly away from it all,
chatting so merrily together, so merrily, chatting so
merrily?
And you had well-night burst into song: “My Troilus, I

love
all kinds of everything!" you said. Oh will you
remember
when together, oh well-nigh together, with a bubble of
laughter, together
we said: "Where have all the people gone? Of a sudden
so quiet,
so lovely at nightfall, and moonlit the way, and only a
few old souls
on homely doorsteps receding, so quiet and lonely, and
hark,
do you not hear the sea?" Won't you, oh don't you
remember
how happily, how gladly we sat us down upon the rocks?
How cool? how fragrant? how sweet was the Voice of
the Sea?
And the fisherfolk cast so silently! How exceedingly
gentle,
how quiet the wave which rippling foamlessly
lapped on the dented shore? And woe alas! I did not
kiss you
whispering a confidence ...

Do not tell me you will forget their faces, their faces so
taken aback,
when we told them where we had been, all while the
fiesta was on!
"And fancy being there, after all these years, with a
cousin I never
met!"
I said. And - "It is a nice experience!" - someone
awkwardly
said.
Oh do not tell me you would forget, oh do not tell me
you would,
when, the day after, fuming and hurt, you had only me
to tell you,
and I said: "Why, damn it, Criseyde, you've drained me!"
Do not tell me you would forget! But hark,
do you not hear the Sea?

Do you not imagine, my darling, oh do you not imagine?
Treading lightly - or doubtfully - as the fiend tempts me,
waxing tender - or gloomy - as the fiend moves me,
going all gooseflesh and barmy! - Oh do you not imagine?
Imagine what it is to call a hearth and a home your own?
Do you have none, oh do you have none for me,
my darling, none for me? Ah! but I have a heart for thee!

*17.9.79*

**Apoloġija**

*Lill-ħbieb tiegħi fuq ix-xogħol u b'mod speċjali lil Dr Edwin Galea, Ll.D., u lil Dr. Patricia Żarb, Ll.D.*

**JIEN BNIEDEM** frustrat:
Poeta
f'qiegħ Bank is-Selħ,
ma' nies mill-aħjar,
inkaljat ...
iżda grat, grat, u grat,
u l-aktar lejn Alla u lejn l-Avukat
li qabeż tant għalija
u bill-ħlewwa reġa' kebbes fija
it-tama fil-ħniena, fil-ferħ, fil-ħbiberija,
u ta' dawn kollha l-poeżija!

Qatt, ma jkun qatt
ma rrid li jkun qatt
li nagħmel bħal Eżaw,
u minn taħt kenn ġwenħaj dellija
inbiegħ is-sehem li lilhi l-Allat taw:
is-sehem tal-għana, l-imħabba tal-ġmiel, il-ġenna tal-Poeżija ...

Naf, naf sew: l-Avukat

kien xi drabi ‘mbarazzat ...
kull min jaf x’insarraf qalli,
dejjem qalli:
int qatt, ma kont qatt,
ikolli ngħidlek qatt
ma’ kont imżejjen
bid-diplomazija.

U issa l-lok għal xi kelma ta’ lewn profond,
u jkolli ngħid li l-Bniedem Kummiedja Divina,
u li jien, mhux l-eċċezzjoni,
Poeta frustrat,
f’Qiegħ Bank is-Selħ,
ma’ nies mill-aħjar,
inkaljat ...
iżda grat, grat, u grat!

*2.11.79*

## Apology

*to my friends at work, in particular, to Dr Edwin Galea, Ll.D., and to Dr. Patricia Żarb, Ll.D. -- a prose translation from the Maltese.*

I **AM A JACK** who am frustrated: a poet, among incomparable folk, like wrecks at the bottom of Extortioner’s Bank, devastated ... but my gratitude’s unabated, and mostly towards the Lord and towards the Lawyer, to whom I owe so much assistance, who rekindled in me my hope in Mercy, Happiness, Bonhomerie, and of all these the Poetry.

Never, it shall never, I will not that it shall ever be that I repeat Esau, and from beneath a Sheltering Wing’s providential canopy, I sell my birthright, which was Another’s Pleasure to bestow: my share of Song, the Love of Beauty, the Paradise of Poetry ...

Know that I know well: to my Manager, the Advocate, things did not at times relate - embarassing! ... all who know me well have told me, always told me: Never, you were never, I must tell you that you never were gifted with - well ... diplomacy!

And now the moment seems to call for a word profound in hue, and I would be inclined to say Man is at bottom a Divine Comedy, and that I, not the exception, am a poet who am frustrated - among incomparable folk, like wrecks at the bottom of Extortioner's Bank, devastated ... but my gratitude's unabated ...

*30.3.81*

## Ħolma lubiena (Maltese)

**MULEJJA**, rqadtli: id-dgħajsa
żżiġġ fuq xfar l-irdum ...
u jien qiegħed nibża' nibqa' rieqed,
għalkemm f'riġlejK! Ma nistax aktar nibqa'
rieqed, għalkemm f'riġlejK: id-dgħajsa
żżiġġ fuq xfar l-irdum!

Ħlomt ħolm tal-waħx, Mulejja, qum!
Ħlomt ħolm tal-waħx, Mulejja, qum!
Dnubiet u faħx, Mulejja, qum!
Ħa nikkmandaK bil-herra: qum,
Mulejja, qum!
U erġa' ħabbatli qalbi
bin-nar ta' MħabbteK,
għax fir-raqda ħlomt li ser jeħduni.

Ħlomt ħolm tal-waħx, Mulejja, qum,

u erġa' ħabbatli qalbi
bin-nar ta' MħabbteK,
għax għalkemm qomt
u nsejt xi ħlomt
il-biża' mhux lakemm jgħib:
irkibni mill-ġdid, Mulejja, u erġa' iddili:
ħallini nisimgħeK tgħidli, nisma' leħneK
ħallini:
"Ibni, Jien dan li rrid!"

*20.11.79*

## Waking dream (English)

**GOOD MASTER** - sleeping! The boat
darts on the edges of the falls ...
and I dread, fear the sleeping longer
though at Your feet! I cannot allow myself the sleeping
longer, though at Your feet: the boat
darts on the edges of the falls!

I've dreamt black dreams, good Master, rise!
I've dreamt black dreams, good Master, rise!
Black sins, black deeds, good Master, rise!
In wrath I must command Thee: rise,
Good Master, rise!
Throb, stir, rebeat my heart-blood
With Thine Own Love's ardour,
Me who, sleeping, dreamt that I shall be carried away!

I've dreamt black dreams, good Master, rise!
Throb, stir, rebeat my heart-blood
With Thine Own Love's ardour,
For though awaken,
My dream forgotten,
Fear, dread lingers, not fades:

Oh! Ride me once more, good Master, furl the Sails:
Allow me Thy Words - I can imagine - Thy Voice
Allow me:
"Son, this is but My Will!"

*20.11.79 translated from the Maltese 26.3.81.*

**NOTE**: The translation conveys the metre of the original. A case where translation may be better than the original. But I am not sure whether the passionate Semitic music of the original - N.B.: Gregorian Chant originated in Israel - is translateable. The Semitic setting can be translated, but it does not sound quite like the original, and set to rhythms in the native sinew. The original will always remain one of my dearest achievements.

## Three interior monologues:
*A Sequence*

### (i) De Profundis: out of the wreckage

**THE LIFE** of the intellect imposed discussion and intellectual honesty true but under the guise of honesty falsehood prevailed imbibing confusion a shadow was thrown over my dearest sentiments a God of Love and Justice and woman's role as a mother the daily beauties of married life as Christ loved his Church sex was sacred and holy but feminism or was it and woman's lib from what I know not and the advice of free love libertines and I have transgressed and begun to doubt my experience of the living God (to which I confess unfaithful) whether it is a subjective illusion or comes from a living God and I am wrecked if I am not a mystic I am a suicide for it is my whole soul my light my peace and priests and parents turning the sword against me and inspiration that I believed came only from the living God but acadawesomes spoke of poets with inspiration like the prophets of old casting doubt on my serenity in the one and only revelation of Jesus Christ that I have begun to feel guilty of being a Christian but Lord where shall I go though I am like a fly caught in the webs clothing the tombs of doubt my soul thirsts for the living God for faith for love O in the prime of our Love Beloved than which nothing sweeter I cried out for the looming Cross but I have fallen overreaching and out of the wreckage I have cried to Thee O Lord for the rain of sanity and love of sober routine and the daily beauties of affection and I am so harassed and tried on all sides and cannot answer that I am overcome by bewildered anguish and futility but if I am not saved though a sinner what hope is there for humanity for I have never worked against Thy Church O Lord though I confess to heresy such as doing evil that good may come and such as the uselessness of prayer and the futility of all yet I have worked ardently for thy Spouse and loved her and out of the wreckage I have cried to Thee O Lord for sanity and faith and a repentant heart and love and a companion for the heart of me weeps to belong and it is not good for man to be alone and the Lord gave Eve to Adam ...

*25.3.79*

### (ii) Diario intimo

**TESTING TESTING** reality-testing faulty it was today a memorable visit to the doctor lit the way my nerves worried him much more he said so kindly than the heavensentcoldintheback and do I keep a hurtfrominsult suppressed inside me pressed he asked so kindly said it is nice to be good and gentle but the limit's the limit and bare your teeth at that he said retaliate not to call me a fool yes but more charitable than you he was father and mother dear brothers and sisters are in Christ not near and He my peace my parting sword and strife I am an island now now I am at a last remove not but in all removes I do kind love both get and forget the fatherly motherly advice refuse at times to my good at times to my ill carouse but the family I love and wish all that harms it drowned deeper than did ever plummet sound may this blasted century's libertinism be damned and frowned oh I love all that's masculine and there are too many tomboys this century but everybody loves awomanthat'sfeminine and ever when the hour comes I everdevelopapassionafresh a year to read the book of Saint Therese the little Saint and then whenthehourcomes you will ever find me reading fondly doting in lovingforgetfulnessmosttender and wonder you will but must believe what help sheasabookmark at which I steal a glance whenever the need arises hour comes true copy lends to all my study however abstruse we two to nothing but our heart's ease carouse oh I am as fond of her as of Saint Winefred Saint of the kindly rash and reeling everbrimming well my dearest Hopkins odd and queer poet's poet for odd and queer men begot and everdevelopedapassionafresh a year and lovingforgetfulnessmosttender then to wake and feel the O-where-is-it-gone suppressed inside you pressed nostalgia for the moment testing testing dearest do I wake or sleep reality-testing faulty but nothing of the moment nothing oh but does nothing of such a moment dearest remain but regrets hopes regards and prayers why nothing then I must Beloved must not I our hearts on each other's lips bid Thee and Thine all for a while regrets hopes regards and prayers ...

*20.7.79*

**(iii) Brown study**
*variations on a love song*

**O MISTRESS MINE** my lovelife's most lovesick and must I confess the wherefore so lonely how silly how green when still in my teen I loved Colleen and knew it would have been returned definitely it would have been had I not an idee fixe that I was called to join the ministry definitely it would have been and in my heart I flirted with her and knew it was returned but I was in a fix because of my idee fixe and I was shy to tell her why though I would have told her were it not for my idee fixe definitely it would have been and now she has gone clean out of my life and all I have now is a pang for the wherefore so lonely how silly how green when still in my teen I loved Colleen and all I have now is a memory that wakens when I knock on a door where once the sister of my heart's dear friend mistook the knock for the knock was in time and she took my knock for her intended's and mistook it she did but believe you me with what a rush was I received and believe you me that never before did I get such a welcome and by heaven above she was ready to swoon in my arms oh the good God what a greeting that was with what heart ache we laughed when we saw her of a sudden sniff stiff and abashed well ah well be good we told her when she went out with her intended be good we told her now Shirley be good and there was a murmur of something terrible beneath the breath she drew with a sniff that stops in a huff and we were laughing with a well ah well and all I have now is a memory that wakens whenever I enter that home where once once did I say oh more than once we sat chatting the old man and I and the wife around doing the housework when once we sat chatting and the subject was unam sanctam catolicam et apostolicam Ecclesiam and the aspect was heretics and I told the old man that my own Da was too squeamish to mention Ecclesia's defects and I agree with him said the old man so emphatically and you have a point there I said in pain make it I said and Joe the Church he began is like a person you love and you know all her faults but you do not mention them in public because you love her and I said just so and the good sweet wife asked me whether I would like some of her cake and I could not refuse the bride and told her later that the taste of that cake was sublime oh those kind people may their charity be their consolation when they go to their Maker the taste of that cake was sublime and we toasted to God's good time and oh the good God enlighten me to mistress mine o mistress mine o mistress mine my lovelife's most lovesick and the taste of that cake was sublime and oh to God's good time and in God's good time whoever you are that's how I love you whoever you are that's how I love you whoever you are my spirit will be wherever you are ...

*8.2.80*

# 1980

## Two songs

### (i) Monk's choir

**Soloists**
**ACROSS THE** bald and bowed and lengthening gaze of the
moon
drifts a long miasma, now broadening, now blotting out,
now drawing a veil.

**Full Choir**
An ancient guilt blackmails our joy,
and lays upon us kisses deadly:
we must repent - or else we cloy -
deeply, late and sadly.

**Soloists**
Across the gentle and bowed and desolate gaze of the
Crucifix
drifts a long miasma, now broadening, now blotting out,
now drawing a veil.

**Full Choir**
You will not make your sin our door,
Satan: our days of sin are ended;
you will blackmail us now no more,
like Ass or Ape appended.

### (ii) Monk's drinking song

**MAY THOSE** who are not Catholics,
sighing sadly all their lives,
proud Cynics, Sceptics, Heretics,
who never kiss their wives,
be treated on the buttocks,
be treated on the hives,
for it was but through loving,
that they were born to bluffing.

And Heaven is a tavern
where we stop to drink together;
and Heaven is a cavern
where blows no doubtful weather.
Zooks to the Pride of Reason!
Sweet Heaven's a high Romance,
and to put his head in Heaven
a chap gets but one chance.

So come you loyal Catholics -
sighing gaily all your lives
till Time will be Time no longer:
all you who love no Antics -
remember us to your wives
and love them all the stronger;
with Love like running rhyme,
we're toasting to God's good time.

*Undated*

## Il-għala għall-gwerra noġġezzjona

**SULDAT** li qatel miet.
U 'l-Mulej Alla qallu:
"X'kellek f'qalbek
meta mal-mewt kont qiegħed tissielet?"
U wieġeb is-suldat:
"Il-ġlied li f'IsmeK kont niġġieled!"
U 'l-Mulej Alla qallu:
"Jewwilla Jien qatt ma widdibtek
ma' daqqa ta' ħarta ddawwar wiċċek?
Jew Jien mhux hekk għamilt?
Il-għala mort tiġġieled?"
U wieġeb is-suldat:
"Sinjur, kulħadd issielet!"

U qallu l-Mulej:
"La ridt il-ġlied
issielet issa ma' nies xewwiexa, għajjura, werżieqa,
erwieħ ħżiena tat-trieq li jiġġerrew
għal dejjem
fuq art l-imwiet!"

Suldat li qatt ma qatel miet.
U 'l-Mulej Alla qallu:
"X'kellek f'qalbek
meta mal-mewt kont qiegħed tissielet?"
U wieġeb is-suldat:
"Is-sliem li f'IsmeK jien wettaqt!"
U l-Mulej Alla qallu:
"Il-għala ma' sħabek qatt ma mort tiġġieled?"
U wieġeb is-suldat:
"Sinjur, xtaqt nara s-sliem ta' wara l-ġlieda!"
U qallu l-Mulej:
"Is-sliem kien dejjem Tagħna r-rieda,
u s-sliem ta' dejjem, u mhux bil-ftiet, nagħtik:
għaddi sa ġewwa, u s-sliem għalik!"

*29.1.80*

## Conscientous objection

*a verse translation from the Maltese*

**A SOLDIER** by whom Life departed died in battle.
And God Almighty told him:
"Show Me thy heart
when Death and thy Soul made battle!"
The Soldier made reply:
"Therein was all the fight which in Thy Name made battle!"
And God Almighty told him:
"Did I perchance fail to warn thee
to give your enemy the other cheek?

Or did I not follow My Own Divine?
Why was it you made battle?"
The Soldier made reply:
"Lord, none but went to battle!"
Then said the Lord:
"Battle, since battle you will:
Black-hooded battle they, black-eyed and black vested
spirits of Evil around street corners who travel
for ever
the fields of Death!"

A Soldier by whom no Life departed died in battle.
And God Almighty told him:
"Show Me thy heart
when Death and thy Soul made battle!"
The Soldier made reply:
"Therein was all the Peace which in Thy name made
Battle!"
And God Almighty told him:
"Why was it you never joined your comrades in the Battle?"
The Soldier made reply:
"Lord, I have wished to see the Day of Peace dawn upon the
Kill!"
Then said the Lord:
"Peace was ever Our Own Almighty Will,
and My Own Peace Eternal, and not in drops, I give thee:
Brother, you're welcome, and Peace be with thee!"

*30.3.81*

## Ħolma (Maltese)

**META MA'** sidri ġriet
rogħda ta' daħqa maħruġa bil-qalb
minn qalbek,
maħbuba,

ma' sidri marsusa,
u nfexxet iddawwal f'għajnejk,
bikkimtni - il-kisra ta' għajnejk
kisritni,
u bla' qatt saqsejtni jien għidtlek, jien dnibt,
u int ma' sidrek rassejtni bil-qalb
minn qalbek,
maħbuba,
fuq sidri minxura
bil-karba li tidħaq u d-daħqa li tokrob f'għajnejk:
għajjien,
fuq qalbek indimt,
fuq sidrek għarwien,
fuq qalbek berikt iċ-ċokon imqaddes taż-żwieġ,
fuq sidrek minxur.

Dan ma kien xej'
ħlief ħjiel mistħajjel,
ħlief xewqa, Mulej,
għax bħalhom m'hemm xej'
li jniffes ġo fija
fi driegħeK, Qdusija,
iqanqal l-indiema
ta' moħħi għajjien,
fuq sidreK għarwien,
u f'imnifsejja mnifsejK,
jonxorni miksur,
għajnejja f'għajnejK,
fuq sidreK minxur. *28.2.80*

## A dream
*translated from the Maltese*

**WHEN, ALONG** my bosom running,
spasms of laughter drawn out wholehearted
out of your heart,

beloved,
upon my bosom folded,
exploded radiating your eyes,
I was stricken dumbfounded - the song that swum in your
eyes
leaves me still so broken-hearted,
and, what you never asked for, I whispered, I've sinned,
and to your bosom you drew me tighter, wholeheartedly,
out of your heart,
beloved,
upon my bosom hanging,
with the cry that rejoices and the glee that cries in your
eyes:
wearily,
upon your heart I repented,
upon your bosom naked,
upon your heart I blessed the humble sanctity of wedlock,
upon your bosom hanging.

That was no more
than hints imagined,
than wishes, Lord,
for nothing better
inspires me, within
Thy embrace, with Sanctity,
arouses the Repentance
of my brain, book-weary,
upon Thy bosom naked,
and in my nostrils Thine Own,
leaves me still so broken-hearted,
my eyes in Thine Own,
upon Thy bosom hanging.

*9.4.81*

**NOTE:** This translation attempts to convey the metre of the original, with its rhymes, rhythms, and alliterative qualities.

## L-aħbar (Maltese)

### QATT SMAJT?

Qatt rajt xi Budda xaħam laħam
jixxaħxaħ għal dejjem ta' dejjem
b'għajnejh magħluqa?

Qatt rajt xi Ajatollah Mawmettan qed jaqsam bix-xabla

kull ma jara?

Qatt smajt xi Ċiniż Confuż?

Qatt rajt xi Brahman li ħeles mis-'samsara'?
Geddumu lejn is-sema, għajnejh magħluqa, sieq fuq sieq,
id waħda qrun u l-oħra tbierek:
ħallih għax issa salv, għax sar jaf li hu Alla,
u ħeles mis-'samsara'!

Fil-pawsa
ta' wara d-daħqa
mewġa mimlija mill-kbir
Paċifiku mliet is-skiet u ħallietna
nirtogħdu beżgħana:
u xterdet l-aħbar
maċ-ċafċifa tħaxwex fuq ix-xtut taċ-Ċiniż Confuż -
rumur ta' l-Etern;
u l-għidut li semgħu
il-Mawmettan u l-Indjan
xtered sa truf il-ħolqien;
u sema' sew il-Buddist,
għalkemm mhux infurmat
minn imkejjen uffiċjali
ta' l-awtoritajiet tax-xandir.

Fuq it-T.V. rajt Komunist bis-suf ħiereġ minn kull toqba
f'ġismu.
U f'moħħi qed nara' nies bla' Alla tiknes kull ma tara
u tħalli wrajha vojt mibluħ jitbekka ...

"Għandi l-għatx!"
u joħloq elf forma ta' ġenn spiritwali!

Jekk għadek qatt ma rajt is-sebħ ta' Kristu,
qatt rajt ruħ żmattata?
Qatt smajt spirtu sfurmat jitbekka ...
"Għandi l-għatx!"
minn ġewwa elf forma ta' ġenn spiritwali?

Qatt smajt?

*9.5.80*

## The tiding

*a prose translation from the Maltese*

**DID YOU EVER** hear?

Did you ever see a Buddha, fat and plump, wallowing for ever and for ever, both his eyes shut tight?

Did you ever see some Moslem Ayatollah, sword in hand, splitting right down the middle all that he sees?

Did you ever hear the confused Chinese?

Did you ever see a Brahman freed from the 'Samsara'? Chin to heaven, eyes shut tight, leg on leg, the palm of one hand a symbol of horns, and his other blessing: let him be, for now he is saved, for he now knows he is God, and has been freed from the 'samsara'!

During the Pause following the fit of laughter a full wave out of the large Pacific filled the Silence and left us all trembling with fear: and the tiding spread with the soft splash rustling upon the shores of the confused Chinese -

rumours of the Eternal! and the hearsay heard by the Moslem and by the Indian spread to the very end of Creation; and the Buddhist heard most rightly, though not informed by official sources of the broadcasting Authorities.

On T.V. I saw a Communist with the hair issuing out of every single hole within his body. And in my mind I see a godless race sweeping all it meets and leaving behind a bewildered vacuum weeping ... "I thirst!" and creating one thousand forms of spiritual craze!

If you have never seen Christ's glory, have you ever seen a wrecked, ruined soul? Did you ever hear a deformed spirit weeping ... "I thirst!" from within one thousand forms of spiritual craze?

Did you ever ...

*11.4.81*

## Beethoven's Ninth

*a note of appreciation*

*for uncle Vince*

**BEETHOVEN** inspired himself from the ideals of the French Revolution, LIBERTY, EQUALITY, FRATERNITY, and it is to his eternal honor, indeed a certificate of his political integrity, that ideologies which preach the same ideals, but practice tyranny, speak of Beethoven as a 'decadent' artist which means an artist who has declined, deteriorated, corrupted himself, sold and prostituted his talent, fallen away from the ideal, the reason being that Beethoven is over-emotional, morbid and sentimental. It is ridiculous that a rebel as masculine as Beethoven should be regarded as over-emotional and effeminate: only a cast of mind which has no place for the spiritual dimension could dream up such trash, and it must have been bigotry unparalleled and perfect of its kind that could have inspired such criticism. But Beethoven's greatest virtue is precisely that he speaks to the heart with great profundity, that he spoke to us of divine freedom, God's love for humanity, and of the dignity of the individual. His individuality made him a rebel by character, but Beethoven was as committed a Christian democrat as the committed Communist, to whom Beethoven is a decadent artist, used to be a militant atheist.

Nowhere did Beethoven preach his ideas more powerfully, nowhere more movingly, than in the Ninth Symphony. No Sermon has ever preached the love of God more eloquently than Beethoven's **SONG OF JOY**. The Ninth Symphony has a profound artistic unity and a profound unity of mood. I would like to sketch broadly the intense drama and dynamism with which the mood, to my listening, evolves and develops with each movement, like an ascent from Hell to Heaven.

The first movement is bitter and sad. The *ALLEGRO MA NON TROPPO, UN POCO MAESTOSO*, is bleak and desolate as

> a waste land, where no one comes,
> Or hath come, since the making of the world.

The movement describes the human soul in slavery, but also describes its dignity in confinement, its majesty in chains, and its greatness in defeat.

The **MOLTO VIVACE** is still unhappy, but the mood of greatness in defeat has given way to one of energetic rebellion, a mood such as prisoners may be expected to feel when planning to escape to freedom. The spirit here rebels with explosive energy against the powers of evil that ensnare it.

The **ADAGIO MOLTO E CANTABILE** is a total contrast to the preceding despair and rebellion. Energy has given way to grace and lyrical beauty, and Herculean strength to tenderness and poetic intensity. The music, I have always felt, describes the divine beauty of the human spirit created in God's image and likeness, and to the listener who wishes to feel its beauty and intensity I recommend the singing of the simple, if you wish the crude, banal and simplistic, phrase - "How lovely! You are so lovely!" - to the melody of the third movement, and to think, while singing, that the simple words and Beethoven's melody address the redeemed Spirit.

It is good to know that one of Beethoven's problems in writing the Ninth Symphony was how to modulate symphonic music, which should be purely instrumental and not vocal, into a mood where, since he wanted to use the human voice, the use of the voice would be artistically acceptable. The extremely easy to sing melody of the third movement provides the modulation for the entry of the choir in the fourth and greatest movement.

Beethoven must have had a very good reason for using the voice in a musical work in which only instruments are usually heard, in which the voice has never before been used. I suggest that Beethoven's reason was precisely that his theme was human dignity. His song was human dignity. What instrument could convey it better than the human voice? The use of the voice takes us by surprise and leaves upon us the profound impression of discovering the Human Form Divine. And whereas many great works of Art have been praised for their "negative capability", Beethoven's Ninth, I believe, should be praised for its "positive capability".

To understand Beethoven's **ODE TO JOY**, however, and to understand the whole Symphony, one should read the poem by Schiller which Beethoven set to music. The theme is God's love for humanity, the dignity and freedom which God bestows on the human person. The following is Louis Untermeyer's translation of Schiller's **AN DIE FREUDE** into English:

**JOY,** thou source of Light immortal,
Daughter of Elysium,

Touched with fire, to the portal
Of thy radiant shrine we come.
Thy pure magic frees all others
Held in Custom's rigid rings,
Men throughout the world are brothers
In the haven of thy wings.

**HE** who knows the pride and pleasure
Of a friendship firm and strong,
He who has a wife to treasure,
Let him swell our mighty song!
If there is a single being
Who can call a heart his own,
And denies it - then, unseeing,
Let him go and weep alone.

**JOY** is drunk by all God's creatures
Straight from Earth's abundant breast;
Good and bad, all things are nature's,
And with blameless joy are blessed.
Joy gives love and wine, her gladness
Makes the universe her zone,
From the worm that feels Spring's madness
To the Angel near God's throne.

**GLAD** as when the sun runs glorious
Through the deep and dazzling skies,
Brothers run with shining eyes -
Heroes happy and victorious.

**MILLIONS**, myriads, rise and gather!
Share this universal kiss!
Brothers in a heaven of bliss
Smiles the world's all-loving Father.
Do the millions, His creation,
Know Him and His works of Love?
Seek Him! In the heights above
Is His starry habitation!

A great poem to which Beethoven composed one of the

most beautiful melodies ever written. It is only necessary to hear the music in order to love it, and the *PRESTO*, that is - the last movement, is one of the greatest moments in music, comparable to the last canto of Dante's **PARADISO** which, in its own right, is one of the peaks in World Literature.

I have written, of course, with the humble simplicity of the ordinary listener, having no other right to speak, I think, than that I am given by the love which I feel for the music.

## Ode: to Beethoven

**WHEN THE** sky was darkest you shook your fist at it.

Your Music plumbs the depths of space.
You were stone deaf, but lo! your Music listens in
to the Light Ages:
The Human Face Divine,
new-swum into your screen,
becomes a Voice
upon the pages.
To the Symphonic Muse
the human voice
is not an orthodox noise -
but let the music fill, be glad and rejoice
that it has identity
in this half-blooded world that raves and rages!
O noble dissident! draw my spirit out
of this inhuman Earth, and call to me, call to me,
voices upon the pages,
that listening I may see, be glad and rejoice,
behold God's image swimming in those eyes
and singing faces ...
fill, fill the Trumpet, sound the fife!

The Human Face Divine,
new-swum into your screen,
becomes a Voice
upon your dissident,
symphonic pages.

*28.6.80/15.9.80*

# 1981-1982

## Two haikus

**1 A Counsel**
**MUDDLE** me in mine
you can; convince me of yours
you cannot. Lay off!

*21.3.81*

**2 Maltese**
**GĦADU** nofs xogħol. L-omm,
dejjem tnaddaf, ġibditlu
l-potti minn taħtu.

*21.3.81*

**2 English**
**HALF-WAY** through! Mother,
spring-cleaner, from beneath him
drew out the potty.

*7.5.82*

## Meditazzjoni Marjana (Maltese)

*lix-xjuħ*

**QALB WAHDA** miżien fuq il-mejda qlub l-omm u l-missier,
twieżen l-għemil ta' l-ulied, u jekk fit-tilwim
twarrab qalb l-omm, jegħleb fil-keffa is-swat
tal-missier. Hekk fik, Madonna, Bint u Mart

u l-Omm ta' Min ħalqek, l-Omm ta' kull maħluq,
naraw id l-Omm iżżomm driegħ is-Setgħani
minn fuq iċ-ċkejknin, u twarrab minn fejn l-imkabbar.
Mara, fejn qatt instema', li fiż-żwieġ imsaħħar,
bejn ir-ruħ u l-Maħbub, il-kelma saret ġisem,
u għammret fostna? Kien għal dan li għannejt
kemm hu kbir il-Mulej, u kull nisel sejjaħlek ħienja.
Għax ried ikun ibnek bħalna, u jgħammar misruq
mill-madmad ta' Mara, sabiex in-nisel uman,
mgħallem mir-ragħad imgħaddab, jagħmel qalb jersaq
għand l-Omm ta' Min nissilha; u dik is-Setgħa
li lilek laqqmet THEOTOKOS, qanpiena
ta' Tama ddoqq għal bniedem, għax għad iżżejnek
bl-isem ta' Omm kull grazzja; għax jekk l-Omm tagħder,
qalb żewġa tirtab, jekk twarrab, qalb żewġa tibbies,
u kollox maħfur, jew miżmum, mat-taħbit ta' qalb l-Omm.
Mara, jekk tagħder int, jirtab l-editt
aħħari: mill-moħba ta' lbiesek jittieħdu l-ulied
fi ħdan il-Missier, maħfura, kull demgħa mimsuħa!
Mara, jekk twarrab int, kemm biża' fil-Jum
aħħari, kemm biki, kemm waħx u theżżiż tas-snien,
għax Alla xitan isir ma' dawk l-ulied!

*8-18.7.81*

## Marian meditation

*a prose translation from the Maltese*

*to my old folk*

**THEIR HEARTS** are one pair of scales on the table, a mother's and a father's, weighing the children's behaviour, and if in a feud the mother's withdraws, the wrath of the father will tip in the balance. Just so in Thee, Madonna, Daughter and Wife and Mother of Thy Maker, Mother of those that are made, we see a mother's hand hold away the

Almighty's arm from the little ones, and withdraw from beside the one that's vain. Woman, when did we ever hear, that in the charmed, mystic bethrothal, betwixt the soul and the Beloved, the Word was made flesh, and dwelt amongst us? It was for this you sang the might of the Lord, and that all generations have called Thee Blessed. For it was His Will to be yours as we are, and to live carried away by a Woman, her sway, that the human race, taught by the thunderous Wrath, might make heart and draw near to her who begot Him that did her beget; and that Power which defined Thee THEOTOKOS shall strike upon a bell of great hope for humanity when it shall find another name with which to adorn Thee, MOTHER OF EVERY GRACE; for if a Mother has mercy, her husband's heart will soften, if hers withdraws, her husband's will harden, and all's held fast, or forgiven, with the mother's heart's beat. Woman, if Thou wilt but commiserate, the crack of doom will soften: hid in Thy garments will the children be carried to the bosom of Abraham, forgiven, every tear wiped dry! Woman, if Thou wilt but withdraw, what fear the day of doom will carry, what weeping, what terror and gnashing of teeth, for God a fiend will be with them so malbegotten.

20.10.81

N.B.: The original attempts to translate a Miltonic voice and a Crashaw-like tone of devotion without Crashaw's excesses into Maltese. The effect is hopefully intriguing in the Maltese but the blank verse of the original would have been of no interest to the connoisseur of contemporary English verse.

## Date
*Maltese*

**WARA** għaxar minuti bla' sabar,
ħsejjes, dħaħen, tpaqpiq, u sturdament,
waslet, fetħet il-bieb tal-'light car',

u dħulija, dħulija, saqsietni:
"Fejn trid immorru?"

"Fejn irrid immorru," weġibt, "mhuwiex possibli
immorru." U ftiehmna fej, w'għidtilha, "Suq,
la naslu ngħidlek."

Fuq il-mejda fir-ristorant newwiltilha nota:

"Irrid li mmorru xi 'mkien il-bogħod, il-bogħod,
xi 'mkien imkien, ġo qiegħ foresta fonda
fejn ma jgħammar ħadd,
u fejn tgħanni biss ix-xmara,
u fejn fir-raxx jittajjar mogħla mil,
sa fid-dawl tal-qamar tidher qawsalla
sa minn tmien mili bogħod,
u rrid li s-skiet ta' dak il-ħin
timlih biss kelma waħda
u 'l-weraq neżlin."

"Mhuwiex possibli," tniehdet bi tbissima,
u 'l-mużka klassika, addattata pop,
lingwa ta' l-anġli mitkellma bla' karita,
damdmet ir-ristorant -
ħsejjes, dħaħen, tpaqpiq, u sturdament.

*19.9.81*

## Date

*a prose translation from the Maltese*

**AFTER** ten endless minutes of headache, fumes, and noise, she was there, she flung the car-door open, and friendly, ever so friendly, said querying: "Where do you wish to go?"

"Where I wish us to go," I replied, "it is not possible

to go." We agreed on a spot, and I said, "You may drive. I'll say when we get there."

Seated in the Restaurant, I slid a note across the table.

"I would like to go somewhere that's far, far away, somewhere that's nowhere, lost in the depths of mighty forests where no one abides, where no sound is heard but the song of the river, and where, in the spray, flung one mile up into the sky, a rainbow can be glimpsed in the moonlight eight miles away, and I would wish the silence to be broken by a word, one word only, and the sound of the falling leaves."

"Impossible," she sighed with a smile, and the classical music, blown pop, a tongue angelic spoken without any charity, shook the restaurant like thunder - headache, fumes, and noise.

*Translated from the Maltese 7.5.82*

## Fuq in-nies

*Maltese*

**FUQ IN-NIES**, ħabib, kullħadd l-istess iħoss:
min jgħoġbok u taċċettah, min idejjqek
u tissaportih, u min idejjqek iżżejjed
tibagħtu jixxejjer, iżda nittama li qbilna -
in-nies interessanti lkoll!

*27.9.81*

## Regarding all sorts

*translated from the Maltese*

**REGARDING** all sorts, my friend, all feel the same:
those you like you accept; those who are bores,
you tolerate; and some, who bore you much too much,
you send to blazes; but I hope we agree -
all kinds deserve your interest.

*27.9.81*

## Little girl in the woods upon an autumn night

**ALONE,** alone, all, all alone,
alone in the big, brown woods!
All by my soul, small puppy and I,
my puppy and me - puppy knows why! -
upon an Autumn night.

There all alone, me and my dear -
how lovely the night drew near!
All by my soul, small puppy and I -
how lovely the stars in the sky!

The sky went out, the clouds turned gray!
The brown trees shook, the leaves flew away!
Me and my soul, and puppy too,
heart beating hard, knew not what to do!

Alone, alone, all, all alone,
alone in the big, brown woods;
puppy and I, both ready to cry,
alone in the big, brown woods!

I knelt and prayed to God so dear:
Good Jesus - help me resist my fear!

*13.11.81*

**N.B.:** Verses composed out of a poem-note written by a child. Though the style of the poem would be beyond a child's, the poem attempts to capture the vision and voice of the child, thus becoming a dramatic monologue.

## Liturgy of ashes

*gregorian verses*

### The penitent

**IF I THEN** weep out my soul in ink, may at last my darling Peace long lost relent, and in my arms relaxing, sigh and say that I am found again, may at last relent and bless me, and the price - all that pain that I cost Ceres - and in my arms relaxing, sigh and say, I love you, say?

Let me then weep out my soul in ink,
pluck all that makes the soul within me sink
low as Guilt, when he sees the Warder, Day,
advancing, suck all that venom out, away,
all that venom out of the veins release
in blood and stuff, and sigh a sigh of Peace.

Bless me, Father, I confess, profoundly sigh, and say: I am the Chief of Sinners.

### The priest

May God the Father, Son and Spirit blend
Faith, Hope and Love within you, and descend
upon you! May their Love your grief redeem,
that in your sleep Faith, Hope and Love may dream!
And from this fullness Grace on Grace abound,
and may Joy seize you! And Heaven around resound!
Sure that you'll be forgiven, you should confess
in sorrow and fear: shriven, the Lord should bless!
Son, lend me your ear, these are God's Ten Laws:
up, up! Consider! Release your faults when I pause!

"I am the Lord your God, who brought you out of the Land of Egypt; out of the house of Bondage. You shall have no other gods before Me."

**The penitent**

Before my God I stand rebuked, and no philosopher can
help me;
the Lord abashes me, and no therapist can, no sage
uplift me;
my God declares me sick, and no physician, no man
who can relieve me, no acadawesome prescribe a
drug to cure me.
The Lord is a God who gives grace to the humble: He
resists the Proud. He will have pity upon me,
and cure me of my disease. Though my malady
be a surfeit of deadly sin, He shall forgive me.
And so I confess, profoundly sigh, and say: my Heart is
vain;
and I ask the Physician to bleed me, and pray that the
Physician may, from my sick semen, Vanity,
relieve me.
For I have made my self, my appetites - of the ghostly
and the bodily senses - my time and my goods
false gods before Him, and I have made God in
my own image and likeness, and I confess that
he who is I is not the Lord,
and I am confident that He will forgive me.

**The priest**

This narrow path make sure you tread secure:
this Faith retain, and this mild yoke endure!

Son, three sins there are which God visits with a terrible punishment, idolatry, adultery, and murder, and offence has two horns, that against God, and that against neighbour. That against neighbour shall we now lay down in the dust prehistoric.

“You shall not kill.”

**The penitent**

Before my brother I stand rebuked, and no philosopher
can help me.
I confess, profoundly sigh, and say: my heart is vain,
uncharitable and unjust, in word and deed, in
what I have done, and in what I have failed to
do, and villainous in thought,
for my brother a door to his ruin, through my bad
example, I have murdered my brother's mystery,
that of his God-like nature,
and I am confident he will forgive me.

**The priest**

This narrow path make sure you tread secure:
this Faith retain, and this mild yoke endure!

"You shall not commit adultery!"

**The penitent**

Before my sister I stand rebuked, and no philosopher
can help me.
I confess, profoundly sigh, and say: my heart is vain,
for I have shown great disrespect for the mystery, that
of my manhood, and that of a woman's beauty,
and I am confident she will forgive me.

**The priest**

Son, you were lost, but have been found again:
Faith makes you whole - avoid the ways of men!
This narrow path make sure you tread secure:
this Faith retain, and this mild yoke endure!

God's Word you have heard being read: "A new Commandment I give unto you: That you love one Another, as I have loved you, that you also love one another. By this shall all men know that you are my disciples, if you have love one for another." You have also heard it being read: "Has no one then condemned you? Nobody, Lord, she said. Neither do I then condemn you. Go in Peace and sin no more, lest something worse befall you."

*Commenced: 9.81*
*Completed: 5.82*

## Thoughts on genius

*"Taste is the feminine of genius"*
***John Langford***

**GENIUS** is talent at the service of a great cause and of a holy purpose. You may have enormous talent and little genius, and you may have great genius but no talent. The devil has more talent than Homer, Virgil, Dante, Shakespeare, Bach, Beethoven, MichaelAngelo, Einstein, all of mankind's supreme geniuses all together, but not one spark of genius. It all depends how you define the concept. The majority of critics would probably disagree, and so will many wise philosophers. Well - take it or leave it!

Tchaikovsky called one of his characters in **SWAN LAKE** "The Genius of Evil," and the impression caused by that one dancer, dressed from top to toe in black flowing robes, crowned with silver, gold, and precious stones, and alone on stage with the music, his time exact as an atomic clock's, all, all alone, in perfect motion: oh that one dancer dominates the theatre as communism did the Earth! Let him but ask you to fall down and adore him, and the mask is off, the illusion of genius is no more, the willing suspension of disbelief becomes disgust, hostile and intense, and the genius of The Genius of Evil shows up as talent, bottomless, infinite, abysmal, lacking one miserable ray of grace, light, divinity and mystery: we see through it as through a petty scheme.

Has genius harmed humanity? Talent yes, but not genius! Genius has civilized humanity; genius has given humanity unageing monuments worthy of the religious species; genius has alleviated suffering, physical and moral; genius has made life bearable; genius has catechized humanity, giving it morality, values and definite religions to fulfil instincts which, unaided by genius, would plunge it in ignorance, superstition and the primitive night of human sacrificee.

Was there ever a genius greater than Jesus Christ? He shows, I will be frank with you, very little talent, poetic or otherwise; the verbal skill of His parables and sermons is that of the most ordinary self-made man who knows what He's after, what He's meant to do and be, and who has a great purpose. We know that He would have, had He wanted, emulated all the poets together with words beautiful as the sun, the moon, the mountains, the rivers, the trees, and flowers of the fields, woods and valleys, the song of birds and the stars. He did not call His bottomless, His infinite, His abysmal talent to His service. He dazzles no one with aesthetic craft, skill or erudition, and His verbal dexterity impresses no expert. But His words are pure genius, and it is the pure genius that fuses them together and makes them great literature, very great - however great, not one book ever greater. There is always some show, mere show of talent, in the books we produce, that pollutes and contaminates their purpose, however holy, and if there be not, we are only the Sons of God.

Did supreme genius ever harm humanity through its power? No, the great geniuses never had a say. They were ignored, unbelieved, accounted mad and foolish, spoken evil of, exiled, despised and crucified: they were all Christ figures. Their blood was the seed of their triumph, and their suffering the power that drove their say through the heart of posterity. It is the politicians and schemers whom nobody wants around, be it their contemporaries or be it posterity, and who have great talent to do their work for them, but no genius to redeem it: these are the great men who, on this earthly level, fool a few people all the time, always get what they are after, and - alas! - reach their infamous ends and their notorious purposes.

*North Vancouver*
*19.2.82*

## Tanka
*to Mike Shields*

**MIKE,** I'd rather not
discuss my book: **Poems in**
**Fancy Dress**; but lines
like these sure should make you feel
something more 'with it' coming.

*3.4.82*

## Tanka
*to Mike again*

**WHAT WAS** that he said?
Verses not mine but given,
whatever their worth.
But my due's my own, and that
Honour's no gift I make **you**.

*7.1.83*

## Haiku
*Maltese*

**GĦADNI** kemm smajt li
Mintoff, minn qiegħ qiegħa, bagħat
globu jixxejjer.

*29.4.82; 3.15 p.m.*

*translated from the Maltese*

**JUST HEARD** that Mintoff,
from the bottom's bottom, sent
a globe to blazes.

*17.5.82*

## The track winds uphill, Phil
*a prose-poem for JGE basaed upon a real-life episode*

**FROM MARGERIE'S** house the track led to the wooden bench where he sat reading the French papers. Curving down hill this way and that, describing a long turn round a valley-like-tumble of brown trunks and foliage, the track seemed drunk in shadow and light, black silhouettes and the white gold of sunset.

Through the trees he could glimpse the sun setting behind a ring of Swiss Alps, and the sunlight penetrated through the branches and lit up the track and the treetops, this way and that. At the bottom of the valley-like-tumble he could hear the water gurgling.

Suddenly he saw Margerie running down the path which curved downhill this way and that. She held a letter.

She ran lightly, negligently, gracefully, in her incomparable lady-like manner, which was such a luxury for the hardened farmhands around. Leafy branches rushed and brushed past her face, and so, too, did the fickle sunlight.

She disappeared in the shadow, then between the trees, then again round the turn, curving this way and that, and her long, flowing hair rose and fell when she reappeared running down the last few hundred yards between the trees which led to the wooden bench. She had an air of conscious dignity and grace as she ran in the light and shadow.

**YOUR** hair shall grow and fall,
and shall discreetly flow;
Shadow and light, upon
your face, shall vanish and grow.

Who had written those lines? he thought.

"Phil!"

"Margerie!"

They had fallen in love on the second day that they were out together. Margerie was a cousin he had never met, a blonde with blue eyes, well-built, and lady-like. He meant to spend the last few weeks of his European tour with her parents on their farm in the Alps. On returning to the states he would be ten credit courses away from his career as an accountant.

"Phil, it's a cable!"

"Are you sure?"

"Oh, it was a good excuse, Phil. They have not found us out yet. But a cable's no joke. Open it!"

The cable was from his mother's lawyer. His father had died when he was a child. He tore the cable open.

***PHIL MOTHER'S PASSED AWAY PEACEFULLY OF A SUDDEN STROKE STOP PLEASE CATCH THE NEXT PLANE TO EXAMINE PAPERS AND TAKE POSSESSION OF HER APARTMENT STOP I'M SORRY SIGNED RICHIE COHEN***

"Oh Phil, darling, how terrible!" said Margerie with a sob of shock. She had not read it over his shoulder. He had let her see it. "And you will have to leave next minute." He had only been nine days.

"Margerie, I will marry you as soon as I begin working. Look, I will be back for Christmas. I am all alone now, and that's very lonely, and I have mother's apartment, and a career to return to. But poor mother! And not even a chance to say good-bye!"

Next day at noon he received a long letter from the lawyer which had been delivered express. He did not open it till he was waiting for his train at the station.

*(22.5.82)*

## Epistle

*to a certain priest*

**IF SOMEONE** say, good Priest, beware
this man! This man, whose looks are fair,
resents your talk, your words too plain,
full of the lore of joy and pain
and big with Love, though stern - austere!
Say that this man, whose looks are fair,
was grateful that he heard your speech,
and glad would learn, and glad would teach.
Father I work, and work I will,
I must, till my sad heart is still;
my sloth confess, with sorrow bit,

and will atone, when funds permit;
but still contend, I urge it still,
that to create is work, and will
defy the Pope that Art is work!
Look! where mean hands of men do lurk
where none but God's should be! Man dreams
no Dream today, but still he seems
what he is not, good, specious, fair,
a Dream-Creation: would he were!
His words are lies that hide his thinking,
but poets reveal the hidden winking!
His life's a coffin, blank and bare,
and dream he must, or else despair!
But Art's unwanted, poor, reviled!
Why! Is it not like Mary's Child?
For which to Court with God I must,
so help me God: my cause is Just!

*10.6.82*

## David's lucky birthday

**MAMA NEVER** told Dave her designs upon him. At bedtime she would pretend that he must have a bath and another boiled egg. And Dave would say, "Mama, I'm very tired!"

"If you say so, darling!" Mama would reply.

"There are no playpens at school!" she pretended. "Playpens, Dave - Plaaaypaeaens!"

"Mama, I want to go to school! I want to go to school, Mama!" Dave sobbed with frustration.

"Poor darling!" said Mama.

It was Dave's lucky birthday. He was six on the sixth. Uncle, Auntie, Grandma, and Grandpa, and his friends, and cousin Pam, and Trish, and Liza, were all at his party. His mouth was stained with chocolate. Clutching the stump of a chocolate bar, Dave went beside grandma and kissed her thank you for her birthday present. Smack!

"I will be going to school!" he told her proudly.

"Why, Dave? You will have to work hard!" said Grandma, still wiping away chocolate from her cheeks, and laughing silently.

`"I want to go to school to become an actor!"

"Why, Dave?" said Auntie. "You will have nothing done for you there!"

"I want to go to school to become an actor!"

"You will have to pay!" said cousin Trish the actress. She had often delighted Dave with her sketches. She could be Mama, grandpa, the president, the postman, and even a Daddy-long-legs, and Dave could not tell the difference.

"No!" said Dave. "If I go to school I will have to work hard. And at school I shall become an actor and I will be paid for pretending."

"At school you will have to give reasons, Dave, and must not say, I want to!" said cousin Pam, the teacher.

"Miss will teach me!" said Dave with adoration. He was in love with his cousin Pamela.

"Dave, at school you will have to do what the book says!"

"No, cousin Liza, I will have to do what Miss and Mama and my head tells me!" and Dave's eyes twinkled with mischief.

"Dave," said cousin Pamela, "what a smart young man you are! On with your shoes and jacket. We're off to the Amusement Park. You deserve it!"

"Yippee!" And Dave screamed with delight. He ran upstairs to his room, two steps at a time, and in two seconds was back again, a smart young man.

A Punch and Judy show was on at the Amusement Park. Punch and Judy were acting Romeo and Juliet. Dave gazed and gazed. He was carried away.

"I will love you forever!" Romeo was saying.

"You are my one and only you, my love, my dream!" said Juliet.

"And you are mine!" said Romeo.

"Till the end of time!" said Juliet.

A roll of Thunder suddenly shook the Amusement Park and artificial lightning blazed through it for five full seconds. A stranger rushed in under a tattered umbrella. He held a pistol.

The stranger took aim and ... bang! Romeo fell gasping in Juliet's arms and screamed loud and long. The loud-speakers were shrieking. Juliet gave one last blood-curdling screech. And then ... silence!

"Mama, mama!" David was screaming.

But Dave soon forgot all about it on the merrygorounds, the horse-riding event, and then over the ice-cream, and besides he was heartily enjoying being made so very much of.

Back in cousin Pamela's large car, the old argument was taken up again. "At school you will become a book-bore!" said cousin Paul.

"At school I will have two girlfriends like you!" said Dave.

"You will be bad at everything except girlfriends!" said Uncle.

"No, Uncle, I will be good at everything except lying!"

"Take little hints and you will be a big man!" said Grandpa.

"School is where my big friends go!" said Dave in doubt.

"Your friends will laugh at you!" said Uncle.

"I know many tricks!" said Dave the terror.

"Dave!" said Mama, aloud.

And Dave was quiet, very quiet.

"I will be a good boy, Mama - if you let me go to school!" said Dave, when Mama was putting him to bed.

"Look in Mama's eyes, darling!"

And Dave opened his eyes wide into Mama's eyes rubbing noses with her.

"Mama loves you!"

"Yes, Mama!"

"Mama will let you go to school, and have friends,

and you will become a big great man - if you are good!"

"Yes, Mama!" Dave repeated, and fell to sleep without saying his prayers.

*August 12th, 1982*

## A guide to the poetry market

*which is also a rhyming haiku*

**POETS,** penny each!
Words, and words-a-heartbeat-each!
Lines-a-jewel-each!

*10.9.82*

## Sonnet, eternal as the grass ...

**ETERNAL** as the grass was said to be,
Hope springs like springs, and Faith will not go under:
full, full, Love fills and flows, just as a tree
brims with loud birdsong, wrapped in lyric wonder.

Eternal as the grass was said to be,
though Hate wields Weight and Might, and War's
loud Thunder,
still purer murmurs ripple low and free
upon Love's lyres, wrapped in lyric wonder.

Lighting the Way that fades, before and after,
Truth, like the changeless skylight, (day or night
or twilight), Love, a great Serenity,

displace unloveliness with Joy and Laughter,
  and spring like springs - though Hate wields Weight
                                        and Might -
    eternal as the grass was said to be.

*10.9.82*

## Warmongers
*villanelle*

**WARMONGERS!** Sport, or suicidal rage?
  Reagan and Brezhnev circling for the kill.
Prehistory's monsters in this day and age!

Their brains, though small, and the book says, not sage,
  scrape the dull clouds, and their doll's arms would kill:
Warmongers! Sport, or suicidal rage?

Look! How they circle! Stealthily they gauge
  each single step. A false one! Will they kill?
Prehistory's monsters in this day and age!

If only beasts, their graves might be their cage,
  and none but theirs, but go with them we will:
Warmongers! Sport, or suicidal rage?

The World's their theatre, and War's their wage,
  the mighty's wayward bauble! Will they kill?
Prehistory's monsters in this day and age!

On the cliff's edge these black belts lock in rage.
  In sport? In suicide? Oh will they kill?
Warmongers! Sport, or suicidal rage?
Prehistory's monsters in this day and age.

*10.9.82*

## To Rex Hudson

*author of Sonnets for the Psalms*

*"And He shall reign ..."*

**THE STARS** are loud and strong,
bright drops of lucent poise in astral light,
and catch my throat like song,
and stud the splendid sky with all their might:
so soft and blue,
a love that's true
and solemn, is the Night.

The breeze blows like a gong.
The moonlit clouds are coming, all in white:
dense, audible, and long,
they come: their step is heavy - might is right!
Stretch out Thy rod,
oh Christ! oh God!
Ride, ride, upon the Light!

Your Book's the Angel's Trumpet!
Your Music's round as a sound argument!
Christ risen, Rex, we lump it:
with "Glory Be's!" my very soul's been rent!
Attention!
Your Book defies convention:
a Resurrection, a new Birth, a Womb -
while men roll megaliths to the mouth of Christ's tomb.

*30.9.82*

# 1983 - 1985

## Prayer for Mercy

**PRAYER** smooths every nerve, oh Lord: have Mercy!
Put me out of my pain, sweet Lord: have Mercy!
Take life, oh Lord, and I shall find it: Mercy!
Cast out the devils, Lord, sweet Lord: oh Mercy!
Worry Yourself in me, oh Lord: have Mercy!
Give me this day a daily Peace: oh Mercy!
The yoke is sweet, the burden light: oh Mercy!
Thy Love makes bright the end of Time: oh Mercy!
Give us this day Thy daily Love: oh Mercy!
Receive me, hide me, quench me, Lord: oh Mercy!
Take life, sweet Lord, and take me home: have Mercy!

*undated*

## At Mister Specservor's

**THAT FASHIONABLE** home, Mister Specservor's
the lean solicitor's, was like a dead end at the crossroads,
spinning with signs and traffic, and nowhere the
pedestrian
may go, a cart, not a home, a car, the latest
from factories where the cars change sizes, every year,
to cater for the fashionable family, every year,
in a word, a dead end without a core, dismaying
to the deep heart's core.

The sitting-room witnessed to bottled energy
that's tame and spent: some plants,
while a few books and records record a desultory
tribute to the unageing intellect. The dining-room
witnessed to lives that live on bread alone;
the bed-room to love that is no more
than what we call 'fucking'.

The 'Bee Gees' upon the wall.
Nothing to indicate that these made Love
between two worlds, not a glimpse of Eternity -
a one-level, too regular, monochromed monophony.

They stop in their souls, these homes, they stop with Death.
But say it. Death. They stop, let drop, let go,
then slap your face with their left, their right,
their left again, and so on, quicker and harder,
till they reach the regular spin. Oh! You'd start back,
abashed. You'd stumble. Tears would start.
And you'd be borne down shuddering to the ground,
your soul abashed.

While Mister Specservor, the host and owner,
sits shrewdly beside you, chattering and glinting bi-focally,
with his biscuits and whisky.

*undated*

**N.B.:** Mister Specservor is a relative of J Alfred Prufrock.

## Haiku, God, how curt you are!

*to.....*

**GOD,** how curt you are!
I - am your friend! even though
you might not be mine!

*19.4.83*

## Principles of criticism

1.

A **GOOD** poet does not write poetry just because to write poetry is fine, nor does a good critic commend a poem because the sentiment sounds fine and poetic. The good poet must be a good aesthete as much as a man of feeling, and the same is true for the critic.

To be successful a poem must communicate a thought, a state of mind, a mood, a scene successfully, and successful communication implies a successful style, a just and proper manner of setting about communicating this particular matter which I am trying to communicate in poetry. And, as every critic knows, words expressive of high-flown, fine, noble, religious, exalted sentiment, or of so-called 'poetic' subject-matter, may be very bad poetry indeed. Parents, for instance, say a lot of 'fine' things, but not one line of poetry, when they are talking as parents do. "And here's the problem," the adjudicator of a poetry competition, in which the award was meant to go to the poet whose entry best expresses a search for the meaning of life, once wrote: "a competition which is offering a prize for a poem expressing 'a search for the meaning of life' inevitably attracts lots and lots of fine feelings ..."

The task of the critic is, primarily, to discriminate between a good and bad poetic style, and to give intelligent and plausible critical reasons why a style is successful or not. To have a style one must, of necessity, have a subject, or as in much modern writing, a mood: it is impossible for the one to exist without the other, or else, following the autopsy, the critic would pronounce a poem dead, spiritless.

To judge whether a poetic style is successful, the triviality or profundity of the theme, the truth or falsehood of the thought, the congeniality or foreignness of the beliefs or opinions expressed, all this is irrelevant. The difference between good and great poetry is another matter, for in great poetry, great profundity is added to great poetic success and literary merit, but to judge whether a poem is a good poem or even a great poem or not by the criteria which we have declared to be irrelevant to literary criticism, is not merely literary bad manners, but the rudest and crudest form of critical prejudice. It is taken as understood, in literary criticism, that to have a style, one must have a subject, but what a subject is worth, that is a questionable criterion, a matter of persuasion, if not, as in much incompetent criticism, of prejudice.

Certainly, the worth of a theme is what distinguishes between great, universal poetry, and good poetry, but the worth of a theme is a criterion which must be applied with extreme tact and caution. What is essential to the laws of criticism is the objective success or otherwise of a style, for that is a scientific criterion about which a conclusion may be reached acceptable to critics of all persuasions. Personal taste is another matter, but personal taste should be allowed very little play in mature, critical appraisal, for if the end of criticism is to cultivate taste, how can one cultivate someone else's, if he does not continually refine his own?

Condensed from a Practical Criticism Seminar which I gave to pre-University students in Malta.

## 2.

**THOUGH** a poem has an essential point of departure, which the poet who is not a poetaster should be able to point out to an audience who has difficulties, a reader may still be fascinated by implications which the poet may have been unconscious of, and the greater the poetry, the truer this is. It is still a very good thing, however, to be clear about that essential point of departure, and not to miss the wood for the trees ..... A message is a good thing for a poem to have, but a poem is not a sermon, and this is where some adjustment of vision may be required, at least among many a layman. A sermon instructs, teaches, and should have, primarily, a message, but a poem, though it might have an instructive element, is primarily intended to communicate experience, and is a good poem, though it might have a message, not because it has a message, but because the style works.

> A poem should not mean
> but be.

**3.**

**IN MY POEM** it was the message which mattered," some poets tell you, when you criticize their style. And then it is amazing how cool and dispassionate such can be towards the feelings expressed in great poetry. With regards to my own feelings, they are eternally more important to me than any form they care to take in my poetry, and I do not give a damn what form they take, as long as they take a form, and the form they take communicates. But however spiritual the message, it is the form, and the form alone, which communicates in poetry, with message or without, and with a message and no form at all, a poem makes ME feel most unspiritual indeed, be the message as spiritual may be.

#2 & #3 were both condensed from my correspondence

**4.**

**AVANT-GARDE** though his innovations may be, it is through the solid foundation of form and structure that Hopkins invites contemporary culture to rethink its break with tradition. Without the elaborate artifice of his rhythms, the artefacts which alchemize what's raw, the make-and-dressing-up-in-style which individuates and heightens, his all-made-by-God-Blessedness could never have made itself felt through a poem. It would seem that it is the art which transforms, and not good will, which is the one thing which communicates, and succeeds, as art.

**SOURCE:** Past Master Submission for publication in **ORBIS**, British Literary Magazine

*undated*

## Popular music, classical music: *terms to examine*

*for uncle Vince*

**POP-CULTURE** is a disturbing phenomenon of the 20th C. In former ages all art was popular and, at the same time, artistic enough to engage the serious attention of the scholar - {we need only mention Shakespeare} - whereas nowadays art which is popular is not 'classical', while art which is classical is not 'popular'. This is a merely capricious distinction typical of a century whose great classics are sadly esoteric, and whose great pops are nauseatingly commercial. The mass-media, besides, have made our culture a cosmopolitan culture, and at its best the century transcends nationalism, while at its worst, the century is featureless. The internationalism of our pop-culture is in the main possessed by the spirit of no people, no nation, no creed, no religion, and a thing of beauty, if such there be any longer, to the mass-media is a good investment, no more than that, and very often may not be considered economically viable either. And is it not one of the agonizing mysteries of suffering that, to make a living out of classical music, an artist must either be outstanding or else stand no chance; while, to make a living out of pop-music, an artist need only be a charlatan?

A precise distinction exists, however, and it is very precisely defined, with regards to music, by any good Dictionary of Music. The three terms - classic(al), classicism - are registered in the New Penguin Dictionary against the following descriptions: "terms commonly used very vaguely, but with 3 main areas of meaning: (1, as distinct from, e.g., 'popular' or 'folk'), serious, learned, belonging to a sophisticated & written tradition; (2, as opposed to Romantic), aesthetically dependent supposedly more on formal attraction than emotional stimulation; (3 = Viennese Classic), belonging to the period & predominant musical style of Haydn, Mozart, Beethoven, c. 1770-1830." The 2nd & 3rd areas of meaning given above do not concern us in our short examination of these terms. Pop, abbr. for 'popular' (originally adjective, hence noun), is in its turn defined as follows: "In older usage it carries the straightforward meaning of 'appealing to a wide audience' - e.g. 'classical Monday pops' ... since the late 1950's, however, it usually refers to a non-classical, commercially promoted type of music of US derivation, consisting almost entirely of songs, whether delivered by solo or group vocalists. Pop in this sense, particularly as purveyed by radio & gramophone records, has assumed the role of a popular alternative to the classical tradition of composition & performance." In the context of this examination it is the more recent usage of the word which we shall talk of.

These definitions, as must be obvious, are not like our uninformed & unconscious critical assumptions, presumptions rather, which we feel so confident of, that we cannot understand why they should be snubbed by the savants, or at best tolerated with a condescending irony. It would therefore, be a very useful exercise for us to pause & to criticize the methods by which we are accustomed to criticize.

Some facile assumptions we readily make are, first & foremost, the distinction itself between classical & pop, & we have already dealt with the nuisance, supplying better definitions to work with. We might add that, while art which is not popular with the high-brows may still have deep human value, art which is commercially promoted, &

of great commercial value, hardly need have great academic value, because when artists, great artists even, produce a work which too many applaud too suddenly, it may easily mean that they have prostituted their talent, & that the popularity of their work will not last beyond the day, or will at best be confined to the uncritical, the dilettantes, & the uninformed. A famous example is Tchaikovsky's **1812 OVERTURE**.

Another facile assumption is that classical art belongs to a former generation, & popular art to ours. Songs in the hit-parade are written by our generation, it is true, but, before they may be promoted to the classical repertoire, they must pass the test of time, & they may then be spoken of as being classics precisely because they have remained popular with audiences, because they have lasted. A song is a minor work, but there is no difference whatever between its promotion to the classical repertoire, & the promotion of one of Beethoven's symphonies. But after 200 years are over, & time has not managed to dull its beauty and appeal, our aspiring teenagers, with an ignorance as understandable as it is imbecile, say that classical music does not belong to this generation, & that this generation has its own. Such music is this generation's because, in a case such as Beethoven's, the music is not of an age, but of all time.

A third popular misconception is that popular music proudly differs from classical in both creative method & inspiration. As long as it is commercially promoted, it will be different from classical music in that its value is primarily commercial, & not artistic. Starting from what the dictionary has to say, there are, however, two aspects of pop-music which, in order to determine its artistic nature, we shall have to examine: first that it consists of songs, & secondly that it consists almost entirely of songs.

Now to begin at the beginning, song-writing is a serious and humble art, as old as King David, & practiced by the great classical composers also; & secondly - there are good songs in the pop-repertoire. The Beatles are good song-writers. But finally, the art of song-writing is probably the least & humblest among the arts of musical composition, an art which all our theory students practice as an elementary exercise, & no one has written better songs than the great classical musicians themselves. Schubert, we know, was very fond of the genre, & wrote beautiful songs as well as great song-cycles, such as **DIE SCHONE MULLERIN**, or such as his songs **TO SYLVIA**; & his songs, irresistible melodies such as those of his famous **AVE MARIA**, were very popular in his day, & still are ... but then Schubert composed great Symphonies also, & so did Beethoven & Mozart & Mahler & Brahms & Tchaikovsky; & Verdi, Puccini & Wagner composed great operas too, operas in which the songs or 'arias' which may be pulled out to be sung again & again, have a dramatic context far superior to that of the tunes which stars in the hit-parade regale us with. What, then, can be said on behalf of pop-music, when we hear that it consists almost entirely of songs? We may say, I suppose, that song-writing is an art, & that the Beatles are good song-writers.

The last & most popular misconception that I shall examine is that popular music is easy to appreciate, & therefore a better art-form because it is more approachable; while classical music is difficult to appreciate, obscure & pedantic, & therefore an occupation for scholars & high-brows. And so I shall end with the famous Platonic observation that all good things are difficult. In art no less than elsewhere we have to work for the reward &, though it is not the rule that, if the labor is greater, the pleasure is more intense, the exception proves the rule. Nor is the labor of the music-listener ever equal to that of the performer, & least of all to that of the composer, but in most cases the relation between the intensity of the labor & the profundity of the pleasure is a simple proportion. The pleasure of the pop-maniac being easily the easiest & the most superficial.

*B'Kara, Malta*
*November 24, 1981*

## Genesis and evolution

**IN A LETTER** dated 13th June 1981 to Cal Clothier, one of my friends in England who is a contemporary, well-known and well-published poet with whom I first became acquainted through a literary magazine, I enclosed the following comments:

> ..... The symbols you use for the 'new imagination, such as With Columbus and Darwin, are stirring, but your subconscious is imbued with the Biblical mythus, whether you like it or not ... It seems that I misinterpreted your Darwin and I must, obviously, excuse your disagreement, since I overconfidently expected a fair amount of agreement ... we have to agree to differ on certain matters, a healthy disagreement surely ... Certainly, Darwin revolutionized outlooks, and thereby created a need to adjust our visions, but not, I believe, to find a "new imagination". In any case, Christianity was never an 'imagination', nor was it meant to be such. I have a strong suspicion that the notorious 'missing link' - which evolutionists are as much at pains to find as archaeologists are at pains to find Atlantis, or cosmonauts were at pains to find a man on the moon - is God Almighty ... I tend to agree with what you say about mythmaking, though not, of course, in the sense that Christianity is pure myth, or at all manmade. Certainly, Genesis, for instance, is myth in the strict literary sense: a fairy-tale with a mystical and metaphysical content which is all that matters. Genesis is written in the stye in which all such myths were written in the days of the sacred Author. And I think I agree with you perfectly that one of the main functions of poetry is to create myths ... I think you will find that the closest I have ever come to genuine mythmaking is in Cinderella

and in The Rhyme of the Beast.

This exchange later spurred me on to compose Evolution, which I completed on September 21st, 1981, and which appears below:

## Evolution

A **RENOWNED** evolutionist lately delivered a lecture on evolution to an international gathering of theologians. For the purposes of our publication it is sufficient to quote his introduction.

**IN THE** beginning, swimming in the cold,
a cell did multiply, increasingly bold,
split, flash and mushroom and, in a blush, radiate
eyes that all over the seas did coruscate
and limbs develop, varieties of crescent,
(illimited varieties of crescent);
and as invertebrates grew vertebrate -
as the illimited habitats dictate -
some numberless infinities of fishes
became their stronger brethren's primitive dishes.

After giving a succinct, pointed, brief and highly imaginative account of man's prehistory over a period of 4,500 million years, the distinguished scientist delivered the following address:

**MOST REVEREND**, incredulous, snowy-haired Sirs,
disown though you may your descent from polar bears,
it's easy to grasp as numbered pagination,
or else you have a weak imagination.
The line goes back to that cell in the beginning,
eyes precocious and watery, its hair thinning;
but, were the **'CAUS CAUSARUM'** that cell's blue gaiety,

would make your image and likeness the cast of
the Deity,
and that's improper - as you know: that's sinning
a sin of class. Fine phrase: "In the beginning!"
Nothing precedes its own Creation. Pause!
Nothing, in space or time, is its own cause,
that cell much less than Man, who's not his Maker,
nor chose his genes: that cell's but a partaker,
that, once created, procreates and selves,
for God the Maker made things make themselves.
But though He be no Magic-Monger, still
His Love's deep hunger, and His perfect Will,
reverb the Word in Time, giving no sign
that Man's a pawn: no palpable design
is felt, we cannot tell, but He is there -
He beats the Time, the When, the How, the Where;
And where these meek (and knowing) Darwins blink
and stumble - there it were well we stop and think
whether the Mighty be the missing Link.

*completed: 21.9.81*
*B'Kara, Malta*

This poem was conceived as a reply to intellectuals, (whether themselves theologians or unbelievers does not matter), whose use of Darwin was too interested. Still later on, in a letter to an old friend in ..., and regarding certain correspondence in the ... papers, about Evolution, which had kindly been mailed to me, I enclosed the following comments:

> ..... I have read the articles on Evolution. Mr X, I think, is a blunderer, and I much prefer Y's, and Z's articles. X does a great disservice to the Pope ... by quoting him. "Although the Holy Father did not clearly and in so many words condemn the theory of evolution of the human body," he says, "he did clearly and in so many words condemn the conjectural opinion of polygenism (man's descent from a group and not

> from a single person, Adam). This almost amounts to a condemnation of evolution because polygenism leads to evolution." After here saying 'almost', which means not quite, he then goes on: "Therefore if polygenism goes against the Catholic Faith, then the Catholic Church cannot accept evolution." Garbage! Let me interpret what the Pope said. He needs it.
>
> The Pope condemns polygenism because polygenism, I think, would eliminate the necessity of God's very especial intrusion in the creation of man, and that is a religious truth defended by all the sane processes of logic, reason and revelation, and since God intruded, then man is descended from a single person, Adam, the first man whom God created, and not from a group, or perhaps God created a group of Adams, but it is convenient to think of a possible group of Adams as one man, Adam. But polygenism does not lead to Evolution, nor does Evolution go against the Catholic Faith because polygenism does. And no Pope will ever condemn a theory of Evolution which leaves room for God's intrusions and which safeguards revealed truth. Of course the Pope 'did not clearly and in so many words condemn the theory of evolution of the human body!" He is incompetent to do so. What the Pope condemned are clauses, or parts, in the theory which impertinently intrude and challenge the Faith .....

I was then asked how it is that polygenism goes against the Faith, and not Evolution. My answer should, I thought, have been clear from the above statement, but for good measure I shall now add the following.

Polygenism, the conjectural opinion of man's descent from a group, and not from a single person, Adam, confounds the evolution of the human body with the creation of the soul. The first is natural, the second supernatural. In saying that man is descended from a single person, Adam, it is made clear that God's most especial intrusion was necessary to create the soul of Man, which sets Man apart from all his ancestors, and this method of saying proclaims this truth. But in saying that man is descended from a group doubt is cast upon this necessary truth, "defended by all the sane processes of logic, reason and revelation". In saying that man is descended from a single person, however, Genesis is not implying that that first parent's body did not evolve from that of a lower species. This is a purely scientific theory, innocent of, and disinterested in, theological polemics, and the Bible's disregard for theories of the nature is complete and entire.

Darwin's theory of evolution surely throws new light upon how we are to interpret that other verse of Genesis:

> In the sweat of your brow you shall eat bread till you return to the ground, for out of it you were taken; you are dust, and to dust you shall return. (Genesis 4:19).

Perhaps, as I noted above, God created a group of Adams. In order to signify the necessity of God's very especial intrusion to create the soul of Man, which sets Man apart from all his ancestors, in order to proclaim this Truth as necessary, and to make this necessary Truth sound simple, obvious and clear, it was nonetheless convenient for the sacred Author to think of a possible group of Adams as one Man, Adam, the first Man, VOM, whom God created.

*February 13, 1983.*

## All fule's lament[83]
**a dramatic monologue**
*to my old man*

**I AM IGNORANCE** itself
I am ignorance pure essentials
the black sheep of the family
a tramp without credentials
that bountiful ignorance largesse
and penniless idiocy finesse
and only feel the insult circle
and only catch the cinders evanesse

and only heard the insult mumble
grumble, growl and tumble
in subterranean tombs and catacombs

and never spied the insult circle
and never caught my da-da stumble
behind the arras pure and simple

because I was a cherub-faced moron without a pimple

but this my heart is everyone's whose heart is sodden
by everyone downtrodden!

you say, ouch!
what trouble has been!
yes brother!
nobody knows the trouble I've seen!
how come you never caught your Da
and never caught Another
behind the arras pure and simple?!

one has to be fair idiocy itself

[83] Without, in any way whatsoever, conveying contempt for the reader, or for anyone in particular except, perhaps, myself, this self-deflating poem composed on April Fool's Night, 1985, is meant to convey quite a real sense of terror at human folly ..

dull ignorance pure essentials
fair bountiful ignorance largesse
and penniless idiocy finesse

but this my heart is everyone's whose heart is sodden
by everyone downtrodden

an insult that can crack the bones
as it cracked Christ and Adam Jones
and I was up to mischief
and never caught my daddy stumble
and left behind my malice

because I do not wish to go insane

because I heard the insult rumble
in subterranean tombs and catacombs
and I have caught a wise man stumble
behind the arras pure and simple

I was a cherub-faced moron without a pimple

because I do not wish to be a blown balloon
in windy aerodromes

because I heard the insult rumble
grumble, growl and tumble
in subterranean tombs and catacombs
and caught my daddy spying
and feared war and fire
and caught my daddy prying
an insult that can crack the bones
and rummage in my marrow stones

and I have learn to say one only word
**"Da-Da! My voices,**
**My voices only told me true!"**

because I do not hope to turn again
because I do not wish to go insane

because I heard the insult rumble
grumble, growl and tumble
in subterranean tombs and catacombs
an insult that can crack the bones
and rummage in my marrow stones

and I have learn to say one only word
like that poor baby shit a turd
**"Da-Da! My Voices,**
**My Voices only told me true!"**

*Vancouver,*
*April Fool's Night 1985*

## Il-karba tal-injorant

***lix-xieħ*** *(Maltese version of* ***All Fule's Lament)***

**JIEN** l-Injoranza pesta
jien l-Injoranza pura essenza
il-'black sheep' tal-familja
jien raġel bla' unur
vagabond mingħajr kredenza

dak l-Injorant kbir ġeneruż largezza
dak il-fqir ċuċ finezza

u nilmaħ biss il-ġamar jiżvanezza

inħoss biss l-Insult idur
nilmaħ biss ix-xrar itir
nisma' biss l-Insult jirbombja
qalb oqbra katakombi
u qatt ma qbadt lid-Da jittrombja
minn fuq il-bejt tal-kaċċatur
u nisma' biss l-Insult jirbombja
ġo dak l-imqaddes Kuritur

kont ċuċ ħelu mingħajr nemex
u l-Injoranza nnifisha
imma din qalb kullħadd kullħadd rifisha

tgħid, aħħħ! x'waħda ġratli!
tgħid, iva ħija! kif weġġajtha!
kif qatt ma qbadt lid-Da jispija
minn wara l-kwinti pure and simple?!

kont ċuċ ħelu mingħajr nemex
u l-Injoranza nnifisha
kont l-Injoranza pura essenza

dak l-Injorant kbir ġeneruż largezza
dak il-fqir ċuċ finezza

vagabond mingħajr kredenza

imma din qalb kullħadd kullħadd rifisha

Insult ixoqq il-għadam
kif xaqq il-Kristu w'xaqq l-Adam
u kelli ħafna brikkunati
u ma ndunajtx il-Pa kemm kien brikkun
u ħallejt il-brikkunati
għax ma nixtieqx inkun miġnun

għax smajt l-Insult jirbombja
qalb oqbra katakombi
u qbadt il-Pa jittrombja
u ma nixtieqx inkun pinnur
fuq bejt ta' kaċċatur

għax smajt l-Insult jirbombja
qalb oqbra katakombi
u qbadt il-Pa jittrombja
u bżajt min-nar u l-bombi
Insult ixoqq il-għadam
u jħuf fil-mudullun

u tgħallimt ngħid biss kelma waħda

**"Da-Da! Il-vuċijiet,**
**Dawk biss qalulhi sew!"**

għax smajt l-Insult jirbombja
qalb oqbra katakombi
u qbadt il-Pa jittrombja
u bżajt min-nar u l-bombi
Insult ixoqq il-għadam
u jħuf fil-mudullun
u ma nixtieqx inkun miġnun

u tgħallimt ngħid biss kelma waħda
bħat-tarbija li ħrat taħta

**"Da-Da! Il-vuċijiet,**
**Dawk biss qalulhi sew!"**

*miktuba f'All Fools' Day 1985, bil-Malti w'bl-Ingliż*

# Part four:
# Lady Vancouver

9 POEMS BY JOE RUGGIER
Lady
Vancouver
WITH A FORWARD
BY
OLIVER FRIGGIERI,
UNIVERSITY OF MALTA
SECOND EDITION

# Lady Vancouver

**9 POEMS**

JOE RUGGIER

WITH A FOREWORD BY
OLIVER FRIGGIERI,
UNIVERSITY OF MALTA

SIXTH PRINT EDITION

**MULTICULTURAL BOOKS**
*"There are many Mansions in Parnassus!"*

114 - 6051 AZURE ROAD, RICHMOND, B.C., CANADA, V7C 2P6

# Lady Vancouver, 9 Poems



**Published by: MBooks of BC**
Unit 114 – 6051 Azure Road, Richmond, B.C., Canada, V7C 2P6
Tel: +(604) 600-8819 E-Mail: jrmbooks@hotmail.com

**Printing History**
Multicultural Books Poetry Series #5
1st & 2nd Editions, March & July 1997 — **ISBN: 0-9681948-0-X**
3rd Electronic Edition Summer 2003 — **ISBN: 0-9733301-0-4**
4th, 5th & 6th print editions, produced as Part Four
of the 1st, 2nd & 3rd print editions of Joe Ruggier's
Collected Poems, June 2009 — June 2018
**ISBN to the current edition: 978-1-897303-26-9**

Foreword by: Oliver Friggieri Ph.D.
Cover art designed by: University of Toronto Press
Desk-Top publishing: Joe M. Ruggier

1st and 2nd editions printed and bound by: **U of Toronto Press**
3rd electronic edition produced by:
**Progress Media Duplication, Richmond, B.C.**
4th, 5th & 6th print editions printed and bound by:
**Lightning Source Inc.; USA**

**2,125 copies in circulation**

# Foreword

*by Oliver Friggieri*

## The poetry of Joe M. Ruggier

**THE DISTINCTION** between classicism and modernism, antithetical though it seems from a purely historical standpoint, has been ably overcome by various twentieth century poets in search of a synthesis. Traditional technical devices have been put to the test and a basic point has been proved: old forms can be efficiently made use of to convey messages which far transcend the confines of time. The principle of universal relevance has somehow assumed new significance and eventually the concept of form itself, however static, became relative and transient. It all depends on the poet for traditional forms to attain the flexibility normally associated with modernism.

Joe M. Ruggier's impressive ability to renew forms and instill in them the vigour of his era can be properly understood in the light of the above. A Poet of great technical power, profoundly versed in the handling of the iambic pentameter, Ruggier involves a whole tradition in the making of his work. He literally plays with words, manipulates phrases and adapts regular rhythms to his innermost needs, thus producing poems equally classical and modern in both content and form. In the process the metrical pattern itself becomes a set of sounds to be explored, modified and re-created. Tradition is here revisited by a new spirit fully aware of the characteristics and demands of modernism. Ruggier never indulges in cheap experimentation, but is keenly interested in establishing a direct relationship with his readers by effecting a subtle compromise between his own musical schemes and those of any sort of spoken diction. He can be somehow heard reciting his pieces, addressing a hypothetical listener, engaging in a discussion of a highly meditative nature.

The overall effect is that a major tenet of modern criticism is fully obtained: form and content are one whole phenomenon. The calculated spontaneity with which he constructs his iambic pentameters enables him to remain natural and authentic, however deep the denotations of his discourse. Metrical precision is almost his most instinctive mode of expression. Traditional classicism is therefore only a point of reference, a model to be immediately substituted by a structure which is completely his own. The opening lines from **LADY VANCOUVER: TO THORA ARNASON** constitute one of the most salient examples of his strategy:

**STREETS** of Vancouver seem the slums of Heaven
when I trudge homebound, pocket weighed with pay
for some love poetry sold from door to door!
Trudge on, trudge on, oh where the grass grows greenest,
where bides the beauty Queen my heart doth seek,
fairest of soul and in her body fair,
that I may keep, like God, an eye upon
a girl I love!

The technical continuity so manifest in this collection is again an indication of the poet's remarkable thematic unity. Ruggier is essentially producing one whole long poem, composed in parts over a period of time, constructed in the light of an underlying principle. The poet has long proved his versatility and vastness of perception, but he deals with every moment of lyrical inspiration with the devotion and enthusiasm of a budding practitioner. He always looks as if he is embarking on his first project, always reaching new heights. This may be due to the recognition of new sources of inspiration, yet his personality as a poet of imagination and experience is pervading.

The most evident component of his world view is perhaps the relationship between dream and sensory experience. He consciously fails to acknowledge any substantial distinction between the inner and the outer layers of sensibility, thus proclaiming his belief that the poet and the man in him are one. He treats the cosmos as if it were a person, an overwhelming figure with human features, a macrocosm which the poet is privileged enough to penetrate through his unique insight. Imagination reigns supreme but Ruggier never loses sight of his own immediate environment, itself the environment of his own hypothetical listener who is never forgotten or ignored:

**ON ONE** side stood the barren, rugged Cliff,
vein'd black and red and blue: varicose veins
of Earth like those of wives, and pelvic grass
like tufts of hair; on one side stood the Sea.
One Room stood in between: one broken Door,
and walls of Stone; another, latch'd, led to the Sea.

**AN INSPIRED DREAM**

In an age when humankind has fatally lost the capability to imagine and to reconstruct an alternative landscape, Ruggier is adamant in asserting the supremacy of creative imagination as a means towards redemption from repetitiveness and monotony. This is perhaps the most modern feature of his whole poetic output. Authenticity is now best restored through confronting one's own inner self, reassessing past experience, rediscovering the power of memory as insight into the future. Alongside the space dimension, even the time scale is radically reviewed. Things are consequently seen in terms of their eternity. Changelessness is what this remarkable poet is actually looking for. On the other hand, the implied impossibility of such a venture is what makes the inspired soul come to terms with reality. Disenchantment is thus transformed into another source of poetic resourcefulness. Dream and common experience are bound to come to terms, although art will always have the final word. The concluding lines from **AN INSPIRED DREAM** assume the role of the poet's original aesthetic manifesto:

**WHAT** did the Vision mean?
My waking ritual done I took the Road:

.... The Rain
began to drizzle; soon it pour'd down hard!
I went back home and made it Art ...

Not less than four pieces in this collection are inspired by death as the poet formally gives tribute to men of distinction. His meditation is not on death as an abstraction, an eventuality or a final inevitable condition, but on death as a new phase in man's uninterrupted eternal itinerary, a stage mystifying all actions and perceptions, sublimating being, defining identity irrevocably. The four elegies, however diverse, are real variations on a central theme, stages in one unique spiritual process. Ruggier is equally sad and serene; he evokes the memory of the dead with the same passion he employs in indulging in a dialogue with the living. **ELEGY FOR PROFESSOR ENRIQUEZ** manifests the degree of tenderness the poet can reach, and is ably transformed into another opportunity for him to underline the basic principles constituting both his poetics and his vision of life. Art and Faith are once more identified as synonymous, whilst the elegiac mood enables the poet to further stress the sanctity of the former: creativity is itself a form of belief, a way in which empirical shape is given to the awareness of divine presence. In idealizing a particular person, a specific exemplary pattern of human behaviour is implicitly idealized.

**ELEGY FOR PRESIDENT KENNEDY**, on the other hand, acquires added strength if put in sharp contrast to the above. Ruggier's versatility as an elegiac poet is easily demonstrated in various ways: the pervasive mood, the poetic form now intimately related to the prose structure, the diction, the message itself are all quite different. Here the poet assumes the role of a social commentator, a moral historian, an enlightened interpreter of events. Universality is once more attained through the transformation of facts into elements of lyrical significance. Death again becomes a point of departure for the inquisitive self to understand and judge the paradox of being.

**ELEGY FOR ROBERT DARMANIN, SJ** is probably the most direct piece of writing ever penned by

Ruggier. Here he strives to restrain his imaginative powers and to come forth with an easily understandable homage to a man of honour. The poem takes the shape of a vignette, finally to lead to the pronouncement of a most decisive verdict which again illustrates the poet's firm belief in the sanctity of Art:

**YOU SAVED** your Soul, my friend, you stroll among
the Stars, a grand achievement like great Artists'.

The most touching excerpts in this collection are indeed religious. **ELEGY FOR REX HUDSON** is a moving tribute to a poet with whom Ruggier shared friendship and from whom he found the recognition he surely deserves as a poet of high standing. The sense of mystery is identified with the artist's awareness. The poet's own creed is best summed up in one line: "Art is immortal, shadowing but the Spirit!" Ruggier has amply dwelt on this argument in his book **INTELLIGIBLE MYSTERY** and many other works of his are likewise strong testimonials to this belief. Equally relevant in this respect is **WATCH-DOGS FOR SARAH**, an equally inspired and moving poem underpinning Ruggier's conviction that the creative act is itself a prayer to the Lord. In **A LITTLE GIRL OF LONG AGO** Ruggier embarks on a cultural excursus actually to further stress the concept that the recognition of the fundamental positive values of humankind are the primary concern of any serious poet. In no other poem is the belief more strongly driven home than in **LADY VANCOUVER: TO THORA ARNASON**, somehow assuming the role of the poet's "summa" in both thematic and technical sense. His prayer to God is equally solemn and decisive:

**OH THOU** Who drivest All,
and Saints and Artists most divine raised up
from the low earth with Love, with Breath inspired,
assigned to each his task, and guided till
complete, and with good Honours dresseth All,
Thou All in All Who for the little worm

feels the Creator's pride, and innocent Love,
Divine Eternal Sprite Whom no one sees,
lonely am I like Thee!

This collection is another proof of Joe M. Ruggier's dexterity in technique adoperated in such a manner as to convey thoughts and feelings deeply felt by the poet and equally identifiable with the reader. Different moments of poetic intuition are here presented as variations on a central theme, thus constituting a cycle, an important landmark in the itinerary of a real poet. Words are chosen with discretion, phrases are put down in a manner as to construct one whole statement, and rhythm is handled with the mature immediacy of an experienced speaker. The collection is actually intended for listeners, not readers, and is meant to be experienced in terms of its successful identification of sound with meaning. A poet of caliber has once more shown that traditional metrical patterns can acquire greater strength if adequately used, and that modern poetry can still retain the musicality and forcefulness associated with romantic and neoclassical poetry without in any way losing either freshness or relevance. The way in which Ruggier succeeds in fusing mellifluous diction and deep poetic insight implies a message to both poets and lovers of poetry.

**Oliver Friggieri Ph.D.**
*University of Malta*

## Acknowledgments

Thanks are offered to Professors Warren Stevenson, Ross Labrie and LeRoy D. Travis of the University of BC, for useful suggestions they have contributed towards the improvement of these verses. Special thanks are owing to Oliver Friggieri – distinguished professor and Maltese poet, widely recognized in Universities across Europe, Britain, and elsewhere for his scholarship and critical studies, particularly in Italy for his studies on the Italian influence on Maltese and other related literatures – for the joyful task he has carried out on my behalf in writing an introduction to this booklet and in reworking it for the second edition.

## **Oh tell me who if anyone does not want to listen ...**
*an elegy for President Kennedy*

**OH TELL** me who if anyone does not want to listen to a sad and pitiful Elegy to the Memory of a Man named President Kennedy between the lines of IT and WHICH deals with the Scandal of the Abominations? Oh tell me who and if, because I am being taken short by the sad and somber Poem, and I want all Humanity to tell me Another!
Oh tell me who if anyone does not want to hear or has not heard the sad and sorrowful Story of a Man named President Kennedy for all of us have heard it and all humanity indeed knows how, having led his Nation to a bloodless victory over the Russians in the Cuban Missile Crisis, in the age of the atom bomb,
All the Abominations, with all their bells and buttons, despised and dishonoured and reviled with sexual abuse a Man named President Kennedy in all their fucking papers, without giving poor John Kennedy so much as a single Honour after the sad dishonoured bastards shot him!
Oh tell me another, *Hypocrite Lecteur*, if you can so much as gasp the why We cannot even so much as declare a Man named President Kennedy a Saint because of the Scandal of the Abominations with all their bells and buttons?
And the poor Man died a Martyr's death; and We cannot so much as give the great sad Man His Honour because of the Scandal of the Abominations! And we cannot so much as make the great sad Man His Honour whether such a thing be done in the Sunshine or in the Moonshine!
And every good and honest sincere Creature's Sacred Heart is wrung and cut and inexpressibly hurt because of what the bastards have done to a Man named President Kennedy;
And every good and honest sincere Creature's Sacred Pride

is wrung and cut and inexpressibly hurt because of what the Abominations have done to a Man named President Kennedy! The dogs of all the Nations bark: the Abominations have listened to a Man's Confessions!

Christians who pose as Christians to slander Christians; Christians who have introduced Abortion into Christendom in the name of Christianity!

May they die suffocated all of them and all of them accursed with the dogma of the Holy Eucharist – with a silent scream like the Child's in the Womb!

And the poor Man died a Martyr's death; and We cannot so much as give the great sad Man His Honour because of the Scandal of the Abominations with all their bells and buttons! And we cannot so much as make the great sad Man His Honour whether such a thing be done in the Sunshine or in the Moonshine!

And the poor Man died a Martyr's death, and all His secrets have been flung wide open by Barbara Fromm; and poor John Kennedy, the unfortunate Man, has fallen into the hands of the Scandal of the Abominations!

Christians who pose as Christians to slander Christians; Christians who have introduced Abortion into Christendom in the name of Christianity!

May they die suffocated all of them and all of them accursed with the dogma of the Holy Eucharist – with a silent scream like the Child's in the Womb!

And they shall none of them receive the most Sacred Chemical unless they render unto a Man named President Kennedy all their little nameless Honours! And they shall all of them roll up all their despite and make it a white-hot poker and stuff it up you all know where!

Oh in all my wildest, sad, most tragic speculations I see the sad, austere, great Martyr in Hades and the Shades with Dante's Virgil, waiting for the sad and somber, great, high-serious Honour;

In which impossible case the Abominations shall all go to be abused with fire at the center of the Stars in the body and in the soul with the worst dogs in History;

and to keep IT Company We shall get IT and WHICH the snakes and the raccoons; and I shall plague the Judge till He hears My Prayer!
And I shall plague the Judge till He hears My Prayer for His Own most good and sweet, most Just Revenge and Vengeance!
And every good and honest sincere Creature's Sacred Heart is wrung and cut and inexpressibly hurt because of what the bastards have done to a Man named President Kennedy;
And every good and honest sincere Creature's Sacred Pride is wrung and cut and inexpressibly hurt because of what the Abominations have done to a Man named President Kennedy! The dogs of all the Nations bark: the Abominations have listened to a Man's Confessions!
Christians who pose as Christians to slander Christians; Christians who have introduced Abortion into Christendom in the name of Christianity!
They all of them must allow all of us the Honour of satirizing them in Our most savage, most unscrupulous tragic Temper, to serve them right for what the Abominations have done to a Man named President Kennedy!
And all of them shall likewise rejoice and be glad; but they shall not get the Honour
That went to a Man named President Kennedy ……

*Winter 1992*

## An inspired dream

**I DREAMT** last night of a nuclear Landscape,
barren and ghastly; wild was the voice of the Sea!
Romantic was the scene: blue hills and clouds
of woolliest white adorn'd the blood-stain'd Sunset.
On one side stood the barren, rugged cliff,
vein'd black and red and blue: varicose veins
of earth like those of wives, and pelvic grass
like tufts of hair; on one side stood the Sea.
One room stood in between: one broken door,
and walls of stone; another, latch'd, led to the Sea.
The earth struggled and jerk'd in orgasmic gasps
of cosmic sex. The apocalyptic tone
of the universe inspired terror and
an insult supersonic thunder shook
Heaven and trembling made me breathe a pray'r
to Jesus! Able I seem'd to float like Saints
above the poles and electronic wires;
and higher if I chose. Beside me sail'd
a strange, familiar Ghost – and heart to heart,
we held a tete-a-tete. But terrified – soon
I floated down and shook the wooden latch
which led upon the gold, incarnadin'd Sea.
A youth who muslim seem'd open'd the door.
Swimming naked upon the eternal shore,
two lovers relax'd – his hands caressing her breasts,
that swum like lillies upon the idyllic Sea.
I then awoke .....
what did the vision mean?
My waking ritual done I took the road:
My good umbrella ... lost! ***Roastmastir's*** ... closed!
My bank ... Sunday! and it was shut! The rain
began to drizzle; soon it pour'd down hard!
I went back home and made it Art ...

*15th October 1995*

## Elegy for Robert Darmanin, S. J.

**I DREAMT** I saw you, Robert, walking down
the aisle in church, and dreamt I saw the Lord
place in your hand your ticket and your wages;
remember'd also how I, a student, sought
your counsel – with what radiant, gentle art
you led me, to sustain my fledgling thought!
I then presented you my published work.
"Offensive thoughts have riled me," then I moan'd,
"since merrily together we hiked on!"
Pensive, you read and asked: "Who gave you these?"
"God the Spirit Eternal Whom no one sees!"
I then replied. Smiling, you purchas'd drink,
gave alms for many a soul you know by name,
a monk who's ta'en his wages, now at Peace,
strolling the streets of Heaven, counting pay,
the rich turn'd poor all tugging at your sleeve!
You saved your soul, my Friend, you stroll among
the stars, a grand achievement like great Artists'!

*24th April 1996*

## Lady Vancouver: to Thora Arnason

**STREETS** of Vancouver seem the slums of Heaven
when I trudge homebound, pocket weighed with pay
for some love poetry sold from door to door!
Trudge on, trudge on, oh where the grass grows greenest,
where bides the beauty Queen my heart doth seek,
fairest of soul and in her body fair,
that I may keep, like God, an eye upon
a girl I love!
Trudge on, and tell me, Muses, whom to crown
Lady Vancouver?!
Qualified am I
to judge, and I remember, God! so many!
Not least my loving Julia's thoughtful care!

A woman that I love she ever is;
how little wonder I that we seemed doomed
to fail! Doomed have I ever seemed … to fail!
In those dark, evil days of eighty-four
I could have welcomed death: rejected, ill,
disturbed, what wrath! what grief! Wished to explode
like bombs! No sooner wedded were we two,
but for ten years have had to fight the vibes
from relatives, priests, and state, in this sin city's
holes where divorce is not the last resort
but social expectation! Negative thought
from those professing positive …
She married me, she paid: I was at zero!
She paid the busfare, coffee, smokes, the rent,
the food, and then proposed a honeymoon!
Said I: "You must be kidding!" For ten years
we fought foul vibes, dear wife, and now we're through!
A home we sweated for, a darling child
we love; all this we have, and more! I am
a wreck no longer: I a Poet am
loved by the people! But for ten years we fought
vile vibes! What wrath I feel! but do not fake
I love you still, for we believed and triumphed!

Divine, inscrutable, eternal Spirit,
what solitude I feel, my aweful Friend,
Thou Lord, Who art Alone: how I delight
to share with Thee a word, to pour my heart,
when heavily it hangs, like songs to Thee
in pray'r and home-made verse, tell Thee my wrath
for counselors of Job, of fraud; my grief
for ungracious elders that the poet want
conformed and measured up to narrowest norm;
for many scandals wrought by plaster saints
who never fooled an Artist, for which sight
they grudged us all the Honour, scorned us all
for being what we are; my sorrow for poor
John Kennedy who fell for his own dear Land,
falling within the hands of the foul scandal,
the vile insufferable bruits of the Abominations!
Divine, inscrutable, Eternal Spirit,
Thou aweful Friend Who art Thyself Alone,
not all who visit Church to Heaven go,
nor all who seem without to Hell, for which
well pleased am I to creed Thy awesome Mercy,
and nevermore confess, to none but Thee!

A little onward lend Thy guiding Hand,
Thou All in All, a little furder on!
I am not chaste but not a hypocrite!
Sweet Chastity, that beauteous Pearl, slid through
my fingers, God, and kissed me 'ciao': Thy Will
was that this Artist be unchaste, and smoke,
and drink, and not drive humans to despair,
as all ungracious pastors do, upon
the steep and narrow, thorny path to Thee!
Have I not thorns sufficient, God? Do I
not pray? not offer? Am I not kind to men?
or not compassionate? Have I not suffer'd?
have I not kept my word? Or is my word
unkind and filthy? Kindness of speech, Oh Lord,
and cleanliness, does that not make the case
for beautiful Verse? Is not the Memory of
Great Men an Honour sufficiently sincere

to my false neighbour? Oh Thou who drivest all,
and Saints and Artists most divine raised up
from the low earth with Love, with Breath inspired,
assigned to each his task, and guided till
complete, and with good Honours dresseth all,
Thou All in All who for the little worm
feels the Creator's pride, and innocent Love,
Divine, Eternal Sprite Whom no one sees,
lonely am I like Thee! As a vagabond doth
upon the streets of Heaven, I sought a lover:
she was a drunk; she stole my money ….. paaah!
but she was lovely! Pity her and bless
her memory, God; and of her malady
may she be healed; *e vaya con Dios!*

Lead, kindly Light,
amid the encircling gloom, lead Thou me on,
Thou All in All, a little furder on,
as the allotted task I still pursue
from door to door, this meaning, healthy task
I prize, to eke myself my public out,
and groan in blood to earn a reader: 'tis
an honourable chore Thou settest me, oh Friend,
but not reflected in sufficient money!
But though I see them seldom, they are all
my choicest-treasured bosom friends: they prize
my spirit, and my living do not grudge –
from soul-destroying labour me redeem!
Honest am I, and I have sighed for all,
for their sincerity, Lord, doth turn me on,
and a good night drives me to sing *"Born Free!"*
Still let me pray for cosier figures, funds
not astral but sufficient, humble wealth
upon this far too mercenary land
that cannot invest in Art, the Soul of Man,
reserves and portions sober, but my own,
that I may work, but not beneath an axe,
and recreate myself, my wife, my child!
Still let me seek that special, bosom friend
that I imagine wildly at each door;

hope for another heart to call my own!

Trudge on, trudge on, oh where the grass grows greenest,
where bides the beauty Queen my heart doth seek,
fairest of soul and in her body fair,
that I may keep, like God, an eye upon
a girl I love!
For though she may not hold me in her arms,
the intimate friend I sigh'd for all this May,
my spirit catches fire, sinks before her,
my sweet Lady Vancouver, Thora of Iceland!

*18th May 1996*

## Elegy for Rex Hudson, 1915 – 1996

**I DREAMT** I saw your dead, corrupted corpse
stretch out a swollen, limp, corrupted hand;
your eyes, where Life-in-Death still squints and warps,
smiled bitter-sweet upon this bloodshot Land.

Cities of North America in your eyes
shadowing no beauty in their nuclear bower;
cities of tombstones where no dream surprise
draws down eternity like a dropping flower!

I saw you chained in a refining fire,
and gently fashioned like a golden rod
to sing eternal song, your heart's desire,
your guilt forgiven, Love your only God!

Oh how many on this Earth of ours
pay lip-service to a high ideal,
all smiling silken sweet, and talking flowers,
their heart's affections' doubtful and unreal!

God writ in vain, in vain the Authors writ
and made us see the writing on the Wall,
and Life goes on, and not a word of it
lives in the Many: what though One doth call?

The pride of Life which breeds the big parola,
and Mammon weaves words lightly seeming plausible,
and beauty made by God stained with crayola ...
Man leaves his muck and calls the Saint implausible!

Has Man no **borma**[84] though he has no Faith?
the common not drop names and talk of Spirit?
not tout the Saints, the Prophets and the Great,
but never live the words of Wisdom in it?

---

[84] **borma**, a term of my invention, similar in sound to **karma**. It stands for the cunning of humanity, the guile and malice of the human race.

Nothing but honour, nothing but paper status,
and all Man does for God is make his living,
and curse true Love as he doth curse the foetus,
philosophize and seize the pay, ungiving!

The private Honour which to Books gave Life
is to the multitude unknown — Compassion
toucheth not the shark, and all is strife;
and all's ignoble beneath a histrionic passion!

But you, my friend, made up to God and Caesar,
and loved the Classics with a candid soul,
inscribed with living words – words were else a teaser! -
your gift a cultured heart, a purpose whole!

How grave it is to sift the wheat, the tares,
momentous to discern in books the spirit;
how sweet to hear thee sing thy sedative wares,
what ravishing Voice, oh Metaphysical Lyricist!

Love and sincerity are not for weekdays,
caroused but in the name, not in the heart,
but you cleansed breath and made speech holy Godways,
and praised me kindly with a glad, fresh art!

For sincerity hath rules of rhyme and rhythm,
and frankness carved in art is not offensive,
and to the butchered heart which troubles fathom
the trumpets of the Angels are defensive!

Art is immortal ... shadowing but the Spirit!
Saint Rex of Minnesota liveth on,
too good to cast away, but to inherit
Fame eternal past opinion gone!

**Joe M. Ruggier**
*Author of INTELLIGIBLE MYSTERY*
*22nd October 1996*

MY **BOOK**, **Intelligible Mystery**, is a study of Mr. Hudson's life and writing, with whom I had a friendly gamble that, had he won the Nobel or Pulitzer prizes for literature, for both of which he had been nominated a few times, we would have shared the money. My quarrels and differences with Mr. Hudson, whom I have known since 1981, were more like the differences between father and son than between rivals, and he and myself had a capital friendship. I shared my creative life with him since 1981. I am sure that on the sad occasion of his passing all his family and friends would find an elegy from my pen an appropriate gesture to the memory of an associate who for 15 years maintained that I was one of the finest poets he know.

## Watch-dogs for Sarah

**I DREAMT** I saw two beasts draw close one night,
my daughter, and each one gently say: "Master,
let me protect your child!" Each held itself
erect – two man-like beasts I saw, shoulders
and face two men, the rest colossal dogs!
I shook their hands. "If this be Heaven-sent,"
I prayed, "protect my child, my Faerie Queene!
Beyond what I can utter, Love is blind
for Sarah Therese my Queen!" And shaking hands
with each I said to each: "I am a Man,
and what I did I did out of a need
I may not utter. The gods demanded it.
Inspiration ebbed and flowed but I made
Pope Caesar Art, and burnt a sacrifice
for greater needs than mine, humans for whom
Salvation lay beneath a lock and key!
With tears let me thank you, beasts of the wild:
protect my Faerie Queene! Let not the stranger
draw close with his contumely and impest her
or intrude upon the dignity of her Spirit
to abuse the awful covenant she shares
with me alone as if these were his toys!
Watch over her with eagle eyes,
Beasts whom the Lord hath sent us,
that she may sleep untroubled, blithe and chaste,
like Prospero's daughter. Trouble her not!
tell her not you lie beside her, watching,
day and night as if you her Angels were!
I pray you though, with fearsome fangs devour
dissembling suitors all. Allow not one
his villainous powers to test upon her mettle!"

Weeks later I spoke to Sarah in her ear
of my sad, unhappy temper: "I do not want
anyone but you to pray for me, my daughter!
I grow tired, beloved, aging slowly,
like the historical peasant suffering much
to make a little …

I wish for no-one's prayer but your own!

They breed all round me, the people's double faces:
the joys of youth are now unhappiness and tears!
Not so the hug you gave, not so the art-show
in those, your blessed eyes!
Angel I need thee, thy hug,
thy sweet, divinest smiles,
the art-show in thy eyes,
and no-one else's prayer!"

*3rd February 1997*

## Dante a posteriori: the faith that moves mountains

**ABOUT ALL** them good Catholics who insist
that Dante did not have a right to do it,
set you down this:
when did the Catholics scruple making insults?
did Dante then transgress in writing Hell?
did he become the chief Imagination
of Christendom to tickle
the repulsive vanity of the religious?
do not real people with real names get lost?
Heaven and Hell not what the Faith's about?
Oh all preciser theologians then,
let me expound a higher dream I had!

Eight hundred years ago
there was in the Antipodes, known nowadays
as Australia, a Mountain flung high up
into the sky two hundred miles, to Spirits
alone known as Mount Purgatory;
and all the dead who did not go to Hell
went there, having perforce to climb the Mount
performing certain labours, before they could
arise to Heaven!
As Time went by a species
arose known to us as the astronomers etcetera,
till Man made what is known to us as progress!
And all to prove that progress is man-made
God chose to blow with His almighty breath
Mount Purgatory off the map in strictest silence,
and like the most high Poet conceal His Hand,
divinest Priest of Culture, lest the bare Truth
of old Dante's divine guidance lay revealed,
and in his vanity and arrogance
Modern Man become like God!
How on Earth

do I know this, oh theologians
preciser than I Am?

I dreamt a higher Dream, oh all preciser
theologians, and my Dream stretcheth farther
than doth the mind of Man!

*9th February 1997*

## A little girl of long ago[85]

*notes for a new Religion presented as a Poem ...*

**A WISE** Man sat upon the Seat of Honour
in Ancient China, and said unto His Daughter:
"I love you much, Beloved, heed what I say!
Know that before your birth I knew about thee,
that you have lived before and I have read
your work which in your last Existence flourished,
and I, your Father, loved your terrible beauty,
the Divinity concealed in your sorrowing spirit.
Knew also of your tragic end and how,
as a good Man sayeth to me, you went
down to the shades below, which made me weep,
My Love, tears that I would weep had my
Own little child been lost. Heed what I say!
A little child thou art but you can read,
and when this book which earnt me fame I wrote
to celebrate my marriage vow, I said
these words to thee alone with all my heart,
though you forgotten were. In your spiritual

---

--[85] First issued in *Lady Vancouver, 9 poems by Joe Ruggier, (1997),* **A little girl of long ago** was re-issued in *Lamplighter most Gracious, collected poems and selected prose, (1972-2009)*, in the original length of 2 pp — now expanded to 7. Reprinted in this edition of *Lamplighter* is this poem in its original length; whereas the longer and more satisfying version is being issued at the back of this collection, with a prose abstract outlining the themes of these ***notes for a new Religion presented as a Poem ...***

Baudelaire's version of pacts with Satan conceals wicked humour directed against the hypocrisy of Society. The critics let him get away with it because it is both humorous and candid. *The Devil is far more sensitive than human beings, to the Arts and to the insult he suffers: it is equally true that he is converting. You do not have a right to snap with an insult as you please not even a poor devil. You are not an Angel so privileged.*

The only purpose of this Author's version of a pact with a devil is Salvation. His intentions are not even as tendentious as Baudelaire. All he is asking is that readers will judge him with an open mind and let him get away with it as the critics allow Baudelaire.

Ear I whispered aery verse the lines
of which concealed my grief and secret love
and with my verse I tempted thee and made
with thee a pact that you my daughter shall
become and may one day rejoice as you
deserve, oh beautiful, tragic, troubled spirit,
and never said unto a single Soul
a single word within my bosom buried!
Know then, my little one, that you are old
enough to be your Mother's Mother!
Let no one then teach you, my troubled Queen,
facts of your Life which with my sorrowing verse
I have said unto you far better than
your teachers can. Beloved Daughter know
that I have chosen you just as the great
Kirin did choose His Women.
Know also, thou tragic, sorrowing, troubled Spirit,
discussing facts of life is then for Thee
forbidden fruit, for in such trivial truths
much lying is and all things seem, and many
little ones like thee have gone astray
by fast ones lost and slain, and been denied
the beautiful Sun, the terrible *claire de la Lune*,
and starlight shedding balm on secret Love,
by trivial truth incullionated. Forget it then,
My Beautiful! Touch not forbidden fruit!
Be happy with what you know and seek no more
save for the useful skills you learn at school;
and keep thy word same as thy Father did!
The eyes of little children, my Beloved:
the Art-show there is all I wish to see –
Lady Aphrodite born from the Ocean;
Professor visiting *del al di là*!
And drink of the good Honour which I have given
My little one whom I have given Fame
for ever for the effect You have produced!"


*26th February 1997 – 26th September 2013*

## Elegy for Professor Enriquez, 1925 – 1997

**GOD BLESSED** you, Uncle, with productive Age,
with honourable work and wife, and with the gift
of travelling perpetual. You now trod
deserted streets of Heaven, in the Peace
of historical dust from where the Saints
and Artists speaketh, and every word is tongued
with fire beyond the speech of the Living.
Love and do your will you who loved the Arts,
your children, church, and people. I recall
your gentle word, your humble origins,
the tears and the sweat of your hard-won,
discreet success on earth, the honest joy
you took in meeting the distinguished – though
you blew your horn but in Humility –
the love of Art you shared with real people,
the sweet peristence of your concern in books,
and your tolerant quiet faith, which mattered more
than blast of war-drums, arguments or force!
You seasoned Faith with love of Art and that's
the difference between God's wine and ours
which troubles the universe with drunken talk!
Much trouble is in the universe for idle words!
Yours is the universe, ours a Death to come!

*19th March 1997*

# Part five:
# a richer blessing

# A Richer Blessing
## poetry & prose by Joe Ruggier

# A Richer Blessing, by Joe Ruggier



**Published by: MBOOKS OF BC**
Unit 114 – 6051 Azure Road, Richmond, BC, Canada, V7C 2P6
Tel: +(604) 600-8819 E-Mail: jrmbooks@hotmail.com

**Printing History:**
Multicultural Books Poetry Series #7
1st Edition July 1999 — **ISBN: 0-9681948-3-4**
2nd Electronic Edition Summer 2003 — **ISBN: 0-9733301-0-4**
3rd print edition, produced as Part Five
of the 1st, 2nd & 3rd editions of Joe Ruggier's
Collected Poems, June 2009 — June 2018
**ISBN to the current edition: 978-1-897303-26-9**

Foreword by: George Csaba Koller
Cover Art: Karen Butchart, (Surrey, BC).
Desk-Top publishing: Joe M. Ruggier

1st edition printed and bound by: **Laser Graphics Ltd.**
2nd electronic edition produced by:
**Progress Media Duplication, Richmond, B.C.**
this edition printed and bound by: **Lightning Source Inc.; USA**

**Over 1,725 copies in circulation**

# A Richer Blessing

poetry & prose by

## Joe Ruggier

with a foreword by

## George Csaba Koller

cover art

## Karen Butchart

**3rd PRINT EDITION (REISSUED)**

brought out by

**MULTICULTURAL BOOKS**

*"There are many Mansions in Parnassus!"*

**Unit 114 – 6051 Azure Road, Richmond, BC, Canada, V7C 2P6**

**This book is dedicated
to my daughter Sarah Therese,
a Heaven in Hell's despite.**

"Better by far you will forget and smile,
than that you will remember and be sad."

## Author's preface

**MY WORK** may be called archaic but it is essentially a neo-classicist revival. There is nothing about my work which is not original and it may be said that Joe Ruggier is responsible for a true rhyme-revival and for a true neo-classicist revival. In my writing I seek to revive conventions which were law before the modernist movement in writing but I am not doctrinaire. I have no patience with rhymesters who think that all poetry should be composed in rhyme. While seeking to revive this beautiful and ancient convention, I have likewise composed in free form, prose-poetry, stream of consciousness, and much blank verse: if I am a rhyme-revivalist at all, I am an honest and open-minded one. One reader commented that my language is dated, going back to the Romantics: people do not write like that any longer. Unfortunately, my dear friend, Joe Ruggier writes like that in 1999, because that is what touches his heart, and much modern writing fails entirely to touch his heart. The whole point of it of course is that he is read by the people. Contemporary writing suffers from those galling and hateful vices: far too much obscurity, tortured sense, and lack of manly feeling. It is not memorable. I am one of the very few practicing authors I know of, if I may say so without being shot for bragging, who refuses to write at all unless he write with his heart. Another reader commented that my work is too formal. I feel no respect for this at all. To what work is my own being compared in being described as too formal? and by whose criteria is it being called too formal? I honour good work only and I do not quarrel with my tools. The eternal truths, observed Maritain, are not to be subjected to a test of fashion, like the art of the milliner, or clothes designer. When the artist, however original, knows that he has understood essential and eternal Truth, what joy is left him but to record his own intensely personal reaction to such a unique experience in a unique and memorable style, in beautiful and musical words, in form which is original and exquisitely crafted. Thus, my style is my joy and my pride. The questionable joy of eternal, ongoing search for the Truths we claim we want to discover, but refuse to accept with humility if we stumble upon them, has been happily taken away from me and substituted by a better. Truth is Truth to the end of reckoning, wrote Shakespeare; and I accept it gladly, humbly, gratefully. If you do not enjoy my style, dear reader, I am very sorry but I cannot help you, because creating it gave **me** deep joy, much pride, and profound aesthetic pleasure: my style is **me** and it is truthful, the only resource I have left which belongs to **me** and is my own, and which I am allowed to manipulate for my own ends. Truth I do not have a right to manipulate for my own ends. My own intellectual theories, of course, are my own intellectual property, but my perception of truth is not a commodity which I have rights to dispose of as I choose: it is only my style over which I have rights to do as I please. I rejoice in the Truth but Truth does not belong to me and my only task as a poet is to write poetry which stays in the memory.

***22nd January 1999***

## Foreword to "A Richer Blessing"
*by George Csaba Koller.*

**JOE RUGGIER** irks me. He is a gifted poet who is possessed by a vision and he refuses to budge. He has never heard the word "compromise." On the threshold of the millenium, he is a nineteenth century man who writes in his inimitable classical style, and he wouldn't have it any other way. He and I have many things in common: we share an immigrant background, an intense devotion to the Blessed Virgin Mary, and a no-nonsense attitude to life. We are both enraptured by poetry, but whereas he has drawn very clear lines and set very strict rules as to what poetry is, I embrace all kinds of poetry with an open heart and an appreciative mind.

When I was struggling through University in the late sixties, I dipped into the collective consciousness of the different epochs of British poetry and in one class wrote about the constraints that the teacher put on our appreciation of these masterpieces of English verse. I called my doggerel "Wordsworth:"

> "Oh Muse of England, arise from Thy Grave,
> And witness the spectacle of Vanity Victorious,
> To Objectivity is Thy Reader made a Slave,
> A Subjective Outlook forbidden to Crave."

Reading Joe's manuscript brought back many of the same feelings I had when I first encountered Wordsworth, or Milton, or John Donne. It was a crystal-clear cerebral celebration, a child-like wonder of eternal truths. Although personally I felt closer to Lord Byron and Coleridge, I would think that Joe Ruggier would be more comfortable with the first three mentioned. His poems exhibit the measured polish of Wordsworth, the deep religious piety and pain of Milton, and the outspoken verities of John Donne.

Joe Ruggier is the only contemporary poet who can write about a devotional practice to the Sacred Heart of

Jesus, and get away with it. Deeply religious, he is also very much aware of the cruelty exhibited by some in his own faith, Catholicism. Ruggier agonizes over the slights and the insults and continues to write about the on-going struggle with his demons, whom he has befriended over the years.

An immigrant from Malta, who has not found his place in Canada, he calls to mind the lyrics of that unofficial poet laureate, Mr. Robert Zimmerman (aka Bob Dylan):

> "I pity the poor immigrant
> whose strength is spent in vain.
> Whose heaven is like ironsides
> and whose tears fall like rain.
> Whose visions in the final end
> must shatter like the glass,
> I pity the poor immigrant,
> when his gladness comes to pass."

The United States has had an official poet laureate, Robert Frost, who read at the Kennedy inauguration, and another, Maya Angelou, who read at Clinton's. In between was a vast wasteland of lyndonjohnsondicknixonronaldreagan, which wasn't exactly famous for its appreciation of poetry. But Jimmy Carter did invite Bob Dylan to the White House, so our unofficial poet laureate was in effect recognized:

> "Ezra Pound and T. S. Eliot,
> fighting in the Captain's tower,
> while calypso singers laugh at them
> and fishermen hold flowers."

Ruggier mentions both Pound and Eliot and seems to have a high regard for both men. Does his appreciation of modern poetry end with these two notables? I'm afraid so, if I was to judge purely from his critical essays in the manuscript, but I do know that Joe has a high regard for some of his contemporaries and he also publishes their poetry through his literary journal and his Multicultural Books.

I resonated with *A Richer Blessing* primarily through

that child-like sense of innocence that many of us have lost, but some of us still nurture deep down.

"Sweet, dark and cryptic are the thoughts that come
to mind of time I spent within the womb;
blessed the one that seizes troubled sense
of the delicious quiet when life blows over;
and ah! proud as I am to be a man,
I long to be a child again."

From **The Dark Night of the Insult**

*A Richer Blessing* is a unique manuscript, an "apologia" if there ever was one, which lists in great detail all the things that an immigrant author has to do in order to survive in a society where he was not born. My friend, Jim Christy, in his recently published book: *The Long Slow Death of Jack Kerouac*, makes a case for Kerouac being an outsider in the U.S. (born in Lowell, Mass. into a French-Canadian family, his mother tongue was the Quebecois joual - he didn't speak English until he was six years old) as being the primary motivating force behind his writings. Also, his deep Catholicism, both of which are shared by Joe Ruggier. The similarities end there, I'm afraid.

Joe still irks me, because he told me once that I should get rid of 90% of the books in my store and just concentrate on the classics. He is revolted by some manifestations of so-called modern literature, and does not hesitate to say so. Yet a noted Maltese scholar, who wrote the foreword for Joe's last chapbook, *Lady Vancouver*, had this to say about Ruggier's poetry:

> "A poet of calibre has once more shown that traditional metrical patterns can acquire greater strength if adequately used, and that modern poetry can still retain the musicality and forcefulness associated with romantic and neoclassical poetry without in any way losing either its freshness or relevance. The way in which Ruggier succeeds in fusing mellifluous diction and deep poetic insight implies a message to both poets and lovers of poetry."
>
> **Oliver Friggieri, University of Malta**

So it follows that if Joe Ruggier's is considered *"modern poetry"*, then romantic or neoclassical poetry are due to make a comeback in the twenty-first century. Be that as it may, rarely does a poet bare his soul with such honesty, ferocity and precision of language and rhythm.

**George Csaba Koller**
*Owner, Black Sheep Books*
*Vancouver, BC*

## Acknowledgments

**THANKS** are offered to Professors Warren Stevenson, Ross Labrie, and LeRoy D. Travis, of the University of BC, for numerous useful suggestions they have contributed towards the improvement of these verses. My father likewise contributed one, very good idea for a poem; and Karen Butchart, a fine artist from Surrey, BC, contributed the cover art, and gave me permission to use her eloquent picture of a *poor Van Gogh* type of ideal. Special thanks are owing to Mr. George Csaba Koller, owner of **BLACK SHEEP BOOKS**, in Vancouver, for contributing a fine critical foreword to this collection. Thank you, George, for your perceptive and tasteful introduction.

# A Richer Blessing

*by Joe M. Ruggier*

## Jehovah

**HERE**, in this dream-Kingdom after Death,
amongst the Suns and Moons of Starry clusters,
resident of a faraway Earth satellite
of a faraway Star, a God liveth here
named Jehovah, old Man with a mighty
white beard fond of his Pipe and Reward,
and most reluctant to make His whereabouts known!
Jehovah licketh the Peace of a new Heaven
and of a new Earth and the House of Jehovah is
a mighty Homeric Palace. The wild beasts
that protect it have Souls one and all, and mighty
are the Forests that surround it, and unpolluted
the Rivers where Jehovah loveth to walk
i'the shades o'the Homeric, and each Star
that He beholds emits a Starry Music,
and the snakes i'the Forest twine and untwine to the sound
o'His Pipe, dancing with effortless ease like a wave
o'the Sea, and the Rainbows are all of them
many-tiered! Jehovah never wore
a condom; Jehovah never hurt a fly;
and His descendants are like the sands o'the Sea,
and to each one Jehovah gave a Castle
ensconced like His own in a Forest! Blessed by All
the Gods of Heaven is Mighty Jehovah,
and His descendants liveth under His Rule,
and His entire Flock kisseth the Rod
of Jehovah and blesseth His Laws, knowing
not guile nor malice. Blessed is He who looketh
upon the Face of Royal Jehovah,
and leaveth the Stone unturned where it lieth,
and the Peace o'the historical dust undisturb'd!

*1st May 1997*

## De Civitate Dei

**SWEET DREAMS** of a new earth I dreamt last night
where everything was beauty far too real!
Great verse by dogs o'the streets remembered was,
and honour by wild beasts defended! Like
a new Las Vegas was the City I
was in nor could the night-clubs in Las Vegas
boast preciser theologians-demonologians!
Everyone else by lovers was accompanied,
and all was *verde*, *verde* and thought the kingdom!
How I adored that primitive honour,
softened by gentle thought and musical speech!
The historical dust itself did verse indite
which "Love Me!" seemed to say, "but dare not say
you Love Me!" At a small round table I
did sit where demon-lovers seemed to pour
wine like a gentle, liquid fire which
transfigured the reins, the heart, the soul within!
A Man who kingly seemed held out a watch,
bejewelled, ticking, tocking, golden watch,
and said: "For you!" but grabbed my extended hand
and held me down remorselessly, that Master
of Kung Fu, and a royaler honour gave!
And in my dream I saw the liquor dance
upon the small round table where He sat
and pour'd it, dance and frothing bubble forth,
take shapes and run like little rivers, touch
itself with gold of sunrise, then disappear
like the darkening streams in woods at sunset!
He took me to a two-hundred-storey-high
and said: "Behold the proudest of my towers!"
I trembled to behold but up we went
where corridors and private corners seem'd
like a million more within the most gigantic
ant-hill, till we reached the topmost floor,
the most beautiful of rooms, the window open,
two lovers wrangling, the Ocean spread beneath!
A Woman half-remember'd but much belov'd
sprang like a blessing out of hiding, and I cried

"Oh are you here? Don't tempt me!" And I wept
to see the wrangling woman jump to death,
her lover following after! My Kingly friend
then said: "We die together here, but beauty
toucheth the heart of all, and evil to him
who evil thinks!" And shocked
I sprang out of my Dream like idle tears
crying: "Oh Lord of all what hope is there
for all of us, for this forsaken earth,
where all of us have slaughtered been in wombs,
and the sweet peace therein has shattered been
for all of us? Why did You not the law
take in Thy hand, and likewise me abort?"
To which an answer peal'd from that high land:
"It sav'd the soul of many a poor devil!"

*16th May 1997*

## The pyramids of Ozymandias

**DO YOU** dare, castrated slave, to sneer at Ozymandias
and call his pyramids an insult? Shoot thyself
with a twentieth century gun! Rid thyself
and the proud Ozymandias of thyself!
and thou shalt rid us all of an insult!
But you shall never be rid of Art!
Do you dare to sneer at Ozymandias, slave,
and call his pyramids an insult?
To us who have no friends in the emptiness
of time and space, no friends in the wide, wide world
of future generations, the brats to come
who shall look down upon us
with a sneer of cold command?
only to rob the pyramids of Ozymandias
and trade the treasures of the egyptians,
the proud egyptians and neighbours of a hebrew,

rob us of all and trade my poor remains?
We who have nothing, nothing, nothing, nothing,
but flesh and soul and love of stone and the simple
joy of our terrible, primitive honours
in the glaring eye of the Sun and the desert
and the awful shock of the Infinite?
Slave it for Ozymandias, for thou art my slave,
and slave until you drop and sleep the sleep
of death in the pyramids of Ozymandias
and yawn it out in many dreams to come,
and let no one but Ozymandias sneer!

*21st May 1997*

## Talking of messages in dreams[86]

**A STUDENT** clasped a book and held the hand
of Life, his Teacher, walking in his dreams!
I dreamt I journey'd on a strange, old road
which led to pots of gold and rainbows, when
a traveller beside me I did see,
a man who lordly seem'd, a god of old
drest like a modern gentleman! He took
my book, he thumbed the pages, slipping back
my book again to me! "Beware!" he said,
"art's a glass slipper, man is not! Beware
of those who look on you as though you were!"
"What means this?" then I asked. And, "there are those,"
he then replied mysteriously, "that will pay
a royal figure could they only see
such heresy ridiculed!" We stopped beside
a house where I was known, and I could tell

[86] This poem was composed upon a dream the morning after I fell asleep with Wagner's music playing. The last piece I remember listening to before I fell asleep was ***The entrance of the gods into Valhalla***.

my friend's intent to wrangle! The old folks
nothing but wrangle did. "What this man is saying,"
then I said, "is teaching universal
as the Beatitudes!" And we were gone,
and all the women join'd us on our way
thorough this life's dark wood, as if to say:
"he's back, he's back, by God he has come back!'
Their laughter bubbled like the running streams,
and everyone was suddenly a-chatter,
flitting like birds in trees, through life's dark wood:
"he's back, he's back, by God he has come back!"
and all the leaves became a secret whisper!
We then came on a road of beaten tarmac
which darkly wove, in the dim distance winding,
and for some reason he had hurried on:
my friend was gone! The traffic gleaming stood
where in a derelict house a man was singing.
"I am Wotan!" said the man. "Sing Wagner!" then said I.
I drifted out of my dream to the tune of his song
as at the end of the well-beaten road
the bridge between time and eternity
could almost be seen rising to the song of the god,
but my travelling bags were gone and voices mutter'd
in my ears: "take not what you may earn yourself!
We pray in times of trouble out of need,
and try in vain to find a substitute;
but prayer solveth not all care!" And at
the sound of that reveille I was awake:
someone was knocking on my Door .....

*24th May 1997*

## Elegy for my friend — FB
*1921-1990*

**I DREAMT** I saw thee, *caro Phil*, sitting down
in simple dignity, like a *Vatican* god,
drest in brown, tatter'd, modern elegance,
an island town which there were none to praise,
*piazza* around a church upon my isles,
my native isles, and both thy arms were cut
and lying down, like those of broken busts,
upon the black, ceramic table where
thou sat. A small, black circle seem'd that table,
black seem'd thy face, thy eyes a smoking fire,
and you seem'd hewn of marble but your eyes,
your eyes, oh friend, reflected War and Peace
and shone. "Phil! Phil!" I wept, "This is no place
to meet, this city of spare parts, but I
am glad, oh friend, to see, to recognize
thy face among the dead, for thou, my Friend,
thou died and told me naught, thou passed away
so silently, as if thou wert a stone
dropt in a deep and placid sea, and thou,
thou wert my Friend, and silence hurt my heart,
as of a Friend's where friendship hath turn'd sour!
But let me then express, if quote I may
a favourite verse, "*L'Amor ch'a te mi scalda!*"
for tears shook my soul, when thou, my Friend,
dids't die away like waves without a word,
a single word, and I picked up the phone,
and thou wert dead!" I ended, dear Friend,
your broken bust together came again,
and came to life, as if life imparted were
to stone, and thou dids't shake my living hand,
and thou dids't lead me where a banquet lay
for two! The wine, the games we play'd, were good,
but better were thy eyes, oh Friend, thy eyes,
thy eyes were shining through the dream I dreamt,
but nothing, nothing, nothing, dids't thou say!
"Oh Phil," I mutter'd, "thou hast naught to say?
say something, something! Do you really have

no word to say, not one, among these tombs
and shatter'd monuments?" "I am at peace,"
was all thou said:
"and with my father! Be at peace with thine!"
thou murmur'd, and thy spirit fled, in shades
of black, upon the light of early morning!

*8th June 1997*

## Requiem for my canary

**I MISS** you, bird that shone like yellow sulphur,
and sang as loudly as the sun is bright:
the rooms were lonely that you fouled and cheered;
you were the substitute of wife and child!
Ah! Pisces, for you were romance and starlight:
why did I forget that husks can seem like seed?
A weary mind made bitter, thoughts upon thoughts
revolving, I did not forget to eat!
But is your freedom final, like my grief?
And do you now inhabit spaces larger
than my three rooms? upon faraway earths
where wise men say many strange creatures dwell?
Dost thou forgive me? thou that hover'd closely?
Wings wildly beating, and thy reins arous'd?

*25th June 1998*

## A personal affair[87]

**WHERE HAS ALL THE BEAUTIFUL POETRY GONE?** Why do poets have to make the ugly, the sordid, and the seamy their exclusive domain? Where are the poetic virtues of brilliant simplicity and lyrical spontaneity wedded to disciplined craft and verbal melody? Where is the magic of assured technique and stylistic achievement wedded to meaningful, paraphrasable content? Why must modern poetry seem like "the creation of a whole tribe of fops got 'twixt asleep and wake?" Why must poets who versify small talk to make it look like a poem be called poets at all if they do not have the skill to handle any other style whatsoever? Why must all such persist in the fiction that this is what the people want when all they can do is remainder books published at other people's expense? All the little names, whom no one will ever care to remember ... authors who do not stand behind their products! ... products in which no author has the guts to invest a single penny of his own! ... fit but to be sold at garage sales to the financial embarassment of other people! ... they all belong to Writer's Unions! As a token of the most strange respect they are paid millions of dollars yearly out of Government and Art Council monies and are allowed to pose as misunderstood geniuses! They are all a strange, eccentric people; & their judgments are highly arbitrary and unsound! All they desire is what all desire ... respect! but they are all hopelessly stilted. Their publication credits, without which I would respect them better, sadly enough, stand between them and sincere respect! Is it not indeed as sublime to be oneself as it is sublime to be God Almighty? Is not Eliot imitation as bad as Milton imitation at its worst and most hideous? Is

---

[87] **A personal affair** appeared for the 1st time in **The Eclectic Muse, 2:1, Christmas 1990**, (pp 2-16), & -- in the form of an extensive Editorial prepared by myself, in my capacity as Managing Editor of **TEM** & Judge of our 1st ever Poetry Contest -- it bore the date 20th November 1990. What appears here is Part 1 of my 2:1 Editorial as it has been extensively & definitively rewritten for my own satisfaction as well as for the satisfaction of readers & contributors who approve of, or otherwise need to consult again, our publishing philosophy.

not sincerity a most artistic quality which is not art? & is not the Grand Style the most fitting garb for true sincerity? Is not the Grand Style the only fitting manner in which the sin of Art should be committed?

Readers of **TEM** have not expressed an unconditional appreciation of everything we have chosen to print, but seem to agree that **TEM** is outstanding in the standard of the work which it publishes, as well as in the fact that it is -- so said one of our close supporters -- on the cutting edge of things in that it is trying to accomplish what so many contemporaries are trying to achieve. This is: to reform the prevailing climate by introducing far more disciplined techniques than are evident in the work of many poets of the so-called modernist movement in writing which succeeded the Eliot-Pound-era.

Evidently, many poets are trying to do what we, as well as **THE RED CANDLE PRESS** in the **UK**, & **THE WORLD ORDER OF NARRATIVE & FORMALIST POETS** headed by **Alfred Dorn** in the **USA**, are attempting, which is to bring about a traditionalist revival and to take poetry back to the people. Poets look up to **TEM**, as well as to other small presses such as the two mentioned above, for inspiration. I would personally prefer to think that both myself as a literary artist and **TEM** are independent of all schools of thought; this would be far too pretentious a stance, however, were I not aware of what others of my own generation are trying to do. In view of this I wish to say that, independent as we may be, **TEM** fully endorses the aims and work of **The RCP** in the **UK**, and **Alfred Dorn** and his **WORLD ORDER** in the **USA**, as among the most worthwhile from among small presses of our own generation.

Entirely immersed as we are in the traditionalist revival we do not exclude well-done free verse: we all want the genre to stay for reasons which will become apparent in the next few paragraphs. While we shall always publish well-crafted **free form**, we ***prefer*** to see quality work in rhyme &/or metre, such as villanelles, sonnets, stanzas, couplets, blank verse etc., & we say this to remind poets of their responsibility to do a good job when they write a poem. We have no sympathy with the work of poets who neglect their craft & want **TEM** to get away from the drivel which so many editors have canonized. We all wish to inaugurate a serious rhyme-revival.

At this point it seems appropriate to talk at some length about the philosophy behind **TEM**. The terms **FREE VERSE** and **TRADITIONAL VERSE**, I feel so strongly, are misnomers for some very precious, extremely special moments, of our literary experience. The term **free verse** does not do justice to the truth -- written about at such length, with such erudition, sentiment and insight, by T S Eliot in his criticism -- that ***vers libre*** is not an escape from form: "for the poet who wants to do a good job," wrote Eliot, "there is no such thing as **free verse**." In the light of this teaching it is evident that when we talk of **free verse** we are talking of a thing which is a paradox by nature. But! while we do need a real paradox to define the thing we are talking about, the term **free verse** is not a paradox. It all but calls to mind the impression of being taken short in all simplicity, and of a simpleton leaking. I would by far prefer to talk of **FREE FORM**, rather than of **FREE VERSE**. The term **free form** is an oxymoron: it is the paradox we are looking for; the term **free verse** does not have the subtlety we require.

The term **traditional verse** is likewise misleading. When I talk of **free form** I perceive in the authors of Scripture the great Masters of **free form**: that is what I mean by **free form** when I am talking of the real thing ... It seems only just to ascribe the honour of pioneering **free form** to the authors of Scripture and to no one else. And the authors of Scripture were certainly not one person. By the authors of Scripture I mean Moses, Ecclesiastes, the Prophets, the Author of the Book of Job, the four Evangelists: I mean all the authors of Scripture in their full variety. I have no wish to rob them of a credit which belongs to them and to no one else.

The Hebrews notwithstanding, the Romans and the Greeks wrote in metre without rhyme. "The concept of rhyme," writes Frances Stillman in **The Poet's Manual & Rhyming Dictionary**, "was unknown to the Greeks, and rhyme was not used in classical poetry." While the tradition of the Greeks and the Romans is still a major influence, **free form** was the peculiar domain of the Hebrews: really, the honour did not belong to Mallarme, or T S Eliot, or Walt Whitman ... it belongs -- and 20th C poets have taken too little care of this -- to the authors of Scripture. [*And while I beg to differ with the Almighty in persisting to write in rhyme & metre, & in asking for craft & technique from the poets whose work I solicit, I certainly intend to render unto the Lord Himself His due.*] While **rhyme**, to quote Stillman's **Manual** still another time -

> ".....first came into use in the Latin Church of N. Africa around A.D. 200 in certain hymns & chants. By the 4th century, rhymed sacred poetry had spread more widely & had become a real stylistic movement in church liturgy ... During the Dark and Middle Ages, rhyme, as well as alliteration & assonance, was a major element in popular poetry, both in the Latin of student songs & in verse in the emerging modern languages of Provence, France, & Italy. By the 14th century, rhyme had become universally accepted in the poetry of Europe, except in Spain. Even in the north, the old, alliterative verse conventions had given way to the new fashions. All over Europe troubadours & minnesingers were entertaining people with their melodic & charming poems in the vernacular, that is, in the modern languages as opposed to Latin, which was still the **lingua franca**, the common language of scholars, of the Church, and of diplomacy ... In the 16th C, blank verse, that is, unrhymed metrical verse, came into use in Italy and England, though Italy soon went back to rhymed forms, under the French influence. In England, rhymed verse had found a modern rival; heroic blank verse would

continue to be used as a major vehicle of the longer poetic forms in English ..."

In talking of **free verse** & **traditional** we then require to sharpen our concept of **free form** as well as to distinguish between **THREE (3) TRADITIONS:**

1] the tradition of writing sublime prose which is the peculiar domain of the Hebrews & in whose work the only rules were rhythm and intensity;

2] the tradition of writing in metre without rhyme inherited from the Greeks & the Romans;

3] the tradition of rhyme which "first came into use in the Latin Church of N. Africa in AD 200 in certain hymns and chants", & for which, it seems, we owe credit to the Church.

If we are then to regard the Hebrew Scriptures as the foundation of Western Civilization, **free form** would seem to be a highly traditional way of expressing ourselves. Why, indeed, should we regard it as exotic & peculiar to the 20th C? What have we done any better than what the authors of Scripture did over 6,000 years ago? Unless we were to look to the Romans & the Greeks as the pillars of our Culture **free form** is **traditional**; while what everyone else used to mean by **traditional verse** ... poetry composed in metre without rhyme or else rhymed verse ... is an exotic way of expressing ourselves imported in part from Ancient Greece & Ancient Rome, & partly introduced by the early Church, which still has extremely valuable lessons to teach us. Poets who try to revive it in their work, as I have sought to do in my own, will no doubt find, what I too have found, that it will do their **free form** much good, which will read better because of the craft & discipline, profoundly evident in the work of the Hebrews, which they will learn from the two other traditions defined above: namely that of the Greeks & the Romans, and the other one introduced by the early Church.

What would the authors of Scripture say were they to judge the drivel which we pass around for **free form**? Would they not probably tell us how well-read they were in the works of the Greeks & the Romans? Why should we allow poets to write **vers libre** and to mistake their insecurity for Milton's "**sense secure**"? "Much skill is required to write well in **traditional forms**," we hear so many poets say between the lines, "but we can always write **vers libre**." Where on earth could the poets have got such an idea?

At **THE ECLECTIC MUSE** we want to take poetry back to rhyme at the same time that we want to take it back to the people, but **free form** shall stay regardless ... it is in our Judgment a highly traditional genre which was the peculiar domain of the Hebrews. Can ***you*** write in **free form** like the authors of Scripture? That is what we mean by **free form** when we are talking of the real thing. Were you an author of Scripture, in other words, we would then have asked to read and publish more of your poems in **free form**. Not being one, we have to insist, much as we would like to help you write well in **free form**, that you show us how well you can handle **"easier techniques"**.

**TEM** shall not tolerate work which displays ignorance of scientific & fundamental metrical laws as well as thematic imprecision. With a little effort, poets at large will generally be able to improve their know-how by looking up in a good encyclopaedia all subjects such as ***PROSODY, RHETORIC, FIGURES OF SPEECH, LITERARY FORMS & RHYTHMS, & POETRY*** in general, & by studying in depth the objective, scientific treatises on these subjects contained in the encyclopaedia. The works of the great critics, while so instructive to students & authors, contain subjective theories about the writing and criticism of poetry: in other words they are not objective & were never meant to be. The encyclopaedia is on the other hand as factual & methodical as human authors could have ever made it, & all poets would reap immense benefit from using the encyclopaedia more often without having to enrol in a creative writing course. My degree in English, for instance, did not make me a poet: it made me a critic! ..... & while my credentials enabled me to give my own writing the critical eye, Joe Ruggier learned much of what he was primarily required to know about the science of writing verse from a small 1-volume encyclopaedia, called **PEARS' CYCLOPAEDIA**, which an uncle Edgar once gave him as a gift. In this pocket, reference handbook there was a fascinating section called ***The Literary Companion*** which was about 26 pp long. Reading these pages over & over again he learnt a lot about poetic craft. He also read other books, & still thinks there is a lot which he still can learn.

Sensitive & perceptive critics of poetry know only too well that any poet worth his salt has a personal affair with his medium, this being largely what thrills us in his work. For reasons such as these we would like to see in the work of the poets we publish the fruits of an intensely personal affair with words. We likewise have to ask all such to show us how well they can use the poetic forms & scansions described in something as dry & factual as the encyclopaedia or poetry handbooks so that our readers can tell that they have not neglected their craft. In writing for **TEM** poets should forget what everyone else has been saying about creating new pseudo-techniques by chopping up their verse to obtain otherwise unobtainable nuances of "***tortured sense***". We find this sort of thing hateful and galling and do not like cadences which creak in such an agony, and with such misery, and in such pain. ***T S Eliot and Ezra Pound have done this sort of thing already and you cannot do it better!*** **TEM** will only publish poets who are willing to work on a far more delicate, far smoother cadence.

At **The ECLECTIC MUSE** we revere **Thomas Stearns Eliot**, whom we regard to have been a first-rate craftsman of language and an exemplary Poet; ***but! we regard Eliot imitation to be as bad as Milton imitation at its worst and most hideous***. We still take the famous lines in **ASH-WEDNESDAY** as our point of departure:

The new years walk, restoring
Through a bright cloud of tears, the years, restoring
With a new verse the ancient rhyme. Redeem
The Time. Redeem
The unread vision in the higher dream
While jewelled unicorns draw by the gilded hearse.

***Briefly, unforgettably, this is our philosophical mandate!*** **.....** as far back as 1972, when I first embarked upon the precarious profession of writing, I had responded to Eliot's prophetic call already. Many other poets have likewise responded to this call in the imperative. It is the work of such poets that I want to see in the pages of my magazine. To all such I badly need to ask the question ... ***What do you know about all the literary forms of all time ever used by Man?*** If you are not at least conversant with a few, nor fully aware of all such, nor allow your knowledge to be reflected in your writing, you then *"lack knowledge of the best that went before"*, and you can hardly aspire to alter the nature of wisdom if you have not assimilated the wisdom of the past.

*30th January 1992 - 14th July 1993*

## The devotion of Catholics to the Sacred Heart of Jesus[88]

JOHN KEATS, the great Romantic poet, wrote in his letters: "I believe in the truth of Imagination and the holiness of the Heart's affections!" His belief became a central theory of the romantic movement in Art and much has been written about it by literary critics. A strong belief that "one uninterrupted blood runs through us all" runs through all the transcendental writings of Ralph Waldo Emerson, one of the most important of North American authors; while the poetry of Walt Whitman, Emerson's greatest associate in the North American transcendentalist movement, points to a powerful belief in a divine Love at the heart of creation through its sex mysticism and transcendental philosophy of merging with the Divine in Nature. Whitman wrote of his own poetry: "This is my body; this is my blood!" In a rather melancholy poem, Thomas Stearns Eliot, the great American poet who settled in Britain at the beginning of the twentieth century, wrote the following lines:

> The nightingales are singing in
> The convent of the Sacred Heart.

The writings of the great poets, in short, and I am speaking of the majority of those whom we do not perceive as Roman Catholic, are extremely eloquent in their testimony to a

---

[88] A talk by myself given at Holy Rosary Cathedral, Vancouver, BC, on 24th June 1998. The factual portion of this paper, which describes the history, the theology, and the practice of this devotion, was condensed entirely from a booklet published by the **Sacred Heart League** of Mississippi, called **The Devotion of Our Time**, copyrighted in 1978 by Sacred Heart League. The booklet is written by Reverend Christopher Farrell, C.SS.R. It seems to me that originality is not called for in a valid description of the substance of this devotion, and that such was not the intention of the author of the said booklet in granting permission joyfully for reprinting portions of his work; but the introduction and the poetry are all my own inventions. (J.R.)

universal belief in the Divine Love at the Heart of the Divine Being, whether He be personified as an all-powerful and immanent eternal Spirit, or in the human person of Jesus Christ. The poetry of William Wordsworth, one of the greatest of the English Romantics, points to such a belief through its highly original construction of a metaphysics of Nature mysticism; and we can easily discern in the work of all such authors the universal influence of the teaching of Scripture: "God is Love!" "Deus Caritas Est!"

The first christians were very close in time to the historical Jesus and some of them remembered the events recorded in the New Testament at first hand. Their spirit was one of passionate interest in the person of Jesus Christ. They were thrilled by His personal love, by the intense charisma of His human personality. They felt the personal sense of loss and sorrow which His apostles felt at the cruel death which Jesus suffered and they were intensely excited by the glorious victory, the personal triumph of Jesus at His Resurrection which proved to them and to all subsequent christians that His claims to Divinity were not a vain boast. The first christians moved in an atmosphere where dreams came true. Their faith was for them a most exciting and most romantic adventure completely unhampered by the sophistication of metaphysics, philosophy, theology, works of art, or a complex and bureaucratic Catholic Church.

As time went by, however, the Church grew and, as it grew, it became more complex, and persecutions, schisms, reformations, and Church Councils began to flourish. Contributing to the growing complexity of christian faith were the great achievements of the christian theologians and artists, the early fathers of the Church, the astounding theology of St Augustine of Hippo in the third Century, the growth of gregorian chant, one of the most priceless gifts of the early Church to us all in the form of one of the most beautiful of musical traditions. Consequently, the simplicity and sheer romanticism of the faith of the first christians began to be obscured by this magnificent growth in sophistication and the inevitable progress and evolution of doctrine. A need was felt to provide a corrective and to reenthrone simplicity in the devotional life of the faithful. Special devotions such as processions in honor of the eucharistic Christ and benediction of the Blessed Sacrament arose. Apparitions of our blessed Mother - Lourdes, Fatima, Guadalupe, to name a few - came on the scene as an obvious attempt on God's part to bring people closer to Jesus through his Mother.

One of the most popular of these devotions centered on the love which is exemplified in the Sacred Heart of Jesus. The catholic devotion to the Sacred Heart of Jesus, in other words, is the product of centuries of christian traditions and devotions. When we speak of devotion to the Sacred Heart we refer to a doctrinal cult by which we worship the person of Jesus Christ considered in his Heart and all that his Heart symbolizes. Every devotional practice approved by the Church is based on a doctrine and devotion to the Sacred Heart is based on the most central of Scriptural teachings: "God is Love" (1 Jn 4:16). This devotion assumes that Jesus is God and that the heart is a symbol of love and honors the person of Jesus through the use of pictures and statues.

In these pictures our Lord's wounded Heart is depicted with a *crown of thorns* around it, rather than around His head, which indicates that his immense love for man was the cause of all His suffering. The *cross* implanted in His heart reminds us of His intense interior suffering which He submitted to even before He was crucified. The *wound* inflicted by the centurion's lance signifies what sin does to Him. The *flames* indicate the intensity of His love for all men. All these symbols point to a direct relationship between devotion to the Sacred Heart of Jesus and the passion of our Lord. Hence, the importance of the stations of the cross, night adoration in church, and the holy hour in the home. One of the characteristic elements of this devotion is reparation and atonement. This is done by receiving communion on the first Fridays, making the holy hour, and above all by striving to love Him more to make up for those who do not love Him.

Everyone wants to love and to be loved in return. It is impossible to read Our Lord's last discourse as recorded by St. John in chapters 14 through 17 and not realize that devotion to the Sacred Heart of Jesus is not based on the words of Jesus. Addressing his Father, He concludes his tête-à-tête with his disciples: "To them I have revealed your name, and I will continue to reveal it so that your love for me may live in them, and I may live in them." (Jn 17:26). The practice of honoring the heart of Jesus is not of recent origin but an outgrowth of devotion to Christ's sacred humanity. Mary, the Mother of God, the apostles, and the great Fathers of the Church revered His most sacred Human Nature. They held in reverence the wounds and, through the centuries, christians have received encouragement and examples from such names as Saints Bonaventure, Albert the Great, Gertrude, Catherine of Siena, Blessed Henry Suso, Saints Peter Canisius and Francis of Sales. In October of 1672, mainly because of the inspirational writings of St John Eudes, the Sacred Heart of Jesus was publicly honored for the first time in a solemn liturgical celebration.

The most prominent place in spreading this devotion, however, belongs to St Margaret Mary Alocoque, a Visitation nun who, between December of 1673 and June of 1675, saw Jesus on various occasions. These revelations form the basis of the famous Promises of Our Lord. He requested that this devotion be further established and that it be distinguished from other forms of christian piety by the special qualities of love and reparation. This devotion, then, did not originate from some private revelation of God and suddenly appear in the Church. It came from the lively faith of men and women "who were drawn toward the adorable Redeemer and his glorious wounds which they saw as irresistible proofs of that unbounded love," as Pius XII wrote in his document on the Sacred Heart. The importance of St Margaret Mary's revelations lies in that Christ wished in this extraordinary way to encourage a devotion which emphasizes God's merciful love for the human race.

Among objections raised to this devotion the following may be enumerated: that it detracts from devotion to the Blessed Sacrament; that it is ill-adapted to the more pressing spiritual needs of the Church and humanity in our times; that it is too sentimental and that it is a devotion for women and children; that it is too passive and overstresses penance and sacrifice and produces no external results. It was precisely because Jesus was not loved in the Eucharist - Mass, Communion, and visits to the Blessed Sacrament were being neglected - that Our Lord demanded the establishment of a devotion to His Heart: "I am giving men an easy means to love me and love me solidly." The Sacred Heart, the Holy Eucharist, and Love are one and the same thing and our acutest problems, personal and social, stem from a lack of love. In this devotion, through which we approach Christ through our senses, the love which we show Christ is an expression of our entire being. People who claim that this devotion is too passive are ignoring the fact that external results are brought about not only by the person who expends his energy on them but also by the plans, prayers and moral support of others.

Of the revelations made to St Margaret Mary there are 12 prominent ones; we call them the Promises of Our Lord. Each one stands on its own merits; and none is to be considered a dogma of faith. It should also be noted that they were made at a definite point in history; hence they must be appraised according to the religious culture of the time. These Promises were made by Our Lord to those who devote themselves to His Sacred Heart and I do not have time, in this presentation, to read them all out to you, and I am sure that you are all familiar with them. However, you may easily lay your hands on them in a good Catholic library. Our Lord told St Margaret Mary that these promises (as well as many others he made) would be fulfilled if those who accepted them truly believed. Thus, the fulfillment of these promises does not depend on a few external practices of devotion, but on lively faith. These promises were made some 350 years ago and all of them are still valid at any point in history. The last one, however, which demands more frequent reception of Holy Communion, and promises the grace of final salvation to those who practice this devotion, is obviously meant to counteract the heresy of Jansenism which was prevalent at that time. (Jansenism taught, among other errors, that God was to be feared rather than loved, and that, out of respect for Him, communion should be received no more than once a year).

Today, many Catholics, perhaps as a result of centuries of first Friday devotions, receive daily and countless others receive at weekly Mass. Friday commemorates Christ's sacrifice on the Cross. Our sacrifice consists in attending Mass and receiving communion on a day we are not obliged to do so. By receiving for nine consecutive months we establish a pattern of perseverance and the presumption is that those who "make the first Fridays" will continue to receive more frequently throughout the year. So, the promise still stands even in our modern religious culture.

We can practice this devotion by a more intense sharing of our everyday life with Jesus such as starting the day off with the morning offering and talking to Him mentally throughout our day. To increase one's personal devotion to the Sacred Heart one should pray more frequently, when alone as much as in community; one can frequent Mass and communion more often; one can pay more frequent visits to the Blessed Sacrament where one can carry more frequent conversations with the best Friend we have ever had; one can practice the holy hour in which one watches for one hour with Jesus, either before the Blessed Sacrament or at home. This personal devotion to the Sacred Heart will gradually rub off on others - family, neighbors, work-colleagues - and the best way to do this is to let our example speak for us. Another practical means of encouraging this devotion is to have a picture or statue of the Sacred Heart enthroned in our home and many Catholics practice the traditional enthronement ceremony in which they consecrate their family to the Sacred Heart of Jesus.[89]

---

[89] It seems appropriate to comment a little about the artistic merit of the traditional pictures and statues of the Sacred Heart of Jesus which are popular among Catholics. One beholds, in these pictures, an artistic, or what many would call a pseudo-artistic, representation of a Man Who seems extremely manly, and Who carries a great secret inside Himself. However, unless one loves Him, these pictures will tell you no stories, and will never yield their secret, and you will say they are bad art. To those who love the Lord, however, these representations are

The enthronement is not an end in itself but a beginning of better christian living and should be kept alive through daily prayer, renewal of the act of consecration, frequent Masses, praying together with one's family and children. Another form of practicing this devotion is the holy hour, both in church and at home. Night adoration of the Blessed Sacrament has been established in many parishes throughout the world. People sign up for a monthly (sometimes weekly) hour of adoration during the night and willingly make this sacrifice in reparation for the sins committed against the eucharistic Heart of Jesus. Finally, many men and women keep on the dashboard of their car a small statue or medal of the Sacred Heart, through which they pledge themselves to drive carefully and prayerfully.

In talking of devotion to the Sacred Heart of Jesus one needs also to mention, in the same breath, the devotion of catholics to the Immaculate Heart of Mary. Our Lord said, in one of His private revelations, "I wish to establish on earth devotion to the Immaculate Heart of My Mother. What is being done to establish this devotion?" Practically in direct response to Our Lord's request in this private revelation, I composed the following prayer, which appears on page 150 of the first edition of **This Eternal Hubbub**, the book I am best known by with my public:

I **OFFER** to God the Eternal Father,
through Thy Immaculate Heart, O Mary,
all my discomfort, all my misery, the pain, the suffering,
the mortification, the humiliation, the work and the heartache,
the frustration, the hurt which I feel deep down in my heart,
all my financial headaches, all the keenest disappointments
which I have ever felt, that they may serve to atone
for my sins, as a reparation for my sins on earth,
so that I may not suffer a harsh purgatory after death,
but may be admitted to Heaven immediately.

---

considerably more consoling and eloquent than much work which is bought as fine art, but would never have been passed off as real art but for deceit.

I offer them also in reparation for the sins of the world,
for the conversion of the world and of poor sinners.[90]

Among other prayers which appear in this section of my poem **The Dark Side of the Deity** called **The Egotistical Sublime, Prayers Composed in Prosaic Moments**, are the following:

### III

M**OST** Sacred Heart of Jesus, grant us Thy Peace,
as You promised us in Your Gospel. Grant me the Peace,
Happiness, and Ecstasy of my Youth, oh Lord,
to guide me, to console me, and to sustain me
through this Life, so full of pain and harsh misery.
O Sacred Heart of Jesus, if it is Thy Will
that I suffer, for the Love of God and for the sake
of the Kingdom of Heaven, for my salvation and for
the salvation of Souls, grant me the Grace that I may
at least be happy. Grant me the peace,
happiness, and ecstasy of my youth; grant us Thy Peace,
O Lord, as You promised in Your Gospel!
Keep Thy Promise with us, Oh Lord, grant us Thy Peace,
and do not deny us Thy Peace any longer!

### IV

L**ORD**, you know what we need and what we do not:
You do your duty, Lord, as you have always done -
You listen to the Prayers of Your Faithful
and give them what they truly need,

---

[90] T**HE** Fable applies to Thee, Lecteur!
Surely thou mayest go to Purgatory until the end of Time,
which is not Hell, not Eternity, not quite for ever,
only a few billion years until the Sun blows out -
(which is the end of Time indeed, a scientifically proven fact,
just a leap and a jump in astronomical parlance) -
and if thou dost not desire such a Destiny for thyself
thou shalt understand why the Author writ this Prayer.

and what they ask You for in humility of heart.

I see evidence of Your Providence all around me, Jesus!
You answer my Prayers in ways
which I would never have been able to predict;
and Evidence of Your Providence
surrounds me everywhere.

Lord, You know how badly I need
To make money constantly,
so that I may honor my obligations,
and pay my debts .....

Help me, O Lord,
To attain the financial aims and goals
which I am required to set myself.
Do not make my day too difficult for me;
Do not let me suffer more than I am required to!

Do not fail me, Jesus;
Jesus, do not disappoint my faith in You!

***In another section of my poem I wrote the following:***

I ... think the time has come
for Thee to take off Thy Mask, and show Thyself
in Thy true Light to all, in all Thy splendor!
Assert Thyself, great Jesus, acclaim Thyself to be
the Artist which Thou art! Free us from the tyranny
of the gross, commercial, uninspired poetaster:
from the deforming insults of pop-culture,
which has deformed us all with the wrong insults -
stimuli which I do not want to feel; the special mercies
of an artist whom I despise as I despise the Borgias;
therapy which has deformed my soul
into a little black hole of bloody pain and nausea
at the unimportance of a man who can only boast

of sexual exploits! What right do artists have, Oh Lord,
to boast of sexual exploits? what right do artists have
to exploit the instincts as if they were Thyself?
All that I wish of Thee, oh Lord,
is a true and serious Honor;
for merit lives from man to man,
and not from Man, oh Lord, to Thee.

*While Part 6 of **The dark side of the Deity** is a celebration of the Eucharistic Love of Christ at the Center of Creation and of human history. It is called **Interlude**:*

**WHEN** Satan hurled, before the Dawn,
defiance at the Lord of History;
and Michael stood, and Glory shone,
whose hand controlled the timeless Mystery?
Who but the Insult was the leveler;
deliverer and bedeviler?

**WHEN** Athens, sung in verse and prose,
caught all the World's imagination;
when Ilion fell, and Rome arose,
and Time went on like pagination:
Who but the Insult was the leveler;
deliverer and bedeviler?

**WHEN** books, in numberless infinities,
cross-fertilize the teeming brain,
and warring, vex the Soul with vanities,
and insults hurtle, insults rain:
Who but the Insult is the leveler;
deliverer and bedeviler?

**AND** when we too shall cease to be,
like all the Kingdoms of the Past,
and groaning, gasping, wrenching free,
we bite, at last, alone, the dust:
Who but the Insult is the leveler;
deliverer and bedeviler?

**WHEN** church-bells fill the wandering fields
with Love and Fear,
the Flesh and Blood of Jesus yields
deliverance dear,
to them who believe in the Compliment Sinsear.

What follows is my **Ode to the Sacred Heart of Jesus**, a poem which, while it celebrates the Sacred Heart of Our Lord, is semi-autobiographical in nature, and is partly a personal confession which I am making to the Lord in a poem, and partly a criticism of our Age. The child in the poem is myself and this section of the poem is autobiographical .....

## Ode to the Sacred Heart of Jesus

1.
**OH SACRED HEART**, Thou heavenly Drink that drowns
acute disturbance; Love-potion breathing power
to tranquillize, and sanctify, and inspire;
Thou milk to pain; Thou drug to paranoia!
peace to vexation Thou! and sweet as dreams
Thou art to those Thy strong, right Hand hath spared
from wrath! Thou climax of a dearest pleasure!
We are Thy fallen sons, oh Thou we try
to reach; only the anger of the guns
hits headlines ..... Thou dost elude our speech!
Ah Lord, my heart is lacerated; my soul
doth ache; my brains are numb with pain; and crown'd
with cruellest thorns, my nerves are cringing songless -
how sore they bleed! what butcher'd, swollen bruises!
and sure I am that I shall go insane
but for this ancient therapy allowed
unto myself, to pray and to pour out
my soul to Thee in sad but sweetest Verse!

**2.**
**I KNOW** a child, sweet Lord, a sensitive plant
that in Thy Garden grew, who read Thy Laws
and tears sprang from deep within his eyes!
This child I know Thy Book ador'd and por'd on
with sweetest inspiration, wild first Love;
and Biblical Art, bedazzling him to rage,
he blaz'd with violent fire to live by such
and craft melodious verse! For years and years
of world without event he toil'd along,
save for the brilliance he could vaunt at school,
save for the ease, the zeal with which he flew
along the paths and counsels of Perfection;
long-suffering years of torment worthless, wherein
a call to charge of souls and Holy Orders
he never could determine! Thy gentle Call
which cost him sweetest lovers, ah! Thou Joker!
and bitter rejection's gall!
**HE SPOKE** one word!
made up his mind and pledg'd his Truth unto
himself and Thee - a priest-like task! one vow!
He had one aim, one business, one desire!
to mount the heights of Art! to fetch Thy Fire,
to carry magic into the lives of others;
and build unageing monuments of Prayer!
No sooner had he vow'd, no sooner pledg'd
his Truth, no sooner said his say unto
Thy artless image, but all Hell broke loose!
but everyone that once upon a time
held him in awe did hold his coat and snigger!
Ah heartless, cruellest power of negative thinking
that nothing but negative foretold! ah demons!
with priests combin'd in secret, and with Hell
alone concern'd, with what facility
you drop your monstrous hints, and with damnation
cut up a soft, impressionable mind!
**AS WHEN**
a little child, fresh to sweet speech and sight
and sound, that rolls enchanted words upon
its tongue, but of a sudden loses all,

speech, sight and sound, flung headlong into Life
deaf, dumb and mute, and darkness buries all
where once was Light, and nothing penetrates
the shell of thought but maims the little snail,
and it becomes a maim'd irrational beast
that cannot respond to Love and Sense at all,
such was that child who once did hear, Lord,
Thy still, small Voice ring clear
within its bodily ear: *"You're going to Hell!"*
Child that he was, he panick'd! he broke down!
He woke one morn unto a waking dream
of joy: once more Thy still, small Voice rang clear
within his bodily ear; and child that he was
thought evil! Oh how foolish to forget:
*Be it done with thee according to thy Faith!*
What power of suggestion hath provok'd
a child unto hard swearing, and his days
hath cast into disasters. Long ago
that child hath crept into his narrow bed,
and sickening pray'd for pardon; mortified,
he beareth still the loss of Chastity;
and all the pains and perils he hath tried
of being without God upon this earth;
without Thee upon this loud, aggressive sphere,
and cast in gloom and blackest desolation!

**3.**
**THAT CHILD** am I, my mind is turning, turning,
and from my inner earth have I cast looks
upon the world out there, where I beheld
a madhouse: everyone's mind was turning, turning!
This age of genocide and global warfare,
where everything's been said and tried and questioned,
but disillusion seals the days; this age,
this nuclear age of space, that sought in vain
eternal youth in drugs and freezers, sought
to re-invent the wheel, and looked to science
for immortality, but does not know
how to cooperate with Nature - least of all
the Christ of Nature, Christ that commandeth storms

to cease upon the shores of Galilee,
where He ate fish from unpolluted waters,
and talked, a Man to Men, and nothing heard
but His own Voice, and voices in the wind,
and the wild Voice of Nature! El Ñiño
scours Mother Earth with mazes of heat and sound:
on any road I walk upon, the ghost
of Matthew Arnold beckons from the tarmac;
and sorrowing I feel two big, black eyes,
from one almighty punch of noise-pollution!

**IN THE** beginning, Lord, thy Plan was simple:
increase and multiply, for thy body's made
for marriage, and marriage is made for children;
cultivate the earth! cooperate with Nature!
But fallen, fallen Man distorted all!
How terrible is the prevalence of Sin
that for so many aeons could inflict
such an ongoing and unholy mess
upon a shock'd, indignant, shuddering planet
that reels from its own scandals like a mouth
that finds it difficult not to react
to its own excrement!

**4.**

**AH! WERE** it not
the sweet, compelling, reassuring Voice
of Saints and Artists, my best friends in the wide,
wide world of time and space; did I not have
the knack to study my own pain like Poets -
I swear I would have buckled beneath my burden!
I swear I would have crack'd and gone insane,
had I not been a Poet! For this good reason,
Thou consummate Jesus, I feel certain
Thou shalt forgive a friend, that thoughtful ever,
his love hath transferr'd early from Thee to creatures,
for Thy sake as much as for his own; and still
find cause to hope - a Hope that springs eternal;
Hope born of new-found Faith in boundless Mercy!
(Thou *dolce Vita*! midnight stroke of '99!

Thou Final Good of fools and intellectuals!)
I think I have good reason to assert —
(three distant beats on some pulse-waltzing drum!) —
humanity's hour for settling down hath come!
humanity is turning twenty-one!

*Easter 1998*

## We adore You, Bread divinest[91]

*A Eucharistic Hymn*

**WE ADORE** You, Bread divinest,
Love's best fruit and Christ's own rite,
        for You the angels sigh and tremble,
        You a man's most precious right.
We adore You, Bread divinest,
Love's best fruit and Christ's own rite.

We adore You, Bread divinest,
Love's best fruit and Christ's own rite,
        of the strong You are the sweetness,
        of the weakest You the light.
We adore You, Bread divinest,
Love's best fruit and Christ's own rite.

We adore You, Bread divinest,
Love's best fruit and Christ's own rite,
        resurrection of the sleeping,
        of the living You the sight.

---

[91] Translation of the original Eucharistic Hymn, "T'Adoriam Ostia Divina", composed in Italian, later translated into Maltese, by Rev. Msgr Karm Psaila, National Poet of Malta, for the International Eucharistic Congress held in Malta in April 1913. The Hymn was set to music by Maestro Caruana, a Maltese composer with an equally impressive musical gift. Dun Karm's and Maestro Caruana's devotional hymns have the effect upon me of evoking eternity drawing closer.

We adore you, Bread divinest,
Love's best fruit and Christ's own rite.

We adore You, Bread divinest,
Love's best fruit and Christ's own rite,
may the world learn how to love You,
King of hearts and chaste delight.
We adore You, Bread divinest,
Love's best fruit and Christ's own rite.

We adore You, Bread divinest,
Love's best fruit and Christ's own rite,
hail, God hidden in Your greatness,
You alone can grip time tight.
We adore You, Bread divinest,
Love's best fruit and Christ's own rite.

*6th January 1999*

## Gift of Faith[92]

*to Dave Norman of the Green Party*

**TALK TO ME** as of old you talked to me,
Divine Beloved: rest upon my heart;
purge it of all unclean unworthiness;
make it a dwelling fit for Divine Love!
Jesus, talk to me! Your silent, sobering Voice
ceas'd long ago to flush my throbbing ears!
Far too many voices thrill tin ears,
far too many idle words have drowned my verse;
and I am left longing for the Music of
a much-lov'd Voice more chaste, more spiritual,
and far more quietly clear! Christ, Lover of Souls,
for ages humans suffer'd what we have
not suffer'd: turning twenty-one, we have
pain-killers, longer life-spans, means of travel,
and aids for greater living comfort; yet
God only knows what we have suffer'd in
this age of paper status, genocide,
and global warfare ... and
for ages men possess'd provisions we
have lost the memory of! Do we recall
the pleasure of a road that's unpolluted
by the blare and noise of car or plane or radio?
or waters clean as those where Aztecs bath'd?
or fish like that which Peter cook'd for Jesus?
Ah, thou miracle planet, Mother Earth,
Satan has turn'd thee to a lunatic
asylum; yet terrible, dreadful were those times
when You had not the civilizing code of Jesus;
for Satan had a free hand then as now!
can anything be more clear? or anything sound
more logical? or anything ring more truthful?
or din its Gospel Truth more lucidly in
my ears than this reality: the World
needs God?! This blighted Earth requires Wisdom

---

[92] A philosophical poem which combines devotional writing with social criticism.

to rule and govern, to transform the pride
of benefits we have discover'd into
a richer blessing unto the end of Time!
The Ancients were not wrong, nor Genius foolish
to seek eternal Wisdom, and the Light
of abiding Truth! For this have I endur'd
poverty and heartless, brutal mockery, anguish,
neurosis and mental pain untold, to give you
this urgent Gospel in contemporary verse,
***carissimo ascoltatore***! Abide
with me, Spirit Whom no one sees, but Who
alone art topmost, Light of Faith and Truth!
There is much to look forward to after death
when you have Faith: Science and Religion
have both agreed we need to die to go
to Heaven! Heaven! ***Il Cielo***! That huge, immense,
vast Universe where everywhere you see
is far away and long ago! There is
a lot to look forward to after death
when you have Faith; and know you can tumble
with your favourite women upon faraway earths
for ever; and for every human ever born
God made a Star ...

*29th August 1998*

## A tale about the origins of the universe

**MUCH** has been said about the Universe;
many theories put forth about its origins,
and of expanding, static, or contracting universes
it has been established
that the Universe is expanding.

Theories have arisen of indefinite expansion,
from an infinitely dense original state,

considered by some to be the origin of Space,
and evolving ever since.

Another describes a pulsating Universe.

Another a steady-state Universe,
which always has been,
and always will be,
changeless as it is now,
with matter being continuously created such,
that as the old galaxies move apart,
the young ones keep the numbers up
at just the right rate to keep the galactic population density constant.

This theory violates the Law
that matter can neither be created nor destroyed,
but on such a small scale
that physicists should not complain.

Recent observations
of an extraabundance of objects farther away
point to a far denser Universe
aeons ago;
which favours the evolutionary theory of the Universe.

New developments postulate
creation and expansion
occurring to different degrees
in different regions
within an infinitely extended space.

I put forth
from my boundless ignorance
a modest theory
that the Universe had a humble beginning
in a family quarrel.

God's Father the Insult,
cantankerous, insensitive old Philosopher,

seeing mud where His Son saw stars,
created primordial Matter,
just as a professor would the dense academic compound;
and, in an effort to control His unruly Sibling,
imprisoned His Son at the very center of universal Plasma
with this taunt of defiance:
"If Thou comest out I shall call Thee Almighty!"

Naturally,
God the Son saw red,
which is another way of saying He saw stars;
but His Divine Mother the Holy Spirit,
a feminine God Who long ago
had initiated Her beloved Son into the Mysteries
behind His Father's back,
infused Her Spirit within Him
and, keeping in mind Her Beauty
and the secret lore She had taught Him,
and feeling Her Presence come all over Him,
God the Son exploded the infinite primordial plasma
just so He could escape to freedom,
as to His infinite joy He watched His dream come true:
insolent Matter slowly began to revolve
in infinite outer Space
becoming clusters of stars.

And so the Universe humbly began,
for Divinities have their differences also,
in a family quarrel amicably resolved.

*2nd September 1998*

## False artists

**WE HEARD** priests and religions are to blame
for all the ills we have sustained. I blame
false artists, thick as lice and billions strong,

that turn the vibes of poor Godot upside down
and inside out: doors to eternal ruin
whose ears are grown too fond of their own folly -
a holocaust of taunts that they invented;
the cruellest whip and scourge of human tongues;
the lines and sentences that those preferred
whom no one needs to touchstones of Taste and Genius,
to Consolations of abiding Wisdom!
Love them, my soul: pray for thy enemies
that they may come to see the Heart of Light;
but honour no one but the very few
whose soul was sweet and tempered, and whose Faith
was seasoned by a deep, long-suffering Love -
not of opinion, the vulgar wind that blows
against thy better judgment! - but Art that rings
like a true penny on the Rock beneath!
Few they were; and very, very scarce it is!

*8th September 1998*

## To whom it may concern

**MY HEART** is hurt by those who with their lips
have said the words, "I love you!" — when their heart
was far away, and when their haughty hips
betray they grudge my presence, soul and art.

I shall not pray to you, my dear, with words
I learnt by heart from churls whose tongues inflict
a hatred worse than whips, but like the birds
shall pray instead defying a churlish edict,

the prayer of love, the prayer of song and cheer,
the prayer of thanks for every cent I earn,
the prayer of silence, where silence means my dear,
the prayer of thought wherein my heart doth burn!

As for the prayer of theological hate,
give them words only and an endless debate!

*12th October 1998*
*Thanksgiving*

## Clutter

**MY MIND** is cluttered by all the snares of Satan,
by silent malice tickling vanity;
women half-dress'd, and all the wiles of Eaton's,
books leading nowhere and inanity!

The pride of publications serves not Culture
for it distracts men's minds from lasting values;
the faithful heart it makes a prey to vultures!
to read real books we have no time to lose!

Give me serenity and clear sight;
give my time back to me to read but what I choose;
give me to feel the real Master's might;
discernment to discard clutter of no use!

Give me the fresh, unclutter'd mind of Homer;
spare me from clutter, in truer land a roamer!

*14th December 1998*

## "Heaven is not worthy the tears of little children"[93]

**TAKE HEAVEN** as it is, a land of wild romance,
where all the gods are toasting by a child attended,
and all the saints are singing songs of perilous chance,
and honest pride and honour are by wild beasts defended!

The heart has mighty reasons and Hell is for the foolish
who never sang like pilgrims to the hidden Life,
and never drank love potions, marrying their pride and
mulish,
and did not cease discussion with the cease of strife!

Take Heaven as it is and not what you might think,
and stop the curtain falling on eternal day!
The gift of youth is sweet in the eternal spring -
despise us not for cheers where the nymphs all play!

Concern yourself with everything, earn the gift of wonder;
mind never the drawbridge falling, nor the dreadful thunder!

*17th December 1998*

## Honours

**LET IT** be said that real honours are
the spice of life. Many a son and daughter
love the lowly; but He Who loves us from afar
would have us care and dote upon an Author!

The man with ordinary needs is with us always:
give him food and give him shelter; teach him care

[93] One of Dostoevsky's most celebrated statements.

for sweetness and light; for honours that are ways
to everywhere unto those who follow dare!

Good honours are what make his small world broaden:
defend them with him; give him better pride
through a higher humility! He should be downtrodden
who walks even haughtier by a great Man's side!

He blasphemes who prays and shoves a great Man's rod
aside: great Spirits are the pride of God!

*20th December 1998*

## My daemon[94]

**MY DAEMON** follows me. I was a child:
his daemon eyes devoured me ever since!
He loves to rule me proudly, goad me wild;
his maddening eyes they rile me, and I wince!

No matter what I do, he is disdain
and negative thought, dogma if I discuss;
ungracious pastor to poetic pain;
dark inhibition in my jail; and boss!

Though he returns but acid, I must say
long years returned me such a yield of art,
and I have learnt such learning through dismay,
that I grow fond; I love to touch his heart!

To our hostilities I see no end;
I tremble! Can I be blam'd to call him friend?

*26th December 1998*

---

[94] the **daemon** who inspires poets.

## Comfort

**WHAT DO** they think of, lined with wealth and pleasure,
who have been called the poorest of the poor?
with no artistic veins, nor saintly treasure?
Shall the downtrodden millions be their door?

Give me the heart of the eternal Tramp
who passes no one by and is not haughty;
the wide, wide world his mirror and his lamp;
nor prays like pharisees, though he be naughty!

I often pray for wealth … a little more
would help resolve the hardship, nor cause harm.
Resolving to turn no one from my door,
I'll see the world, and make the earth my farm.

Yet never shall I forego for comfort mild
the joys of Art in my romantic wild!

*26th December 1998*

## Shall it be sex or art?

**SHALL IT** be Sex or Art? which is more precious?
lines that are relics offered to my dear?
Sex ought to be the climax of all that's gracious;
Art the long shadow of God's own Love and Fear!

A violent storm doth rage within my belly;
my blood boils endlessly; I am not chaste.
The hand of God doth stir the Babe like jelly;
but humans cheapen God to chemical waste.

And what's the Art we know but a disaster!
a horrid taunt flung in the teeth of Order!
sincerity made of paper! saints of plaster!
and not the Fireside where we sort disorder!

I pass a motion ***World Art*** be taken lightly;
***L'Amor*** high-seriously and more uprightly.

*26th December 1998*

## The holy Shroud

**WHAT** vision, and what darkness, and what knowledge
passed across Your weather-beaten face
when the small robin drew the thorn and blood
decorated his vest[95] - I cannot tell!
All Time swam in Your sight, and You beheld
infinite space, and superhuman silences
weighed down upon the unbearable pain. Did you then
count the majority that went to Hell,
despite Your bitter Sacrifice? and did
apocalyptic troubles crush Your brains? and did
the names of those who made You worthy honours
ring in Your spellbound ear, two thousand years
ago upon the Cross, in that last abandon?
Did spirits visit You within the tomb
whence You arose a Superman? or did
You painfully awaken from the dream of life?
and slowly stir? and slowly, very slowly
count Your five wounds and dress them? wiping away
the blood and filth upon the winding sheet
which bore Your stain for generations still

[95] Condensed into a mere line and a half, this charming, romantic image derives from a much longer poem in Maltese, by Rev. G. Delia S.J., "Il-Leġġenda tal-Pittiross", (*The Legend of the Robin*). Delia was a popular and highly reputable poet writing in Maltese.

unborn? Ah! what ridiculous parodies
are screened in cinemas of that most real
supernatural **VOM**[96] that You became Who meant
the very least Word You spoke ...

*3rd January 1999*

## To Dante

**WE HONOURED** people, but they went to Hell
whatever we said, whatever they all said.
Often 'tis folly barest truth to tell,
to speak out loud a limping line and bad.

Dante, your Hell is cosy with the glow
of Love, and softened by poetic beauty!
Classics instead of words will soothe my brow,
and working my salvation is my duty!

Ah Dante, if you could the noise I hear
switch for inspired silence, in that space
where one's alone with a poem one holds dear,
in that most awful loneliness of Grace,

I would then say: "By God I've been new made;
Honour upholds me, and His Light and Shade!"

*12th January 1999*

---

[96] A term which signifies SUPERNATURAL MAN. It is used to very fine effect by Dante in his **Commedia.**

## Our deserted oceans

*to my old Man*

**WHO HATH** not gazed in awe upon the Ocean?
or whose breath heaves not at its boundless motion?
For over eighty centuries sheer romance
hung o'er the Ocean, food, adventure, chance;
and lands beyond the sun held potent magic
of the unknown, a beauty wild and tragic.
We have shortchanged the coast for aerodromes;
the lovely sea for square, blank, inland homes.
One hundred years ago did liners throng
the waves, Marseilles, Bombay, New York, Hong Kong,
a thousand names; a thousand more arose,
Swissair, AirFrance ... jet aircraft by the nose!
Planes used fine fuel then, the tankers now
pollute the Ocean, aircraft the ozone brow.
Earth's bowels are burnt aloud above our head,
and make for global warming: man is mad!
Vessels then consumed a moderate fuel.
Jet aircraft now burn and unload their gruel
in millions of barrels a minute transformed to heat
and sulphurous fumes; and millions think it's neat
to travel in a rush, where travelling once
was restful ease and sober, rare romance!
Old Wordsworth saw it coming, Humanity
at odds with Nature, and he blest the sanity
of those at peace with God and mother Earth.
The seas now lose their spell; we inhale dirt.
Our deserted Oceans need love and care:
use much more but much more wisely, and be fair!
In less than fifty years we short exchang'd
what Heaven harmoniz'd, plann'd and arrang'd,
for speed, the brainchild of two murderous wars
which blitzed old ways of life, and clos'd the doors
upon them, before we could weigh and assess
the dire consequences and the murderous mess!
Dazzled by speed, our joy is slowly sinking:
is it not time we stop, take stock, and thinking
retreat like monks, pray for support and guidance?

weigh all the progress made, the boons of Science?
do nothing more before we see the Light
shine through the plunging, dark, polluted Night?
and soften'd by Wisdom, utilize the proud
discoveries we made and boast aloud,
into a harmony resembling rhyme,
a richer blessing unto the end of Time?

*19th January 1999*

## Story of a self-publisher[97]

**MY SUCCESS** story is humble but inspirational. I have heard of authors who write constantly and make it a point to publish at least one new book a year. I work differently. When I started I was possessed by an overpowering feeling that I had to write, to generate content, to create style and to compose in style, to create writing which exemplified the rules of good writing, and to create a few hundred pages of good poetry: to produce a repertoire. In those days I hardly worried about publishing credits. In a sense, publishing credits hardly ever came my way, and were hardly worth holding my breath about -- they came occasionally, rarely, and I hardly ever managed to publish more than one poem at a time. I still remember publishing my first poem. I felt disillusioned. After such intensity and suspense, I had managed to publish one poem, in a book that most professional critics would have described as Vanity Press, and I felt: "God! what a long way I still have to go!"

It was more important for me not to write in a vacuum. For this reason I considered it more important to correspond with as many contemporaries as I could manage

[97] An autobiographical success story which I hope may serve to inspire aspiring authors.

to write to. Corresponding with practicing authors gave me a feeling that I was not working in a vacuum. I always managed to obtain reasonably honest feedback, feedback from poets who were in the thick of it, who were themselves struggling hard to get published, who empathized and knew precisely what it takes, and some of them were famous ...

When I first chose to become an Author I felt this priority keenly, partly to expose myself to knowledgeable criticism and feedback, and partly because I did not want to work in a vacuum. In the course of my writing career I have been able to maintain an international correspondence. Authors of such divergent personalities as **Margaret Toms** & **Roy Harrison**, contemporaries from the UK who have both made good names for themselves as poets; **Mike Shields**, Editor of ***ORBIS POETRY MAGAZINE***; **Len McCarthy**, editor of ***CANDELABRUM POETRY MAGAZINE***, & **Philip Higson**, a distinguished ***CPM*** contributor; **Lydia Pasternak Slater**, {UK}, sister and translator of the poetry of Boris Pasternak, the renowned Russian novelist & Nobel Prize Laureate; **Rex Hudson**, Nobel & Pulitzer Prize nominee about whose life & poetry my book ***INTELLIGIBLE MYSTERY*** was written; and many other acquaintances, some of them desultory, most of them involved in my magazine- and book-publishing enterprise, have exchanged letters with me at book-length. We did not always see eye to eye and stayed together merely because we shared the precarious profession of writing with all its vicissitudes.

I have managed to stay on top of an extremely demanding correspondence. I have found correspondence a rewarding and satisfying occupation which has earnt me true friends and hard-won respect. These letters comprise private collections into which I have poured all sorts of reflections about life and art. I derive pride from the fact that I have been able to sustain such a wide and discriminating exchange with my contemporaries. As my circle of correspondents grew, so did my successes, so also did my disappointments and blunders, so also did my repertoire. More than this, though I was at times criticized unjustly, I always managed to hold my ground, to make a cogent reply to criticism, though not always a faultless one, and to improve my writing, slowly but steadily, without suffering loss of face or nerve. In the process I managed to create over two hundred pages of poetry which still holds power over my imagination. I likewise managed to create possibly a few thousand letters which are in their own right -- especially since I do not keep a diary or journal -- an invaluable autobiographical record.

I likewise managed to publish my first major book, **INTELLIGIBLE MYSTERY**, which grew out of my correspondence with Minnesota Pulitzer and Nobel Prize nominee Rex Hudson, and which deals with Mr. Hudson's life and poetry. My second book, **OUT OF BLUE NOTHING** -- a cycle of 24 philosophical sonnets -- was partly conceived as a friendly reply to Mr. Hudson's poetry. When I started composing it I had over two hundred pages of existing poetry to my name and my intention in starting from scratch was to compose a work completely streamlined to sell. Having to date sold over 6,000 copies, **OUT OF BLUE NOTHING** has now attained national bestseller status for a Canadian book of poetry.

Professional, well-paid, & satisfying though my first self-publishing adventure was in 1985, **OOBN** - my 36 p. cycle of 24 philosophical sonnets published in the Spring of '85 - is not a book as a book is defined by UNESCO, {viz: a minimum of 49 pages}; nor was it ***properly*** published by a professional house. This is how the book came to be .....

My primary motivation in writing it was to celebrate my wedding in December of '84 & to distribute a privately photocopied booklet to wedding-guests as a souvenir of the wedding. Naturally I desired to pay my wife-to-be a good compliment. After the wedding, & after I had been cut off Income Assistance, {presumably because my wife was perceived as earning enough to support both of us}, my wife made me a gift of an edition of 500 copies of **OOBN**, to be printed by Laser Graphics, following a format which I had designed with the assistance of Mr. Brian McGregor

Foxcroft. Very simply the book was offset-printed, collated, folded & stitched, from a camera-ready copy of my own typing & artwork. This was in the Spring of '85 .....

Once the book was released, having nobody to market the books for me, no source of income whatsoever, & nothing to do save what I was inspired to do, I chose to employ myself & to conduct a market survey on my own & I took to the streets and sold the books door to door. Since '85 I have sold out all 500 copies except, I believe, for a few; and since mid-November '89, I have sold out four more editions of over 1,000 copies each. I am now selling the 6th Edn: a further 1,080 ... I work 2/3 hours per evening, 5/6 days/wk, between 6:00 and 9:00 pm, when I am likely to find people at home. I work methodically. I take care of the job as if it were a salaried position. I can remember working in the snow at very short notice in Autumn '85 ... to drum up a little money to take my wife out on her birthday. On my worst nights in '85, though at the time I only worked desultorily & irregularly, I invariably made $5.00 per hour; on an average to better night, I would make anywhere from $10-$20 per hour. The customer list which I made in '85, which I have retained on file, helped me to sell out ***THE VOICE OF THE MILLIONS*** in '88, & to commission more stock from profit.

Whatever the fortunes of my marriage have been, I still find ***OUT OF BLUE NOTHING*** as truthful now in '99 as it was 14 years ago when I wrote it to celebrate the Day of my Date with my Destiny, the reason being that my book & its message are not so much about Joe & Julie but a little more universal than that. That my poetry sells as indicated has been one of the most joyful discoveries of my life.

***The Voice Of The Millions*** is a 100-page collection of my Selected Poems featuring poetry about many subjects some of which are: music, book-binding, crafts and professions, death, romantic love, nuclear warfare, the supernatural, the assassination attempt on the Pope which occurred in '81, the third World, fairy tales made into poetry for grown-ups, {viz: ***CINDERELLA** and **BEAUTY AND THE BEAST***}, fillers in the form of serious and humorous haikus and tankas, contemporary affairs, dreams and Reality, and various other subjects such as Evolution, Vancouver and British Columbia. In this collection I specialize in fresh lyrical forms, as well as in the free-verse - {as well as rhymed and metrical} - dramatic monologue.

Published by ***PIERPONT PRESS, WISCONSIN, TVOTM*** was released in November of '88. In conjunction with my Publisher the first printing has since then been sold out. The book has now been substantially improved, and while ***PIERPONT PRESS*** have done some marketing, I bought stock from them to sell it door to door in Vancouver. Latest reprints have been retailing for $16 and are now sold out. The 1st, saddle-stitched edition retailed for $12.50.

Using these methods and building upon these practices, I have published 7 major books in North America -- two or three more than that if I were to count publications which were published in Malta prior to my immigration to Canada. Unlike most authors I do not feel the necessity to write and write and to publish one new book a year. Using my methods I have created at least a dozen unpublished manuscripts. When I need to publish a book the only criterion I consider before publishing it is whether it is going to be good business. I then publish the book, revising and reworking it carefully before publication. I then market the book and do not publish another one before I milk the marketing of the first book by selling it thoroughly and scientifically. Using this process I have taken **OUT OF BLUE NOTHING** into a sixth definitive edition where every line is where I want it to be. The most valuable addition I have made to the 6th edition of this book is notes on the meaning of the poetry. My readers are responding to these notes with much warmth. When I need a new book, presumably because my marketing strategy needs a blood infusion, I simply turn to my existing Mss and put a new book together. Thus, I currently spend most of my time in marketing and do not always feel the need for new writing.

Among the writing chores I perform as part of my current job as full-time author/publisher the following may be enumerated:

1. revising, reworking, editing, and rewording old manuscripts to prepare them for publication;
2. staying in control of my voluminous correspondence;
3. coordinating the publication of literary work by other authors;
4. editing my poetry journal in my spare time with the valued assistance of diverse voluntary associates;
5. writing information packages for my publications, my poetry journal, and mailing them in large numbers;
6. staying in control of occasional important correspondence which crops up;
7. negotiating contracts, and the correspondence they involve, for new books that I may be requested to write: I am currently attempting to negotiate a contract for creating a major work of translation from Maltese into English as requested from me by the Professor who holds the Chair of Maltese at the University of Malta;
8. business-letter writing which I have to do all the time in my capacity as sole proprietor of **MULTICULTURAL BOOKS**, my traditionalist press of which I am 100% sole owner;
9. I compose lots of new aphorisms and new poetry which I store on computer.

Apart from these home-based occupations, I have worked as a poetry instructor at Maple Ridge, where I was invited to teach a poetry workshop and paid an honorarium by the Ridge Meadows Arts Council. I have likewise served as Judge in the traditional category of the 1995 Poetry Contest organized by **THE ROBERT RUARK FOUNDATION INC.** in 5 categories: Light verse, Limerick, Free Verse, Traditional, Haiku, a role for which I received an honorarium. Since 1989 I have been the Managing Editor & Sole Owner of **MULTICULTURAL BOOKS,** my own small press which, since 1985, has released & marketed 27 Titles, viz: 14 issues of ***The Eclectic Muse, Out of Blue Nothing, In The Suburbs of Europe, Savitri, A Children's Goat Book, Walking the Dog, If You Wish The Wind To See, Poetry for Children,***

***This Eternal Hubbub, regrets hopes regards & prayers ..., Lady Vancouver, Selected Poems of Roy Harrison, Poems by John Laycock, The Egotistical Sublime.***

I am likewise the Editor & Publisher of **THE ECLECTIC MUSE**. **TEM** is a small magazine which has made 14 appearances between 1989 & 1997. Vol 1, No 1 appeared in Christmas 1989. The latest issue, which is the 14th, is 5:2, July 1997. **TEM** features contemporary poetry from Canada, the United States, Britain & elsewhere; translations into English; as well as very short stories, articles, & reviews of poetry books received by the Editor.

Between 16th November 1989 to date I have been involved in door to door marketing on a scientific and methodical basis. My starting points were ***OUT OF BLUE NOTHING*** **{2ND EDN}** ***& THE VOICE OF THE MILLIONS*** **{2ND EDN}** in Kitsilano Area. Hours of work: 5-9 p.m. The **gross,** 16.11.89 -- 21.01.90, was: **$2,100**. At the time of printing this writeup - 16.06.97 - I have worked in N. Vancouver District & N. Vancouver Seymour; Greater Vancouver --- Kitsilano, Dunbar, Kerrisdale, Shaughnessy, UBC Campus & Point Grey between **Blanca** & **Alma**, Cambie & Oakridge, Commercial Avenue, parts of S. Vancouver & of N. Burnaby; W. Vancouver & Victoria. This is the 9th or 10th time around that I am working these routes. **Net Income**, 16.11.89 - 14.06.97: **roughly $6,000/Year**. The **gross** till 31st December, 1995, was: **$47,002.86**. ***OUT OF BLUE NOTHING*** has also gone into a 6th Edn and has attained national bestseller status for poetry. ***IN THE SUBURBS OF EUROPE*** has gone into a 2nd. I had marketed, door to door, 500 copies of ***OUT OF BLUE NOTHING*** between 1985 and 1986; 250 copies of ***INTELLIGIBLE MYSTERY,*** between 1985 and 1988; & 200 copies of ***THE VOICE OF THE MILLIONS***, between 1988 and 1989. Techniques used were door-to-door sales for ***OOBN*** & ***IM***; Tel sales to old customers & new prospects for ***TVOTM***, which was marketed under contract with my US Publisher. These were all time-limited jobs under the self-employed category. Likewise, I have always been responsible for the professional typing, word-processing, desk-top publishing or otherwise of all my books published in Vancouver or the States between 1985 and 1997. I have always worked hand in hand with my printer to prepare the texts for publication.

One thing I wish to say about Sales is that the socializing it involves, as well as the challenge of a commission base w/high-income potential, are aspects which I positively enjoy. Though I would personally prefer the security of a salaried position, I find my door-to-door marketing strategy an extremely healthy, athletic & pleasant occupation. It is likewise flattering & very meaningful to have so many people read my work. I truly consider persuasive selling to be a basic life-skill, & I can certainly recommend Sales to everyone as an excellent source of supplementary income.

I am fluent in English, Italian, Maltese; some French, and some Spanish. My qualifications include the **Writing and Publishing Certificate,** obtained from the Canadian Center for Studies in Publishing and the Writing and Publishing Program at Simon Fraser University at Harbour Centre, where my tuition and living allowance were paid for by Manpower for one academic year, and from where I graduated in June of 1997. Other credits I have are my diploma as a Word-Processing Operator, paid for by Manpower for 3 months: two timely grants which out of a poet positively turned me into an established publisher - some of the finest gifts which I have ever received. Hats off to Manpower and many thanks! To my name I likewise have an Honours degree in English Literature from the University of Malta, where I was awarded a double-first in 1977. I also hold several Advanced Level certificates obtained in Malta from the University of London; together with many Ordinary Level Oxford University certificates.

As a child & adolescent I idolized all sorts of writers such as Enid Blyton, Jules Verne, Thomas Hardy, Keats, Alexandre Dumas, T S Eliot, Shakespeare, Sir Arthur Conan Doyle, Agatha Christie, & many others, and I had an unusually intense relationship with Authors: something which finds expression in Part 2 of ***OUT OF BLUE NOTHING***. Now that I am an adult I still find Jules Verne and well-done romances relaxing; but I no longer have favourite poets and composers so much as favourite poems & musical works. As far as paintings go I have no book-knowledge whatsoever, but know my mind well. I prefer Art which is well visualized, and tend to stay away from the so-called Abstract or Avant-garde which only serves to emphasize what far too many 20th C Artists, amazingly enough, have been able to get away with through no particular merit of their own but for deceit ... I find Sacred Music, especially Hymns & Gregorian Chant, profoundly moving and therapeutic, the healing power of which I need as badly as I need sleep. I feel contempt for the arrogance of artists who throw traditions overboard in an attempt to alter the nature of Wisdom, something which Eliot never did, never said, & never implied. Other than that, I really enjoy the classical composers, poets and artists, with a predilection for Shakespeare, Dante, and the Baroque, whether it is found in the Art of the brothers Van Eyck, the poetry of Hopkins, the novels of George Eliot's middle period, or even the sonnets of Roy Daniells, a Canadian poet of genius who died in '79. My favourite English novel of all time, let the women note, is George Eliot's ***MIDDLEMARCH***, a book which I can read, and reread a few years later, and still be moved and compelled by its potent magic. Flawed as it is by a disastrous conclusion, ***THE MILL ON THE FLOSS*** comes second. Richard Wagner has likewise composed three of my best loved musical works: ***THE RING OF THE NIBELUNG; THE MASTERSINGERS OF NURENBURG; & PARSIFAL*** - and his endless melody proclaims him an artist of the Infinite ...

Given that at the present time I do not feel a great urge to create major new work destined to be released in book form, I usually prepare to write by jotting down notes in point form, also by making mental notes, which I then mull over indefinitely -- drinking wine or beer in the process -- and slowly, but surely, fill and flesh out, sometimes freewriting them one by one and letting my unconscious do the hardest work, until I eventually achieve the finished product. Some of my best writing was written after a long process of mulling over and putting down on paper in one flash of resulting, eventual inspiration.

I must confess that when I say that I mull over a piece of writing indefinitely and let my subconscious do the hardest work I procrastinate. What tells me that I am ready to write is the pressure of massed ideas at the back of my mind coupled with the pressure of eventual inspiration fusing these ideas together coupled with my intense expectation to get the job done. Thus I write under interior pressure building up over time spent in digesting and assimilating many scraps of inspiration, but procrastination is something I have to be very humble about. I plead guilty.

Usually I bog down when I do not have sufficient mental notes to freewrite and flesh out or else when I do not have that eventual flash of inspiration which puts a piece of work in proper perspective or else when I have rewritten for ages and know that a certain passage needs even subtler, more prolonged reworking and I do not feel up to it because:

1. I need more interior growth;
2. I have been looking at the bloody page for far too long and this makes me feel dull and uninspired and not up to the task of doing a major reworking.

This phenomenon occurred during the preparation of my fifth book, **THIS ETERNAL HUBBUB**, for publication. This was my fifth, and the contents of this book are more or less where I want them to be, but not the Author's Preface, which was written in retrospect. After squeaming and agonizing about the entire book for 15 years, I likewise agonized about the Author's Preface, which was the most recent thing I wrote. Though I have been told by perceptive readers that the Author's Preface is intense and haunting, I know -- because this is what my conscience tells me -- that some parts need reworking, rewording, amplifying, clarifying, etc. -- and having looked at it and the entire book for such a long time, I was not up to the task of doing the job

100% satisfactorily before the book came out. The book, nonetheless, had to come out: I had given out my word to the public, to the National Library, and to my distributor, **JOHN COUTTS LIBRARY SERVICES LTD.**, and I had to start selling. I think that the reason why I bogged down here is easy to understand.

There are moments when a dedicated author has to say, this book has to come out, and only by releasing it can I discover its real shortcomings. I have much to excuse me in thinking so regarding **Hubbub**. I had been at work on the contents for 15 years and my book reflects much interior growth. I could have waited another year but I was having an extremely hard time with the totals on my paycheques. The book had to come out, start selling, obtaining some pointed feedback from readers who were inclined to be constructive, just so that I could start making money at the same time that I could hope to work towards taking the book into a 2nd, revised edition where everything, hopefully, would be worked out to my satisfaction. There are times when an author simply has to put out a book so that he can be privileged to know exactly where he stands with it and only by incurring the expense of putting it out can he ever hope to find out its shortcomings and take the book to where he wants it to be.

What transpired next after this publication was my course in Writing and Publishing studies at SFU Harbor Center. I learnt a lot and thoroughly enjoyed myself. I obtained exposure to scientific methods of generating content which I had not been using, though I had heard of them before. This Manpower subsidized training course was for me a fine gift indeed which helped me achieve professional growth.

I do not think I cover all the stages in the process though I certainly cover all the stages in my current writing process. I merely leave out the stages in the process which I used to compose my early poems, the procedure and writing and content-generating techniques which I used in my apprenticeship as an author. One of my best-loved poems among my readers is **THIS WINDLESS NIGHT**, a poem which deals with my inability to find a fitting subject for a poem -- "I want to write, this Windless Night, / And where shall I begin?" -- and makes a poem precisely about the inability to generate content for a poem. I managed to do this by writing a poem about a windless dark night and using that same windless dark night as a mystical metaphor for the state of my uninspired soul. I leave out these early stages in my writing process, how I began to write poetry and succeeded when I was still an apprentice, because this story is simply intended to be an account of my current success.

What worked in this process is the level of linguistic and original intellectual achievement of my existing corpus of writing. By corresponding with my contemporaries I have created a corpus of work whose contemporaneity and substantiality may not be contested. As I have pointed out before my second book has attained the status of national bestseller for a Canadian book of original poetry, something which I would never have achieved without honest scientific feedback from contemporaries with whom I have corresponded.

Another factor that worked in this process is that I have scored an unimpeachable marketing achievement: single-handed, I have sold over sixteen thousand poetry publications. I hardly think there is another practicing poet in Canada, and possibly elsewhere, who can match my sales volume. Considering I write serious philosophical poetry, this is quite something. Not bad, ugh! Amongst things which don't always work well is the size of my money. I need to earn at least four times what I earn.

All publishers agree that no one can market books as well as the author. My marketing strategies -- going door to door scientifically and methodically selling books to the public -- while keeping me healthy and in good shape, have obtained impressive sales credits, though not always the security of a decent income. Why can't someone give me an award? I keep asking people. I have a national bestseller to my name and I have thoroughly **earnt** that credit.

My process certainly changes according to the task at hand. Letters which have to be written, but which do not have to be marketed, get written differently, and I write good letters. On the other hand, readers who read books which I have written to sell, do affect my process also. Their suggestions are important to me and while I do not and may not be expected to take all their suggestions, I often take note of the truly pointed suggestion, such as the suggestion many readers made me to publish notes on the meaning of the poetry in **OUT OF BLUE NOTHING**, my bestseller. They were right and these definitive notes may be perused in the 6th edition of my sonnets which was published as Part 3 of my fifth book, **THIS ETERNAL HUBBUB**.

To enhance productivity I would simply ask to publish more of my existing manuscripts, to market them until I milk the market, and to keep writing new poetry. I am now also turning to writing for business for the national magazine market. My big issue is that I do not always feel the need to generate new work but certainly require to optimize my business, and to generate a respectable income. That, I suppose, is the bottom-line of any workman's endeavors.

The way I write certainly differs from the way I cook. When I cook I use whatever ingredients are at hand. I love exotic dishes and I use raw materials, that is ingredients stocked inside the cupboard, to create a complex but tasty dish. When I write I want to excel and while my cooking is imaginative and often generates food which I delight in, it likewise generates dishes which are not that tasty and nourishing, though perhaps original. But I cook only when I have to and I am an amateur cook. If I were to cook the way I write I would possibly be sought after by the most expensive restaurants, considering that I want to see none but the most expensive ingredients in my writing, which as such take many hours to mull over. Likewise, I could also starve to death waiting for the meal to be prepared.

What most concerns the readers of this success story is that success like this can be achieved by any truly gifted self-published author working graveyard. The Italians say: "Night is the mother of good counsel!" I have found nothing better than late evenings or the night for obtaining real inspiration after a long afternoon of activity. Prayer and fasting can always be recommended to everyone as a source of inspiration. Going door to door selling books to the public for exercise and some money can also be done in the afternoon as a means, not of becoming rich, but to secure oneself a steak for supper, an inspired evening and inspired dreams. And always your best ideas will come when your head is clear and the air you breathe is fresh and nothing is better than to write something real after you have exercised and earnt money at the same time -- late in the evening and well into the night!

***June 1997***
*4,755 words.*

## Ungracious pastor

**JUST** tell me who the Hell you think you are,
ungracious, testy, pharisaic bitch
who said I have no right to make a rhyme,
and when you spoke the prayer died upon
my lips! Ah! negative, inhibitive Prophet
of gloom and doom who makes a show of just
how chaste you are! Artist whom no one needs
offending God, illuding no one but
yourself as to your state of grace! Author
of true religion that served us in nothing but in
damnation, how well I relish sending
your true religion to a thousand tarnations,
and your bad faith that stinks,
concerning myself only with the one that heals!

*16th February 1999*

## Easter vigil at the Cathedral

**OH GOD**, my God how crocodiles have hurt
my two poor eyes but never made me see!
Oh how my heart was aching, Jesus Christ!
Oh how my mind was hurting, and a word
I could not tell! Good Friday came and went:
the heart-felt hurt alone remains! Ah God,
my God, why has this thing befallen me?
that I have loved You well and there are those
who paid to watch us quarrel? Jesus Christ,
how I wish to run away, to talk to no one,
bring out my heart and mind with no one ever,
to be sincere with no one but with You!
I am but one Poet: Christ! say but the Word —
I did but say the Word to You! Great Jesus,
when wilt Thou talk to me? I said it to
a multitude - they said it not to me!
Oh how my heart was aching, Jesus Christ!
Oh how my mind was hurting, and a word
I could not tell! Good Friday came and went:
the heart-felt hurt alone remains! Great Spirit
Who can enchant me in the depths of Hell
and hold me spellbound with a word: I did
but say the word to Thee! Great Jesus, Mercy!
Say but the Word to me! I said it to
a multitude - they said it not to me!
I never made a claim, great Jesus Christ,
to better inspiration than the one I had,
but the effects were wholesome - ah God, my God,
how ugly were the special mercies that
I obtained as a return! Jesus Christ
say but one Word to me, and never again,
to no one else, unless they tell us a Verse
as right and tight and wholesome! Jesus Christ
come quickly, for my genius fails me, and
the light of day itself is treacherous!
Rain down upon me a gentler saving Grace!
You have heard all my prayers, Jesus Christ,
You have heard all of them, whether they were

bad dreams or brighter, dark or sweet and light,
whether they served my interests or didn't,
and every prayer I have prayed you answered,
and all bad dreams materialize no less!
May I conclude by philosophical
induction You do not have selective hearing?
Let me infer You love me! Jesus Christ
console me, as You did this Easter Night!
Such an impressive, poetic and serene
effect! That powerful, round, resonating,
romantic voice of the Bishop, his shepherd's staff,
his eyes on quiet fire, and his voice
that carried far the tale of a risen God,
around the proud Cathedral, softly lit,
in tones that rose and fell like lovers' breathing!
Two men stood by him saying nothing.
To myself I said: great God, so many artists,
how few are any good, and all I care
about is good effect! I got it here,
tonight, at Holy Rosary, one good dose
of Heaven in a good poetic effect,
what true Religion is all about to me!

*Easter 1999*

## Blessed Faustina

*Joe Ruggier's appreciation*

**MILLIONS** of people in this world of ours are all busy judging one religion only, Catholic Faith. They are all busy judging us, in other words, and everyone's favourite charge is that we invented Catholic Faith in bad faith, in order to keep people under, to hoax them, and to fleece them of money and of power. The correct answer to the charge that God and Heaven are a man-made achievement is: be proud of real achievement! The computer is a great achievement but a man-made Heaven is a far greater one. Eternal youth is far too good an honour to forego. Whenever we try to point out something like that to some people, however, they will tell us "judge us not that you be not judged!" But we are all being judged by bad judges of Catholic Faith a lot of whom are judging all of us in bad faith and I have a right to use my judgment.

I pointed this matter out to a very dear friend of mine, a man that I shall never attempt to persuade to read the catechism because he will never fall for it and I prefer his sincerity to a book's. I was pushing for one gracious admission only and he made it to me: "I do not understand Catholic Faith and I never did!" My reply was as follows: "That is all I want to hear. That you do not understand Catholic Faith does not matter in the least and as long as you admit it like that I shall say that you are in good faith. Do not ever make a mistake like that. Never judge what you do not understand because I will have to charge you. I have no wish to make you Catholic like the Catholics. I wish to teach you the religion of the arts with my own book which I have written about it and about Catholic Faith, **This Eternal Hubbub**. To work out this religion properly you have to learn to judge works of art very well that your career in the arts may be entirely well done. This is one heck of a darn good true religion: it gives you the feeling that you are judging souls as long as you never ever dare try to do something like that. You judge works of art only and fall in love with their beautiful spirit. It shall be done with you according to your good faith and not according to the Artist's. Works of art yes, you may judge, because a mistake can be condoned, you will learn a lot, and it will bring out your judgment, but only as long as you are willing to learn, and only as long as your good will is there to be enriched, refined and ennobled by their beautiful spirit, for real works of art displaying miraculous technique are primarily miraculous in the excellence of their spirit but only as long as your good will is to it to be enriched by them. People you must judge never, because you will make a terrible mistake once only and then you will be told it by the Judge: "you have made a mistake which I can never condone!"

And this is what the religion of the arts is all about in brief, and all the saints and real prophets of all time, and all truly great artists may be described for our purposes as masters of true religion who recognize the boastful Claims of one self-appointed Judge and only one: Jesus Christ."

It is now time to talk about our subject, the life and writings of Blessed Faustina, an obscure twentieth-century Catholic nun from Poland whose writings were declared to be inspired writings and herself declared blessed by her own compatriot, Pope Woytyla. We are going to try to make a good judgment about her own Gospel but her soul is not ours to judge. Blessed Faustina claims in her own book, **Divine Mercy in My Soul**, that she had a tremendously intense personal relationship with Jesus Himself in Person, whose Own words to her she reports in writing on innumerable occasions. The Lord's messages to this mystic visionary were spoken in perfect confidence. Jesus seems to have bound her conscience to complete secrecy and confidentiality and this Woman of God would have considered it an unethical irreverence towards the very Person of her Divine Lover Himself to publish her own writings for her own advancement before the time was right, just for the sake of being published, noted and hitting headlines in the media. So much so that till many years after her own death very few people knew anything about the very existence of these writings.

Blessed Faustina had extremely scanty schooling, no university credentials at all, and when she took her religious vows there were so many worthwhile and beautiful things that she was entirely ignorant of that her fellow sisters in the convent shamed her and would never let her hear the end of it. Her own book she sat down and wrote under inspired dictation with a terrible and real pain of ghastly effort: she was a simple soul whose education fell far short of ours. In spite of the terrible simplicity of her message, however, in spite of the tedious and laborious repetitions, and the flowery and overflowing gushiness of a lot of her words, her insights and theological precision, which the poor Saint never claimed to have obtained from anyone but the Lord Himself, are awesomely authentic and substantial, and the sincerity of a Saint it is a sacrilege to judge or to question. Her message can be summarized in a little nutshell: how terribly painful, how awefully disturbing and how incredibly difficult a thing it is found by so many souls to trust God's Mercy, that a true and lasting faith in the awesome Divine Mercy will gain unimaginable things, and without trust in God's Mercy all is lost and you're a goner, no matter how many Eucharists you may swallow or how many sins you may confess, but a nutshell is a very poor substitute for a good book.

The Lord described Faustina as His Secretary and told her lovingly that He had beheld her before His own visionary Eyes in the Garden of Olives two thousand years ago and that He felt consoled by her own peculiar brand of extremely intimate and personal compassion that she felt for Him. And no doubt she was in her own way a soul gifted with loving powers but precisely in need of such a dignified and transcendental spiritual uplift. Many around her persisted in putting her down unscrupulously, callously and mercilessly, they would never let her hear the end of their accusations and they even accused her that she was of the devil and had made pacts with Satan. They all set themselves up, in short, as her self-appointed eye-openers. They should all have stuck to cork-screws and can openers in the form of sharp metal tools but her two poor eyes they should have left alone.

An extremely reputable priest observed to me that private revelations like Faustina's are not for us. We do not have a need for them and they are largely a waste of time. No, I said, I do not buy that. You appreciate a beautiful honour for what it's worth. There is a certain romantic and mystical beauty to Faustina's writings emanating from the complete privacy and intimacy of her personal relationship with Jesus which extremely few knew anything about till years and years after she died. She would painfully drag herself to her room in silence, and she would find Jesus Himself sitting down at her small table like an old, old friend, ready to give her something to think about, to write about and to pray about. What a beautiful private honour![98] I have made up a really good joke about her book, I concluded. Great Artists and female secretaries - never trust them alone. But do you really want to say something like that to people unless they read the book?

*23rd April 1999*

[98] Faustina's numerous visionary experiences, which she records in her book, would no doubt be considered extremely simple-minded by many people, and many doctors would call them schizophrenic. It is only necessary to have such experiences yourself, however, to realize what a terrible, possessive power these experiences exercise upon the souls of faithful Christians, particularly if they genuinely love Jesus. Simple-minded as Faustina's experiences were, it may be said that these experiences were Our Lord's loving way of educating a simple-minded Saint, and raising her to heights of spiritual perfection that many people can only dream of. The correct answer to the charge that reading work like Faustina's is a waste of time is that reading such writings is meritorious in the eyes of God however tedious and mortifying it may be to many people.

## The dark night of the insult,
## The rule,
## & The reliquary

*a sequence of three mystical poems*
*dedicated to the memory of my favorite Saints:*
*John of the Cross, Teresa of Avila*
*and Therese of Lisieux*

## The dark night of the insult

**SWEET,** dark and cryptic are the thoughts that come
to mind of time I spent within the womb;
blessed the one that seizes troubled sense
of the delicious quiet when life blows over;
and ah! proud as I am to be a man,
I long to be a child again!
Oh when
one leaves behind that magic thrill of Youth,
that miracle of tight, untroubled sleep,
of energy unwearied in the blood,
that not-to-be-repeated thrill, first love,
whether such love be love of verse, or God,
or woman ... he enters upon the dark, cruel night
of the insult, where the laws are laws of the jungle,
and many a friend dissembles, slits your throat,
kills and buries upon that gloomy night,
and no one the wiser!
No matter what the honours are,
that night, that night where he must travel blind,
is deadly and brutal! Not one honour made,
not one gift that he is given, but it cuts
both ways and deeply and each cut is grievous!
Not one light he is afforded but it doth
conceal a troubling mystery! Not one joy
that he rejoices but it stops upon
a choking sorrow! Not one dollar earnt,
but far too many rascals fleece a better,

feeding him venom! Not one work of art
he may create, sublime a gift as art
may be to give to men, but in return
he shall be given acid! Not one Light
shall shine in darkness, not one Joy shall freshen
and heal his butchered mind and heart and spirit,
but he shall be confounded and confused
by fancy lights, and sorely vex'd and taunted;
but those shall come along
who shall inject a piercing, stinging sorrow
and choke him on it! Not one resolution
made in good will, but his good will shall clash
upon ill will as if in mortal combat,
and his own will shall never know what's best!
Not one good suggestion he is made, but far
too many shall make another, though it were
unwanted! Not one counsel given but
that counsel's Machiavellian and it serves
none but the giver! Not one leap and bound
but he shall stumble! Not one fall sustained
but there are those who in their heart shall pray
the prayer of the pharisee against him!
Not one consolation he may receive,
or gladly give away, but he shall become
an argument in the mouth of his enemy!
Not a joke, not a smile, but he shall be plagued and slighted
with a sincerity he doth not need!

"Either we shall listen to the over-wise,
or to the over-foolish, giant gods!"
wrote my good friend John Keats
two hundred years ago! Blessed be God
alone for these afflictions, for He is topmost!
and through that Night alone shall He rain down
His Wisdom! and the dreary, ghastly mind
of adults shall He bless with splendid Judgment!
Blessed be He for that refining fire,
which we shall call a Purgatory on earth,
which turns the dreary dust of adult Man

to something rich and strange beyond belief
and wildest dreams!
His gift to me - an interesting mind,
which Kingdoms is the World may never take;
and master works of Art whose complexity
is far more eloquent than men's sincerity!

This is my prize, for He has done me proud:
I ask you, reader, much as your interest
is far more precious than the paper words
are printed on, that you beware, on pain
of deadly enmity, of sacrilege against
my innermost person, for this Book, I say,
is worthless paper, and your love, your pleasure
are far more precious, but each work of art
I give you is inscribed deep in my Heart;
enjoy, but butcher not, nor crush my dreams!

*21st January 1999*

## The rule

**TO BE** remembered live thy own divines.

An Artist is a Law unto himself,
yet he may not propose unto himself
a Law which is unlawful, nor shall he
allow himself to be conformed like herds
unto an arbitrary Rule: he shall be
a Man conformed to US; and he shall snub
himself with his own insults!
He shall pray and fast
for inspiration: surer methods are not known
for such! Yet should he be an unbeliever,
let him look into his heart, and write: the God
that he professeth not regards his heart
alone - just as the critic beholds a Housman's;
or Dante Virgil's! Let him, if need be,

stay up all night to watch and pray like Jesus,
and to create his Art away from day,
and let him sleep late so long as he remembers
that he must work to eat: his task shall be
to fashion Art out of his mind and heart,
and to create his market, that he may not
leave anyone else in a financial lurch
for marketing his book! He shall therefore learn
that basic life-skill, selling, the product being
his works of Art: let him spend time on this!

He shall remember that by the fruit we know
the tree; he shall place his work and time
to serve humanity; he shall not praise the Lord
with an insult to whosoever he
may choose, or I shall give him sixpence ... He shall
use Honour to honour God, and to honour a Man,
just as Beethoven honoured God and Schiller,
or Milton honoured God and his first parents,
or Wordsworth the God of Nature and those at peace
with Nature! Let him likewise defend the Honour
of his immediate kin!
Let organized
Religion be held in deep respect by Artists:
it is a valid source of sound instruction
for many an ignorant man; yet 'tis far better
to lead a wholesome Life in wild Persuasions,
than be a wicked Catholic. More precepts do not
arise within my mind, and these are meant
religiously, a rough and ready Rule
by which well-meaning Artists should abide:
may Heaven grant me strength and fortitude
To live my own precepts.

*16th February 1999*

## The reliquary

**A POEM** is made of flesh. You have no right
to hack a poem. You hack a heart of flesh,
you draw the precious blood: a sacrilege
that fouls a man's privilege from birth,
his unique, innermost Person. The Saint will cast
a shred of cloth or bone in metal for you;
the Poet lays bare his soul. Which is more precious?
The Relic that has no value in your sight
or God's without a prayer? Or that where words
are felt experience? and every verse a bite
of flesh upon your lips? I would, if I
were you, pour out unceasing prayer, as if
the Universe depended on it. Be proud
of your computer, but much prouder be
of man-made Heavens: eternal youth and passion
are honours too sweet to lose. Yet what of this
legacy of verse a Poet leaves you? Beware
of sacrilege against his innermost Person:
a foul that only fools admire! Saints
are Saints: they are not fools, they care; but if
you care to read me, do not disturb my atoms!
Judging of poems you judge of souls: beware!
Are you unworthy? Fear and go to school!
A Poet feels an intimate delight
in distant readers: wild though he may be,
he cares about you! Invoke his name and Spirit,
and he is with you always! He longs to meet you
in a closed, intimate space where no one else
will ever intrude or hear! Farewell, my reader!
no friendship's deeper
than that between true authors and good readers;
but once you buy, display a deeper care
for the Poet's equally authentic Sanctuary -
you treasure a heart of flesh!

*19th February 1999*

# Part six:
# Songs of gentlest reflection

# Songs of Gentlest Reflection

a prose & poetry collection by

**Joe M. Ruggier**

with a critical introduction by

**Ron Johnson Ph.D.**

**FOURTH ENLARGED EDITION**

(reissued as Part 6 of this edition of my Collected Poems)

(includes two critical reviews)

brought out by

**MULTICULTURAL BOOKS**

*"There are many Mansions in Parnassus!"*

Unit 114 – 6051 Azure Road, Richmond, BC, Canada, V7C 2P6

**Songs of Gentlest Reflection, by Joe Ruggier**


**Published by: MBOOKS OF BC**
Unit 114 – 6051 Azure Road, Richmond, BC, Canada, V7C 2P6
Tel: +(604) 600-8819 E-Mail: jrmbooks@hotmail.com

**Printing History:**
Multicultural Books Poetry Series #10
1st Edn May 2003
2nd Electronic Edn Summer 2003 — **ISBN: 0-9733301-0-4**
3rd Enlarged Edn (includes two additional critical reviews) —
Spring 2004 — **ISBN: 0-9733301-1-2**
4th print edition, produced as Part 6 of the 1st, 2nd & 3rd editions of Joe Ruggier's Collected Poems, June 2009 — June 2018
**ISBN for the current edition : 978-1-897303-26-9**

Critical Introduction: Ron Johnson, Ph.D.
Desk-Top publishing: Joe M. Ruggier

1st & 3rd editions printed & bound by: **Laser Graphics Ltd.**
2nd electronic edition produced by:
**Progress Media Duplication, Richmond, B.C.**
this edition printed and bound by: **Lightning Source Inc.; USA**

**Over 775 copies in circulation**

## dedication

to honour God
and to honour a Man

**IN THE** Beginning there was only one Man, and Nothing belonged to him except his Word of Honour ... and if you take from a Man his Word of Honour, what sort of a Man is He?! We see that one Man's Word of Honour unfolding, over Time and over Space, and over thousands of Years, in Sacred Scriptures, Books, Texts and many Religions, in works of Art, as well as in Historical events, and public as much as private Revelations .... and so it is that, whether Creation happened according to the modern Astronomer, or whether it happened according to the Bible, it happened according to that one Man's Word of Honour .... that One Man was God ...

## Songs of Gentlest Reflection

by Joe M. Ruggier

a critical introduction
by Ron Johnson Ph.D.

**WHEN WORDSWORTH** published his first "Preface" to *Lyrical Ballads* in 1800, he stated that he wished to ascertain "how far, by fitting to metrical arrangement a selection of the real language of men in a state of vivid sensation, that sort of pleasure and that quantity of pleasure may be imparted, which a poet may rationally endeavor to impart." Wordsworth hoped that his use of everyday language, a new concept in poetry, would give readers as much poetic pleasure as did the traditional poetic language in use up till then. As we know, his 'experiments' were so successful that they ended the use of formal poetic diction forever. This move to transcend the restrictions of traditions can be found in other art forms as well, such as in the work of the Impressionist painters, and in the structures made by such architects as Frank Lloyd Wright and LeCorbussier. Artists found that reliance on the forms of the past was stultifying and debilitated their work. Today, in poetry, we consider innovation in expression to be as important as insight or intelligence.

**AND** with good reason. If all that artists had to say could be said equally well in an essay or a sermon, there would be no need or place for them. A real artist is one who has a vision of a reality so complex and multifaceted that, in order to express it, he or she must go beyond the conventional methods of communication. Thus, we get a sonnet with too many syllables in the twelfth line; a painting in which the wash fails to conceal the undercoat; a novel that uses an inordinate amount of obscene language. Rather than being missteps, or errors, these are clues to subtler understandings of character and philosophy than can be reached through words and pictures alone. The poet must rely on ambiguity, contradiction, grammatical misdirection, and puns, as well as the more easily understood devices such as image, metaphor, and symbol. In this respect, we have to accept everything the poet writes as being an indispensable part of the poem. Each word, each mark of punctuation or lack of it, every rhythmical or arhythmical line is there for a purpose. We have to read beyond the signification of the words before we can start to grasp the poet's vision. Often, as with courtship, the more difficult the task, the more valuable the prize. And just like courtship, a poem captures us with a promise of beauty, tests us intellectually and emotionally, and rewards those of us who stay the course with enlightenment.

**THE POETRY** of Joe Ruggier does just that, but he makes his readers work for their reward. When we first read him, we are struck by several features of the poetry that seem strange to our modern tastes. The rhythms are not always smooth to the voice of the mind; the diction seems to vary between the sixteenth and the modern century; and the focus on Christian concerns seems to our modern perspective to be too pervasive. But all these characteristics of expression work together, presenting us with a unique poetic mentality, one that is capable of giving surprising insights into the nature of poetry and the imagination.

THE TITLE *Songs of Gentlest Reflection* tells us that the poems will examine his private world, a world of personal experiences and feelings, and beliefs about poets and poetry. In the opening poem, addressed to Saint Teresa, we discover a mind warring with the conditions of its world, yet finding comfort in faith. The poet says,

> ...Ah! Saint Teresa, in spite of all
> the falls sustained, in spite of all the graces
> lost and gone, like the black stars around the Virgin,
> spirit-stirring is the thought of Homeland!

His hope is based upon his belief in the sacredness of poetry:

> ...and Heaven is the Land
> of Song! Never shall I doubt my heart again;

truths of Imagination are Truth indeed!

Comforted by Saint Teresa's prayer and by his view of the imagination's truth, the poet is convinced that poetry is a significant part of God's reality. Lighthearted playful images such as "God's tobacco, which causes neither heart / attacks nor cancer!" and "The ways of God are not polluted, / neither by noise, nor smog, nor chemical fog, / nor traffic!" are often juxtaposed with a startlingly beautiful consequence, as in this example:

...Think what it shall be like
for authors to work upon the word-processor
that God shall give them, and to have their work
recited by the Wind!

Although they sound strange to our ear, directing our attention to the images of the modern world illuminates the different perspectives through which we view life.

**THE JOY** underlying "Saint Teresa" is quickly dispelled when we reach the bitterly ironic "Lucifer". In this poem we find an ambiguity that appears intermittently from here to the end of the collection; it also brings to the foreground the conflict between the poet, the conditions of his life, and the attitudes of people surrounding him. "Lucifer" is a morality play dialogue between God and Lucifer in which Lucifer demonstrates more compassion than God. It contains several unusual details, such as the fact that Lucifer had a mother and that he can feel compassion for a mortal. The exaggeration in the poem is that there is a man in a worse state even than the Fallen Angel, and Lucifer feels pity for him:

My dreaded Heart of Hatred
feels one little, tiniest pang
of pity, compassion, and remorse
for one Man only:
He Whom the human species crushed completely;
He upon Whom a mortal tyrant
inflicted punishment worse

than God upon a Demon!

It is tempting to believe that the "one Man" is Christ, particularly since the references to him are capitalized. But the unusual features of Lucifer having a mother who punished him, and a youthhood ("my heart of green debris", although 'green' could refer to envy as well as youth) suggest several interesting identity transferences. Lucifer may be the poet himself, with all the attendant misery, yet still pitying Christ's death. Or, the poet may be the Man, so miserably punished that even Lucifer pities him. This ambiguity of identity occurs in several other poems, such as "To My Friend", and "You are Jesus", so that we must consider the ramifications of this particular device.

**IN THE** poem "To My Friend", darker elements of the poet's complaint hinted at in the first several poems are set out more specifically:

Oh Friend, I am ill, wronged and lonely;
the hole wherein I lay my head
is lonely, and your Presence distant ...
Discharge me, distant Friend, from all charges
against my honour:...
Judge me not, distant Friend, nor taunt me,
nor ever be my Judge:...
Liberate me from the cruel judge who judged
and judged and did me wrong and pillaged me!

In a brilliant series of imperative verbs, the poet tells the Friend what to do to make him feel better:

Take my heart, nameless Friend, in your two hands
and hold it tight:
unfold it, stretch it in the sweet luxury of the Spirit,
uncrease it, relieve it of the cramps
of a thousand, countless wrongs,
and heal it of the cuts from expert demon-butchers.

The ambiguousness of the Friend -- is he Jesus? God? -- increases the intensity of the appeal in that *anyone* can be the Friend, just as anyone whom the world has wronged can be identified as the Son of Man (who has nowhere to lay His head).

**THE LAMENT,** or complaint theme, is reiterated in other poems, most notably in "You Are Jesus". In the most direct statement of his imaginative connection with Jesus, the poet asks, "Is it in me presumption, Friend, / to compare my hurt to Thine?" Jesus, the personal friend, is complimented, scolded, appealed to, and finally asked to be the one to save the poet's honour: "Leave nothing upon my death-bed / but a red, red rose, ..."

**IN "EUCHARIST"**, Ruggier explores the philosophical basis for poetry. As do many of the poems, "Eucharist" ends with a prayer:

> ... receive my prayer
> ... that unto him or her I love,
> beneath the exquisite Fake and Curb of Art,
> my Work may carry likewise healing touches
> of saving Power and restoring Grace ....

It is an apparently simple request, but it brings together Ruggier's thoughts on the source and efficacy of poetry. Like the Eucharist, he says, poetry is a "fake" whose outward appearance conceals and represents an inner reality. The rhetorical connection between the Eucharist and poetry is made at the start of each of the first two verse paragraphs in which the verbal repetition cannot be missed:

> When readers honour verse they honour but
> sincerity made of paper, printed matter
> which neither stirs, nor breathes, nor is not made
> of flesh or blood ...

and

> When lovers of Christ receive the Bread, the Wine,
> they honour but a crumb, a drop of wine,
> which neither stirs, nor breathes, nor is not made
> of flesh or blood ...

The honour given to poetry, he says, "Impowers the experience / of Beauty, Truth, and Goodness, Peace of Stasis, / Aesthetic Beauty, and Sincerity." Likewise, "the Honour made / unto that exquisite Fake , by mutual pact / between the Lord and him or her He loves / whose Heart doth understand, impowers likewise, ... / the sweet, cathartic, restorative experience / of saving Grace ..." The key connection between art and the Eucharist is that they are both ceremonies accepted as representing a truth from an unseen source. Our acceptance is the act of honouring, which then "impowers" the experience.

**ONE TRICK** of syntax Ruggier uses works especially well. In the line "Gentle Jesus, loved not wisely but too well,..." it could be construed to read either "Gentle Jesus who loved..." or "Gentle Jesus who was loved ..." The grammatical weight leans towards the latter reading, but when both readings are thought through, both add considerable depth to the idea being examined. Jesus and the poet become paralleled through the ambiguity of the line, which in turn further underscores the essential connection between poetry and the Eucharist..

**AFTER** having developed the idea that both religious ceremony and poetry are imperfect physical realizations of imaginative truth, it would seem logical that the poet would include in it his ideas about children's make-believe worlds as well. Perhaps taking his cue from Wordsworth, Ruggier explores the child's situation. "Terrible indeed / it is to laugh at little children and hold them up / to ridicule against their better judgment," he says in "A Song of Gentlest Reflection". "Kneel down and ask a child to teach you judgment; / pray to the little ones for vision; / ... / ... Be a staunch believer / in the profound equality between great Artists / and little children: ... " The abstract qualities that we believe in, such as love and sincerity, can be found in their pure state in the child's world.

**THE MUCH** more poignant poems about children, however, are concerned with his daughter, Sarah Therese. Beginning with "Child, the Gentlest Loving Faults" and continuing with "To a Child" and "Lady Aphrodite Sweetest Daughter", we trace the feelings of a father towards an adored daughter who has been cruelly taken away from him. At first, the poet gives her words of advice and wisdom by which she may live her life: "Ah little child unfallen, go not astray: / ... Smell the flower of your own unpolluted conscience / before you consult deceitful priests or bibles!" But then, in a poem that becomes chilled with angst and pathos, "Lady Aphrodite Sweetest Daughter", the words are frightening: "Child, you were taken out of your father's arms / with a crushing, chillingly vindictive / unspeakable cruelty! Daughter ... / give me nothing but your hand, nothing do I crave / but your eternal Love!"

**IT WAS** perhaps while in this mood that the poet wrote "Virginia Woolfe", a brilliant examination of artistic impulse and suicide. Certainly, the keeper of the light-house had become an intimate part of Ruggier's life.

**IN AN** earlier paragraph, we looked at the subtle concepts of "fake" and "honour". As we came to understand them, we became sensitized to the connections radiating between essence and form. In the poem "Mary", we are given a third interesting concept: witch. The poem begins praising Mary by restating her history:

> Woman
> Whom God the Messiah, from pre-existence, chose
> between the lines, out of a beautiful book,
> for His most intimate friend in Time, and made
> You Alone His Mother, high divine Priestess
> of Messianic Culture ... did You likewise, Mary,
> choose Your own Son out of a beautiful book?

But we quickly see that the poem is meant not to praise, but to validate her. "Those there be ... who do not honour You because You are / not God,". The validation consists of love: "many a Poet loved You, / and many an Artist, and many a wise, old Sage, / and many a Man adores You, Mary ... / ... / Gods of the new Religion salute You, Mary, / divine, blessed Mother, Woman-God, / divinest Witch in Christendom ..." "Witch", when applied to Mary, invokes and imbues her with all the natural powers and magical influences of the earth. By connecting Mary with the earth, he is saying that Mary-earth is the source of life; God-heaven is the ruler of that life. Earth brings forth life; God rules. But when he mentions his daughter in the final three lines, we once again are forced to see the figures of Catholic theology as a kind of code for the family.

**THIS CODE** seems to be reinforced in "Divinest Mary". The poet parallels Mary and Elizabeth in the first verse paragraph, and then speaks to the Virgin as though she were a tangible woman in the second. God, in the third paragraph, is a judging God of whom the poet wants no part. In that the concept of the Virgin Mary does contain within it all aspects of woman -- child, lover, and mother -- the poem becomes a beautiful appeal for love. The final four lines are a remarkable tribute to the memory of young love.

**IN SOME** senses, the poems in this collection are rather like a dark mirror. As we look into them, we can make out the face of the poet peering back. At times, perhaps, we see something of ourselves there. But always, stretching beyond the poet's visage are large vistas of intellectual landscape. It is this combination of qualities -- the sensitive, troubled heart and the inventive, inquiring mind -- that makes us return so often to Ruggier's poetry.


Professor Emeritus of English Literature
University of BC — August 2000

## Acknowledgments

THANKS ARE offered to Professors Warren Stevenson and Ross Labrie, of UBC, for useful suggestions they have contributed towards the improvement of these verses. A few of these poems — namely: **A Poem for Saint Teresa**, **To My Friend**, **Helen or the Three World Wars**, **The Skiff**, **Denial or the Arts**, **Mary,** & also, after the 1st Edn was released last Summer, the poem **Eucharist** — have appeared in **The Neovictorian/Cochlea**, a traditionalist journal edited with much expertise by my esteemed associate & ally Dr. Esther B. Cameron of Madison, WI. In many ways warm, courteous acknowledgments are owing to her. My poem **Mary** also made a reappearance in the *Divinity* issue (June 2003) of **Romantics Quarterly** — likewise a traditionalist journal edited by Marilyn Rae & Skadi Macc Beorh & based in Florida. Once more warm thanks are due to Marilyn Rae as much as to Michael R. Burch for allowing me to use, in this enlarged re-issue, their two, independent, fine & sensitive reviews of this book which were published in 2003. Gratitude is owing also to my two patrons, the Rev. James Comey, (of Richmond), and Mr. Tony Dyakowski, (of Vancouver), for their timely financial assistance with all of the expenses involved in reissuing this book. Special thanks to Ron Johnson Ph.D., retired UBC Professor, for creating such a fine, perceptive and sensitive critical foreword to this collection. Thank you, Ron, for your kind and gracious introduction, but above all for your precious, joyful interest in my work and for your positive thinking ...

## Songs of Gentlest Reflection

*by Joe Ruggier*

## A poem for Saint Teresa

**L**et nothing disturb you;
nothing frighten you.
**A**ll things are passing.
**G**od never changes.
**P**atience obtains all things.
**N**othing is wanting to him
who possesses **G**od.
**G**od Alone suffices.

*St. Teresa's Bookmark*[99]

**AH! SAINT** Teresa, I am struck with wonder
what a beautiful Woman you are, and how well
intelligence becomes you! I read your prayer,
Saint Teresa, and to myself I said,
my dear Saint Teresa was saying it
to me! Divine assistance cuts and burns,
I said unto myself, but never fails:
my soul took courage from the thought, and to
myself I said - though I have naught but books,
and though I seem to have lost all, the Lord
still is my portion; God, Alone, suffices,
and His Help goes very far and counts for much,
though He is much reviled, unsought, and worked

[99] On the evening before I sat down composing this poem, I asked Julia, my wife, to give me a holy picture, which I saw in her hands, of the Saint in caption, having all my life been fond of Saint Teresa. I turned the picture over and saw nothing printed on the back. I went home. While undressing, my sixth sense nudged me to try turning the picture over again, and I saw the words of this beautiful quote printed on the back. I do not believe that my eyes would have played such a trick upon me and could only conclude that the Saint herself had pleasant, playful intentions. In any case, this incident, which led directly to the composition of these verses, filled me with such joy and real pleasure, and with such a deep sense of Divine Presence, that this quotation is one of my favourite quotes till this very day, and I immediately sat down and composed this deeply joyful poem .....

against! Teresa's gentle reassurance
my soul inspired with a gentle touch
of ethereal grace divine that rous'd my heart
of hearts like living waters. Loving thought
and recollection came to mind. If truth
it is that brains have feelings, mine did feel
a gentle, cool, refreshing touch of Grace
and healing, as of a wound that hath begun
to close. Ah! Saint Teresa, in spite of all
the falls sustained, in spite of all the graces
lost and gone, like the black stars around the Virgin,
spirit-stirring is the thought of Homeland!
Sweet is the thought of sweet Success and Rest,
in the House that God shall give me, surrounded by
God's handsome Women, whose intelligence
becomes them more than mortal beauty, and
whose beauty is immortal! Sweet is the thought
of God's tobacco, which causes neither heart-
attacks nor cancer! Nor doth God's medicine fail!
Nor doth God's music ever cloy, anymore
than music of the spheres did ever cloy
the Ancients, though they had no symphonies,
nor instruments, nor orchestras! God's poetry
works like magic; His art has healing power
beyond ours! The Ways of God are not polluted,
neither by noise, nor smog, nor chemical fog,
nor traffic! His means of transport carry first
the Spirit to better Worlds by far where Peace
abides and reigns; where Peace comes dropping slow,
as if to seal the bitter, bitter Wound
with flesh and blood! Think what it shall be like
for authors to work upon the word-processor
that God shall give them, and to have their work
recited by the Wind! Though the round Earth's
foundations falter, God's rewards shall never:
His Bank shall never fail nor cause inflation,
and it is backed by gold indeed! Drink to me
with thine eyes, Teresa: God's wines are fresh,
and subtly subtle; and Heaven is the Land
of Song! Never shall I doubt my heart again;

Truths of Imagination are Truth indeed!
Ah, God! my God! and dear Saint Teresa!
Watch over me, sustain and guide me! raise
me up from dust! and purify, and cleanse,
and heal me! Make good your promises! Deliver
and rescue me from evil! As I said
unto myself at the beginning: Divine
assistance cuts and burns but never fails!
The Lord my Portion is! and Hope in Him
is Hope indeed! securer than the Rocks
beneath! and Faith in God is Self-Reliance!
and Faith and Hope are never wishful thinking ...

*22nd August 1999*

## A song of gentlest reflection

**SWEET** music is not noise
but the sound and real extension of silence -
but silence may be sweeter;
and when I am dreaming let everyone step
more softly.

Whatever sublimities may be expressed,
**L'Amour** is sweeter and all sublimer,
and where Love is there are no sins:
it is not Love
which alters when it alteration finds.

Honours and people are all deceitful,
but acrimony, sanctimoniousness and despite
are of the devil
and good honour is better and far sweeter.

The eyes of little children, my beloved,
see things beyond our ken: say but half the word -

a little child will understand incredible matters
that you can't; doctors of the Church in infancy,
and better than all the visiting professors
from overseas that you or I invented.

A little child's conscience, my beloved,
is straighter than God's Gospel. Terrible indeed
it is to laugh at little children and hold them up
to ridicule against their better judgment.
Only one sin does the poor child commit,
the one with which the taunting adult
belies the children's vision,
their unpolluted conscience and their finer judgment.

Kneel down and ask a child to teach you judgment;
pray to the little ones for vision;
to dream a sweeter dream ask the children
to teach you let's pretend and make believe;
if you are sick of lies, where nothing but lies abound,
beseech the little ones to tell you a beautiful lie,
and never believe anyone else's.

Be a staunch believer
in the profound equality between great Artists
and little children: the little beastie makes
the adult swear and shed many a useless tear,
and understands love only and much sincerity;
and shall likewise understand great, private honour
when you adore it, give it one and teach it one.

*6th October 1999*

## Child, the gentlest loving faults ...

*to a sweet thirteen*

**THE GENTLEST** loving faults are sweetest when
you send your conscience flying. Where Love is
there are no sins. Do thou but heed my thinking,

my fair little one: let no one judge thy conscience;
let no one rile thy funny bone. Despite
is of the devil; priest's acrimony a far
more wicked sin than gentlest loving fault.
Punish it with the sign of Cain. But so that
you may say I am a good philosopher,
loving though it may be, that gentlest fault,
Acrimony a far worse sin than Cause,
on Earth abstain as best you can: it's better
for Wisdom's sake; and solitude is sweeter.
Think no ill, my child, and let thy conscience be,
and come what may - be thou an altruist,
for where Love is there are no tomes nor sins:
but gentlest loving faults are far sincerer
than all the Earth's when they involve neither
another nor children born nor those unborn,
but gentlest you, and thy sweet self alone!
Child, Wisdom is far sweeter than crass error,
but if you err, that error's slighter far
you err in solitude than with someone else
combined, and other lives involved: stuff Judgment!
stuff acrimony, sanctimoniousness and despite!
stuff conscience! stuff the priest-like Cain and all!
Let none disfigure little children's love,
nor children's error, nor mangle a romance:
let no one judge you, child, nor rile your conscience
with a priest's foul interest in sin alone,
or a neurotic saint's last night's hangover!
Child, cherish Divine above romantic Love
as being more romantic still. Fight for
His trust with Divinity's good secrets as being
far sweeter secrets still than the foul Earth's
indecent entertainment flung to all ears.

*9th October 1999*

## Lucifer

**THE LORD** said to Lucifer:
"This is a day of reckoning!
Lucifer, say, and mince it not, nor tell a lie,
how many souls are lost?"

And Lucifer replied:
"Devil though I am I know that Thou art God,
nor am I quickly fooled! Behold my Heart
of green debris and crooked, wrinkled Hatred,
and this the Sword my mother stabbed me with!
No one, no one, not one among the souls
that I have lost could ever draw it out,
and their lament is cries countless,
and I am proud, Lucifer is proud, most proud of it,
for Lucifer, Lucifer the Master Demon, Lucifer saw
how in Thy splendor, God,
Thou didst not crush him all completely!
My dreaded Heart of Hatred
feels one little, tiniest pang
of pity, compassion, and remorse
for one Man only:
He Whom the human species crushed completely;
He upon Whom a mortal tyrant
inflicted punishment worse
than God upon a Demon!"

"Lucifer, Lucifer!" replied Almighty God:
Ah, Lucifer, chosen though you were
to punish the ungrateful soul that never loved Me,
ah, Lucifer, magnificent in defeat,
I made Thee magnificent more by far
eight thousand years ago,
and better by far it were you never fell
through no dread Fate or Destiny, no Will of Mine!
Ah, *Lucifer le miserable*, how deprived you are!
And I am very sorry, Lucifer,
but though saved you may not be,
the Lord of All has crushed you not completely!"

*11th November 1999*

## To my Friend

**OH FRIEND**, I am ill, wronged and lonely;
the hole wherein I lay my head
is lonely, and your Presence distant.

Foxes have holes and the Son of Man
has nowhere where to lay His Head
but for the bosom
of your intangible Presence!

Lay your heart, nameless Friend, close to mine.
Take my heart, nameless Friend, in your two hands
and hold it tight:
unfold it, stretch it in the sweet luxury of the Spirit,
uncrease it, relieve it of the cramps
of a thousand, countless wrongs,
and heal it of the cuts from expert demon-butchers.
Breathe upon it, oh my Friend,
the precious breath of your diviner Spirit.
Dress it, oh my Friend, with the ointment
of your heart's precious blood.
Refreshen, oh my Friend, heal and gladden
my poor, cut, cramp'd, aching, troubled
and sorely butcher'd spirit,
and set me right but once
from nameless, countless wrongs.

Your private matters, distant Friend,
are not my business; protect my own
as in a distant cloud.
Discharge me, distant Friend, from all charges
against my honour:
I am ill, and wronged, and lonely!

Judge me not, distant Friend, nor taunt me,
nor ever be my Judge: my hand is loath and cold.
Liberate me from the cruel judge who judged
and judged and did me wrong and pillaged me!

Oh Friend in the wide, wide World
of Time and Space, your cruel silence taunts me:
make your Presence felt,
and let the Music sound from nowhere!

The Son of Man
has nowhere where to lay His Head
but for the bosom
of your intangible Presence!

*16th November 1999*

## Of Catholics and Artists

*for Esther Cameron who had the grace to ask for it*

**WE MIGHT** as well, oh friend, talk cowboys and indians --
fear the wild west: it is a dangerous country!

Precisest theologians in truest religions
have never dreamt what values Artists vaunt:
cults of the style are cults of Persons; cults
of the message - coercion of the flock!

When the good Artist yields the unforgettable,
praise his style: fear, tremble before his meaning;
messages often are far too sublime for words,
and those there be who ought to know much better!

Sacrilege against the Person of the Artist
is a ridiculous foul that only fools
admire. Works of Art are the Sacrament
of the innermost. Hack never what's made of flesh;

of blood! Concern thyself with saving grace
alone; and with damnation God alone ...
just as Augustine saves the soul of Plato,
Aquinas Aristotle, and Dante Virgil!

The pride of culture is a profound and lasting
consolation to untold men of good will -
no pride stinks worse nor more pathological
than his alone whose subtle state of grace

has made him haughtier far than the great Artists!

*9th December 1999*

## To a child

**LITTLE** child, little child,
little child of long ago,
little child you are honoured
in the philosophy of Plato the great philosopher,
little girl of long ago
whom God Himself chose out of a book
just as the great Kirin did choose His women,
or just as Jesus chose His dearest mother!

Little child, little child,
blessed, divinest, sincerer child,
beware of born, grown-up deceivers
and subtlest counsellors of fraud!
Fear the revengeful, the vindictive,
senior, very christian ladies and gents,
who will use beautiful honours
to revenge themselves on the souls of children!
Beware, little child, of those
who will count all your money, fleece you of money,
and give up their own money
to pillage and to murder the sweet child's vision
and your better judgment!

Little child, little child,
the art-show in your dark, sincerer eyes

is diviner than all the sights on earth
a little child will ever see!
Ah little child unfallen, go not astray:
yours is the best brain I know!
Consult your own better judgment, little child!
Be thou a life-long student of your earliest Vision!
Smell the flower of your own unpolluted conscience
before you consult deceitful priests or bibles!

Ah my false honours, little child, are better far
than the sincerity of a thousand christian faces:
devote thyself, dearest daughter, blessed Seer,
to thy own heart and earliest, tenderest love!

*29th January 2000*

## Eucharist

*To my Jesus, il miglior fabbro*

**WHEN** readers honour verse they honour but
sincerity made of paper, printed matter
which neither stirs, nor breathes, nor is not made
of flesh or blood - and yet because dead poets
and living men, as by a mutual pact
unspoken, hearts upon each other's lips,
honour the exquisite Fake, that mutual pact
between the dead, and living man, of Honour
spontaneous, silent, and unspoken, betokens
not imperfections of the mortal Maker,
but Spirit immortal, dressed in the flesh of sharp
Perfections holier far than their own Makers,
which for the Honour made that exquisite Fake
impowers the experience
of Beauty, Truth, and Goodness, Peace of Stasis,
Aesthetic Beauty, and Sincerity!

When lovers of Christ receive the Bread, the Wine,
they honour but a crumb, a drop of wine,
which neither stirs, nor breathes, nor is not made
of flesh or blood, and nothing but a crumb,
and wine remains, and nothing but a Fake.
Because the consecrated camouflage
of bread and wine is honoured by the blind
and silent eye of Love, the Honour made
unto that exquisite Fake, by mutual pact
between the Lord and him or her He loves
whose Heart doth understand, impowers likewise,
like contraband in holy camouflage,
the sweet, cathartic, restorative experience
of saving Grace, wherein that subtlest Master
conceals His carnal flesh and precious blood
for gentlest Food and subtlest, healing Potion.

Gentle Jesus, loved not wisely but too well,
will You likewise allow a Poet - one who
believes in God, himself, and demons, just so
all may believe whatever made no sense
to them at all, to us made Sense stupendous -
to dedicate to You a Rubaiyat?
and drink in silence with his eye to You,
and to the Saints, as lovers drink? ..... Tell us
another one, good Master, but will You likewise,
as You bless and honour consecrated bread
and wine, honour and bless and consecrate
his Book and works of Art? Thou Who did bid us
receive with trepidation ..... receive my prayer
likewise, that Work which like sweet contraband
my Heart, my Soul conceals, might likewise never
be spurnt by Thee, nor held in spite, nor in
dishonour, that unto him or her I love,
beneath the exquisite Fake[100] and Curb of Art,

[100] In my poem the term 'Fake' is not a term of disparagement. It would be tragic, in the context, to miscontrue my meaning. To me, the false honour accorded to beautiful works of art, or what certain factions **choose** to say is a false honour, is nothing but courtesy towards a man's innermost person. If I have to go door to door to sell my work, in

my Work may carry likewise healing touches
of saving Power and restoring Grace .....

*12th February 2000*

## Professor Lizard SunBasker the world-treemendous Shakespeheerean expert leaves his last interior monologue in his last Will and dying Testament

**I AM PROFESSOR** Lizard SunBasker, the world-famous expert on the poetry of William Shakespeare. My IQ is well above the common man's IQ, and this I know very well indeed, that I am not a fool, nor am I quickly fooled. "Know thyself!" is law to me and to my wife, Dovetails the Beloved, as much as it was law to Socrates. Now why, I ask you, should I ever so much as rile myself or judge myself to know myself? or why should I ever so much as rile or judge my conscience, like some poor religious caterpillars that I know?

I go by great works of art. I honour genius only, wherever I see it or wherever I can read it and appreciate it. I have always trusted the tale and not the teller, and their own great Jesus Christ said as much to them also, for by the fruit you know the tree. I honour above all the great William Shakespeare, to whom Professor Lizard SunBasker and his wife, Dovetails the Beloved, owe nothing but luck, luck, luck, good luck beyond all telling. We have had one heck of a fun-filled life, my own dearest wife and me. We

---

particular, I certainly have no use for the sincerity of people who wish to be sincere in any other way. Such a thing, to me, is sacrilegious. By the term 'Fake', in the context of my poem, I intend to signify a 'blind eye' such as we may cast on those we love with a kind intention .....

are not millionnaires. Who has ever made a million from loving one Poet? But the house alone is worth one cool million in the most luxurious posh quietest area I know. My bank account says $783,469.87 Canadian and I am still sucking one heck of a pension. We have travelled like kings. We have watched Shakespeare acted at Stratford-on-Avon. I have lectured on my Willie at 131 major Universities. My books about him are still selling. All the women I ever taught adored me and hung on my words like the young virgins in the Bible and ah! every now and then I flirted and I loved it! My dear dear wife, she was never ever jealous of me, and I never ever grudged her another man, every now and then. I owe it all to the great William Shakespeare.

I swear it by God, if there is a God. Professor Lizard SunBasker has a conscience and a code of honour and a loaded revolver beside him as he writes. If I do not give that one great benefactor and favourite genius of mine his honour, his credit, his due, and everything that belongs to him and not to me, if I do not understand myself and in so doing get to the bottom of a cosmic riddle in the light of the work of a genius, by God above if there is a God, I'll fuckin' shoot myself and fall down dead in this ditch I have dug in my own garden. For I cannot believe that such a great genius would give me such a reward without trying my intelligence to the utmost.

God, if there is a God, I am not a genius and I know it, and I am not a foolish man and I know it, and I am intelligent and I know it, and I am extremely superstitious and I know it: I believe in the power of one man, dead and buried for five hundred years, to bring into my life nothing but success, romance, wealth, and good fortune. Ergo! I believe in the supernatural agency, adequacy, efficacy, love, concern, and self sufficiency of the dead with regard to the affairs of the living. I kiss my hands to the dead. My heart is proud of the dead. I am grateful to the dead. I owe it all to the dead.

I am in love with the words of the dead and the words of the dead have brought me nothing but love, romance, and success. The only god I have ever believed in is Shakespeare. If I do not get to the bottom of all of it in my old age I'll fuckin' shoot myself now with this loaded revolver and fall down dead in this ditch I have dug in my own garden. Now why, I ask myself, do I adore the work of that one dead poet? What is the secret of his power over me, my power over people, and the luck and success he brought me? William Shakespeare is the only great genius I know who would have understood everything about Dale Carnegie a lot better than Dale Carnegie ever understood poetry as well as I do. And this is it, Professor SunBasker: Professor Lizard SunBasker, kid me not! You honour that Poet because he feeds your pride, never insults your intelligence, and nourishes your narcissism. My students honour me because I feed their pride, never insult their intelligence, and nourish their narcissism. The greatest genius who ever understood man's ego and narcissism and the lesson he gave me gave me power over people.

We are all the way we are without being necessarily made of quintessential vanity or falsehood. Why should I ever so much as think my Shakespeare was vain, false, fake or a fraud, the only god I know who brought it all into my life? Why should I ever so much as think that I am vain, false, fake or a fraud? All my top students got away with top-notch credentials and all of them hit it lucky with romance and well-salaried careers. I swear by God if there is a God I believe in myself and the genius of Shakespeare but what did the great William Shakespeare believe in if he believed in anything at all?

Answer, the great William Shakespeare believed in himself and his work, just as I do, and I am not a genius and I know it. Ergo! that man's book is my Bible, and being the only one I ever went by, if I do not stick with it now in my dying hour, I swear I'm a goner: if in my fuckin' old age I do not understand a cosmic fraud far worse than the poetry of my Shakespeare, I'll shoot myself now, and fall down dead in this ditch I have dug in my own garden.

But what did HE believe in? We have the public world he saw and one tremendous theatrical histrionic public Honour; we have the private MAN whom no one saw and his one tremendous and far more beautiful private

Honour! ERGO! save appearances because appearances save faces, but all that glitters is not gold, and often have you heard that told! Appearances deceive and public Honour may be a tale told by an idiot! Ergo! that one Man's greatest proudest Honour was a great private Honour and that one Man's private Honour is the only code of Honour I ever went by! Ergo! I shall from henceforward go by my own private sense of Honour only and as God's Bible says set my own house in order! I shall be sincere with the dead! I shall confess all my sins to the dead!

Gotcha, Professor! Whatever I have done, I have never harmed anyone, neither myself nor another, never judged anyone harshly, neither myself nor a Christian, whether I believe in God's Bible or whether I don't, and the only commandment I have ever broken is the sixth commandment. Gotcha once more! There was good sport in it, for my dear wife Dovetails my Beloved and for myself, and having no other God to forgive me, I forgive myself all my adulteries, by my books and by Shakespeare's: great Shakespeare, I honour **YOU**! I owe it all to YOU! confess all my sins to YOU! and kiss my hand to your bones!

Now with my own eye I spy in the great Shakespeare's public world of men and women a great public Honour, his own great, invisible, and far more beautiful private Honour, and as in the breathtaking panorama of a great romantic movie, Christian Europe as it was Christian before the Schism and before the Reformation, and before the Reformation all Christianity was Catholic and took the Faith for granted like William Shakespeare. Gotcha! Professor SunBasker, gotcha once more! He was the great dramatist historian of Christian Europe before the Protestant Reformation. His men and his women, that chameleon Poet of Poets, they are all screwed like the Catholics, they are all great like the Catholics, they are all lovers like the Catholics, they are all ordinary people like the Catholics, they are all powerful people like the Catholics, they are all wicked but for a few, like the Catholics, they are all bad philosophers but for a few, like the Catholics, they got it all wrong but for a few, like the

Catholics, they are all outrageous people just like the Catholics, a lot of them repent in the nick of time or else on their death-bed, just like the Catholics, and only a few of all those are good saints, just like the Catholics.

Professor Lizard SunBasker, I can hardly believe what you have just established! Professor Lizard SunBasker you know it in your mind from intuition and from the equally reliable tale of internal evidence! Professor Lizard SunBasker, Geoffrey Chaucer was one heck of a beautiful poet also, and he wrote the line, take the moralitee, good men, and let drop the chaff: apply it to Shakespeare! You have nothing to go by but public Honour and private Honour. Save appearances always like Shakespeare but go by private Honour only! From the insufferable verbiage and the unforgivable cosmic fraud pick only what is in your best interest! Go only by the lines that truly wish you well from the pen of your best well-wisher ever! Confess all your own faults to the best lover you ever had in all your life!

Professor Lizard SunBasker, you did so much in your life that was right: I swear I'll shake hands with you to the last that you got this one right now. Great Men like Shakespeare were never chosen so to go to Hell! Great Men like Shakespeare were never made by you or me! Great Men like Shakespeare go to a Heaven a lot more real than I ever thought or imagined! Professor Lizard SunBasker, you dine with Him at Journey's End! For the Sun of Shakespearean Romanticism is beautiful and it shines golden, gorgeous, and eternal!

*27th February 2000*

## Lady Aphrodite, sweetest daughter

**BEFORE** she was born I thought of her,
before I married a maid I softly prayed for her,
before I formed her in the womb I knew her,
and in the dark I gently called her, 'Daughter',
writing for her lines of sad but sweetest verse.

Child, I've been through hell, I have seen hell,
I suffered the second Death on your behalf —
I went to hell to bring you back upon my shoulders:
daughter, I was hurt and I was lonely.

In the eternal darkness
I waited for her with profound compassion,
Canadian toque and book in hand, a sad, true lover
sorrowing and hurting for the love, the hand
of a Woman, the First Lady of the Poets.

Daughter,
fear me not, be not ashamed, think no ill,
judge naught: were they not all of them
little children once upon a time?
Little One, sorrow never again.
Fear not again. Never cry again.
Woman whom I chose out of a book,
Lady Aphrodite born from the Ocean,
professor visiting *del al di lá*,
goddess reborn and reincarnate by a dogma
I myself defined ...
remember always - how cleverly you crept,
how wordlessly and how silently you stept,
out of the darkness into your father's heart,
and out of your mother's womb.

Child, what suffering I suffer'd!
With you in his arms your father was proud,
and all his ghastly wounds were healing.
Child, you were snatched out of your father's arms
with a crushing, chillingly vindictive,
unspeakable cruelty!

For your dear sake, daughter, I forgive,
but kid me not, be good to me, I deserve
your pity, mercy, and your love.
I never did you harm, never did wrong by you,
nor ever thought ill of you,
and what my heart commandeth me I did.

Daughter, give me your heart.
Now that thou art growing into a Woman,
give me nothing but your hand. Nothing do I crave
but your eternal Love!

*30th March 2000*

## Virginia Woolfe

**WHEN YOU** wrote ***To The Lighthouse***, Virginia,
did you then, that downcast, London day,
reread ***Time Passes***, analyze, and then reanalyze
that terrible and sorrowing loneliness you felt,
surrounded as you were, my dear, by such
vindictive people,
in such petty, facetious, homely images
so well-concealed?

Did you then ask yourself, Virginia,
whether someone else was waiting
between the lines of that simple
and terrible and beautiful work of art,
someone, perhaps as lonely as you were,
perhaps the majestic Keeper
of that majestic Lighthouse
in that ghastly and terrible and magical Landscape?

Why did you not ask yourself, my dear,
whether the Artist in the Lighthouse was,
perhaps, a lot more human than yourself or me?

Do you know at all, did you ever have a clue,
Virginia, who that Majestic Artist was,
might be, or may have been,
who kept the Lighthouse and his far-flung flashlight
displayed and shone full on upon your face,
that downcast, sorrowing, terrible night,
with himself, in the shadows of that Lighthouse,
so closely hidden and so well-concealed?

Did you stop to consider, Virginia,
human though you were like him or me,
suicidal though you were like myself,
unbeliever though you were like so many,
unsuspecting though you were as a child, my dear,
innocent and wicked though you were, Virginia,
just what a simple and terribly beautiful Art
the Artist in the Lighthouse sprang upon you,
with his far-flung flashlight on you?
just what a subtler ring of honesty and truth
and beauty your work of art possesses, perhaps,
than you ever thought it might that terrible day
on which you killed yourself, my dear?

Did you travel, Virginia,
and on your knees, maybe, say thank you
to that majestic Keeper, and kiss his feet,
the great Artist in the Lighthouse
with his far-flung flashlight on you,
and himself in the shadows so well-concealed?

Did you ask yourself, Virginia,
just who on earth was he, that majestic Keeper
that on your feelings wrought such magic?
or did you then merely publish
that simple yet terribly beautiful book
which made you famous,
with an uncalled for feminist curse, perhaps,
on a man such as your friend the majestic Keeper
in the shadows of that Lighthouse,
with his ghastly flashlight,
the flashlight of that great Artist in the Lighthouse?

You should have simply asked yourself, my dear,
whether someone else was waiting there,
perhaps as lonely, perhaps as sorrowful as you were,
perhaps with a heart himself, which your heart only
craved as his own, or whether your heart
told you things your mind did not understand,
and never left me to moan and to mourn,
a few thousand miles away, as I always cry
for a personal lover, a personal friend,
a favourite book, and a personal loss,
your sad, bitter, unconsoled, and lonely end,
with nothing, perhaps, in your dying ears,
nothing perhaps but a voice which hopeless eyewash,
revengeful mockery, and shameless effrontery
may have seemed to you and me? tragic heroine?
tragic romantic idol by a book-lover well beloved?

And who knows, my dear,
if anything wiser would have occurred
to my dull mind and me
in a dilemma just as painful and just as terrible?

*2nd April 2000*

## Mary

**AH MARY**, divinest Witch[101] in Christendom,
divine, blessed Mother, Woman-God,
alone of all Your Sex resplendent, Woman
Whom God the Messiah, from pre-existence, chose,
between the lines, out of a beautiful book,
for His most intimate friend in time, and made

---

[101] The term "Witch", in my own language of the heart, is no more a term of disparagement than the word "Fake" was a term of disparagement in my poem, **Eucharist**. It is intended exclusively as a term of affection and endearment just as a beautiful poet may be called a sorcerer, an enchanter, a bewitcher, or a magician ...

You Alone His Mother, high, divine Priestess
of Messianic Culture ... did You likewise, Mary,
choose your own Son out of a beautiful Book?
Did You likewise, perhaps, pre-exist, a Maid,
as Wordsworth wrote, whom there were none to praise,
and very few to love, in hidden, forgotten
lives, maybe many lives, but honoured by Plato
the Visionaire, in his Philosophy only?
Were You, perhaps, divinest, blessed Mother,
in previous, hidden existence, introduced
to Your Own Divine, future Son, as to Your Lover,
at a top-secret dance, the dance of God,
of Time, Eternity, and of the Hours?
Mary, Woman-Priest of the re-incarnate God,
marriages such as Yours are made in Heaven,
and such-like Lovers are all chosen out
of beautiful Books! Those there be, divinest Mary,
who do not honour You because You are
not God, but many a critic honours the man
he pleases, and many a reader talks of Dante,
the divine Poet, or the divine Artist
MichaelAngelo, and many a Poet loved You,
and many an Artist, and many a wise, old Sage,
and many a Man adores You, Mary, though
he may not boast that he is Yours -- so what?
and many a Child, and many a beating Heart!
Gods of the new Religion salute You, Mary,
divine, blessed Mother, Woman-God,
divinest Witch in Christendom .....
The Peace of God be with You, Mary, the starriest
Calm of Art, as of the reddest rose in June!
And sweet, gentlest reflection be my portion
in return for the Poet's softest speculations!
Let Sarah Therese, my dear daughter, speak ...
Helena of my own Book, unique, only Child
of my own Culture .....

*22nd May 2000*

## Helen - or the three world wars[102]

**HELEN,** for whom all Greece arose to fight,
when love of Woman holy was and dear,
to build a Land made of God-aweful Light,
and all the gods in Homer breathed near —
all Greece was but the choice, experienced Two
who for their kinfolk, poets, gods, and land,
made War an art unspoilt, and noble true,
and Homer guided with a steady hand!
Helen, we mourn instead the billions dead,
butchered at Auschwitz, and overkill unfair,
in three world wars where we all sank like lead,
and still we wear the black of silent care!
Helen, did Greece have such a cross to bear?
Whose Honour, or whose Dishonour, was sincere?

*7th June 2000*

## How to convert a man

**IN ORDER** to convert a Man ... it's not
enough to pray for him, nor quite enough
to give him good example - things which are,
quite often, holy fake and pious lore.
You need to give him food to eat. You need
to change the Poetry he feels. You need
to change his Art: to rub, and to massage
him hard and long and well with the oils of
the Good News. Send me, I say, a Poet
to wish me *buon voyage* on my departure,
for this is where you need a real Artist.
Believe me, oh my Friend, the case for Art
is great - and it's high-serious: nothing does

---

[102] World War 1, World War 2, and the Cold War.

it have to do with culture as you know it!
Only beware, I say, of many Masters!
Beware of letting far too many Artists
carry out operation conversion on you!

*July 1st 2000*

## You are Jesus ...

**I AM NOT** unloving, oh my Friend,
yet my loving skills are far from perfect,
nor quite as skilled as Yours. I never became
a beautiful Poet, nor ever created Verse,
to taunt You, gentlest Friend, yet You know,
my Friend, I am one who like Yourself
has been cruelly, murderously, heartlessly taunted.
Is it in me presumption, Friend,
to compare my hurt to Thine?

I adore You. I look up to You. However madly,
oh my Friend, I ever fought so many upon
a point of Honour, I honour You.
I gave the Books to You. After whatever
I ever taught so many people with a book,
I do not want the Honour, dearest Friend,
unless it comes from You.
I never, oh my Friend, considered myself
worthy of You. I do not dare, nor ever did.

I am not unworthy, Friend,
of human friendship, nor of honest praise
proffered without forced smiles upon
the people's clean white teeth, nor am I
unworthy of honest tears, but of You
I am not worthy.

You are Jesus whom the trillions honour.
You are Jesus the *forçe majeure* of History.
You are Jesus, the gentlest, the kindest,
the most compassionate, the most merciful.

Oh my Friend, cruelly have I been provoked,
murderously have I been wronged,
provocatively I cursed and swore, oh how I cursed
myself for swearing! Oh my Friend, well I know
that Jesus wept. I have likewise wept!

I am mad at You:
I cannot for the life of me believe
that such wrong happens with Your collusion!
Yet I love You. Yet I beseech You
in my bitterness, never to let me allow
much bitterness to include You too.
Yet I love You
with unskilled love. I refuse
to think so ill of You. I beseech You ...
make it sweeter, make it perfect,
make it skillful.

Noise and attention are sweet and have their uses.
Silence and solitude are sweet and have their uses.
I am of both these a lover, both hold attraction,
both may be used
for much good, as much as for much evil,
and likewise, oh my Friend, that sweetest love,
the love of creatures, authors, saints, or fine artists.
But You are Jesus whom the trillions honour …

For my child, my child, my sweetest child
Lady Aphrodite, I offer up
this silent death to You. Count me, oh my Friend,
as the friend of the dead, for I know well
I have been honoured by the great Jesus Christ!
Let me, if You love me, bawl at You a bit;
feed me only out of Your hand.

If I am dying I beseech You, if You are my Friend
let no one come near me, neither spirit, nor priest,
nor relative, nor do I wish to hear anything,
neither prayers, nor songs, nor psalms, nor Masses,
nor music, nor words of absolution,
but the saints of Heaven chanting,
from the depths of their being, over and over,
just that one word, just Your name ..... Jesus.

You are Jesus. You are gentle. You are kind.
You are compassionate. You are merciful.
You did not hold against Me
crass error, mistakes or faults. It is Your will
to save our face whatever ...

You are Jesus. Help me bear my hurt.
Dress my cruellest wound. Help me for Your sake
accept Life's cruellest, most murderous,
heartless burden. Oh my Friend, may I die alone,
as if I were, I may say, a wounded animal
in a hole, but one which was faithful to You,
that no one, upon my death-bed, may taunt me,
nor tempt me, but the sound of the Heavens
chanting, from the depths of their being,
over and over, just the one word, just Your name ...
Jesus.

Like Yourself, if I may say so
without too much presumption, but in a real,
real pain, I am, oh my gentlest Friend,
far more sinned against than sinning ...
Leave nothing upon my death-bed
but a red, red rose, just so that no one may say
of me, that man was lost, that man was a demon!

*July 4th 2000*

## Lord Joe of the Rood

*to the art-councils*

**ONCE MORE** I measure out a loving skill,
an amorous practice – the arts of love:
*Arte d'Amore*! Once more I am bereft,
a beggar at the door of Love unquiet,
and lonesome take the road, and lonesome trudge
the pavements! Your Honours, I swear that I am not
Jude the Obscure, Lord Jim, nor Oliver Twist,
nor Jesus Christ, nor His Lady-Love Griselda!
Songs of gentlest reflection are composed
by poets to soothe their pain, and not for Councils!

Ah Thou! Thou Well too deep for thinking! Thou Well
wherein Thou cast me, I was born disguised,
aborted with red tape, with special needs,
and in my mother's womb I strove with shadows,
shadows, perhaps, from a past life, perhaps
the hands of God, perhaps the pain, the plunge
of God's harpoon, the call to silent war,
to future victory!
Just so oppressive are
the times, great God of all, that though we say
this is Peacetime, yet this is Wartime, and
your friend, who though a baby boy in playpens,
already felt Thy thought snake through his thought,
your friend, I say Your friend Lord Joe became,
thirty years later, a war-poet though
he never went to war – just so oppressive
are the times, you nasty gods!
I cannot say,
great God, you have been callous: I forgive
You all, for all the many gifts You made me!
Oh Thou, who art far greater than thy gifts,
than mine, treat me well! Use me with loving care!
I prayed. Lord, I prayed to suffer. You did but take,
and never stopped, and what You gave, You gave
with one hand taking, and nothing have I done
but suffer! Halt! I say. Thou Rascal, stop!

Breathe upon me, if you must, a loving breath!

You are reputed that you are the God
of Peace, and if You are, be Thou the God
of Peace, and of the loving Land of Song
and endless Sunshine, Land of perpetual mourning,
Land of the endless elegiac wail and mourning,
Land of the silent keening for the lost,
the trillions lost to silent death, to grief,
to cruel care, but with a peaceful Music
that neither vulgar is, nor joyless, yet weeps
in Peace with God in weeping!
Light the Peace-pipe!
Trim my wick and light the Flame! Reach me the Torch,
the smoking Olympic Torch aflame!

*25$^{th}$ July 2000*

## Divinest Mary

**DIVINEST** Mary
Who took care of the Christ-child
when He crept and hid His greatness there,
beneath a Woman's heart,
just as the child in your womb, I say,
just as the child in Elizabeth's,
at Your glad greeting leapt for joy,
and Your spirits both rejoiced,
your's and Elizabeth's .....
and just as likewise the child in ours,
as much as in your womb, or in Elizabeth's,
are our Hope, all the Hope
we shall ever be given,
the Promise of a bright new Day .....
divinest Mary
give me children!

I hate You not.
I wish You no ill nor harm.
Mary heed me not
if I was ever provoked to swear.
Mary heed me not
if I bitch and loathe myself
for bitching, and then a Woman-God like You.
Slap me hard once, but forgive me.
Mary, I am ill, far too ill of the thought
of such loathsome things.
I adore You, Mary,
as a Man adores a Maiden
made all of gold and sunlight.
I am spotted compared to You.

Be it done with me
according to Thy Word, divinest Mary.
Not the Word, I say,
of an extremely great supernatural God,
above all and topmost --
which always made me feel
so very little, Mary,
so cuttingly discouraged,
so cruelly bruised beneath His heel:
but the Word of a Woman-God,
which makes my heart
leap and rejoice like Yours
when the child rejoiced
beneath Your heart and beneath Elizabeth's!

Just a verse, divinest Mary,
made of naught but breath between us,
made of naught but of my love and Yours.
If I publish it, divine blessed Maid -
as is the vogue with poets -
be not taunted,
be not insulted,
and if You say, tear it,
I'll tear it, Mary;
but ever I shall retain untarnished,

fleshed out and etched in the heart's red blood,
the memory of my sweet golden love
for eternal youthful You.

*31st July 2000*

## Between God and a poet .....

**THINK** only of our Love, and not of Art,
for there the treasure lies! Give Me your heart,
oh Son: I'll plant therein great work galore!
Pore on our Love, not on pedantic lore!
Consider that a verse, or Heaven's Grace,
are but the breath between us, laced like lace —
lost on thin air but for your heart involved;
lost on thin air but for your hand resolved;
lost on thin air but for your pride omitted;
lost on thin air but for your love committed!
Be not pedantic, nor sedentary —
a scholar gypsy is the thing to be:
that you may understand, not men alone,
nor works of art, but books as well as men!

*10th August 2000*

## Reply to Him I love .....

**I WAS** happy, happy I was indeed,
composing verse with no ill thought of harm,
of evil, of a just revenge, at peace
with You, innocent jokes between

the lines of my prayers, a little child
that looks up only …
                    Christ Jesus, I lost my Peace,
my Peace I lost indeed, though I wrote,
dutybidden, about revenge, though down
I looked, since down I had to, upon
a chosen People.
                    Christ Jesus, never!
King of Mercy, no! I was
thrice happier in the dark
than I am now that I see better.
Christ Jesus,
why did You let so many mortals taunt me?
I lost my Peace. Christ Jesus, why did You let
the cruelest temptations snare me?
I lost my Peace. Why did You play
such games with me?
                    God's Art
is subtler, gentler far indeed than ours!
His work is interesting more by far than ours!
intelligent more by far than ours!
Mine … is incomplete without You!
You are ahead of me indeed! Great books
are but the memory of a sweetest love
He bore Himself unto entire Peoples.

Christ, I am ill, sick, too sick indeed, of insults
inside the memory of beautiful books,
wherein I wish for compliments only;
wherein I want only good honours!

Christ Jesus, he revenges not who picks
a gun and shoots, but he who murders heart,
and soul, the memories books enchant us with,
whether he murder with a scandal, sin,
or just another hell on printed paper,
him it is who truly is vindictive!

Christ Jesus, shoot … revenging no one!
Christ Jesus, if You ever

took compassion upon poor devils,
shoot and reign!
Christ, I defy You thrice again,
shoot and reign … revenging no one!

I suffered injustice …..
I am not afraid of justice!
I suffered stinking cruelty …..
I am not afraid of Your unkindness!
I suffered a mortal's vengeance …..
I fear not the Lord's avengeance!

It was my love, my love it was indeed, to Church
to go, distraught, abstracted, bereaved of Him
I love, dissatisfied with hackneyed prayer,
with Church, my hair on end, my clothes unkempt.
A poem which is a cry is just as sure
a prayer, better by far than all the prayers
that ever were. There are those, Christ Jesus,
who think poets are blind in sin
and blindly think
their works of art are some good honour …..
Let such be called a farce, Christ Jesus,
ridiculous as much as those,
upon my very soul, who comb their pride,
their worthless work of art, caring neither
for Your love, nor mine …..

But knowing, knowing, knowing, as I do,
oh Thou my Friend, that my poor verse is naught
but breath between us, made of Your Love and mine,
I fear being false! I fear, fear
letting You down, or else dishonouring You!
Christ, take them, have them, but on the day
of Vengeance, revenge me not, dishonour me not,
put me never to shame, spare me at least
a worse one: charges against my honour …..

Oh Thou, my constant Friend who stays,
Who guides my trembling hand regardless,

though sleeping, dreaming, walking,
as some say,
my head in air .....

*12$^{th}$ August 2000*

## The honest unbeliever

**JESUS,** if I know not at all
if in Truth You be, or if You live,
and move, and all Your limbs exert,
and somewhere have Your Being, yet You are
a gentle, compelling, reassuring,
compassionate Force in History, because
You are just such a Force upon the souls
and hearts of men.
Jesus Christ,
if at all You be, I never heard You say,
"Hello Donnie! Get on Me Johnny!
Jesus will give you His flesh and His blood
to eat!" Christ, how I ramble,
but I never hurt anyone, I was never
at all truly unkind to anyone, to the poor, the bereaved,
to the sorrowful, the sad, or the miserable;
yet have I always loved a good book, good music,
honest fun, an honest woman, and honest drink!

Jesus, if at all You are,
if the Spirit - which worked within the Human Spirit
for thrice ten trillion years - is at all
a living Man's living Spirit,
a personal Being, and a living God,
Jesus Christ, talk to me! -
knock on my door in the middle of the Night! -
tap on my bloody bedroom window! -
wake me up or God above be darned! -

introduce Yourself! -
You are famous enough to fool me not,
though perhaps You assume
what shapes You please, passing us poor mortals by
upon the Road, unnoticed!
- the invisible Man, the silent God!

Great Jesus, I make no sign of the Cross,
lest a consummate fool revenge himself
on my gift of intelligence, for it is all I have
and a fool I'm not! Great Jesus,
for similar reasons I suppose
I'll have nothing to do with blessed barns made of brick —
for I respect him who said:
my altars are the mountains and the ocean!

I enjoy, if anything, beholding the Cross of Christ
gently caressed by a Wordsworthian philosophy,
and His knocked out and gnarled, ancient Form
tangled with weeds and green, ancient moss,
Wordsworthian winds in a Wordsworthian jungle ...
oh! they may all be gifted with love for the Jesus they've got,
but what if they have no other gift at all? Is this then
a case of sour grapes? Jesus?! You never
answered me ...

Yet if You are, if this be a prayer
but no one will say so, if the living Power
at work in Human History is truly a living Man's
real Power, I conjure You,
I swear it by all that the trillions held dear,
heed but Thou my human prayer!
pity a poor devil's confession of weakness!
for God Almighty's sake talk to me!
Mr-All-is-Silent-Dead-and-Buried-All, talk ...
darn You!

*30th August 2000*

## All Love is sacred .....

**IN THE** jumble and din of modern cities,
immense shopping centres cast in iron cages
and technological jungles, where the constant,
nuclear boom of cars, and planes, and radios
deafens and deadens the sense, by day or night,
bringing the eyes to the constant verge of tears
caused by filth, smog, far too much light and colour,
and noise-pollution, with a cruel, sadistic
wrenching upon the very nerve itself
of sensitive feeling ..... ancient Love remains,
perennial as the grass, a holy corner
which the Heart calls Home, where a man takes refuge
with prayers inside his Heart: Eros, Agape,
Thanatos, good Love and bad, or the four Loves -
all Love is sacred ..... !

*13th September 2000*

## Black stars

**MY HEART** is full of fear at the thought
of many Graces lost - the moment when
the Spirit of the Lord bent over me,
when I lay ill, in bed; - the moment when
the little children asked me to play more music; -
the moment when I had Church at my feet; -
the moment when the Saints of Heaven listened,
whilst I read verse; - that when the Lord Himself
questioned, and talked with me, upon the beach .....
Yet merciful reflection chides me gently ---
"God is compassionate and knows not hatred.
For each Grace earnt a dozen need be lost,
as in a game of Chance. Child, fear not,
for Graces well you've earnt, and each Grace earnt

to Me betokens labours undergone -
for I help only those who help themselves!"

*17th September 2000*

## False judges

**READER**, apply this verse, not in empty jest,
but only to those who earn the insult best.
Where true thinking, and true teaching, most abound,
like petty Popes false judges most are found!

From Ulysses to Artemidorus, from Aeneas to Turnus,
from the proudest Pride of a Nation
that ever requested a kind word and assistance,
from Lazarus to Dives, from One who leads the Opposition,
from all the Great Russians with love or with hate,
am I an Artist?
or did you ever, with works of art,
break legs with expertise? .....

In the name of some true religion, false judges
pull off nothing but fast ones upon the souls
of poor artists who love their books,
and the good honours their Saint
or their great Artist make them!

In the name of some awesome, divine intoxication,
they thoroughly hate Shakespeare and Dante
for a professor ...
They who are not the Pride of the Poor.
They who are the unjustest, inhumanest Scourge of the Poor.
They who do not hear the Cry of the Poor.

Their church is the church of the tortured nude,
the church of the most brutal white collar crimes against

humanity,
the church of the aborted adult,
the church of the uglier sisters,
the church of nasty gods of the inhuman task,
the church of bashful cunning and of the shamefullest thing,
sinister and scandalous, infamous Church
of seventy-seven times seven obnoxious insults,
which mistreated me and which maltreated me,
the church of the mortal sins,
the church of the obscene penance,
the church of the revengeful man,
the church of the slanderous tongue,
the tribunal of the inhumane,
the church of the fraudulent theft,
the church of the vested interests,
the church of the unsociable boor,
the infamous revolter of the Pride of little Children,
who never did anything for them but mistreat and maltreat
them …

Such is the favourite true religion of demons
who enjoy rendering themselves thoroughly hated,
thoroughly despised, and thoroughly obnoxious
for whatever Jesus they've got ... devils
who render themselves obnoxious, despised, and hated,
are devils in a state of just revenge: let them weep
for that true religion they've got
for the next two thousand years.
Remember
the Word of Him Who wrote:
"I do not want Sacrifice - I want Mercy!"

I say to myself,
poor devils have rights to do something also,
but I shall go to Hell on behalf of the poor devil
to whom I choose to make that good Honour only.
Over and out.

No one wants this church of theirs,
this church of such a dishonourable penance!

My books are the only law my conscience goes by,
amongst so many judges, pulling off lies and fast ones,
sqaundering my riches, squandering my gifts,
in the petty church of the prodigal parent
who reenacts Romeo and Juliet,
and the Capulets and Montagues,
with all that obscene authority ...
my gifts are at least as precious as divine Grace;
false judges are not worthy of my repentance.
And I was always far more terrified
of all that terrible authority
than of a work of art.
Will You at least, oh God, give me the Peace
with my writing? It is the only Joy
I ever truly rejoiced, who knows what Joy is like.

False judges are all a ridiculous, insensitive, and heartless people,
who do not understand the ways of the Heart,
yet put on airs at your expense
because you show them poetry,
and you think they are going to rejoice with you.
You meet with nothing except Dives and Grigios,
traitors, prodigal squanderers of all your riches,
butchers, manglers, and murdereres of little children's faces.
Maybe your poetry was the only soft spot you ever had for them.

Does not a Child have rights to murder?
Shall not an Artist
defend Himself like King James against false judges?
They put on airs at your expense,
they show off with borrowed honour,
lifted wisdom, plagiarized inspiration,
they lay burdens upon your back, they snub you like heck,
and yet boast with your words, pillage, defame, and murder you,
with all your gifts and riches ....
Exit their true Religion. Enter the Religion of Art.
Art is made of flesh and blood

and they all draw Blood
and revenge themselves in the Blood of poor Artists:
good as my good honours are, I am not Dives.

To their church of dreadful hatred,
spiteful revengeful mockery,
and cruel, vindictive, sadistic maltreatment
of infants, from the God of undying Hatred.
For all the Artists they hated
with a vindictive hatred,
for all the Hatred I feel for the likes,
because they do not want Us to love them
so that they will give us a beautiful honour.
The God of undying Hatred
loves His friends who honour Him
and loves His kinfolk only ....

My books are all naughty boys.
I give them all rights to misbehave:
great Artists are superior parents;
and I am a good Father
to my chosen Daughter and to the book I write.

This one book I wrote is the only dangerous book
I ever wrote, the only beautiful book
which I ever found offensive, it is the best book
I could have written to inspire respect
of beautiful work in spirits which are not foolish.

The church of the false Judge
who pillages, defames, and murders,
is the cruellest vengeance
the people ever suffered -
family is a Vengeance,
marriage is a Vengeance,
world Art is a Vengeance:
does not a poor Artist have rights to revenge himself?
Is this not all it takes to point out
just what a serious issue works of art are? .....
Harakiri upon false judges!

I would be damned, if I had done
something like that without love-death.
I have no wish to assert my rights over such a thing
if such rights are going to give me
a sinister and infamous reputation.
May the Lord resurrect the devil whom We shot
and I hope the conclusion to the book
shall be an invitation to the Dance ...

I abhor the word Hatred ...
I detest the word Vengeance ...
I care a lot more for loving thought
and loving feelings, who prefers to say -
"I hate!" ... like a child. I care a lot more for saving faces.
I care a lot more for being spared
the false accusation and degrading laurel
of falsehood ....
I have no rights to assert over such a book.
I have no rights to save my face by seeing a church
removed.
I merely assert rights over the Love inside my heart.
I ask for the Love of God.
I plead for my birthright to be at Peace
and make a prosperous living from the skill of my hands.

I am shocked, utterly scandalized,
just how well many people hate,
just what a real vengeance they were plotting
upon my poor soul, all my belongings,
my intellectual property, my birthrights,
and everything I possess ...
am I so foolish as to publish the vengeance I took
with a vain-glorious taunt upon my lips?
or am I so foolish as to plot top-secret assassinations,
in a church of false judges and spiritual aides?
Let them never so much as breathe
a single prayer on my behalf .....

Reader, apply this verse, not in empty jest,
but only to those who earn the insult best.

Where true thinking, and true teaching, most abound,
like petty Popes false judges most are found!

*17th September 2000*

## Beggars at the gates

**WE ARE** all beggars at the gates of Love:
God locks and joins and interleaves our hands,
which interlaced, are interwoven so
that we need no one, yet each other need!

*22nd September 2000*

## Mystical soliloquy 1

**TRULY** I'm tossed upon the horns of thought .....
you cannot imagine how very badly I wish
to leave Church - Christ!
                                        yet Jesus
I love, Jesus Christ, Jesus is not like that!
Gentle Jesus, Who keeps us waiting,
waiting for us also, with a patient, benign,
gentle, merciful, fathering, forgiving,
persistent Love, like the warm, golden sunshine!

I can hardly believe I flung
such hard swearing at Him.
Lord, we are strangers ...
You must come to my aid, if You wish me
to know You. I know not how best I may please You -

teach me .....
How may I best, oh Jesus, be good to You?
I know not what humours You best of all,
but only tell me ...
which prayers You enjoy hearing best!
which poems You like best!
which music You appreciate best!
which food best agrees with You!
which compliments you best enjoy being made!
which praise best cures that proud holy hurt
that with my thoughtless taunts I wounded!
Oh Sacred Head surrounded
with crown of piercing thorn ....

I feel so content to be on my own
talking to myself with only You for audience -
with You I feel secure! Your Spirit's attentive silence
is a safe, reliable place to pour it all into ...
Lord, I am frail, confess
to frailty of the flesh - honest to God!
that I am feeble, weak, loose.
Yet I aspire to practice
what in my Book I preach
as being the Law by which my conscience
is obliged to abide.
None may ever say I am inhuman.
Nor anyone give me the damning laurel -
faultless Artist ... ; nor yet that I am frigid,
and this much, Lord, is strength ...

I can hardly believe my ears,
I can hardly believe that in wild moods
I spoke so ill of You, gentle Jesus
Who let me carry on ...
I want my spirit to turn back home to You,
I want to recover my chilled youthful Love for You.
I want nothing that belongs to You.
You shall lose nothing on my account,
not Your honours, not Your titles,
not Your money, not Your gifts -

only Your Love, oh my chastest Jesus,
for what long years I longed
to be like You, and failed .....

*28th September 2000*

## Poetry is .....

*to my Mother*

**LIKE** cooking, like darning clothes, poetry is
a loving skill, a stitch in time, like all
good deeds - a nobility in the blood, much like
the genes themselves, fruit of the womb prepared
at conception, with lifelong labours purchased.
Gifts of the Spirit, knowledge of Art - together
with negative ability - are both
required theological virtues,
the Arts being a viable vocation for
the millions, who have naught besides. It's bad,
it's wrong to say that poems make nothing happen:
like grains of mustard seed, great poems are acts
of Faith - Faith in oneself, as much as in
a mightier Spirit capable of moving mountains;
prayers for and upon the Soul of Man.
Itself by Man created, Dante called it
'the grandchild of God': great Art created jobs,
and employment for masses upon masses
of worthy people. It is the '*Caus Causarum*'
of what one may call the most momentous event
of all, the silent, interior conversions, the changes
of heart, of dreary, habitual thought, which with
a change in Art, like change of scene, brighten
upon this Earth the light of common day,
and which God only knows, and only He
can keep thereof the records, documents,
and profoundly historical chronicles.

*2nd October 2000*

## Man, insentient man

**HOW SADLY**, oh my God, I saw You look today,
how red, how blue, how black Your Face,
how bitterly sore and ghastly,
what an ashen look upon Your fallen Face
suffused with silent, sculptured tears,
Divinity of old, Thou, Ancient of Days,
how icily unspeaking, how lonely, chill,
and far, head and flowing, bardic hair
in silent death to the ground bowed down
beneath a cruellest sorrow
upon the furthermost mountain-top ...

I dared not ask, Immortal.
I dared not break the spell,
lest my question, well-intended,
serve as nothing but a taunt
where the silence hurts, but speech
nothing but an accursed torment is!

Did the Evil One revenge himself,
perhaps, upon a child You love?
Or a Soul You once loved, once favoured,
or a Child with priceless graces gifted,
ungrateful turn, and a callous spike
drive in that tenderest Heart?
Or lovers, perhaps, who upon each other
dote, and each the other love, and praise, and favour,
but that love only use
as a cutting taunt to You?

Or did Insentient Man
nudge You, where Alone with Your Art
like a pot You brewed, but nudge You
only to send You sprawling,
like a rejected Book?

Lord, I am mortal, carnal, infirm,
but I pray, may neither my child, nor myself,

be that child, that soul, that friend, that lover,
that insentient beast ...
where well I know, Eternal, that beautiful art
is a soft spot the Divinity bore Itself to Man,
I love, I honour, Lord, my own sense of Honour
celebrate and cherish, and my pain
forget a little on Thy cut, tormented side,
but Thou, Thou hast no Honour but Thy Love .....

*21st October 2000*

## 15 poems of place

*A sequence of fifteen poems in free form*
*about homes I have lived in, in Vancouver,*
*over the past 20 years ...*

### 1. 2010 Mahon Avenue - 1982

**THE LAST** two nights of '81
we spent in our new home
in North Vancouver, purchased before
we came to Canada ...
It was a wee place,
with quite a few rooms, but for eight people
quite a tight squeeze. A brook tumbled beside
the house, gladdening the sight and
the ear.
Our relatives, perhaps,
felt happy at seeing six song-birds in a cage,
with mother-hen and father-cock fussing
around them, but of a sudden,
after six to eight months or so, the terrible
recession settled in, the value of property
rocketed down and the mortgage rates

shot up ...
all of us had our aspirations,
artistic, professional, employment-wise, or otherwise,
and none of us had adequate employment.
We could not afford the bills, and father
had to sell the house at an astronomical loss
which represented mum's and dad's life-savings ...

I still weep a little inside myself
when I remember.

## 2. Hoskins Drive

**IT WAS** much larger, and temporarily ours.
It belonged to an uncle-in-law
and his departed wife, mother's sister ...
They were not rich, but almost.
We heatedly argued and argued,
amongst ourselves, how far better for all of us
their advice and counsel would have been
than the one we took before we came to Canada ---
until uncle-in-law, who is now departed, said:
"Sorry! but the house is for sale ..."

## 3. Lillooet Road, North Vancouver

**IT WAS** a townhome with three floors.
I shared a room on the third with roofs
delightfully sloping ...
I had lost my job
at the gas-station, as the recession settled in.
I did business, with my typing services.
I corresponded with my new friend,
the poet Rex Hudson, as my plans to write
a book about him grew upon me,
and fleshed themselves out in my mind.

I shared a few last letters
with my Maltese girlfriend,
as our geographical separation,
and economical considerations,
became impossible to overcome.

I read poetry with undying passion
at the Literary Storefront,
downtown Vancouver,
where I was respected, looked up to
for inspiration, and for an honest opinion.

I tried hard to relate to my family,
to my new friends and audience,
to my new society.
I tried hard to obtain a second degree,
and to find a suitable job.
I often visited Capilano College,
close by my home ...

a sad man with many interests,
lonely and lovesick ...

## 4. 3070 Dryden Way

**FATHER** could at last afford a mortgage,
in a neighbourhood where streets were named
after great poets ...
The house was spacious,
with a garden and many private corners.
I had been admitted to post-graduate studies,
at UBC, till matters went out of control
and I had to leave, giving up, perhaps
prematurely, out of a loss of heart and morale,
and taking refuge immediately in social assistance.

It was at this point that I moved on my own
for two or three months till,
this pet project coming to grief also,

I moved back to Dryden Way where
I was allowed my own private, quiet quarters,
a small front room on the ground floor,
with its own separate doors to the street,
far too chilly, far too cold to sleep in,
but where I finished, thank God and with the help
of many a generous friend, composing my book
about Rex Hudson, a fine piece of work,
acclaimed unanimously by the poet and by
his friends, who published the work for both of us,
my first in North America.

I immediately commenced work upon my second,
my tribute to my future wife, my twenty-four sonnets
which I allowed only my wife, a few friends, and my friend
Rex Hudson to see, but which were destined
entirely to sell after I had put aside
my voluminous collections of belles-lettres,
and over two hundred pages of good poetry
to my name.
                                        It was at Dryden Way
that father got me hooked upon rolling
my own cigarettes, and making my own smokes
with the cigarette machine and empty tubes,
with filters and all, an innovation in our
tight circumstances which dramatically
reduced my smoking from five or six packs
to one pouch a day, where it has stayed ever since.

## 5. East 12th

**IT WAS** special. It was blessed.
It was hilarious. It was a farce.
To live on your own you need no roommates ...

I moved in with someone I required not,
a Catholic who did me in,
borrowing my last two hundred dollars,
father's money, and moving out on me,

with money and all, leaving me alone
with a man and his girlfriend, who
moved out also.
Before
I moved back to Dryden Way,
where I was destined to finish work
on my first book, I received Blessed Light
one night in the middle of the night,
Joy, Holy Fire, Truth, Inspiration,
a spotless loving Feeling, a faultless Insight.

I would not do myself a favour, friend,
to say how, or what, or why, or what words
were exchanged between my soul and
the invisible heavenly Friends Who consoled my ears,
alone in my lonely bedroom, but those were the words
that cured me of a lifelong error in perception,
that set me on a safer, sounder path
of knowledge, thinking, feeling.

I almost regret having left that Place
where my innermost Mind saw Sense
and which my Heart ought to have called Home.
To live on your own you need no roommates.
Great God I could shoot myself in the leg
for avoiding the Angel that followed me
right to that door ....

## 6. Dundas Street, East Vancouver ...

... **WAS** my first marital home, a one-bedroom
with a tiny balcony, and an inconceivably
boring view - a deadly space
riddled, from the start, by poverty
and unemployment, by the slow, accursed stain
of universal guilt in the very sound
of the one word, "divorce" -- but for
the fresh promise of new, interesting love,
a relationship to work out, a new child

to conceive, to hope for and hope in,
and the hope of a brighter future ...

Ah! that deadly cave, that cruel cage
was a poet's! and there and then
I sold my beautiful guitar for a thousand,
forgot my music, threw overboard my expensive lessons,
published my book with the money, the sonnets
I wrote for my wife, with instant success
as a poet ...

I do not regret it --
no one around me felt what I felt for my music:
no one cared to help ...
But next time
a friend like my estranged, hardworking wife
shall offer to pay for my ticket
on our honeymoon, however costly,
I shall never say no again
out of a mistaken sense
of compassionate pity ...

## 7. Forbes Ave., N. Vancouver

**MY SECOND** marital home was a two-bedroom
on the ground floor of an old house with a lawn,
and marked for demolition, where my daughter
was born, where I wrote her
a prize-winning sonnet ....
Memories crowd my mind,
unemployment, the intensity of my love
for my child, selling books door to door
in the snow to take my wife out on her birthday,
my intense financial embarassment, trying
to find a publisher for my selected poems,
and on and on.
The neighbourhood
was far more fun than Dundas, and I was friends
with the neighbours, upstairs, and they bought

my writing, as well as other products from me.
We were very close to a Catholic Church,
as well as to my infant daughter's future school.
We were also close to a nun's convent,
where I used to take my infant child,
and she would look at the roses
and smile at me ...

My wife and myself, before we moved out,
had hopes to buy the entire property, upstairs
and downstairs, and we could not afford it.
Ah! poor Julia! and my poor feet and my back!
The house was sold to a man who had some money,
and with the money he demolished it and built
a complex of four, beautiful townhomes,
probably making somewhere around a million ...

## 8. West 3rd, N. Vancouver

**MY THIRD** marital home was my wife's first mortgage,
a major feat of financial juggling and economic
management of the family income.
It was a ground-floor,
corner-of-the-building suite, with two bedrooms
and access to the small but gorgeous
garden on the side of the building. The mail
arrived punctually, and quite early in the day.
I would rush to pick it up as soon as I woke up.
My poetry journal, at that time, had been
established, and I lived for my mail.

I was selling my publications door to door
with notable success. One of my authors,
who had won a prize in the magazine's
first contest, visited me from Seattle.
A member of my door to door public
had given me a Siamese kitten,
a weakling with severe emotional problems,
having been forcefully separated from its mother.

It was sad to watch the kitten die.
At the time
I was also assisting, on somewhat compassionate grounds,
a businessman, likewise with severe health,
and emotional problems, with his business -
to no end and to no avail. It was so sad
to watch my friend eventually die
of alcoholism.
But I had become
a well-known BC author with a first-rate
reputation, though my marital problems,
sadly enough, persisted in escalating ...

## 9. 1737 Larson Road

**LIKEWISE** a major feat of economical juggling,
my fourth marital home was my wife's second mortgage,
a full-blown house with a full-blown yard, green hedges,
and garden ...
My daughter was growing up,
and happy as I was in our well-earnt home,
where I had two rooms all to myself,
to use as office space and as a music room,
the terrifying problems, which eventually led
to the breakup of our union, escalated
with horrid facility, and I sure as heck
believe in the jealous Devil ...
I had established myself
as author and small press publisher. A lot
of other authors, as well as members of the public,
looked up to me for my expertise,
as well as unique marketing techniques,
and the authors considered the credits
I gave them extremely professional
and credible. And our new address
looked so beautiful as a publisher's headquarters.

Julia was often lenient when it came to money,
but it is no wonder God hates divorce.

I could have ended up on the street,
and Julia could so easily have lost the house
to me and to the lawyers, and myself
could easily have lost my fledgling daughter's
future sympathy ...
I preferred to settle
for a reasonable figure, forgiving
Julia a far larger settlement against all the bills
she had been paying ...

## 10. West 4th, N. Vancouver

**I CHOSE** the apartment for being so very close
to my daughter's home, a large one-bedroom where,
for the first time in my troubled life, I had
my own space all to myself, two canaries, two finches,
office space for my professional work, a large
bedroom with an extremely spacious,
walk-in wardrobe closet, and many other
advantages. I invited a few friends over
and composed, at West 4th, some excellent poetry -
published in '99 - but it was an extremely expensive
apartment.

Things went out of control again
when, after eight months or so, my money
from my marital settlement fizzled out -
after I agonized how best to spend it,
being actually obliged to spend it all
by the Ministry
and spending too big a portion, sadly,
on an entirely unsuccessful business venture -
and I had to move, as quickly as I could,
to less expensive quarters.

## 11. Burquitlam

**BURQUITLAM** was far too lonely, and although
the major routes were totally as noisy
as in any other modern city,
the neighbourhood was far too uneventful,
decidedly boring and deadly.
The apartment was smaller
and cheaper than West 4th, and the landlord
very helpful - until he extorted far too much money
from me when I had to move. My canary and finches
died. It was so sad and lonely.

I experienced trouble with my neighbours,
upstairs, and underwent a break in,
losing good stereo equipment to the thieves,
just before I got the opportunity to move
close to my parents.

## 12. 5937-B East Hastings

**BEFORE** I ever so much as saw it coming,
though the rent was low, though my parents
were my neighbours, and though the apartment
was one of the most splendidly spacious
one-bedrooms I ever rented, the hydro bills
were far too high and I had to pay them all,
slowly, out of my welfare cheque.
I was otherwise
very happy with that place, a large, ground-floor suite
with splendid location, until the new landlord -
a tight-fisted businessperson for that matter - argued
that it was an illegal suite and that he required the space
for business improvements.
I had already applied
for a subsidized home with BC Housing
and several other associations, and the fact

that I got practically kicked out on the street
by businesspeople was, if you ask me,
the best blessing in disguise I could have asked for then.

## 13. Plaza Hotel

**IT WAS** a pleasant, relatively inexpensive
room to stay in, with a single bed and a small stove,
and somewhat cramped, until such time as I could obtain
proper, subsidized housing.
I was on good terms
with the manageress, a senior, extremely lively,
busy and active lady in her eighties,
with an agile mind, extremely pleasant,
British manners, and some form of interest
in books. She gave me kind permission
to bring my desk and computer equipment
into my room, the only amusement I had ...

The neighbourhood
was full of lower class types of folk,
but the fact that I had almost been shoved out
upon the street was in my hands the most persuasive
argument I had to put the pressure upon
BC Housing and convince them that I was
in emergency, and my stay at Plaza Hotel
lasted for less than two months .....

## 14. Stratford Gardens

*6035 Pandora Street - 1st Feb. '99/1st Nov. 2000*

**THE PLACE** had good spirit,
good karma, good feeling,
and my parents were my neighbours.

My mother prayed hard for me
to obtain a subsidized home from BC Housing

when I was almost out on the street ...
early '99. My father visited at times -
to fix a light-bulb, and twice a week, at nine
in the morning, he would call at the garden door,
leave me early morning coffee in a bag,
leave me snacks for the day,
before he went to work in Surrey.

It was sweet, consoling, comforting,
reminiscent of childhood, tranquillizing,
to have my old man look after me
gently and silently, with the strength of love.

I had a holy corner.
It was full of devotional items, rosaries and images,
where my heart prayed and called the place home.
It was tiny, it was a hole in a wall,
but it was mine, my one-stop, afterdeath retreat,
where I had silence, solitude, forgiveness, comfort, peace,
and my parents were my neighbours.
I could call on them and eat.

I felt sad to let it go.

## 15. Richmond Gardens

**MY SUBSIDIZED** apartment on Gilbert Road
concludes this minor saga, or semi-poetic diary,
of constant motion, constant search, and constant
relationship, a splendid, bright and spacious,
one bedroom, which I moved into on November 1st, 2000,
offered by Canadian Mental Health Association.

I have all the space
I ever aspired to have all to myself
for an affordable rent. I merely hope,
as I write, to drum up within myself
the intellectual and emotional energy -
and I have had an unusually eventful

interior life, full of the joy of artistic creation -
to keep plugging away at my professional calling -
author and small press publisher, until such time
as I can manage to raise money, perhaps
only in small sums at a time, to keep investing
into my small business, and to be honest
and not delude myself, I can honestly say
I could shoot myself in the leg for not managing
my money better and accomplishing far more
than I actually did, with my finanacial management skills
honed just a little more finely.
Richmond, I find,
is just as busy, interesting, and active a place
as Burnaby is, and not at all a boring place,
though the long bus-rides try my patience, but
I think that, after Richmond, my next stop shall be either
fame and riches, or else back home to Malta,
my native country .....
I have, as I write, two splendid applications
for financial assistance, lodged with
the Canada Arts Council, and a lot to look forward to,
if only I were to get as lucky with such people
as I feel that I honestly deserve ...

## 16. Coda ...

"Poets, learn your trade:
Sing whatever is well-made ..."
**(W. B. Yeats)**

**BEFORE** I composed this tin-eared sequence,
I gave myself this counsel,
just a little while ago ...

Friend, to think hard, deep and close is fine,
and equally fine to write in a subtle,
relatively obscure, complex, or difficult convention -
complexity saves your face
from the simplicity of the impious,

from the false honours of the far too sincere -
plague upon them!

Do not revenge yourself on complexity
and subtlety, but every now and then
be a little facile and even, perhaps,
facetious. You can still compel
and command a sensitive interest
where the heart understands.
Never mind if sometimes
you need to compose simple, unmusical verse,
that may sound somewhat tin-eared and silly,
even though it may not seem well-made
and the pedant may call it "the comics".

You do not need to get an hernia
to convey through honest work an honest feeling
nor should your reader get one
as his reward for trying to catch your effect.

*Commenced on 27th November 2000*
*Completed on 12th December 2000*

## Lamplighter most gracious ...

**HOWEVER** I complain, things turn out,
food's on the table, a little pocket money,
barely enough perhaps, and a book to sell
is in my hands always .....
As when
my neon tube was the only good light I owned,
and it ran out of neon gas while I was writing,
and beneath my breath I would pray,
a little sulkily:
"Jesus! Gheezus!
to pay for it will stretch me - but

You care, and if You but wish
to help me, so You can and so You will -
fix the light for me, Jesus:
I need it - can't work without it!"

And hey presto, forthwith
my neon tube would flicker alive again,
as my personal sense
of intimate union
with my invisible Friend
deepened and grew
more intimate!

Love You, Jesus -
love You, Lamplighter most gracious ...

*27th November 2000*

## Faultfinder, faultfinder ...

**CHILD,** my child Lady Aphrodite,
this vision flashed upon my inward eye:
one hundred thousand souls and more I saw
burn in the fire, and the Spirit of the Lord
came down upon me, communicating, as it were,
these thoughts that struck inside my heart.

"Child," or such was
what I understood, "these are the unfortunate
who lost their skin not through My Judgment,
nor through anything I willed for them. Devils they are
who love Me, living their earthly life
chained, as it were in a dungeon, to the feet
of a false judge in a top-secret box, who lost their head
in a state of grace, caught in the eyes of the evil one
only through negligence and faultfinding. Child,"

the silent, unspeaking voice seemed to say,
"the Judgment is not for them as terrible as they think it is.
Notch it to experience, count it as one, terrifying chapter
in life, consider what faults, real or imagined,
or small, or hefty, you've been forgiven - forgive
and forget, rise and forebear, and ever thank God
and bless your luck you went not there."

Faultfinders, faultfinders, I sighed in a ghastly pain,
but with a breath of thanks, little you know, faultfinders,
what brutal white-collar criminals you are
against humanity, against the suffering, inward,
soul of people a lot more sensitive, and
a lot more human than you: leave us alone,
faultfinders, leave us alone, all meddlers finding fault,
who seem but to blot out and blotch
the very love of God and light of day
like a black, scandalous door swinging shut
in the face of all those who are born free ...

*13th December 2000*

## Unforgettable sensations

**FLESHED** in the intricate depths of my own mind
and marmoreal senses, as on a silent screen,
the shadows gently fill with chequered shade,
where fairies dance and thornless are the roses,
and gracious nymphs and muses naked play
in the embroider'd maze. Like swan-song wild
at sunset, peace, youth and passion play upon
the classical faces, cast in Love and Death,
exchanging Heaven's language, each to each
unfolding tall ones with a Blessed ending ...
Jesus and Mary, Orpheus, Pan and all
the gods of fable piping four Quartets,

Hellfire springing gently from beneath -
small, ruddy flames in loving dance whereon
the gods stroll hand in hand ...

*21st December 2000*

## Poet and "failed" musician .....

**IN MY** book **regrets hopes regards and prayers .....**, a collection of prose and poetry released in August 1996, I published two essays, both exercises in musicology, or music criticism. These were **Beethoven's Ninth: A Note of Appreciation**, and **Popular Music, Classical Music: Terms to Examine**. Not being myself, in any way, a professional or fully-fledged musician, nor even a fully trained performer upon my instrument, classical guitar, I might still recriminate myself to my dying day and cry over spilt milk all my life long, that I did not -- while the feeling was still fresh inside me, while the inspiration still possessed and haunted me -- write a book of essays in music criticism about the music I have listened to all my life, a lot of which I still listen to and which so many people love so well.

There are a few things I have learnt, as much as from the joy of my successes as from the anguish of my failures. What I offer below to the aspiring musician who is willing to learn from mistakes which I made in good faith -- errors which I know far too well that the majority of my own contemporaries and teachers make all the time -- are a string of self-counsels, or rules in the philosophy of performance upon a musical instrument, which I have gleaned and learnt over the years, not owing to any outstanding success as a musical artist, but more from the sheer anguish and bitterness of failure ...

As an author of twelve books, published in Canada, I have formed a reputation as a poet in BC, in Malta (my country), in Minnesota, to some extent in Wisconsin, in small poetry journals in Britain, and elsewhere. I own my own poetry journal, my own small press, and have also published other authors in book form, one of the most notable being John Laycock, from Britain, now deceased, who fought in World War 2.

I sold over 20,000 copies of poetry publications and related literature between 1985 and 2000. I sold 6,000 copies of **Out of Blue Nothing** and 2,000 copies of my book about Malta, **In the Suburbs of Europe.** The professor of Maltese at the University of Malta told me that there is nothing like my book about Malta in Maltese literature and that it shall always hold pride of place therein. All my other books sell competitively.

I have pioneered in Canada rhyme-revival and neo-classicist revival. I have been honoured to assist Rex Hudson, the late Nobel and Pulitzer Prize nominee from Minnesota; the late Mary Meisel, a poet from California; and John Laycock. I have created a poetry journal, of which I have released 25 issues and in which I have published and encouraged many budding and deserving authors, many of them from BC.

When I came to Canada on December 28, 1981, not a single poetry journal I ever wrote to, between 1981 and 1985, when I self-published my first book, would condescend to buy one single poem of mine in rhyme and metre. A total, complete and perfect bigotry existed against work in rhyme, even though I had written well in free form, stream of consciousness, blank verse etc., and between 1981 and 1985 this bigotry settled over my head.

I then self-published, in 1985, my sonnet-sequence, **Out of Blue Nothing.** Since the first edition of 500 copies came out, I have sold another five editions of this book, six in all, around 6,000 books, making this book a national bestseller for a Canadian book of poetry, turning the tables around in my favour, and giving the lie to people who used to tell me that people did not want this sort of thing any longer. Oh no! I had consulted the people and won!

With the creation of my poetry journal, **The Eclectic Muse**, in 1989, the tables were turned completely, a serious and real rhyme-revival had been inaugurated, pioneered in

Canada by myself and my clan of poets, and since then 25 issues of my journal have been released.

Having described my successes as a poet, I have to be extremely humble about my failures as a musician. Ever since I was a child I wanted to study music. In Malta, there were no qualified classical guitar teachers when I started. Eventually it was decided that a guitar worth $18 should be purchased for me and I was sent to learn plectrum guitar under the tuition of a jesuit monk with no qualifications. An equally fraudulent music teacher, a stranger who was the best friend of my mother's sister, presented me with a plectrum guitar method, signed by her to me in flowery terms, which can only be described as a piece of junk.

I then obtained a teacher for myself who taught me how to read music and play plectrum guitar and under his guidance I worked my way through one album by Nick Manoloff and worked my way on my own through another collection of guitar solos likewise compiled by Nick Manoloff. I was dissatisfied and in my heart I knew that a lot was missing. I did not obtain for myself a qualified classical guitar tutor till ten years later and only through the generous eye-openers of my English poetry tutor and his likewise distinguished father (the personal friend of Maestro Segovia whom I mention below) ... and only after I had picked up countless bad habits and done considerable damage to my ear.

Himself a pupil of John Williams, my new tutor taught me the Segovia technique properly. Under his guidance, I picked up new skills fluently, was beginning to play well, had learnt some music by heart, and could even play **Recuerdos de la Alhambra**, and some other concert pieces, proficiently. By this time, also, I had purchased, with my family's assistance, quite a beautiful student guitar from Manuel Rodriguez in Spain, and had also paid it off with my own money.

I then came to Canada, in December of 1981. After a month I obtained a scruffy job and went on taking desultory lessons and practicing. Lessons, however, were expensive in Vancouver, compared to Malta. When I lost my job in late 1982, till I got married in December 1984, I could not afford a single guitar lesson, since I was receiving social assistance and still making no money, neither from music, nor from my writing. Again, when I got married, I was cut off income assistance, presumably because my wife was perceived as earning money. My wife and I decided to sell my classical guitar for $1000 and, with the money, I self-published my first book. I succeeded instantly and since then there has been no looking back but my musical education was over. Just because it was decreed that I ought to be a "saint" and not an "artist", and because I was too young to know better, I had effectively been aborted, deceived, and defrauded to my face of a proper musical education, to the extent that, for my entire fifty years of life and more, I have been chronically unable to settle down to a suitable career.

Though it spelled success for me as a poet I still regret that decision. Things could have been worked out differently, more cunningly, without me having to sell my guitar or give up music. Added to my success as a poet I could by now have also been a proficient classical guitarist. I had learnt a lot of basic music making and the lessons I learnt as an amateur musician and music lover have done me proud in my work as a literary artist.

A noteworthy incident occurred in 1982. In Malta I had a great friend - the father of my English poetry tutor - who was a personal friend of Maestro Segovia. When Segovia visited Vancouver in 1982, having no doubt been tipped about me by our mutual friend, he asked for me after the recital. The usher, unfortunately, pronounced my name Joe Ricci, instead of Joe Ruggier (Roodgeer), and I was new to Canadian mispronounciations. I was also still overawed by my surroundings and failed to take the precious hint. Had I only taken the hint I might have met and made friends with Maestro Segovia and he might have taken me under his wing and helped me. He is now dead and gone and all I can do is sigh and breathe a prayer.

Rule number one. If your blood is an artist's and an artist of Maestro Segovia's stature asks for you, allow yourself to be overawed by nothing whatsoever, clench your teeth and bluff your way right through it until you meet him, however scandalous and outrageous the bad pronounciations are. Rule number two. Never allow yourself to be ruled by relatives, however apparently well-meaning they seem. If you wish to make your own way as an artist be ruled by your own instinct only but always seek to blend it, not with the advice of well-wishers you happen to live with, but with inspired judgment. Trust your own artistic judgment and seek to bring it out untill it is a lot sharper and more reliable. Trust your own *amour-propre* as much as your own feeling of romantic love for your subjects and area of specialization.

Rule number three. Do not allow anyone to despise far too far what you know well and learnt all on your own with nothing but your own skill, good will, and gifted ear. This is a corollary of that famous rule of thumb, do not try to teach an old horse new tricks. What I am implying is that my qualified tutor, back in Malta -- hats off to him for managing to teach me the Segovia technique -- was totally wrong in coming down so hard on my plectrum performances. He merely set me down hard on the way to despair and demoralized failure. The way to go was to ask me to deliver a plectrum concert to an audience of complete beginners on the grounds that, all over the World, beginners are started playing plectrum guitar as a warming up aptitude test (a test which I had passed formidably) … on the grounds also that I was doing "something right"—that "something right", whatever Maestro Segovia or John Williams were saying, being "the Joy of Music!" This would have made my courage soar without making me look down on my previous teacher, as long as it were made clear that I must learn far more competent technique. Now what on earth is wrong with asking a student to give a plectrum concert, to a suitable audience, of an entire album which he learnt to perform on his own, which gave him so much joy of music making, and likewise gave pleasure to people who listened to him play it, though they were not professional music critics? Where on earth is the joy of music, let me ask, and where on earth is the protection of a student's artistic rights, if a qualified teacher can crush, beneath the heels of world famous artists, his own student's personal achievement so remorselessly, though it can only be described as an elementary achievement?

Rule number four. Learn to seize and clutch at a good opportunity. I was performing, once, a beautiful piece of renaissance music, on my Spanish guitar, in the fields, just beside my home in Malta, before I came to Canada. A gang of fifteen little children or more, most of them very probably only around six, seven or eight years old, rushed towards me, as soon as I finished, crying out loudly, "again!" It was the first time in my life a real audience had requested an encore from me. I do not know what unholy instinct made me sulk and feel so inadequate, pack up and go. I do not know what the hell of a self-destructive, fatalistic mood and temper comes over us sometimes, worse than a simple timid awe, or fear of inadequacy. Those children could have been the angels of Heaven. I could have made it there and then as the leading classical guitarist on the island of Malta. What critical acclaim is more solid, let me ask you, than that of the children? I can still shoot myself in the leg. I still feel like having failed a test I was meant to pass, through my own, most grievous fault.

A similar opportunity occurred in Canada, in 1982, when I was working at a gas-station, in North Vancouver, a job which involved night duties. I used to take my writing papers and my classical guitar with me and, when the night was quiet, I would either write or practice guitar. My boss had found out that I was becoming a proficient performer. Once he actually visited, with his wife and two sons. He offered to take care of the cash, operating the till himself, pointedly requesting that I play music for him. Mr. Ruggier ... shoot yourself in the leg once more for self-destructive tendencies! He could have been your first impresario in Canada and Maestro Segovia could have been your second!

What follows below pertains more closely to the theory of music criticism and to the philosophy of performance upon your favourite musical instrument. The bad theory that I am about to criticize is not my fault because the vast majority of music teachers, however highly esteemed, however well they think of themselves, however qualified they think they are, practice it as an accepted, enlightened, and acceptable pedagogy: it is truly shocking, it is utterly scandalous, just what bad pedagogy, and what bad theory it really is, but it is not my fault.

When a student, however gifted, whatever natural flair, grace and good will he may bring to it, obtains a qualified teacher for himself for the first time, it is the custom among many such qualified people, if not among all, to tell the poor student that it were far better if he knew nothing at all, just how incompetent his own training is, and usually to drop a lot of famous names with their student and, in due course of time, slowly teach him how to play piles upon piles of music already extremely famous and performed to perfection by many other performers, some of them extremely famous also.

I am not saying that my own teacher did not teach me well. He was a splendid teacher; but I had to fight him to teach me. I merely bear witness here and now that these pedagogical methods should be entirely forbidden and totally disallowed. Why? That is just what I am about to do, tell you why, and you will see what good critical sense my own theories make. I may well be a "failed" musician, but neither my literary successes, nor my musical failures were ever wasted on me, neither in the music I breathe into my poetry, nor as a musicologist, and music theorist and critic.

When Maestro Segovia first demonstrated his craftsmanship and superb technique to the world of music and launched his unspeakably eloquent world-wide appeal for gifted composers everywhere to compose beautiful music for Spain's beloved instrument ... he had done it. No one could ever hope to do it better and success like that can never be repeated. Naturally, once Maestro Segovia established himself, and he was born in the era of vinyl records and long-playing musical albums, he had established himself for real and his music was effectively immortalized. Vladimir Bobri eventually published the book, **The Segovia Technique**, which defined with finality the classical guitarist's credo, on the basis of which so many musicians, who would otherwise have wasted their time in the ranks of the unemployed, are now gainfully and pleasantly employed. What I am putting forth is a pedagogical credo of equal power if it were to be universally accepted.

Teach an intelligent, gifted, willing student to play the famous and extremely beautiful pieces performed by all the famous names you know only in so far as they are going to help your student improve his technique, craft, performance skills, judgment, and overall musicianship, and not one jot or tittle further. In other words, no one on earth should ever be made to feel that he needs to play ***Diferencias sobre guardame las vacas, Recuerdos de la Alhambra, Preludes No 1 and No 4 by Villa Lobos, Granada***, and such like music, just as Segovia plays it, or just as John Williams plays it, or as well as Narciso Yepes plays it, or like Julian Bream. No one can. No one ever will play these pieces as lustily as Segovia. And if you did it will be no use because you would not receive the honour however badly you would like it. The honour goes to Segovia.

Believe me it is ridiculous that I could fall into a trap like that especially because I knew that the trap existed. And I say this to many teachers. You are driving many sensitive budding musicians to despair about their skills. Encourage the gifted student to learn how to play only the barest modicum of music which has become so famous, performed as it is by all the big names in the industry. Once the gifted, sensitive student has learnt his stuff, he should positively be forbidden, in the most imperative, strongest, most forceful terms, to go on playing such music. Let's face it ... such music does not belong to him. It does not belong to you or me. The honour for composing it is not ours nor the honour for inspiring it and performing it to unparalleled perfection before the millions. The answer is forget it. Chuck it overboard. If you really wish to enjoy it listen to Segovia, but, if you really wish to get yourself a better honour, play something else and perform those hackneyed pieces only if you become very famous yourself and the public requests them from you.

It is a lesson in basic honesty and justice. Turn the honours over to their rightful owners. Play only those pieces over which you enjoy exclusive rights to perform and no one else has a right to perform it. Play the world-famous pieces only if you become as famous as Yepes, Williams, or

Alirio Diaz, and only if the public requests them from you. Be yourself and never take any notice if someone tells you that you cannot play like Segovia. Do not heed such shameless trash. He cannot play the pieces you are playing either anymore than you can play like Segovia because the rights do not belong to him. Never break the laws of your profession, for nobody and for no reason, by which I mean rights law. If you are trying to play like Segovia you are effectively breaking the law, because the rights to that honour do not belong to you. As I wrote earlier, I may well be a failed musician, but the lessons were not wasted on me, and I am a professional poet and a professional editor and critic. If this vein of theoretical and pedagogical thinking were adopted universally by qualified teachers I think that the effect will be one where we might be able to stand back and admire dozens upon untold dozens of artists who are all of them a lot more different and original and we shall be able to sit down and enjoy.

The answer is, perform your own compositions and transcriptions only. On a humbler mode you can try your hand at Segovia's trick. Make friends with good composers you know and appreciate and ask them to send you some compositions to perform for them as long as they can give you exclusive rights to perform them. Try your hand at transcribing melodious tunes you hear for your favourite instrument. I once transcribed for classical guitar an extremely melodious church-song which my friends in Malta used to sing in chapel. It was a very successful transcription and it worked like magic in chapel during the silences. I held the congregation spellbound while performing it. And in Malta only, though it was not the Land of the guitar like Spain, there was, God!, volumes of beautiful and original Maltese music which could have been successfully transcribed for an instrument as eloquent as the classical guitar. Had I attempted it twenty five years ago, I would have been hailed as a musician in my own country.

That is what it means to be an inspired artist as it is given unto you to be an inspired artist. Be limited by your own identity. You will become a real artist with a profound identity. Do not ever attempt to emulate or assume anyone else's nor ever allow the academic establishment to drown your identity beneath the art, achievements and honours of another nation's. These simple rules and do's and don't's of pedagogical theory should positively become dogmatic inflexible rules and taboos of the music teaching profession. If they were to be universally practiced as such they would have the effect of producing gifted, intelligent performers who are all far more interesting artists, because they are all playing different music which no one else is playing. They will have the effect of rendering all those extremely famous pieces a lot less hackneyed than they sound just now, such that it will really become a joyful experience, capable of restoring the beauty back to the music, to return to listening to those world famous pieces on your stereo equipment, or else listening in the concert hall. And we shall all be able to hear a lot of new musical pieces, perhaps not at all as famous, which no one else is hearing anywhere else, because you will be playing your own music, over which you have exclusive rights of performance. The whole point about my plectrum concert is that no one else was playing that entire album so well with a plectrum if my teacher had only protected my rights to perform it ... You were not an expert and the music gave you and others joy; and when you became an expert you became a wretch. Without resorting to inexcusable French, the bottom line, I repeat, is your money's worth and mine, as much as it is bringing the joy back into music.

*December 29, 2000 – May 15, 2009*

## Love-talk ...

**TALK** to me as true lovers talk,
a gentle, healing, silent talk,
where words - like 'honey', 'darling', 'love you' -
mean more than baby talk is true.
Tell me only, if you have to,
I love you simple, plain and true,
me a fish, silver, slim and little,
beneath the coral, fine and brittle.
Snap it not, drop no trap nor bait,
but simply stand, and gazing wait.
Nude in their element fishes swim,
unashamed, nor trapped by fashion's whim.
Ah! my heart's nude darling, when I think of you,
I'm no less human, no less true .....

*14th January 2001*

## Hedges .....

**BOOKS** which are far too great are terrible:
they kill the little birds, they slit their throat -
the little robins chirp their brittle song
and die. They trim the gorgeous, luscious bushes,
they leave them bare and nude and dwarfed and naked.
I beg, beseech, I plead, if you love, but love
the Arts, kill not the little birds, slit not
their slender throat, and murder not the joy
of song which silent sings within the throat,
in the forgotten wilds.
Pray for one book,
one book, perhaps, with an eclectic muse,
where all the subtlest complexity of thought
revenges not the singlest, slightest chirrup,
and no one dies of suffocated song
or feeling .....

*14th January 2001*

## A proof of love

**NOW WHEN** I was fresh and easy, I would go
to Church ... devotion fill'd my soul with tears.
I guessed not all Gospels could so tiresome grow -
the same words repeated for twice a thousand years.
But middle-aged I have become aware
of all the paranoia, boredom, pain,
where with lame hands I grope ... of empty air
and dust, and chances lost, and littlest gain.
Yet here I am, my God, where I relax
in warmth of heaters, and Thy glowing smile,

where words, repeated, securer are than cheques,
the Love which then I felt, now lost awhile.
Thus we gave God, Whose Love doth not change the story,
a proof of Love — seal of eternal glory!

*21st January 2001*

## The arts once more ....

**YOUR** face, my thane, is as a Book where men
may read strange matters."
So wrote the Poet ....
sure - he was a lover true and honourable!
Such is the love of God - or men - to me.

The love of God,
the love of God,
the love of God
is a Book, inspired, divinely beautiful -
and likewise love of people ... and all the true
religions there ever were, or yet to come,
are works of Art: I have no other conscience!

Oh Friend, say I, beware of saints whose follies
are more obnoxious than a demon's; beware,
I say once more, of the simplicity
of the impious ... the false honours
of the far too sincere: the over-wise,
and likewise the over-foolish - plague upon them!

Complexity redeems my face
from such and such disorders ...
but barely to conclude, I write my own
good book myself assisted by the reader,

by the sincerity and love of my own friend.

Love works three ways: one's own, one's friend, the Lord's
where Hell and Heaven married none do harm.

*23rd January 2001*

## 1: To the Poet ...

*After re-reading CHRISTABEL*
*and KUBLA KHAN*

**GENTLE,** honourable creature who works on air,
old friend of grief, old friend of love, of care,
hurt by the critics, hurt by the niggler's lance,
hostage to fortune, hurt by roulettes of chance,
hurt by the grocer's principle - ah! my friend,
on earth, on earth, there be no rest, nor end!
Over-criticized, mismetred, mistranslated,
over-read-into, misquoted, misinterpreted!
Creature of love ..... responding but to love
and adoration - by Heaven above,
I say, modest but proud, be glad, rejoice!
You have an honour: not with boastful noise -
but what on earth is honour worth but hate
if you do not rejoice? do not create
nothing but work of beauty, truth and goodness,
that in your work your heart rise back and bless
itself, your thoughts, your days, and loveliness
come back to you immortally .....

*30th January 2001*

## 2: The bad author

**HE TORTURED** sense and tortured style.
He tortured words and tortured sounds.
He tortured understanding, hearts and minds ...

He wants good dollars for aimless chat - small talk
lop-eared to look like verse ...
which anyone may have for free
around the next street corner.

He cared naught about the life-long waste
of reams upon untold reams of good white paper,
expensive ink, and tens of thousands of hours
of precious time, his own and his consultants' ...

He cared naught that on earth there is
real hunger - for real food as much as of the spirit,
nor that one of the poorest could have become
himself a proficient artist, with so many supplies,
and with similar opportunities ...

He is unaware that nothing but bad feeling,
nothing but bad understanding,
shall come back to him in Art ... eternally!

*1st February 2001*

## 3: words, my Lord ...

**I SAID** unto my Friend    good music is good doctrine ...
free us, oh my Lord    from the cold war of words
bring back unto old eyes the loveliest gems of Light
the joy unto my smile    the laughter back
unto my life        and with the coal
of inspiration retouch my trembling lip
and the bonniest song bring back
into my face
            pass around the wine of Love
for Love as of old    sweet Love
                        once more    and of all
these
nothing but Love remains
                exchanging with us only
classics instead of words .....

*4th February 2001*

## between editors .....

*to Jan Nathan*

**LITTLE** do a million authors know
what lofty hopes what ideals
what vision and what passion
good editors begin with early in life

until harassed by the mundane as much as
the Scriptural call to make ends meet
they are driven inexorably to pettier chores
which all conceal regardless a love-affair
between the lines .....

as the editor steers as best he can
towards far lesser evils involved as he is
in the clash upon clash of egos upon fragile egos
which editors protect dutifully and as best they can
at the cost far too often of their own joy
in their own writing or in books they'd far prefer to read

and so my heart really goes out to you
Jan Nathan sparkling successful
editor and woman of the world with I am sure
many a loftier aspiration and likewise your own
right reasons as I offer
this modest token of my appreciation
for a golden publication credit
just as a well-wisher
might pluck three red roses
from his garden if he had any
and send them along with his greetings
upon a thank you card

*10th February 2001*

## From Canada with love -

**THE GOOD** God Who hears the cry of the poor
displays Himself in our splendid social services ...
thanks be given always
for Theodore, and Jennifer, and Judy,
for Mental Health Associations - and for subsidized homes.

But Buddha, Confucius, the Hindus, Mohammed,
Baha'ullah, and likewise the God of the Christians,
all Saints and Artists also, conveyed their Love in a Book,
inspired, divinely beautiful, where words are supported
by deeds, and words and deeds are Law ...

Is it then within me error to assume
that the only true Religion there ever was
is a divinely inspired Book supported by deeds
and Love?
He Who conveys His Love through authors -
He is not vulgar ... He is not narrow ...

But the poor, ah! the poor sustain a great wrong,
unable as they are to stand up on their own feet ...
Everyone postpones, procrastinates and fritters away
their time. Everyone refers the poor to someone else,
or to a separate department of social services.
Everyone puts off seeing and serving them,
just because they can only be seen *gratis*. Everyone
gives them appointments, seeing them for a few minutes
only.
Everyone will talk to them properly next time ...
All their pressing urgencies are invariably postponed
or deferred to someone else ...
no matter how good their own ideas are!

Ah the poor sustain a great wrong
and might never be able to stand up on their own feet ...

*26th February 2001*

## Denial or the arts

**THE RICH** have art ... and though the cloister's more
enticing than the world that Satan paints,
the rich are not the poorest of the poor
like the drug-addicts - without the arts or saints.

Hence, if a rule of life may be devised
for Artists, it would seem they ought to inherit
what by the rich and by the poor is prized,
that rich they ought to be in flesh and spirit![103]

Thus wrote Teresa[104] - squeaming whether Art
is in the self-same spirit as the vows
and counsels of Perfection - that the Heart,
and ways of Love thereof, are holier cows

than denial ...
words inspired from above:
*"do not renounce that which awakens Love!"* *7th March 2001*

---

[103] A spiritual counsel given with Church approval by the Clergy in my native islands unto countless Maltese. I venerate Saint Francis with his Gospel of uncompromising poverty. Likewise Teresa of Avila, John of the Cross, and above all the Beatitudes: *"blessed are the poor in Spirit!"* but poverty is not viable spirituality for artists who all aspire to and need money to work well. The spirituality that shines through this concept is far more viable for artists than uncompromising poverty of the flesh and of the spirit. The sublime Genius of the Gospel is indisputable but I insist that many another head can think straight also on parallel if not entirely congruent or literal lines.

[104] **Spiritual Testimonies**, No 26: (Avila, date uncertain), *Do not renounce what awakens Love.* **The collected works of Saint Teresa,** in 3 volumes. Vol 1. Kieran Kavanaugh O.C.D., and Otilio Rodriguez O.C.D., translators. ICS Publications. Institute of Carmelite Studies, Washington, D.C. paper, 517 pp. p. 399. In this spiritual testimony, Teresa squeams and agonizes whether a painting, extremely ornate, which she had hanging on the wall, in her room, is consonant with her vows, and with the spirit of mortification which she embraces. The Lord's loving reply to her is very straightforward: "What is greater, mortification or charity? You must never do something like this, neither to yourself nor to your nuns. Do not renounce what awakens love! Satan has in this manner deprived the Lutherans of everything they've got to awaken their loving feelings. My own Christians must in every way strive to do much better." The conclusion is simple and a good argument for the value of the arts: Love is greater than denial.

## Critical appreciation

**THE PRAYERS** we so often pray — missing,
thereby, the point of what we say, or else
the skill and craft between the lines, beneath
the words, concealed, the subtle texture, diction,
quite often expert phrasing — reveal too often,
but unto lovers only, the finest skill
which would ennoble and dignify the work
of finest craftsmen, which in famous works,
as much as in these prayers, is taken quite
for granted, overlooked, and underestimated,
but for true lovers is all there to see:
each phrase, each separate metrical contour,
each with its varying time-signature,
and different onomatopoeic timbre —
the texture, heartbeat, diction - and the music ...

*"You died, Jesus - but the source of Life
flowed out for souls, and the ocean of Mercy
opened up for the whole earth. Oh fountain of Life,
immeasurable Divine Mercy, cover
the whole earth and empty Yourself out
upon us. Oh blood and water which gushed forth
from the Heart of Jesus as a fountain of Mercy
for us, we trust in You. Holy God,
Holy Mighty One, Holy Immortal One,
have Mercy upon us and on the whole earth.
Jesus, King of Mercy, we trust in You!"*

Thrilled by the Lord's self-appreciation, We
return to this set piece, perceiving,
in the crabbed, expert twists of the phrases,
the cruel contortions of the Lord's gnarled death
upon the Cross, and in the plosives
and quiet sibilants, the silent gushing forth
of Mercy, like the gushing forth of blood,
deep within the heart and soul of the
receptive faithful who, in a real spirit
of reverence, faithfully recite these prayers,

and quietly experience the powers of Grace
which the words, although subdued, describe ...

*7th March 2001*

## Merciful breath of God .....

**MERCIFUL** breath of God that nuzzles like mist
upon my walls, upon my bed and carpets,
pictures and books, upon and all around
the holy images within the corner
where my soul prays and calls my subsidized home
my own sweet home, where I compose my verses --
ah! thou kind, thou benevolent Spirit,
intangible Presence inside whose ear
I pour all my secrets, Who all my passes
knoweth ..... will You such terrible knowledge
use against me? or will You my solace, and
my shelter be?
Home sweet home! sure lot
where all my memories are, my holy images,
and all my verse is written! You, kind Spirit
who lives in residence here, witness of all
my secret passes, all intimate signals
between the lines of all my books - protect
my mind! protect my rights! my innermost person!
be Thou benevolent to me!
May I live
a blameless life, within this hermitage;
and may my heart with blameless love be blessed!
Spirit, in Whose Presence I create
my work, I am extremely sensitive
to works of Art, in whatever medium!
I am extremely sensitive to real people!
And likewise am I sensitive
to love between the sexes .... none may say
I am inhuman! but I would You were
to make me just as sensitive to Nature ....

I do not have Wordsworth's feeling!
nor Shakespeare's flawless insight into character!

This fresh Religion which I have created,
this cult of my own Book, which binds my conscience,
is made of nothing, oh my Friend, but breath
and Love between us: all I have ever said,
or written down, about the Arts, means but
what I say now - Faith is Artistic! and
my books are but good Honour between me
and Thee! I am not Wordsworth, Sir, nor are
the Arts, perhaps, quite Nature; nor am I
Shakespeare - but what I here define, and here
once more lay down, sure is high-serious thinking:
Faith is Artistic, boil'd of an Artist's blood!

Thanks be to God for my own home, where I glean'd
such Truth! Thanks be to God for my own sweet bed!
Allow my will to make its Peace in Thine,
my heart, my mind, my soul less turbulent be,
resigned, contented with my share, my lot
in Life, and with the Love which I know well
You bear me! Protect me from the evil eye!
Cleanse a child of unclean spirits!
Save me,
but only when my turn comes, not before!
I love my Life, wish I would do well, and better,
upon this Earth before the clock of Time
is counted, and my Time is up .....

*28th March 2001*

## Upon Vancouver's pavements green ...

### 1. to the dead ....

**SPIRITS** of old friends -
revolving, tunnelling and burrowing all night like squirrels
in the gloomy recesses of green, virile forests -

may there always be a blessing of friendship
and sunshine between us .....
may we always be friends and blood-brothers,
sharing the wine and the peace-pipe
in a shady oasis .....
may you always be there - my friends,
and may the Lord likewise be there,
a white Light still and moving,
tunneling like squirrels beneath the palm-trees
in an infinite maze of make-believe .....
may your blessing descend always upon me,
and likewise may it come back to you,
like sunshine through cloud
upon a good conscience
at the far end of the rainbow .....

*7th April 2001*

## 2. thoughts ...

**THOUGHTS** that arise within this nutshell of
my brains patter upon my brains like peas,
like small, sharp shrapnel whose incision hurts
and cuts the tender meat ...
Let there be Peace
between us, and merciful Love. My mind is small
compared to Thine. Thy thoughts, in mine, are all
much larger ... Give me Verse that has the power
to soothe my hurt, and Thine. Give me song
that has the power to heal my wounds, and Thine.
As Your Spirit shudders within my own
from shock and scandal, cleanse me I pray of unclean
spirits. Teach me, of Your Wisdom, discernment
of Spirits ... with Your Precious Blood dress up,
oh my beautiful Saviour, my own butcher'd Heart.

*14th April 2001*

## 3. prayer for recognition ...

**IF I SEE** You upon the roads walking beside me,
accompanied,
perhaps, by heavenly partners, by inspirational
associates ... if I see You pass me by upon the pavement,
and all You want, perhaps, is but one cigarette,
with a Heavenly Princess beside You ...
spare me
the degradation of not recognizing You,
help me break the terrifying silence - and let me
pass the test, oh my gentlest, dearest Friend ... help me
but merely talk to You as I soothe my wounded Spirit
in the blood and balsam of Your subtle Love ...

Lord of camouflage visiting from the Beyond,
Prince Charming that can'st so well
conceal Your Existence upon
Vancouver's pavements green .....

*14th April 2001*

## 4. to the people ...

**I LOVE** you. I admire you. I adore you. I look up to you
at each door I knock upon. I need you. You reward my
respect,
though I would like your money, with that unfailing,
astonishing
Canadian courtesy of yours, that golden quality
which never ceases to amaze me, in which I am forever
your student ... You reward me with a well-earnt,
spontaneous, flattering purchase of my poetic wares,
with an unforced smile upon your courteous face---
without for a fleeting instant
one forced smile upon your clean white teeth ...
I wish you well. I would that no harm will ever befall you,
neither here and now nor in the hereafter ...
And as we part and bid each other good-bye,
tense feelings as of an old friendship,

as if we had not met for so many and so many years,
hum between us, taut and electric,
and we shake hands as if we might never
see each other again and as if we regretted it,
as if this were the last time ...
and I bless you all with all my heart.

*17th April 2001*

## 5. this outrageous revenge on Nature ...

**AH! THIS** very path I trod upon in total torment
right through this derelict technological jungle
this heartless outrageous revenge on Nature
which dispels whatever peace I may be visited with
and breaks the very bones within my skull
as if they were being broken one by one
with studied sadistic cruelty
with noise and blare of cars, machines, planes, radios
this way of life is an outrageous revenge on Nature
this way of life is the loveless, terrifying outrage
against the delicate ways of the Heart
and I can but rebel and choke
cry out in silent hurt weep without being able to show it
the long silent weeping of the years and drown and
suffocate ...

Ah! where are You? if You are in any way responsible, Sir--
why do You not help us? or has Satan himself
imposed upon us in Your Name his own mad theme? .....
God in hiding -- where are You?

*18th April 2001*

## 6. upon Vancouver's pavements green ...

**IF I COLLAPSE** and fall down dead upon the pavement,
if I drop down dead right here like a cone falling from a
tree,
will You be there to greet me, with Proserpin gathering
flowers
beside You, in the classic-laid rose garden? upon the gold
brocade? Will Mary the Beloved be there likewise?
Will You be there to meet me? to kiss me upon my cheek
the kiss
of merciful Love? to grab by the stem this sensitive Plant
which is withered, and to snap it tight once more,
to snap it proud and right? to slip into my dead grasp
my ticket and my wages? my cheque for my next
twenty-years' tuition? and my certified copy
of the word-processor designed by God for me?
Will You be there to help me recoup my losses? to tell me--
be it done with you according to your Faith?
according to the great Hope inside you,
in the shadow of which you lived?

... will anyone I know
carry me away upon a Shield?

*17th April 2001*

## Impediments in the blood

**I HAVE**, my Lord, a clot within my blood,
a spanner in the works, which stops the flood
of thought and feeling, and which only You
could have placed there ... to thicken, perhaps, the brew.
Salvation lieth in the Sacrament
of dripping Flesh, Whose Love is vehement -
it lieth not in Art, but giveth place
to works of Faith, wherein God Himself displays.

Deep is the turbulence of Love misplac'd
inside me, yet I pray -- let it be lac'd
and grafted on to Thine: Thou art the Vine;
we sing the verse aloud, we sip Thy Wine.
Let it be said, all work is work, and work
is hard, but serving God I did not shirk.

*25th April 2001*

## For my beliefs

**I HAVE** endured
a lifelong, bloodless martyrdom
in the hysterical silence -
I have borne ten thousand deaths untold
for whatever God may be ...

A sob shakes in my voice as I write,
as if my voice was gone. A tear rises in my throat,
as I lie down in bed, hiding my face in my pillow -
the long, silent weeping of the years
with no one to hear, no one
who cares to hear ... is Love not greater than Denial?
I fondly ask.

Bear with me, oh my gentlest Friend,
Who listens saying nothing,
Who never minds the insults ...
that I let You down on such and such an occasion,
where I could have arisen
to such and such an inspiration,
to such and such a nudge of Yours,
resulting in such and such
a better work of art which I may
have written, or created,
if I had made myself accessible to Your finer Spirit,

if I had done but what I say ...

bear with me, be patient with me,
counsel me well -- I am worth Your while,
I believe in myself and Thee ...

pardon me if I do not always go to Church:
my gift to You is the heart of countless People;
and my lifelong hurt I offer up for Lady Aphrodite.

*21st June 2000*

## The trickster

**HE DEALS** in and upon
confidence, emotions, and respects,
the private thoughts, and the love of many ...

He sells the books of all the Faiths there be.
All are equally important as long as they fetch in
the Almighty Dollar, but his own Faith,
and all the Faiths of all the authors,
individually, or altogether,
to him are of no importance whatsoever
unless they sell ...

Mindful then of the mundane
as much as of the Scriptural call
to make ends meet,
we strive to be far truer dealers,
far truer lovers, and far more honourable great artists .......

*21st June 2001*

## Teach me ...

**TEACH** me how to rejoice like little children
when a child is by its peers complimented.
Teach me so to appreciate Your compliments -
You Who are the Kingpin of my Art.
Revive my taste for loving sounds of Music,
for haunting shades of Verse. I waste. I wither.
The blood's congealed and thick within my veins
and does not beat like youthful blood. Ah! God,
if I do not rejoice like little children --
You who snared my mind and snared my love ever since
I was myself a child in swaddling bands --
if I do not rise to such and such occasions:
teach me how to rejoice like little children
when a child is by its peers complimented.

## Like a lamb to the slaughter

**I SAW YOU**, framed in the entrance
of my apartment building, a senior, face unsmiling,
sombre and gaunt, a taut, infirm old man
with serious, worried gaze,
as you dutifully said good-bye to the priest,
after shaking, perhaps, his hand .....

Did he, the priest, perhaps,
anoint someone you love with the last rites?
Sir, I must say, you seemed so much
like a trusting child, full of faith,
compared to that supercilious, sulky,
sarcastic-seeming priest,
who had such a cynical, self-satisfied smirk
upon his haughty, upturned face, and did not care
for my respects, nor to shake hands with me!

Are you sure he was worthy, I ask,
of your blindfolded trust in him?

I pitied you, I pitied you deeply, truly,
my heart crumbled upon itself with compassion,
with a sob, with a lurch for you,
poor fellow Christian for whom I felt so keenly,
as I invoked the Mercy of God
upon you and upon those you love,
as if you were a lamb, being led
blindfolded to the slaughter .....

*24th August 2001*

## Mete for thought ...

**OH FRIEND**, my faults are spotted countless,
but likewise are the extenuating circumstances
which mitigate, diminish and soften guilt ...
I am wronged, ill, hurt and lonely.
You are good to the poor, the abused, the oppressed: judge me not!

I will, gentle Friend, that I be a man, that I keep my word
with You and with people, that I earn my living well,
that I be rich in flesh and spirit, likewise that I
take good care of these gifts, be kind to the poor,
that I entertain and please myself in Godly fear ...
lend me then, I say, Your helping Grace.

Lord Jesus, *mete* for thought,
food of souls and bread of Angels,
fill my heart and soul with all good things
and feed me the food that leads
unto life everlasting ...

*3rd October 2001*

## Osama Bin Laden

**AT THE** start of a new war, wrong beginning
for the new millenium, at home, where he is a hero,
people are saying ...

"You are a great man, Osama bin Laden.
Remember the honour of a billion Muslims
is at stake! If you are taken ... die bravely,
happily, in good cheer, and you will see
how merciful is the Lord Allah!"

In the West he is a villain, essentially evil,
wanted dead or alive, to be shot, perhaps, on sight!

Muslims enjoy dying for Islam, believing
that martyrdom merits instant salvation,
yet they ask for it by dragging countless
unwilling people into their frenzied bloodlust,
and vortex of self-sacrifice. Moses, whom they honour,
said clearly, "Thou shalt not kill," and this is what
the Christians, despite their many, glorious martyrs,
understand ...

North America believes in Freedom,
and nowhere is Freedom, being "born free",
a more delicious nectar than upon this Continent,
yet many here are worse, perhaps, than atheists ...

Everyone has a grain of sense and reason, a glimpse,
a little light, some fraction of an authentic insight,
yet who is it can entirely unravel
the endless tangled string? without damaging faces
or the dignity of individuals? Who is it can undeceive
the millions ...

And who on earth wants terrorism to thrive
in this age of atomic warfare?

*10th October 2001*

## Sex, did you say?

**HOLY, HOLY**, Holy - my heart and soul
and bodily senses, Lord of Power and Might,
yearn for the touch of Your vanishing fingers -
the med'cinal glow of Your restorative rays!

What we then call sex
is just so much a privileg'd sacrament,
and the unworthy practice is just so much
sacrilege against the very flesh and temple
of God's own living Spirit!
I plead guilty,
I plead human, infirm, and fallen, fallen, fallen ...
Yet why on earth should I ever cease
from pouring my heart to Thee in ceaseless prayer,
though I own my humble state of imperfection,
that Thou, my Judge, at least may say: "Your sins
are heavily outnumber'd by your prayers!"
Further,
I aver ... sexual love is love indeed,
whereby one loves a partner like oneself,
and although distinctions rise, such as ... good love,
bad love, I think that human creatures, should
they be depriv'd and filch'd of such and such
their loving joys, they shall - like the proverbial
unattended flower, take umbrage and despair,
demoraliz'd, discouraged, and this - I say -
as long as men may breathe, or eyes may see,
as long as hearts may likewise beat -
none has a right to do to none!

*3rd January 2002*

## Reflections upon the resurrection and ascension into Heaven of Jesus and Mary

**IF JESUS** was
the greatest of the Prophets ...
as so many say He was ...
would it not have been
bottomless disaster
were not His claims all true,
or were the Resurrection
a fabrication, or interpolation ...
how on earth could the greatest of the Prophets
be held accountable for allowing
such wicked, shameless trickery?

Hence -
we pray, therefore,
to the Lord as much as to His Mother,
to Him as much as to Her Who
like His Goddess bore Him
... take us to Heaven
in the sincerity of the thought
... take us to Heaven
in the sincerity of the sentiment
in the success of all our projects and endeavours
in the salvation of the millions ...

*13th February 2002*

## Upon the visit to Vancouver Archdiocese of the relics of Thérèse of Lisieux, Doctor of the Church ...

**AH! THÉRÈSE** - Child of God, to whom I render'd
life-long honours, prayers, thoughts and practice ...
when your venerated relics, in your hour of great honour,

visited this Archdiocese, in your fateful hour
of Heavenward, predestin'd glory --- escorted,
as they were, a glorious sight for all to see,
by the Canadian Mounties, and by the Faithful ---
I felt ... must I confess? ... the horror, the pain,
of my own, terrifying, life-long ordeal,
accompanied by a constriction of my stomach,
and of my appetite, my demoraliz'd heart and mind.
Ah! Thérèse --- I love you still, though at the time
I wrote no poetry - at which my Christian friends
complain'd!
I simply offer you now this poor, limping sample
of my Art, as my due to you, and the sincerity
of my heart and of all my prayers ...
whilst I invoke the Holy Spirit's warm, smiling sunlight,
and the thrice blessed rays of sanctifying Grace,
to penetrate and flood the drunken, dense, gloomy
and sunken stupor of my soul and innermost being!

*6th March 2002*

## Mystical pleadings ...

**LORD ...** in my heart, where You have descended,
see the hurt, see the pain, see the heartless
brutal murder ... yet another agony in the Garden,
where all of us heap'd and mangled lie!
Let Your joy seize in my veins
like wildfire across the Heavens!

Let the refining fire of Your Holy Spirit
rinse and wring and purify and purge and wash
my every corner, as the invisible fingers
of the Holy Ghost
gently scour and stretch and heal and reconstruct
my heart and soul and every living fibre,

reach around each sinew and mend each beating tissue
with the gentlest healing touch
of self-effacing Grace!

*Veni, Creator Spiritus* ... Friend at my side!

*13th March 2002*

## The Priest ...

*.... to James Comey & Anthony Boniface ...*

**THE PRIEST** is a good kid ...
though not, perhaps, exalted, though not great,
he is a natural as a saint, failings and all.

He is proud of his long, flowing vestments,
his prophetic role, though he can do naught
but preach the Gospel, or ... woe unto him instead!

He is proud of the faith, the trust, the attentive ear
of the faithful, who love him as a brother,
even confessing to him their private follies.

He is proud of his own voice, soaring
above the organ music ... proud of his achievement
as a major, or minor character
in theology, likewise proud of his task as almsgiver
and friend of the poor .....
                                                            yet - he asks
that you pour out unceasing prayers
even for him who can likewise die
the second death ... and all his pride become
but dust and ashes on his tongue, capable,
as he is, equally of doing much harm,
as much as much good.

Let him not, nor anyone, be grudged, nor denied
his proper reward, nor set yourself up
as Judge between those who love each other ...
one Law for all - equal and fair!

*27th March 2002*

## The skiff

**MY SKIFF** - with which no ships compare -
has weathered storms of Ocean:
in blackest night the beacon's flare,
in steep commotion,

is but the one, consoling Sense,
the verse that shakes my Heart;
for Food the Ocean's Providence
beneath the curb of Art!

Thou reddening Glow! Thou blood-red Core
upon the Wild neglected,
that ghastly Shadows casts ashore
by Time collected -

within the Flame upon the Wick
I dream that I behold
my Genius dance, my Fortune click
with cards of Gold!

Hail, holy Fire! through whate'er
perilous Seas - the Raft -
oh Thou! Thou burnest everywhere,
but not as daft

as Thou art faithful what Thou wilt!
I love the drift and sound:

Thou reachest but to Castles built
on solid Ground!

The Critic thought he haughtily steers
top-heavy, mighty Ships,
but with the Spirit interferes
from holstered hips!

Likewise the pious Rationalist
but clouds the faultless Feeling -
with Reasons fine as fog or mist -
that subtlest Reeling

which in my Heart of Hearts is burning!
Ah but my Life-raft's light,
and the vast Ocean's overturning
bury it quite

may never, and only upward bobbing,
throbs like my Adam's apple,
and Vision brings the Joy of sobbing
and makes me grapple -

where in the Flames She smiles and dances,
black hair blown by the breeze,
where my Beloved counts the chances
and me strip tease!

*11th September 2000*

## Songs of Gentlest Reflection

*reviewed by Michael R. Burch*
*on www.thehypertexts.com*

**JOE RUGGIER** is a man I would admire even if I didn't care for his poetry. Although it has become fashionable for poets to bemoan the "state of the art," then toddle off to Starbucks to indulge in sympathetic cappuccinos, Mr. Ruggier has resolutely defied both the modern poetry "industry" and the apathy of readers by selling his poetic wares door-to-door, to the tune of several thousand books. In the process of singlehandedly outselling most of this century's theoretically Major Poets, he has embraced just about every out-of-favor aspect of poetry imaginable: meter, rhyme, form, praise, elegy, spirituality, even (gasp!) Catholicism. Talk about courage under fire.

But poets are creatures we find it hard to pin down, and Joe Ruggier is no exception. In his newest book, *Songs of Gentlest Reflection*, our heroic hardcore rhyme revivalist opts for free verse, and inquiring minds immediately what to know: why? In a letter I received from Mr. Ruggier, he mentioned his deep appreciation of T. S. Eliot, who was a traditionalist and a classicist, yet chose to write free verse. Ruggier went on to say: "Personally I think ... my work in rhyme and meter is superior in craftsmanship to my free form ..." (which I find interesting because I feel the same way about my own poetry). Why, when a poet's abilities and muse incline him to form, meter and rhyme, does he employ free verse? I would venture this in the way of explanation: when what a poet has to say is more important than how he says it, free verse is a natural medium. When the muse speaks through us--not our words, but hers--form, meter and rhyme more often result, especially when the poet has the talent to be inspired. But a poet cannot very often say precisely what he means in form, meter and rhyme.

In prose, of course, one can say exactly what he or she means–to the extent that words and the writer's abilities allow. Free verse is, to an extent, a compromise between traditional poetry and prose. Poets who specialize in free verse will probably disagree (what!–me compromise?, pshaw!), but let them write their own essays of defense, repudiation, whatever. I think it stands to reason that the more a poet intends to say exactly what he means, the less he can employ form, meter, and rhyme. Great poets seemingly bend or break this "rule," but perhaps this is simply a testament to their talent, audacity and flexibility to "go with the flow" without seeming to do so. Does anyone actually believe that Shakespeare never changed poetic horses midstream when an attractive rhyme presented itself? Or, looking at things from another angle: if Shakespeare had unlimited ability to say exactly what he wanted to say in form, meter and rhyme, why did he sometimes resort to prose?

All modern poets write prose. Why am I writing this review in prose? Simply because what I want to say is more important to me than how singingly/swingingly I say it. It would be damn hard to recast this review as a cycle of sonnets while keeping its meaning completely intact. If I had any chance at all of breathing the breath of poetic life into this piece, it would certainly have to be in the form of free verse.

Is it possible, then, that what Joe Ruggier means to accomplish in *Songs of Gentlest Reflection* is more akin to telling than singing? I believe this to be the case. In his letter, Mr. Ruggier also made the point that "vers libre / sublime prose was the peculiar domain of the Hebrew Bible." Since divinity is a primary theme of *Songs of Gentlest Reflection*, free verse does seem appropriate. Onward, then.

I have come to the conclusion that the repetition of words is an underrated, misunderstood, even misapprehended poetic device. Reading James Joyce, Henry James, Archibald MacLeish, Conrad Aiken and other "repetitious" writers has taught me to distrust the monomaniacal workshop mantra against the repetition of words within close quarters. If one is to receive consistent advice from a poetry workshop attendee, it will invariably be a warning not to repeat words; repetition of words is considered a disease, nay, The Very Plague, of beginning writers, which might have come as a shock to Joyce, James and gang. I find it interesting that in the first few pages of *Songs of Gentlest Reflection*, words like "gentle" and "sweet" appear quite frequently, often in rapid succession. This tells me several things: that Joe Ruggier does not attend poetry workshops, that he is something of a poetic rebel, that he has an important mission which demands the setting of a certain tone early in his book, and that he's not afraid of modifiers (as many poets are these days). It's unfortunate that so many modern poets (A. R. Ammons comes to mind) seem to distrust words to the point of not using them for their normal purposes. "Sweet," for instance, is a word virtually abolished from the modern poetic lexicon. On the other hand, Eliot said that poetic time is relative, and Shakespeare used the word "sweet" whenever he felt the urge. Shakespeare was the most liberated of poets, and I have never understood the strong distaste of modern poets for perfectly good words. So I'm encouraged that Joe Ruggier is unafraid to defy poetic convention. Isn't that what poets should always do?

In his opening poem, "A Poem for Saint Teresa," we find other indications that Mr. Ruggier is determined to resolutely defy poetic convention. He employs archaisms ("rous'd"), inversions ("Teresa's gentle reassurance / my soul inspired ..."), and frowned-upon interjections ("Ah!"). We begin to despair that he will ever earn a passing grade in a poetry workshop! And the workshops have given us *so many* great poets; surely that is why we are at a loss to remember their names . . .

In his second, near-titular poem, "A Song of Gentlest Reflection," Ruggier tells us:

> A little child's conscience, my beloved,
> is straighter than God's Gospel.

Here and in the following lines, Ruggier is closer to Blake than to Eliot, and Ruggier displays something of the forthright moral indignation of Blake whenever children are mistreated or unappreciated. As an admirer of Blake, I find this commendable. In lines like:

> Kneel down and ask a child to teach you judgement;
> pray to the little ones for vision;

Ruggier falls somewhere between Blake and the teachings of Christ himself; then his poem resolves to something original yet familiar:

> beseech the little ones to tell you a beautiful lie,
> and never believe anyone else's.

Here, I hear echoes of Blake's "little lamb, who made thee" and Jesus' "suffer the little ones to come unto me." Ruggier compels us to delight in the innocent wisdom of children, while simultaneously presenting himself as their staunch advocate. As a result, we see the moral potential of poetry. I'm not a fan of organized religion, but I am a fan of this poem. Ruggier is very persuasive here, and bad poetry is almost never persuasive, unless it persuades us to run away screaming.

Another thing we find often in good poetry, but seldom in bad poetry, is wisdom. In Ruggier's next poem, "Child, the Gentlest Loving Faults," we find pearls of wisdom:

> let no one rile thy funny bone. Despite
> is of the devil; priest's acrimony a far
> more wicked sin than gentlest loving fault.

And later:

> let no one judge you, child, nor rile your conscience
> with a priest's foul interest in sin alone,
> or a neurotic saint's last night's hangover!

As he demonstrates in "Lucifer," Ruggier can sound not only like Blake and Eliot, but also like Milton:

> Behold my Heart
> of green debris and crooked, wrinkled Hatred,

And again in these lines:

> Lucifer saw
> how in Thy splendor, God,
> Thou didst not crush him all completely!

In an interesting poem, "Eucharist," Ruggier draws a parallel between the communion of poetry and holy communion. Readers honoring verse "honor but sincerity made of paper" while people taking the sacrament "honor but a crumb, a drop of wine." This is the insight of a poet, that "dead poets and living men ... / hearts upon each other's lips, / honour the exquisite Fake." I come to poetry for such revelations. I have often thought of poetry as a form of communion between poet and reader. I've even ventured a poem or two on the subject. So I find this parallel fascinating.

There are other poems in this collection that fascinate me. For instance, in "Lord Joe of the Rood," the speaker (whom I take to be Joe Ruggier), pulls a Job, albeit with a bit of cranky humor:

> I cannot say,
> great God, you have been callous; I forgive
> You all, for all the many gifts you made me!

and

> I prayed. Lord, I prayed to suffer. You did but take,
> and never stopped, and what You gave, You gave
> with one hand taking, and nothing have I done
> but suffer. Halt! I say. Thou Rascal, stop!
> Breathe upon me, if you must, a loving breath!

If there's a God in heaven, he must be wincing and chuckling after that tirade! These are peculiar lines, the better for their peculiarity. But what about these lines from "Divinest Mary:"

> Mary, heed me not
> if I bitch and loathe myself
> for bitching, and then a Woman-God like You.
> Slap me hard once, but forgive me.

After railing at God, our hard-beset poet asks to be bitch-slapped by the Virgin Mary! What can one make of a book like *Songs of Gentlest Reflection*? I am at a loss to say exactly, but I will say this: if you like your poetry smooth and creamy like cappuccino, this book may not be your cup of java. But if an eclectic mix appeals to you, I recommend that you settle down with this book for a heart-to-heart encounter with a poet like none you've encountered so far. Joe Ruggier is not a poet we can easily classify. His poetry leaps from archaism to inversion to modern English and back again. If he were not a poet of considerable talent and insight, I might be inclined to suggest that he settle on one century's language or another's, but then I'm reminded of the title of a book edited by Annie Finch, *A Formal Feeling Comes*, and of a book of poems by A. E. Stallings entitled *Archaic Smile*. There are certain subjects which lend themselves to otherness, to unique, oblique or antique modes of expression. When it comes to "things religious," sometimes a less-than-modern tongue seems, as Goldilocks exclaimed, "just right." Every day, English-speaking people all over the world pray in a language something like this: "O Lord, we implorest thou that thou wilt be with the space shuttle astronauts as they prepare for reentry into the earth's atmosphere." So perhaps Ruggier's language in *Songs of Gentlest Reflection* is entirely appropriate. He speaks about timeless issues, why should he pin himself down to the particularization of a single moment in time or language?

When I have finished reading a book, my impressions of it are often quite different than when I first picked it up. When I started reading *Songs of Gentlest Reflection*, I was a bit put off by what I saw as the flip-flopping of the language from one century to another. But the more of the book I read, the more I put aside my childish, workshop-ish ways, and began to see the book in the light of what I call "the rightness of words." When children are insulting each other on a playground, they use a different language than the one they use when asking their parents for allowance money. When construction workers who curse every ninth word enter a church, they immediately don a new language, as easily as they doff their hardhats. In *Songs of Gentlest Reflection*, Joe Ruggier writes elegantly and passionately in a language we all understand: the language of prayer and communion. And he speaks powerfully and compellingly for children; not, as so many writers do, from the standpoint of how they must be shielded and protected, but from the standpoint that they must be acknowledged for their uniqueness, for their unique way of knowing and accepting things that seems so alien to us, their parents.

So when we read poets, it's important for us to relax and not let our inhibitions get in the way of their words. Robert Frost said "Poetry begins in delight and ends in wisdom." As readers, we have to again learn to surrender to the delights of poetry. *Songs of Gentlest Reflection* is a good place to start. It will help you smile and wince your way to wisdom surprisingly like a child's, coming from so erudite a poet.

## Songs of Gentlest Reflection

*(reviewed by MARY RAE: Managing Editor of ROMANTICS QUARTERLY Poetry Magazine).*

**JOE M. RUGGIER**, editor of the poetry journal, **The Eclectic Muse**, and author of numerous volumes of poems, has brought forth a rich and lively collection of poetry and prose in **Songs of Gentlest Reflection**. Many of Mr. Ruggier's poems are reflections on divinity. His work has a natural flow, yet the subtlety and quiet elegance of his phrasing leaves the impression that the reader has been thinking with, rather than listening to the author. Here you will find beautiful poems such as, "You are Jesus…", "Divinest Mary," and "Mystical Soliloquy 1," as well as "15 Poems of Place," that are meditations on the places he has lived and which have deeply impressed his life. Also in the collection you will find essays such as "Poet and 'Failed' Musician", a fascinating account of his journey into the world of classical guitar study.

Mr. Ruggier's collection, 90 pages of varied poetry and essay, beautifully printed in a pleasing 8.5 X 11" format, is a pleasure for any reader.

**Songs of Gentlest Reflection** is available from:
MULTICULTURAL BOOKS
307 Birchwood Court, 6311 Gilbert Road
Richmond, BC — CANADA, V7C 3V7
Tel: (604) 277-3864 E-mail: jrmbooks@hotmail.com

# PART SEVEN: In the Cannon's Roar

*Work previously unpublished (strictly selected)*

**In the Cannon's Roar, by Joe Ruggier**
*work previously unpublished (strictly selected)*


**Published by: MBOOKS OF BC**
Unit 114 – 6051 Azure Road, Richmond, BC, Canada, V7C 2P6
Tel: +(604) 600-8819 E-Mail: jrmbooks@hotmail.com

**Printing History:**
Multicultural Books Poetry Series #28
1st print edition :
produced as Part Seven of the 1st, 2nd & 3rd editions
of Joe Ruggier's Collected Poems, June 2009 — June 2018
**ISBN for the current edition : 978-1-897303-26-9**

Desk-Top publishing: Joe M. Ruggier

this edition printed & bound by: **Lightning Source Inc.; USA**

**Over 225 copies in circulation**

## Just that one Man .....

**WELL** I know One Whose Honour's rooted in
the Laws of Nature and the Laws of Thought,
the Laws of Science and the Laws of Art,
the Laws of Logic and of all the branches
of Morality, Ethics, and Theology,
criticism and profoundest Metaphysics .....
He is the Friend: born for His Own Salvation,
born free, and born to save untold Millions —
Whose Honour hinges on the thinnest breadth
of unthinkable structural precision
in the Atom, in the Poem, or in a Star
in the most distant Galaxies and Pulsars .....
Yet I seek this Man in Nature or in Art,
in all the highest places, or in the faces
across the street ..... Yet I imagine He
bears Satan a close resemblance also ..... Yet
I feel this one Man's hypothetical damnation
would be announced by horrid acts of God,
thunder and lightning, hurricanes and earthquakes,
tidal waves, and volcanoes - underwater and above:
so deeply rooted is His Honour in
the Laws of Things Whose every aweful step
is punctuated by the music of
the Spheres .....
Such is Christ of Whom all Time
doth say: "He was a Man!" — Such is "the Friend"
of Whom no Man is worthy to call Him "Buddy";
yet Everyman's proudest Honour is subsumed
within the Lord's great Honour .....

*26th July 2003*

## This noble bird .....

**I'M** not a glutton, but I love good food
and eating well ... but once I'm done, do not
touch food again till Nature calls.
Frankly,
I find the cycle time-consuming — but
I've often thought: "Just count how many chickens
die to keep one Man well-fed for Life!
How many chickens die to stock one packet
of fresh chicken hearts, purchased, perhaps, at Safeway's!"

I am not superstitious nor a squeam —
Mankind has been created worthy of
such sacrifice, but my indignant gorge
arises up lamenting ...
"Waste not — want not!
Do not blaspheme an animal's love anymore
than you should the Creator's Providence!
Created only one step higher than
the Animal Kingdom — remember that your needs
are similar and, although Chicken is not
my favourite food, I admire this noble Bird
better than I admire You ....."

*8th September 2003*

## This flower'd asylum ...[105]

*"The Easter Lilly, a beautiful flower,*
*from all Eternity marks the hour*
*when God the Son was laid to rest,*
*straight as the spears round His nest."*
*— Terry Towson*

**THESE** gentle candles kindled ruddy red,
tossing their heads before the Sacrament,

---

[105] This image is a semi-metaphorical reference to Church ...

are Love trapp'd in my sacred Heart and beating
quietly within my temples ..... for the Heart
of all the people's sacred.
Like soft incense
burnt in a censer — sweet Peace comes swinging slow,
a gentle propellor from beneath upon
all Being's vast and endless Ocean where
to drown is sweet within this flower'd asylum,
this haunt of song and loving, lonely cheer.

This flower'd asylum's a victory for the Arts!
Despis'd by zillions it equally is to zillions
the heart's delight where the alternative is
that terrible nuclear boom of Century Twenty
which to Lovers means only ... lonely as a cloud
amid a crowd: Where have all the babies gone?!

*28th January 2004*

## Reflections about stylistic matters ...

**I SEEM** to live
in this eternal instant ...

All the styles of all Time
co-exist within my consciousness
and although primarily I support
rhyme-revival & neo-classicism
my policy is eclectic ...

As such it does not make
for a homogenous stylistic surface
but I do not rule anyone out
nor revenge myself on anyone
with Procrustean-bed criticism[106] ...

---

[106] **Procrustes** was a giant who owned a castle where he imprisoned many whom he tortured in his torture chamber. This chamber consisted of a room with a bed inside which fitted nobody. If his victims were too

A few friends have honoured me
for being truly various, diverse,
eclectic ...

*28th January 2004*

## Requiem for my computer

*Composed on All Soul's Day 2004*

**DISPLAYING** symptoms of extreme senility,
my old computer ground to a slow halt.
A Dinosaur — it would not copulate
with newer parts: its mere 120 MHz
were not sufficient power to drive all of
the clutter, programs, data, newer gadgets …..
I spent a thousand to rejuvenate
and to springclean it — but everything slowed down,
including common tasks in the wordprocessor:
one session on Internet lasted two hours.
I was sad to watch my old man go: I had
feelings about him; but it was only a machine …
I agreed with my computer dealer — "Prices
are down. Stop throwing away your money; buy
a brand-new system …..!"

*2nd November 2004*

---

tall to fit inside this bed Procrustes would chop their limbs off until they fitted. If his victims were too short Procrustes would stretch their limbs out upon this bed until they fitted. The concept — **"Procrustean-bed criticism" ...** is a well-earnt censure of Art-critics who do to works of art and imagination, by attempting to make them fit some preconceived notion, theory, intellectual, dogmatic or doctrinaire system or other, precisely what Procrustes did to his victims ...

## Who pick and choose

**THE** Eye of Faith perceives most wondrous colour
beyond the scope of what we mean by sight.
Nerve-shattering is the leap from black and white,
for those born colour-blind, to such strange seas
of sight and thought within the Solitude
of God.
          The Eye of Faith perceives the Lord
as in Himself He is: His litanies;
His Sacraments; His rosaries and all
His holy beads and titles—and as He is,
for what He is, accepts Him all in all
with all His pointed thorns.
                                        So many also
discuss the Saints and Spirit and great Books,
over caviar and wine and cheese … their hearts
are touched by Grace but not committed; it is
of God, but We are fickle—We refuse
to accept God as He is who pick and choose.

*10th January 2005*

## Elegy for Julia Sit

*BC's 'First Lady of Motorcycling' gone — The Province,*
*Friday, July 15, 2005 (C14)*
*Biker-safety advocate dies in crash — The Province,*
*Wednesday, July 13, 2005 (A9)*

**CHAIN'D** tight   in Mammon's fetters   both of us
   me to my computer   and selling poetry door-to-door
   you to your restaurant   and motor-cycle
there are times when I almost wish
                                        I would die

upon the road

to punctuate in blood
my honour as you did
lock tight
my freedom with your freedom
your honourable sporting spirit with my own
and carve my name upon the pavement
as being the spot where a "poet of the people" fell

I never met you, Julia Sit
yet your tragic, youthful passing
compelled my imaginative sympathy
making my creative juices flow
only too happy to oblige a mutual friend of ours
who requested that I compose a verse for the occasion

we all admire you, Julia Sit
none of us bear you ill-will or wish you harm
we are all touched by the story of how you went to meet
your lover
precisely a year less a day from his own tragic passing
as if by a divine, intelligent design

we all have faith that if a merciful God there is
He will indeed stand upon His Honour, being just so much
the God of Mercy as He is reputed to be
we all have faith He shall be good to you, Julia Sit

and just in case another life
peeps through the hollow eyes of death
I have exercised my own insurance Policy
and said in your behalf
a quiet, peaceful prayer
just as your lover might
place upon your grave a red, red rose

the endless road snakes on ahead for all of us
to greet far other feet than mine
and far other wheels than yours

*20th July, 2005*

## A character …

**YOU** drive me round the bend with your chit-chat,
a proud, expensive bird taught how to chatter—
tomes of small talk lop-eared to look like verse.

Friend, when you talk you dream you're writing books,
where all the implications need working out:
you ask, a long time later … "what was your question?"
You are expensive … own a car, a rich home,
a holiday home, and rent a third apartment:
are you worth, I ask, the paper that you write on?

The reason behind the professoriate is
to honour artists … yet many artists worked
for love of God or neighbour, whereas professors
bask in relative riches! They boast good reason
that to support the arts they must not lose
their shirt, but I ask … are they genuine?
or simply hirelings servicing themselves?!

Despite your grocer's principle you have
a heart beating through a handful of perfect lyrics!
Friend, you have been, to me, a constant friend
for years two score and four, introducing me
with success to various, valid sources of income;
giving me odd, well-paid secretarial tasks,
or paid, editorial work; doing me various
editorial favours; as well as driving me
home from my printer's with boxes full of books,
although you claim'd you're not my feed, nor unfeed,
assistant … and various other little things,
which mean so much, where you displayed concern,
much as a father would, for my lonely life
and impoverished plight, such as our joint
getaways together at your holiday home!

I endorse your 'summary',
that … "we both care and give a damn for poetry!"
The kernel is sweet. You have earnt with honour

the title, 'friend'. I have 'a friend'. A 'friend'
is a 'friend'—a thousand times a 'friend'!

*18th September 2005*

## Cheering up ...

**BESIDE** my bed a home-made shrine revives
and gladdens my drooping spirits: as though the birds
of Heaven sang inside my head, besides
my bed, to rouse me up from Pluto's gloom!
When shall I learn to leave alone the wounds?
revisit the cheerless Past no more? and dwell
no more on "regrets hopes regards and prayers"?
cheer up? arrest myself no more with the dark,
dead hand of gloom? Resolve on good resolve
have shattered all around me on the ground-swell
of angst and of futility! I go to bed ...
resolved about tomorrow! When I wake up,
and the good mood is gone, I pace around
for hours, timing my next cigarette, before
I recover the mood in which my good
resolve was taken! I have not learnt to rule
against "spectator syndrome" — becoming myself
a good musician by listening to less music!
Good Lord! I've known myself to nurse and take
to heart the desolate pull of all those Graces
lost and gone! like the black stars around the Virgin!
I sulked. I swore. I sang no song to Jesus.
A gloomy Galilean glared at me!
I shook myself together, tall and straight.
I sang once more. He smiled and set me free!

*21st January – 3rd February 2006*

## A counsel

**THE SPIRIT** of Hamlet visited me by night,
saying … ""All artists need to learn this: in
regard to something so terrifyingly essential,
to the salvation of a poor artist's soul,
as a little praise is, and an honest compliment,
all artists need to make assurance double sure
a thousand times over that they are not being paid
false compliments, nor dishonest praise!"""

For years on end in my psychotic condition
I experienced serious problems discerning
sincerity from falsehood …

An outstanding Shakespearian expert
in sincerity and falsehood
Hamlet knows …

*3rd February 2006*

## Reflections, in the style of a journal-entry

**I ATTENDED**, last night, Mel Hurtig's presentation, at Canadian Memorial Centre for Peace, about the terrifying, world-wide escalation of the nuclear arms race. It is totally alarming to consider just what untold billions of dollars are spent world-wide on nuclear arms buildup by superpowers such as the USA, China & Russia, described by Dr. Hurtig as a threat to world peace. I feel personally shot and extremely upset that I am in many ways a successful poet, a poet of the people positively with people behind me, and the only free gift North America ever made me is a disability pension, as if all there is to life is just not dying, or as if you are trying to tell me that we need weapons but not poets. I cannot help feeling the perfect Gospel Truth of poet Longfellow's mighty stanza …

Were half the power that fills the world with terror,
were half the wealth bestowed on camps and courts,
given to redeem the human mind from error,
there were no need of arsenals or forts …
**(H. W. Longfellow, The Arsenal at Springfield)**

I insist that this is the obnoxious climate we are living in, a nation that spends untold billions on weapons, but capable of giving me, a successful poet, nothing more than a disability pension, as if you are trying to tell me that we need weapons but not poets … tell me another!

*4th March 2006*

## Old Dante's damning powers

**MANY** people, in particular modern Catholics, are scandalized by Dante, particularly by his **Inferno**, wherein Dante positioned real, historical figures among others which are mythological. I once told some Catholics … "Church teaching about Hell is dogmatic theology whatever you say. Why does Dante make you such a terrible insult with Hell? Because he hates you? Or because he wishes you better? The critics, the poetry lovers, the professors understand Dante correctly, and so do the artists … the artists, in particular, are right to love Dante so deeply because they know that his honour is a sincere honour to them and they understand him most correctly in that they understand that his intentions are to save them!" The poem below is where my further reflections led me **…**
**Joe Ruggier (27th May 2006)**

**OLD DANTE'S** damning powers are as God wants —
he snubs with Hell only where he wishes better.
If people do not like them, people should
control their own — damning powers being,
most likely, the only supernatural power

most people have. Dante's **Inferno** speaks
to their condition: they read it and reread it;
and in regards to Hell, Church teaching is
dogmatic. If, however, it does not speak
to your condition, you may read **Purgatory**,
the most human, the most touching, among
great Poems, where, suffer what you may, the edges
are all solace, the consolation of all the faithful
who are not perfect … to whom the Lord may say:
***"I'm going to torture you upon the violin!"***
and we learn Love, and Holy Spirit, and enter
Heaven musicians like Yehudi Menuhin:
a school for all — **Purgatory** the blest!

*26th May 2006*

## Sunday 1st October

**IF I** go not to Church today I swear
I do not so
to spite You but to spare You spite! Jesus,
what on earth is the use, to me, to You,
that I should go to Church beneath an axe?
obliged and forced beneath a servile fear?
honour compulsory dragged out unwillingly,
and not transported by the Spirit?
and in my heart feel nothing but my venom,
my blasphemous wrath that rankles like a canker —
corrosive as a poison? Jesus, I go
but in good cheer: if not, I need abstain
to spare us both ill-will …..
Jesus,
my love and my devotion,
and amiable disposition,
Your Love, Your Grace, and Your Compassion,
are a free gift we make each other both —
in Spirit and in cordial, candid Truth!

Why should we wrangle though my love is drooping?
or just because Thy Presence seems so distant?

*1st October 2006*

## Lamentation

**AMONG** my sorrows I count the loss
of musical training. When, over twenty years
ago, I could play, upon classical guitar,
concert music, and threw it all overboard —
(arguing that my writing was ready for the public
but not my music) — I was, *qua poet*, an instant success!
But now, that I am trying to recover
my music from the ashes, it is as if
my gift is saying …
"You gave me up for another Woman
many years ago without asking yourself
whether you could have kept us both …
I am not an easy Woman, and you may not
have me back for the asking!"

*9th January 2007*

## Another Christ

**I TOLD** the priest: "Are you another Christ?
By "another Christ" I understand
an Artist like Dante, or like Shakespeare,
with His Own work of art, His Own Gospel,
His Own Kingdom, and His Own People!
You are by comparison
***Alter Christus pour les plus enfantes!***"

To which the Bishop answered:
"You can tell from this just what a lowly man
I am, but I am a Man, and this is what I mean
that God loves humble people and perfects Himself
through weakness — for He gave me power,
and I invent this not, to hold a sin
or loose a sin, and if I do either one
my word of honour is binding in His sight.
By this you know I am a Man—
despite my lowly station compared
to illustrious people such as you describe!"

*11th January 2007*

## God's Own "literacy campaign"

**ALMIGHTY** God turned on His microphone
and loudly spoke to all Humanity …

""I, Who in silence and in solitude speak,
without words or printed matter, straight to your Heart
and Soul, wherein you apprehend immediate Knowledge —
listen: if you have ears for what's aloud
or silent … let the leaven of revealed Religion
shine like *rheingold* through your troubled Spirit!

The ***literacy campaign***, which I launched,
over eight thousand years ago, when I invited
the chosen people to read **GENESIS**,
the very first book of Scripture penned by My servant
Moses,
has run its course … right now, eight thousand years later,
papers dribble out of everyone's nose, the tune has caught:
everyone is asking everyone, "Read It!" and "Read Me!"
**"Iqra!"** — the Angel said to Mohammed.
Books are being published by the hundred thousand:

the professions are at sixes and seven; likewise the
churches
and world religions … overwhelmed, one and all,
by far too much of one good thing!
Take a hike, folks!
The ***campaign*** was My eternal Will: the ***credit*** is
exclusively
My Honour and My Due — Almighty God,
the grand old Man of Letters! Time to stop reading, Folks:
take a break! What are you doing with all this Knowledge?
I want to know: what have you learnt? where is it taking
you?
Absorb what has been done, the best that has been done!
Rediscover the beauty and the wonder of the very best
that's been achieved over the centuries. Spring-clean so
many
thousand libraries, and everyone's living sight,
of crippling crap and clutter. Positively, in everyone's
best interest, recycle what is not destined to last
beyond the day. Essentially absorb and rediscover
the little left over, which everyone can digest
and manage better:
the very best alone come down the road of History;
before you may impower a more effective—
far less paralyzed Future!

I repeat, I dare say, Folks, take a hike! but …
don't you dare 'throw up' another 'book' before I give you
the all-clear, in this ongoing 'cultural revolution' …
I, your truest Lover, God Almighty,
known among fellow authors also *qua* Mr. Godot!"'"

*2nd February 2007*

## Instruments …

*to my parents, who always said prayers approved by Church Authority*

**MUSICAL** instruments are
delicate, sensitive, complex creatures.
Methods most scientific
need practicing for years
before you may extract
from a musical instrument
the effect you want,
manipulate, bend and tickle
its inert spirit to your own purposes …

Prayer is but man's attempt
to hear from God the music
he wants God to let him hear.

I can hear the Lord Jesus say
to many people:
"I am an Instrument
most delicate, sensitive and complex.
You have no right to extract from Me
the effect you choose, nor manipulate My Love
with your prayers, nor strum My mighty strings
unless We agree, and unless We agree
you have no right to tickle Me
with your words and with your honours
and not even with all your prayers …"

Vandals who pray to Jesus as they want,
flinging insults, flinging compliments
as they choose, and take Him in their hands
to pick what tune they please …
cause untold wreckage in an Instrument
worth untold millions — which explains precisely why
Jesus has become "a false penny" …

Therefore we need to learn
how to "manipulate, bend and tickle" God
into giving us what we want! He Who is
no one's common "Buddy"
requires to be "tickled"

strictly in ways He approves Himself …
"sincerity" being governed by Divine ***Science***!

What I describe the masses doing unto Jesus,
people do unto each other all the time —
which is why so few relate harmoniously …

*21st April 2007*

## Priesthood …

*to James Comey*

*"To what green Altar, O mysterious Priest,
lead'st thou that heifer, lowing at the skies?"*

**PRIESTCRAFT** was with us since the dawn of Time:
Osiris, with his priests, foreshadow'd Jesus—
Christ's Priesthood being but the culmination
of tradition old as the ages …

just as Dante's poetry
is the perfection of the Troubadours …

Oh why is it never praised in these terms —
just as Dante the Beloved
is so well-acknowledged and annotated?

Indeed, to save one Man, the Lord can damn
all Christendom …   (Jesus in the Garden,
and dangling on the Cross, pray'd through His death-throes
to atone for all sin by inviting divine Wrath
to spend itself on Him: the insult no one had
a right to make Him, just because He was
one Man, was to condemn Him all alone
to Hell, so as to save the millions.) …
                                                            There are
obnoxious Priests, wicked, or insincere,
or dirty.  Those
there be who go to Hell out of mistaken
zeal or sincerity: the Judgment is not

for them as terrible as in their mind
it seems to them to be! Those there are also
who out of the intolerable despite that they
despise each other, serve each other in nothing
but in damnation … and those there are also who
detain one billion Christians, chained to their feet
just for the numbers, whom they teach ***beautiful ZERO…***

The Spirit spoke within my heart, saying:
"Power for Good becomes power for Evil
in the wicked Priest: his warped and deformed
spiritual power, authority and insight
lead some to ruin worse than common errors —
but among the countless negatives
the positives are likewise countless,
and countless are the souls whom the Priests steer to God!
Here's how some Priests, the Friends of Jesus, go to Hell:
sincere devils loved and consoled by Jesus,
because in Life the Priest consoles the Lord!"

*3rd June 2007*

## Required sacrifice …

"**WHAT** makes the Mass required ***Sacrifice***?"
I fondly ask …

"For twice a thousand years," Jesus seems to be snoring
through the tedium of the Mass —
"Myself, the Lord Jesus, suffered nothing but
endless, tedious repetition, Myself, repeating Myself
over and over and over, until the hatred
I feel for My Own Words, for My Own Voice,
suffocates Me with tears …
for twice a thousand years
I did nothing but sit and stand and sit
and stand again, to greet people,
to welcome people, to make everyone feel good —

as if inspired lice dwelt in My nether region!
Son, this is the reason that I want everyone,
out of respect for Me, to suffer repetition,
to sit and stand and sit and kneel and stand again,
during the required mortification of the Mass,
where I am with you in the tedium and frustration …
so that you'll suffer and know just what discomfort
Jesus still suffers on your behalf—
just so you will make Jesus, Who loves you,
a sincere compliment —

and whilst you sit and stand do not forget
that you were told: ***"do this in memory of Me!"***

*3rd June 2007*

## An awful judgment

**I STOOD** before the Judgment Throne,
an artist, with one hand up front,
the other hand behind. The Judge
said simply: "Friend, to make you feel
My Love, I've nothing got but Art,
a Book which all men call 'the Bible',
and I am nothing but an Artist,
just as you are. All that I want
from you is that you strictly make
your readers feel the Love, just as,
to save you, I made you feel 'in love'!"

*5th June 2007*

## Axioms in reason …

**WE SHALL** not cease rejoicing
with all the celestial spheres,
and the end of our rejoicing
shall be to arrive where we started
when we have finished plumbing
all the great honors we do not vaunt,
nor brag of, nor possess.
We shall obey the Voice within us —
saying: "This is but an axiom in right reason …
if you do not have an honor,
then, for a sincere honor,
rejoice with everyone who is rejoicing,
knowing, with perfect clarity,
your hour shall come, and that God
does not forget anyone who returns His Love.
Know therefore this is but logic in right Reason:
if, for a sincere honor,
you do not rejoice in this fashion,
all your sins shall be retained and held against you!"

*4th December 2007*

## Shakespearian salute

**SOMEONE** remarked: "Shakespeare has two faces!"
"William Shakespeare," I retorted,
"is not an Artist with two faces:
He has hundreds! and in His Work
there is one only god —
His Divine Majesty the Lord William Shakespeare!"

Many think, indeed, that Shakespeare
liberated us all from institutions,

from all Churches, from all Church Doctors,
Saints and Catechisms, from all the laws
and precepts of the Church, of any church,
indeed from all Commandments
and the entire moral order, Shakespeare being ***a beastie***
beyond Good and Evil and beyond ***the Priestee*** …

Their love of the Lord Shakespeare is indeed
wicked, sly and malicious, capable of
corrupting the Master Himself should He not
beware; but I agree —
God set this Poet absolutely FREE!

*4th January 2008*

## Rich in means and rich in Mercy

**I WENT** to Church, one Sunday, deep in my heart
reciting: ***"Make me rich in means and rich***
***in Mercy!"*** High across the Altar, a banner
displayed the message:
***"You cannot serve God and Money!"***

Did ***a beastie called the Priestee*** find out
what I was thinking, and seek, perhaps, to lodge
the cutting insult deep in my tenderest temple,
my brittle skull? He could not do it better …
I have no doubt that Priests there are all sorts,
and as we know them, all are human, all
imperfect. My own experience clearly says:
the Priesthood has, at times, a damaging
and harmful impact upon the lives it touches;
though the rule is — this impact may be more often
beneficial …..
I see in my mind a multitude
of Christians gone to Hell, aborted adults,
pet lambs caught in a sentimental farce,
rendered subservient, crushed, and good for nothing
by the ponderous resources of true religion —

to whom the Priest teaches little, though
they need rehabilitation and full-time social workers!
He seeks only the subservience of Christians,
just so they may not make satanic priests
an insult … most of them uncles and aunties,
cousins, nephews, nieces, moms and dads,
grandmas and grandpas, living a loving life,
huddled close to their loved ones, for warmth and comfort,
gone to Hell strictly to serve the Lord's
Machiavellian purposes.
The professors say,
***they are casualties upon the road of History!***
They are, up to a point. What I always say,
echoing the Apostle's famous epistle, is:
***"They are of all people the most to be pitied …***
***(it is not good for them to be good kids***
***the way they are; it is far better for them***
***to be wicked as God wants wickedness to be.)***
***They led a life of virtue — with virtue being***
***the Lord's peculiar honor, (and so also said Church) —***
***but after Death they lost their proper reward!***
***Great Hope lay in their hearts … they died lamenting,***
***and went to Hell for all their true Religion!"***

All Christendom bleeds for the sad loss
of all such Christians. Though genuine cases, they
go to Hell regardless because they are ***foolish***:
***guardians*** whom no one needs of the Lord's great Honour;
naïve and unprepared, totally without Life's cunning.
This is the taunt which taunts the Lord precisely.
However true it is that Jesus be
the quintessential Machiavel, Man alive
never arose to His most real Principles!

Christ has a Heart and loves His Christians, knowing
that they are not to be idealized,
but that they are a genuine case. He knows
they go to Hell pawns to His purposes,
in an eternal game of inscrutable chess,
and knows He is responsible. When
His Christians go to Hell, Christ weeps and weeps,

and there is nothing the Saints can say which can
console Him! Jesus tells them: **"Bear it with Me
in silence, and leave Me alone to My weeping!"**
The Saints understand, murmuring:
**"Poor Jesus lost a Soul He loved!"** Upon all
such souls Jesus passes one Judgment only —
**"Just look at that! how many little Children
Satan has carried away to Hell from Me!"**

Christians
who lose their soul like this have none to blame,
not even Artists, but ***a beastie called the Priestee …***
who prepares them for damnation, caring little
that we feel crushed by the ponderous resources
of true religion, that after two thousand years
of this treatment, we are suffering from ***revulsion***.
He persists, much as he knows we do not want
to be insulted like this, to crush us beneath
the overbearing insult which taunts us, without
lifting a finger to help us bear it.

Still I prayed, defiantly:
***"I've suffered far too much: give me a break —
make me rich in means and rich in Mercy!
I do not want Sacrifice. I want Mercy —
the one and only council of Perfection!
I do not want Money that I may serve Money!
I want Money to serve God and myself better!
Make me rich, e'en as God Himself is rich,
rich in means and rich in Mercy!"***

Is this why, perhaps,
God says we cannot serve God and Money: that we
may all serve Him, whereas He may keep the money?
I doubt it, though I know He is, and needs
to be, the quintessential Machiavel …

Beware
of those who will say: "He is telling you
a tall one! Priests are all a beautiful people!
The Christians are all smiling, going to Heaven,
one by one!" Do not believe their phony cheer …
I know whereof I speak! I know I was,
at my own peril, a "good kid" like that in Youth:

if Jesus had not taken me under His wing,
through poetry and music, I could
have lost my soul for all my true Religion.
Nor did John of the Cross critique the Priests
in vain; nor was his Teaching lost upon me!
I call on all such Christians: feel for yourselves
compassion and pity as I felt for you,
that you may cease being slaughtered …

*6th - 13th January 2008*

## adequate recompense

in the style of a journal-entry

**PEOPLE** who love me offer at times as much as eighty dollars for a book I'm selling. If they do, they do because they know I need to live well. They do out of compassion knowing I am skillful, and knowing what a tough job I copped selling books door-to-door.

There are those around me who want to say, applying the Gospels unto myself but not unto themselves, that I received my reward already.

My answer is: after the heartache, the stress, the weariness and the toil, the hard labor — wherein I best resembled Tolstoy, bending his back to work in the fields, like the peasants — the prayers that I prayed for each and every new reader that I made, the tears and the sweat that I put into my door-to-door campaign, the only recompense I consider just and adequate is the Salvation of each and every single reader, and … the Lord Himself, giving me new blood for all the blood I lost to readers!

*13th January 2008*

## Appreciating Segovia

**AT SIKORA'S** the other day,
the classical music store close to Harbour Centre,
I asked Roger: "Do you have any more sets of 10 CD's

for a bargain price of $30?" Roger checked,
fetching me 10 CD's of guitar music
played by **"Segovia and friends."** I said:
"nothing can beat 10 Segovia CD's for $3 each,
even though it may contain music I already have."
I added:
"No guitarist I know can match
Segovia's sound. Segovia goes
BANG
BANG
BAAANG
B A A A N N N G G
and you hear the wood booming in the forest ...
**PALOSANTO!**
Segovia's sound is mighty, robust, strong, powerful,
it has physical strength and beauty. Rubinstein
has a sound like that. Ashkenazy on the piano
comes near but not quite.
I've been listening
to Laurindo Almeida, whose disks I bought
at Sikora's. Almeida is a good musician,
and his effects are most interesting,
especially when he matches guitar with voice,
but his sound is juvenile and adolescent
compared to Maestro Segovia.

Likewise the Los Angeles Guitar Quartet,
who play the signature tune on Studio Sparks,
on FM Stereo. It is extremely interesting music,
extremely melodious, extremely well-played,
but their combined sound is thin
compared to the Master's ...

*31st May 2008*

## To Rumi

**I WAS** impressed by praise your editor penned
for you: "*this ocean of sublime jazz*
*perhaps with no parallel in world literature!*"

Islam and its culture remind me of just that,
sublime jazz! As I read on
I could hear it in the atmosphere--
making me think of sex, at the same time
making me think of God, lifting up my mind
to higher things!
That is precisely
what jazz ought to be like, I thought,
and I cheered you, old Rumi, who, centuries ago,
in the middle ages, understood so well
something so primitive, and yet so modern!

That is just what I am missing when I listen
to jazz music, the sublime jazz of Islam!

*25th June 2008*

## A professor's love: an appeal to the Judge

**A GOOD** degree, your Honour, is the love
of the professoriate! A good professor's love
is crooked like a hook raking in the money
in night-clubs in Las Vegas, but love it is
whereby, upon the strength of good credentials,
and all the useful things professors teach,
countless folk find gainful employment,
supporting themselves and their families,
and working well with everything they learnt
at University. I know that the love of the professors
who gave me my bachelors was crooked:
they gave me the honour without giving me work;
but I know that my degree was a gift of love!

On the strength of my bachelors only,
and everything I was taught to obtain it,
I was capable of becoming a poet of real stature
and a publisher, and I know how well I work,
as author and publisher, with all the skills
I learnt at University …
Talk to me of a professor's love, your Honour:
a good prof deserves it!

*8th July 2008*

## Child of Nature

*for my friend, Virginia Quental*

**SHE** dwells in the big modern City.
Her third floor apartment looks out
upon the filth and noise of concrete and iron jungles
every square inch of which proclaims the Death
which Mother Nature died
that egoists may make their so-called **'PROGRESS'**:
the forests of the Earth all gone, the climate changing …

Were we to stand and to observe
ten minutes silence for the death of Nature
would never atone for **VENDETTA** so obnoxious!

But my friend Virginia is a child of Nature:
embracing poverty in the Gospel Spirit,
she lives by Art, she lives by Love —
where her modest dwelling boasts countless canvases,
a rooftop garden assembled with her own hard work,
and sunflowers as bright yellow as Van Gogh's …

vaunting
sincerer honour
within
the deep heart's core.

*9th November 2008*

## The quintessential Pop-Song
*a parody*

**aaahhwwssshhh!** the sentiment between my legs!
great God! just how my stereo needle's stuck!
how true it is I do not understand variety!
how true that I know not how to vary!
how to do something else for a change!
aaahhwwssshhh! the sentiment between my legs:
great God! — just how my stereo needle's stuck!
but still I thought I'd show you
just how well I can invent a pop-song also!
just how well I know how to parody
the unvaried, obnoxious theme!

*30th November 2008*

## Thomas Stearns Eliot

an early re-assessment for the new century

*by Joe M. Ruggier*

**A PROLIFIC,** hardworking author who witnessed, whatever his labours were, to the traditional value of working till you drop — plagued, also, by neurotic disorders which he handled by becoming active as an athlete — T. S. Eliot did not, by comparison to the sheer extent of his professional labours, write much original poetry and, as a matter of fact, published only one slim volume of major, selected poems. Yet his selected poems display Housman's unerring sense of when to write, and when enough had been said. Eliot knew precisely when his inspiration was in flight and when it was that it said, "you have said enough". Besides, like the fine, outspoken critic that he was, he was not altogether prone to vanity, knowing clearly that others had rights to criticize him just as he did them, and his criticism conveys an exemplary feeling of clean-breasted honesty. Again, his attempt to revive English drama displays much pluck, bravery and courage, and bears witness to the Spanish saying that "God loves a courageous soul". Yet his plays are not on the whole as memorable as his serious poetry.

At this point, I cannot help recalling the following passage, taken out of his famous essay, **Tradition and the Individual Talent**, which sums up certain major aspects of his poetic creed:

> **YET** if the only form of tradition, of handing down, consisted of following the ways of the immediate generation before us in a blind or timid adherence to its successes, "tradition" should positively be discouraged. We have seen many such simple currents soon lost in the sand; and novelty is better than repetition. Tradition

> is a matter of much wider significance. It cannot be inherited, and if you want it you must obtain it with great labour. It involves, in the first place, the historical sense, which we call nearly indispensable to anyone who would continue to be a poet beyond his twenty-fifth year; and the historical sense involves a perception, not only of the pastness of the past, but of its presence; the historical sense compels a man to write not merely with his own generation in his bones, but with a feeling that the whole of the literature of Europe from Homer and within it the whole of the literature of his own country has a simultaneous existence and composes a simultaneous order. This historical sense, which is a sense of the timeless as well as of the timeless and of the temporal together, is what makes a writer traditional. And it is at the same time what makes a writer most acutely conscious of his place in time, of his own contemporaneity.

As profoundly truthful, and as positively moving, as I find this teaching to be, I cannot help feeling that, unlike Homer, whose brilliant mind, at the dawn of Time, was singularly uncluttered, Eliot, like the rest of us today who are sensitive at all, suffered psychologically from being required to toe the line to all the great minds, all the great discoveries of all time, and his mind, like ours, was overpowered by the clutter of the ages — a psychiatric phenomenon of which his poem **"The Waste Land"** is such a powerful correlative. What is positively miraculous is that out of this waste land of thought and feeling he managed so powerfully to *"construct something upon which to rejoice"*; that out of the freest of his free form we are always overpowered, compelled and thrilled by the astonishing emergence of unique craft and profoundly interesting structure.

T. S. Eliot worked stupendously as a magnificent technical innovator and re-invigorator of language who approximated poetry to conversation using a striking free form technique. In spite of this apparent freedom of form, however, Eliot worked beautifully in rhyme and metre also as displayed internally within all his free form from his earliest (Prufrock) to his maturest (Four Quartets) …

Read as one long poem with the various parts marking distinct stages upon a spiritual journey, the entire corpus of Eliot's selected poems reads like a continuous uninterrupted account of one man's spiritual growth and journey from the 20th Century ennui and angst of Prufrock to the heights of mystical, Christian contemplation. We start in a valley, a deep ravine or abyss, and finish on a mountaintop, amid the breathtaking heights of spiritual ecstasy and consolation. We see in his work the face of the proverbial, bored and unhappy professor, in search of the Peace and Joy of the Gospel — (just as we see this face also in Rex Hudson's work, in Hopkins' and Jacques Maritain's, as well as in Roy Daniells', Canadian poet and UBC Professor of authentic genius who died in 1979). Reading Eliot we are blessed by the feeling that there is, indeed, hope for everyone — *"che puo' salvare l'anima anche te!"*[107]. Each poem in the sequence provides a gorgeous objective correlative for an interior state of mind, heart and soul. The sense of profound interior structure and relational sequence is paramount and Eliot's work conscientiously exemplifies the truth that to be great, one must always heed one's conscience and what the Divine Spirit is trying to say at every point in the journey, in guidance …

Eliot, however, is a striking example of the truth that too much fame and popularity are not good for you in your own lifetime, for the simple reason that the reaction against you will settle in, and Heaven defend you, then, from the crushing insults which readers who have been oversold about you will surely raise. The alternative to this type of acclaim, which in Eliot's case was decidedly spontaneous and unforced, is a renown which gathers slowly, gently, and which does not come all at once, but stays with you after death, and grows with time, like the proverbial waters which, although still, run deep.

---

[107] *"that you can save your soul you also!"* — a line from an aria by Mozart.

Too much fame, perhaps, with all of its unholy pressures, is what prevented Eliot from becoming an orthodox Catholic like Dante, or like Thomas Merton, or like Jacques Maritain. Had he done so Eliot could easily have been declared a Christian Saint and even Doctor of the Church. He was great enough for these honours in a myriad ways and his fortunes with posterity would have been enhanced and assured. The only reason that so many saints and inspired authors feel that the arts are a false or spurious honour is precisely and in all simplicity because audiences are always tempted to discuss the arts in a spirit of idle talk and boastful vainglory and not in a spirit of prayer to the Divine Author Himself of all valid inspiration …

A lifelong practitioner of the unswerving, the uncompromising, the conscientious, and the exemplary, T. S. Eliot, perhaps, made one last-minute concession to idle talk, to vainglory even, (like the foolish women talking of MichaelAngelo in **The Love Song of J. Alfred Prufrock**), and this one lapse sadly cost him securer and far more glorious honours. One wishes that, just as audiences are inspired, often quite spontaneously, to say that an author is as great as Eliot, they ought to feel equally inspired, while contemplating an author like T. S. Eliot, to pray as if everything depended upon their prayers …

Bearing in mind my qualified reverence and lifelong admiration of Thomas Stearns Eliot I shall herewith desist entirely from questioning and probing his integrity any further. I endorse without question the astute, priceless discernment and the brilliant simplicity of St. Augustine's sentence … *"Many who seem without are within"* … and I shall conclude this reassessment with a story drawn from experience. As a university student in Malta I was, in many respects, naïve and vulnerable. Because my staunch Catholicism positively aroused resentment in my classmates, even as my high grades aroused their envy, I endured many harsh, unkind criticisms, and I was badly in need of emotional protection. I found this protection in the work of T. S. Eliot.

I was very happy with the arrangement … a great Anglo-Catholic emotionally protecting and rescuing an inexperienced Roman Catholic: capital! I love him! It could not be better! I positively used to reply to all the unkind criticism I was enduring with well-chosen quotations out of my great mentor's books in such a way that no one could tell me that either myself or my sources were narrow-minded. I shall never, in short, forget just how truly the shining Spirit of Eliot asserted and reasserted me, affirmed and reaffirmed my poor, naïve, vulnerable spirit in those days of inexperienced Youth, positively giving me precise spiritual guidance, and it is for these reasons that I insist, always, that I owe this Poet a debt of gratitude. It would be sacrilege for me to cast a shadow on his motives and intentions. I shall never forget just what spiritual direction, comfort, moral solace, and emotional reassurance I derived, extracted and earnt myself, in those days, between the lines of all of Eliot's pages, and I positively feel for this poet what Dante felt for Virgil:

> "tu duca, tu segnore, e tu Maestro."[108]
> *("you are Guide, you are Lord, and you the Master.")*


*3rd October 2004*

---

[108] Dante — La Divina Commedia, Inferno, Canto II, line 140.

## The decay of artistic beauty and integrity

*by Joe M. Ruggier, Managing Editor of TEM*[109]
*to my devoted friend and reader Dr. H. Ragetli*
*who asked me to write upon this topic*
*and who contributed to this discussion many seminal ideas*

### Preamble

**AMONG** the most popular of heretical misconceptions, to my way of thinking, an error whose age-old copyright belongs to certain fundamentalist religious factions, is the well-known cliché that *"we do not need artists!"* Though this attitude, at best, turns the stomach of many people, being nothing but *heresy, quintessential heresy,* there is really not much we can do to stop such *looney tunes* from *catching.* Just as crass an error, from my point of view as a full-time arts activist, is the bigotry that *"great works of art are not a real honor!"* and that *"Artists are good for nothing!" ... quintessential heresy and anathema,* the trademark of various foolish Christians! It seems to me that a good answer is that the Universe has billions of galaxies and, within each galaxy, there are, positively, billions of stars, perhaps trillions, perhaps with untold blue planets circling round them, which we may never hope to travel to, populate, and own. What do we need them for? The Creator, however, generates them all the time, purely to please Himself with the pride He takes in Creation, the sheer *academic delight* He derives from *creativity.*

Artists are mirrors of the Divine Creator. This analogy, in my interpretation, illustrates what I feel is the correct teaching: that we all need Artists who are productive, joyful and proud of their *Work,* just like the Creator; such Artists have a key role to fulfill in society. If Artists wish to publish as many great *Works of Art* as God created *Stars,*

---

109 originally released as an editorial to **The Eclectic Muse**, *Volume 14, Christmas 2008;* herein refined according to critical suggestions made by my associate, Mr. Virgil Kaulius.

positively beyond what anyone can ever hope to use and appreciate, it does not matter: pleasing Himself Alone, God derives pure *academic* delight from *creativity*, and likewise *Artists*. The only condition is that they must be joyful, and proud of their creations — giving us nothing but their best — just like the Divine Creator. I venture to add: as long as human creators are joyful and proud of their work on this basis, *as long as they shew us God*, you should invest money in their work; if they do not, do not invest a penny. It is, at best, totally impossible for an Artist to please everyone, but he is called upon to please God by shewing us God, Who pleases Himself Alone!

**The Decay of Architecture**

What needs saying is that the decay of language has occurred by and large because extremely few of the authors who manipulate language for their own purposes, and who are practicing now, seem to be motivated along the lines recommended above, and as a result insensitive indifference to artistic beauty has led to what comes across as moral decay, deterioration, degradation, and corruption. Language is not the only area displaying this decay. It seems to me that a perfect analogy, drawn from another area, is the joylessness displayed in the modern architecture of our big, ugly, modern cities, with their *long, unlovely streets*, the terrifying appearance of their *tombstones*, as perceived from an aerial view, and all their horrible high-rises, every one of them an eyesore and all grouped together without any care or eye for taste and architectural beauty, wherein each balcony peeps into someone else's bedroom window.

Some time ago I discussed these concerns with my brother, saying that artistic beauty is in my best interpretation a sincere honor, and that, where there is sincere honor, there is present God! I concluded that our *big city planners* seem to have no clue what artistic beauty is, what the sincere honor is, or What, and Who, God is. My brother remarked immediately, "Do you not appreciate what they are up against? In order to build a sky-train route just as they are building in Richmond now," Richmond, British Columbia, being my home-town, "the expenditure is

1.5 billion per kilometer! In order to justify such a terrifying expense," he concluded, "they urgently require areas with an extremely high population density!"

Naturally, economical concerns must always be dealt with, but I have no doubt that utility and convenience are not the exclusive concern, and this is where artistic speculation, and a dedicated artist's viewpoint are a-propos. Purely from a viewpoint of artistic speculation and imagination, I can see, in my mind's eye, a city such as Richmond being built totally underground, with only farmland and farm-houses on top, and a few sky-train routes, and only a few high-rises, extremely sparse and far between and all of them as awesome as the World Trade Centre, with 300 feet of soil, perhaps more, to all of the acres of farmland on top, and with biking trails, hiking routes, and a few other facilities for those who wish to enjoy the sunshine. Underneath, to keep away the humidity and the water, since Richmond is practically built on top of the ocean, there should be, all around, at the bottom, the sides and underneath all the farmland, a wall, at least 500 feet thick, of metal casing, cast iron or stainless steel, or else concrete, constructed in such a way that it would insulate everything entirely from the humidity and from the ocean, and would positively hold everything together. Also, there should be a depth, from underneath the farmland to the very bottom of the entire structure, of at least one mile, perhaps even two miles or more, with this space being devoted to various levels, or layers, each the equivalent of around 35 storeys, roughly the height of the highest high-rise in Vancouver. Within these levels, and within the entire structure underground, our big city planners could build high-rises, and immense shopping centers, with hundreds, perhaps, of parks and indoor gardens, to their heart's content, and the underground high-rises in their turn could serve as reinforcing columns supporting the entire structure, each of them being as awesome as the World Trade Centre.

I assure you that, however expensive it is to build a *City of God* along these lines, such an awesome achievement of technology and architecture would bring the wonder, and the artistic beauty, back into our eyes. It may also be proof, practically, against Atom Bombs, nuclear Weapons, and an attack such as that sustained by the USA on 9-11. Around 300 feet of soil on top, perhaps more, with 500 feet of iron casing or concrete all around, perhaps more, might be sufficient to absorb the explosion of such deadly weapons; whereas one Atom Bomb only, dropped on one of our modern Cities, would probably demolish most of the high-rises in any such city, escalating such a calamity to a world-class disaster worse than any *Krakatoa* or *Tsunami*!

I fully understand that the above is nothing but an artistic speculation. In the creation of such an awesome achievement of technology and architecture there are problems which can only be resolved by expert men of science and top engineers. A proper feasibility study needs to be undertaken before anything happens. Many things need to be determined, such as how deep to dig, how far from the surface the bottom of the entire structure must be … as far as we choose or only as far as the bedrock extends? and how high should each layer be? as high as high-rises of 35 storeys each? or only as high as regular houses? Among other problems are the issue of proper ventilation and air conditioning underground, the strength of the concrete fortifications surrounding everything, as well as the optimum way to use the underground high-rises as pillars in their own right supporting the entire structure. An artist is competent to provide imaginative viewpoints. Only top engineers and expert men of science can resolve all the technological problems.

**The Decay of Language**

This brief paper does not deal with the decay of language only, as the original title primarily suggested: it deals with what seems to me to be the deterioration, the degradation of artistic beauty and integrity, of which the decay of language is only an aspect! Regarding the decay of language as such, one aspect is *"small talk lop-eared to look like verse"*, a galling relic of modernism which it seems to me that most authors writing at the dawn of the 21st century ought to throw overboard. Another aspect is *"tortured sound and tortured sense"*, likewise a galling relic of modernism …

Another aspect of the decay of language is *political correctness* and many sorts of undesirable euphemisms — such as substituting *hearing impaired* for the straightforward description, *deaf*; or the euphemistic phrase *mentally challenged* for the straightforward description, *insane*, *mad*, or *lunatic*; or the attractive phrasing of *the Ministry of Justice*, which substitutes for the more accurate *Ministry of Law* — where the *Law*, however *legal*, may indeed be *unjust*. The attractive phrase *freedom of choice* likewise means one thing to pro-life individuals, another to pro-choice individuals.

All of us are involved in the decay of language, not the Artist only; and all of us are guilty. Artistic Beauty is not a question of Beauty alone. It seems to me that it is also a matter of existential survival in which all Civilization is at stake: the decay of the *Word* is leading directly to the disintegration of society. The perversion, for instance, of the word *Choice* in the attractive slogan, *Pro Choice*, to cover up and justify the murder of the unborn, for whom there is ***No Choice but Death***, seems obvious and striking. It seems even more ironic and sinister when compared with a statement in the Fisheries Act, which equates *"Fish eggs with Fish"* (R.S., c 119, s. 1; Statutes of Can. 1985, c. 31). Another such perversion seems to be the equation of the Death Penalty with Murder, because of the frailty of human Justice.

As an instrument to name, identify, describe, define, formulate, communicate, and transmit thought, the *Word* is of existential importance. As such it enables and empowers organized human existence and creativity, provided it is used respectfully and truthfully. It seems that deliberate deceptions, slogans, and half-truths corrupt the vitality and creative value of the *Word.* The creativity and impact of the *naming* function of *words* may be sensed when one considers the task of primitive man, in this case the Biblical Adam, to give names to the objects, creatures, and phenomena all around him, in Creation. Likewise, the consequence of *the loss of meaning* of the *word* may be observed when one contemplates the confusion which resulted from such loss at the site of the tower of Babel.

Indeed I am convinced that these observations and statements are of universal value and may not be brushed aside as sectarian opinions. The neurosis we are experiencing is the deterioration of the beauty, integrity, and reliability of the Divine Word into the frivolous triviality of the commercially inspired word, a ***word*** without honour, in our modern mass-media.

It seems clear to me that words, the intelligence intrinsic within language, more than architecture and more than music, directly impinge upon our perception of reality, the intelligible substance of things. Rhyme, as a phenomenon of beautiful language, points directly, as many a fine critic would argue, to the intelligence intrinsic within words. A great Poet, such as Dante, does not abandon his sense, his meaning half-way in order to make a rhyme. A great Poet drifts along, making an act of faith in the intelligence intrinsic within language as his guide, his meaning pointing out his perfect rhymes, whereas his perfect rhymes reinforce his meaning, both aspects, intelligent sense and intelligent rhyme, being securely married to each other … much in the same way that authentic human intelligence works flawlessly when married to the intelligence displayed by the most reliable, computerized technology of today. Conversely, today there are no great poets and thus all rhyme and reason have deserted the English language. This phenomenon seems to underline just how true it is that we are *wrecking* language, we are battering, corrupting, and disintegrating the intelligence intrinsic within words, the intelligible substance of things.

All of us, poor children of the Spirit, sincere, bereaved lovers of artistic beauty, are living in a World where, for every book we produce conscientiously, everyone else brings out a score. Whatever our motives are, however shining or corrupt, everyone else is publishing, and, for every book we offer to anyone for reading, everyone is asking us to read a score. Every day, in our private apartments, we have to put up with the mindless language of TV, as well as with the plague of information and unwanted advertising that comes through the mail, and we are called upon to determine what goes into the garbage. As a mere exercise in vanity and mutual back-scratching, everyone is speed reading everyone else. No one has the time any longer to read for comprehension and understanding. No one has the time any longer to read the truly beautiful classics, Longfellow or Walt Whitman to name the top poets of North America. Is this what we are calling a service to Culture? It is anything but: no one has a right to plague, torment, mistreat, maltreat, and victimize anyone in this fashion! We are witnessing right now the deliberate corruption and destruction of language! We need right now a Cultural Revolution: don't you ever dare dream of doing anything like that again to anyone with **books**!

**The Decay of Music**

Music, another dimension of intelligent communication, seems to be another area of creativity now displaying the damage caused by the same *wrecking*, the same *battering and disintegration* carried on all around us. Classical music, much maligned in our day by certain factions, seems to be where all the *variety* is: different genres, many instruments, countless styles, countless performers, and countless composers. In classical music we can listen to symphonies, operas, oratorios, concertos, serenades, sonatas for single instruments, quartets, quintets, octets, and more. We can listen to many instruments, more often than not different solo instruments, accompanied by an orchestra, or chamber orchestra, in a concerto for Harp, or Piano, or classical Guitar, or Violin, or Cello, or accompanied by a string quartet or quintet, or unaccompanied. We can listen to countless distinguished performers, musicians, or conductors, all of them bringing something unique to the sound and to the interpretation. Classical music is truly where all the *variety* is within music, and this *variety* directly addresses, it seems, our perception of *the intelligible substance*, *the intelligence intrinsic within music*.

Yet we are told, by countless ***amateurs*** and ***teenagers***, that pop-music, with all its objectionable connotations, is *friendlier*, more *popular*, *easier* to digest and assimilate, and should always be introduced for *variety*. Truly, my friend, pop-music consists of songs, only songs, and nothing but songs; and whereas song-writing is an art, I am convinced that it is nothing but an extremely humble and ancient art contained within *classical music*. The vast majority of songs that we are regaled with in pop-music, contrasted to the songs and operatic *arias* contained within classical music, deal with one subject only, *erotic desire*. Is this what we are going to call *variety*? and what we are describing as *friendlier*? Truly this is nothing but oppression and social boredom, and serves to underline the truth that, if you wish to learn music at all, you ought to do yourself the favor of learning music well, beginning with **The Dictionary of Music** as your first, constant and reliable guide. Again, we are wrecking sound, we are wrecking *Music*.

I do not love classical music and loathe pop-music. I merely adore good music and deplore bad. Classical music often comes across as *cloying, stale* and *conventional*; whereas some good pop-music is by comparison extremely *fresh*. In my extensive, home-based collection of musical recordings, I have a small cross-section of songs, Italian songs, English songs, some of Nana Mouskouri's, as well as spiritual songs, (*soul-music*), created in a popular contemporary idiom, a lot of which I have been listening to since I was a youth in Malta. It is impossible to be immersed so completely by the media in an art-form without becoming extremely critical at the same time that one falls truly in love with a little of it. The result is that, whereas I am convinced, as always, that pop-music consists of songs and only songs, ***canzonetti***, I adore this brief selection of songs that I listen to at home, finding them indeed *fresh, re-invigorating*, and truly a *change*.

I am convinced, however, if my readers can excuse an opinion so radically different from the majority's, that pop-music, for the reasons described in the previous paragraphs, is evil, positively an instrument in the hands of Satan. It seems to me that the reason that it has not been condemned is, not that it does not deserve uncompromising moral censure, but primarily because there are countless sincere and honest people working therein and we must never crush the good with the wicked, which is what Jesus Christ's parable of the wheat and the tares is all about. Aside from all this popular musicians have indeed created a few popular songs, whether they are pop-songs as such, or whether they are spiritual songs disguised behind a contemporary idiom, (as in *soul-music*), which come across as *fresh,* incredibly *beautiful*, wherein the issue we most deplore is that these red, red roses of musical inspiration should have been plucked out of a soil contaminated by so much blood, human sacrifice, and nuclear waste, as if one were positively to cultivate diamonds out of the bedrock at Auschwitz, stained as it is by blood and human waste. My conclusion is simple: we positively adore a little of this music for its *beauty* and for its *freshness;* but we deplore the obnoxious connotations which, were it not for our act of critical, redemptive intervention, would have positively made it an instrument in the hands of Satan. Apart from the ethic that this is what our selective, critical faculty is intended for, it seems to me inevitable not to deplore the astronomical amount of time required to comb and rake this enormous wasteland of useless music just so we can preserve such a limited crop of truly beautiful flowers. Is it worth our while?

Finally, may I conclude by pointing out a few rules in identifying what is truly "**good**" and "**beautiful**" in popular music? My suggestions are simple. Always look for *rhythm*, *melody*, *harmony*, qualities which are common throughout all music, both popular and classical, but above all, in popular music which is destined to endure, you ought also to look, in my ethical assessment, for *words* which lead our *conscience* and the *soul* to the **greater good** in one's life, a concept which is borne out so convincingly by the beauty of *soul-music*, cast in the disguise of a contemporary idiom. A great song ought to display a subject of enduring worth — and it ought to be ruled, before we conclude, that erotic appeal, whereas it often features as an ingredient in great Art, is in no way a criterion of lasting artistic worth and aesthetic beauty, and, more often than not, contradict God's laws and His plans as expressed in any Scripture, in any major Religion, being nothing but an instrument in the hands of Satan in so far as it has been prostituted shamelessly and immorally through popular works of Art.

**Conclusion**
In one of my daily prayers I pray as follows: *"Lord, make me a Man such as I am in my prayers, in my thoughts and imaginations, and in my books and all my dreams; such that my prayers, expressed in my own words, and my literary creations, likewise couched in my own language, shall never be interpreted as being a taunt and a temptation to You, Oh Lord, but shall strictly be perceived as being a sincere honor to me and to You!"* This perception, in my opinion, is precisely where the decay of language, of all artistic beauty, seems to be rooted — people who do not mean what they say; people who bring the word of hope to your ear but do not stand behind it, never fulfilling their promise; people who pay each other false compliments which no one in his right senses should ever take seriously; people to whom *maximizing profit* is the only issue that matters and who allow this concern to override all other legitimate considerations; people who compromise their principles, having no clue what a *sincere honor* is; people who are not ladies and gentlemen as they are in their dreams … this is precisely where the decay of all artistic beauty is rooted! This is not the way of sensitive human beings! of real ladies and gentlemen with beautiful imaginations! This is not the way in which the heart-searing beauty of God's Bible has made an astounding comeback in every generation for the last eight thousand years entire! This is not what we mean by *the sincere Honor!*


*July 15th 2008 – May 7th 2009*

## The parable of the talents, reflections

**SO AS** to judge people well, the Divine Judge is constantly marrying, merging, and flexing criteria. The Judgment, in His Hands, is not a rigid instrument or intolerant mental outlook, abiding strictly by absolute and inflexible rules. It is on the contrary a most flexible and plastic way of perceiving, constantly adapting itself to individual need. This flexibility of judging criteria is what animates the rich mosaic of Gospel parables about Divine Judgment. Whereas Compassion is as always the heart of the Law, binding in everyone's conscience as Mother Teresa taught us through her own example, as much as through the equally shining example of all the rich who, acknowledging her Compassion, honoured her with gifts of money, God's Judgments, whereas they always hinge around Mercy and Compassion, constantly adapt themselves to missions, to vocations, to callings, which are not necessarily like Mother Teresa's …

Mother Teresa's compassion consists in feeding the poorest of the poor to help them die with dignity — and is binding in conscience. She needs countless hands to help her look after the poor, with neither the strength nor the means to eat well, let alone enjoy culture. A real Artist's compassion, on the other hand, consists exclusively in helping his public accept, bear, cope, and live with a difficult insult. We may need only a few such great Artists, but an Artist's brand of sincere compassion is binding in conscience no less than Mother Teresa's: absolutely everyone is called upon in conscience to accept a difficult insult; since everyone, at some stage of his interior growth, requires qualified help to cope with such an insult; since difficult insults damn and people save their dear soul when you help them bear an insult. Taunting the public with nameless insults is the most terrible pastime there is. I do not think the Artists are to blame alone: many do it who are not Artists!

Dante made Hell a great work of Art: his intentions were, not to crush you, but strictly to help you accept, bear, cope, and live with such a difficult insult, this being Dante's sincere brand of awful compassion … he suffered that terrible insult himself before he grew up to help you accept it. Artists may not share our belief in Hell, but they all interpret Dante correctly. They understand clearly that Dante's intention was, not to crush them, but to help them cope with this terrifying insult. It is the Catholics who fail to interpret Dante's intentions correctly. Were you to say that a sincere Artist's compassion is not binding in conscience like Mother Teresa's, I will retort ... *man does not live by bread alone! Mother Teresa can say what she wants! but I know that she was also fond of composing poetry!*

Certain factions argue that the parable of the talents is a false honour to punish Artists for being false. It is not. This parable is the sincerest of honours to the Artists and to all intelligent people. Works of art, in so far as they are good works at all, are the light within you: you have little right to bury great works of art underground, for the Gospel says clearly —"*let your light shine before men.*" With good reason this parable is indelibly carved in the conscience of world Artists who clearly sense that the Lord was alluding to them. It speaks to their condition. It is also the most real of Judgment criteria with many a lasting lesson between the lines to be implied and extracted.

The only intelligence possessed by a computer is the knack of the microchip to distinguish between zero (0) and one (1). Stupid! but only consider what a computer is capable of achieving when its dull intelligence is programmed by Man's Genius! The parable of the talents is about the basic gift of perception, which everyone is born with in doses of one talent at a time, to use his gray matter and put two and two together, whether this be in Math and Arithmetic, or else in Business and Finance, or else in the Romantic sense of pairing lovers, or else in Scientific inquiry, or else in the Artistic, Theological, Philosophical, or Metaphysical domains. It is a real Honour to Artists, who are often the wiliest and most resourceful of people, possessing, to an eminent degree, the ability to put two and two together productively, just as Jesus says they must in this parable — the core talent, if nothing else, wherein the artists excel through the productive harnessing and application of human imagination! Moralists, priests and theologians think within straightjacketed experience; artists think outside it.

Were Man's genius to harness everyone's basic gift of perception as we have harnessed the computer's, the result would be that we shall free the human mind from error, as Longfellow says in one of his great poems. People going to Hell by mistake would become a thing of the past, an exception entirely unheard of. But people who are not capable of putting two and two together are unreliable. They are not an asset, particularly where money is involved: they are often best ejected from a professional team.

And such is the parable of the talents, that brilliant synthesis that God wills everyone to use his brains, his wits, all his gifts and talents, all of mankind's great works of art, all of humanity's resources, all of them ***gifts*** at our disposal, as well as all of our own, individual resources — productively, under pain of being cast off if we do not. It is the sincerest of honours to Artists! to intelligent people everywhere! a criterion of Judgment deemed valid by all our modern business practices! *"Business is business and you must not interfere: unless you put two and two together productively, as Jesus is asking, unless you* **produce**, *I shall fire you - it is Business with a capital B!"* Unless you are productive nobody wants you in his team: you will only waste his money causing your employer untold embarrassment; but the heart of the Law is Compassion, now as always.

This is just how inspired Jesus was, two thousand years ago, just how far He was seeing, with what clarity of vision He perceived business as we know it two thousand years later, and just how lonely He was, what a misunderstood Genius, how limited and how extremely primitive were His materials and His public, with no one around Him whom He could trust with His inmost prophetic vision, no one around Him who could possibly understand all that He saw. And He talked to His followers of the only thing they could relate to: His Love! The first Christians were ignorant because they had absolutely no other viable option. In our day learning opportunities are countless. Many modern Christians are ignorant because they do not want to learn: they have been judged and have been found wanting and in contravention of the parable of the talents!

Purely to amplify this judgment, the Christians boast countless beautiful honours, countless Saints and Artists. All these great honours are talents, gifts at their disposal. Many Christians do not have a clue what on earth they must do to make so many talents work for them by putting two and two together, such that they shall earn their living productively with great people, as everyone within culture understands all too well how to do, and such that they shall save their souls with great people. This is just how true it is that many Christians are foolish, that they are committing a real sin against the parable of the talents.

Another nuance from between the lines of this parable is … in the salvation of great people there is at stake the salvation of countless people, as well as expensive wine and cheese. Whereas there is a poet in everyone as well as a merchant, God Himself would have to be a fool, One who is precisely not putting two and two together, to save common folk only, as certain factions argue, and not great honourable people, especially if such are great by God's standards. All I am asking is, put two and two together: as long as God saves Dante, and Shakespeare, and MichaelAngelo, He stands to haul over three billion fresh fish from the Ocean; but were He to save a fool, what shall God reap in return? Where are the fish? Where is the wine and cheese? To save your soul with honour as He saved Dante's, God needs to see "*plenty fish, and plenty wine and cheese*!"

What, for instance, is the justification for purchasing and restoring an Organ worth one million dollars for the Catholic Cathedral in Vancouver Archdiocese? It is precisely to be found in the parable of the talents. If this expensive organ is used productively, as Jesus says in this Parable — in the sense that it serves as a focal point for employing fine musicians, such that it will help many gifted folk to earn their living praising God, if it serves as a focal point for recitals and concerts which are money-makers for the Cathedral, (such that the Cathedral can hope to recover the investment), if it serves as a focal point for all the Christians at the Cathedral to praise God, according to the Scriptural line *"let everything that breathes praise the Lord!"*, if it is an asset to the Cathedral and not a liability, being used productively as Jesus is saying — in this case it is not Vanity. It serves, in such case, the ideological goal of the "greater good" of the community, wherein Catholic community has often been described by knowledgeable critics as a **team**, displaying team work, rather than as an environment for a few individuals of genius only! The expenditure is justified by the logic of this parable. If such an expensive instrument, however, is not used productively, if the expense is not justified, it can be argued that the expense is wicked Vanity, with many people saying: *"Why did you spend so much money on an Organ? You cannot even play the darn thing!"* It becomes, in this case, a purely secular concern!

Countless modern millionaires know also and all too well what all the religions say about compassion. They understand far too clearly the Lord's Parable about Dives and Lazarus: they are keenly sensitive to that nerve-wracking condemnation. Modern millionaires, like Bill Gates in the USA, or Jim Pattison in British Columbia, are by and large an asset to society, helping make the world go round, in so far as they invest untold millions in business, in so far as they employ countless people, in so far as they donate money through their nose to numberless charities: they answer in their own way everybody's petition in The Lord's Prayer — *"give us this day our daily bread!"* They are witness that nobody has a right to hate anybody, neither the poor the rich just because the rich have money and the poor do not, nor common people the Artists just because Artists possess expensive gifts which common people cannot boast! Once more the Parable of the Talents is the sweetest justification of the rich Man and all his ways. He understands this Parable all too well, knowing precisely how to make it work for his own purposes and countless people's.

Countless taskmasters are demanding Church to give away all She owns without counting the cost. Nobody gives without counting cost. The line by Saint Ignatius, *"to give and not to count the cost,"* is incorrect theology, nonsense devised by the Saint purely to fleece an Artist: the correct theology is the Parable of the Talents. *God is the lawful Owner of a Universe where everywhere you look is long ago. He gave us nothing but one lousy, defective Solar System.*

*The rich are obliged in conscience to use money productively according to the logic of this parable, and to give to charity out of their income only according to the need and to their capability.* As if anyone at all is *a god all goodness and all mercy and a foolish Man as I am implying!* As if one Jesuit only giveth and doth not count the cost!

The parable of the talents is also about redeeming ourselves with our own skill and prayers. Certain factions, totally insensitive to the fact that everyone has a similar need, seek to save their soul by victimizing and sacrificing everyone they know to their personal need. ***Nonno Crocefisso and Nonna Crocefissa!*** *(GrandPa crucified and GrandMa crucified!)* What are they up to except victimizing everyone they know to their own great need, the Salvation of their soul? Don't you dare save your Soul like that! Your neighbour has a similar problem: you must save your Soul with your own skill and prayers, just as Jesus implies in this Parable, knowing that, when you reach the point where you cannot do more, God will reward you for helping yourself! Salvation is never a solo flight either!

Mother Teresa does not necessarily need anyone to join her physically to feed the poor with chopsticks, one by one, where she will also have to bed you, clothe you, lodge you, feed you, and train you! Herself and her nuns, moreover, are obliged in conscience to use their money, the compassionate gift of countless rich people, productively, as Jesus says in this immortal parable. If they do not, they shall risk losing their money, begging again with many rich people telling them to get lost. Mother Teresa, however, needs you to obtain real credentials, whereby you can earn your living convincingly. When you earn your living productively, do something about it: GIVE AND DO NOT BE STINGY! There is never any harm in giving! We all know what the Gospel says about giving: compassion is binding in conscience, the Sacred Heart of all Law, human and Divine, in all World religions, just as Mother Teresa says! Give of everything you have, materially and spiritually, in that spot of earth occupied by your own two feet!

All I am arguing is the sweet and rational application to Life of Our Lord's Parable of the gifts, as a valid criterion of Divine Judgment, as well as a sincere honour to Artists, in whose conscience this profound Teaching is indelibly inscribed! An Artist's conscience clearly dictates that, if he possesses one gift, he must earn another, and if, owing to the necessities of his work, he must throw one talent overboard, he must replace it with another ten; that Life is a great, precious gift and must be made the most of … This is the insider reason why the Arts, and the Culture Industry, are big business: it is entirely owing to this driving factor; but the conscience of all this big business is Our Lord's parable of two thousand years ago! All Christians require it spelt out that this immortal Parable is the Conscience of the Artists, that an Artist's conscience is equally truthful, and not Mother Teresa's only! Who on earth puts the idea into people's head that countless human beings working within Culture are all evil and without a conscience? What do people take the conscience of the Artists for?

Countless Christians do not right reason. They think with the mind of Church or the Priest's without making the slightest real contribution. No one needs subservient people who say "Aye!" to anything we may say. We strictly require Christians who use their gray matter productively, Christians who make a valid contribution to the Cause with authentic thinking of their own. What I am arguing is a fundamental concern of metaphysics — human perception! Precisely what does human perception consist of? According to my interpretation of Christ's parable, it consists of the skill to put two and two together productively within whatever branch of knowledge you may be operating! The Genius of rhyming language, for instance, a Genius taught unto us by Church Herself, consists of putting two and two together by making your poem rhyme like Dante's. It is anything but **stoopid** when well-done.

The parable of the talents is above all the parable of human perception, the one and only tool of human perception being to put two and two together as Jesus is asking. You do not need any other gift of great Genius except this one and only gift of basic I.Q. The wicked servant in this timeless parable was being precisely a **stoopid**, a **stooptu.** Whether he was truly so, or merely acting, his divine Master sent him to Hell on the spot, (this being just how right professors are to do it to their students!) — not for not being a Genius, but for not putting two and two together, that basic gift which everybody is born with, in doses of one talent at a time, this being the only gift of Genius that is being called for. Within the arts, within culture, all such **stoopids** are dismissed instantly, with no explanation offered except that they are **stoopid**, without a single credential, degree, certificate, mention, or diploma being awarded them. This is precisely what an Artist's conscience says unto an Artist: "You have no right to be or act **stoopid**. You possess no less than anyone a gift of basic I.Q. Use your brains productively, putting two and two together as the Lord is asking. You learnt your mother-tongue by putting two and two together even though you were a baby! Stop being or acting a **stooptu**! You are not such a thing and you must clearly show it!" It needs be said that a good Artist's conscience tells God's Truth unto an Artist no less clearly than Mother Teresa's.

Christians honour only the coins of Faith, Hope, and Love: not being capable themselves, they often fail to honour capable people adequately. Many Artists honour these Virtues also, but within Art the Law is different: Artists honour the coin of Intelligence only, because Intelligence and Ability are great Virtues just as Jesus is implying — they grow out of being practiced! Jesus implies clearly, a nuance of doctrine which is at the very heart of this parable, that one is born with talents through no merit of one's own: merit and personal virtue arise exclusively from the good use to which one puts the gifts one is born with. It needs saying that Faith, Hope, and Love are surer guides unto eternal Salvation than Human Intelligence, but Christians and Artists must be accepted as they are, and this parable speaks to the condition of the Artists. I stress the most subtle complexity of Scripture despite its disarming simplicity. The Gospels contain grist for all. Everyone reads through his own lens, picking therefrom teaching which speaks to his condition, his own vested interests, but the Sacred Author compromises Himself never ever, in nothing He says, and with no one whatsoever.

## Reflections on Our Lord's second greatest commandment, "love your neighbor as you love yourself", and Whitman's "Song of Myself".

**WHEN** Jesus formulated this fundamental and universal teaching, He was assuming that no one among His Public was a fool. He was assuming that everyone listening loved himself truthfully and sincerely. Jesus did not say: *"Love your neighbor more than you love yourself."* Nor did He say: *"Love yourself first and foremost and only then your neighbor."* He said: *"Love your neighbor as you love yourself!"* The tacit assumption is implicit and unmistakable. The two parallel clauses, *love your neighbor, love yourself,* are of perfectly equal importance, carrying equal weight and emphasis. The Lord meant clearly that we are all obliged in Conscience to love ourselves truthfully, without self-flattery or deception, that we are also obliged in our Conscience, without asking questions, to transfer and extend this same truthful and sincere love to our neighbor.

There are nowadays factions, among modern Christians, who do not have the slightest clue what is meant by loving oneself truthfully and sincerely. They honor the Lord with a murderer's insult to themselves. They positively damn themselves with an insult at the moment of death just like Graham Greene's Scobie, a fictitious protagonist in Greene's novel, **The Heart of the Matter**, who, after committing many adulteries and receiving the Sacrament in what he sees is a state of sin, commits suicide so as to rid God of the nuisance, strictly because he considers himself totally unworthy, of no value whatsoever in the eyes of God. The Lord Himself cannot stand this sort of thing. He knows best just how many countless Christians He is losing to this factor. He knows also that it is a terrifying Judgment upon Himself, that He is responsible!

Let me then ask … Can a Christian who honors God with a murderer's insult to himself be relied upon to love a stranger called his neighbor truthfully and sincerely? The answer is, of course he can't! Christians of this type are trouble makers causing nothing but friction within society.

They have no right to hate their neighbour with the hatred they bear themselves. They require desperately to learn authentic sincerity. They ought to go to jail for hurting themselves and for transferring the hurt to their neighbour.

This, then, is precisely what we all need great works of art for, to provide for everyone an exercise in being sincere all the time, to plant in everyone's heart **a poem called sincerity**. Many Christians read nothing but official Church publications, they quote nothing but the Catechism, they pray out of books only, they sing out of books only, they listen to nothing but mediocre sermons from mediocre priests about a Gospel two thousand years old … are they being sincere?! The answer is, No! It is the artists who are by comparison being sincere, these days: they are living the parable of the gifts and talents in a most authentic fashion!

In the Arts, in the Universities, in the Culture Industry, we honor countless great people. Do we honour all such with a loaded revolver against our head because we are nobodies? Never ever. Great people are all somebody but so are all of us and we honor all such with a sincere honour to ourselves. Do you expect a man to work hard for fifteen years, to obtain three degrees, and then to work for the rest of his life, promoting the work and message of great people, without feathering his nest? without making himself a sincere compliment and a sincere honor? with no trace or hint of proper reward except perhaps in a future existence?

We want all great people to be honored with a sincere compliment unto oneself: this is mere social justice, neither selfish nor altruistic! You have no right to make great people false compliments, nor yourself either. That you are not a genius gives YOU no right to commit against yourself a sin of hypocritical deceit, this being what it means that Charity begins at home: with YOURSELF right where you are. You are obliged in conscience to truthsay yourself under oath of perfect truthfulness, candor and sincerity towards yourself. You are somebody and so is your neighbor. You have no right to deceive either party. You may kill yourself if you do, just like Graham Greene's Scobie, and countless poor Christians damning themselves with an insult at the moment of death … a sin against all

Hope and worse than suicide! How can I trust you to love me well unless you love yourself well as God wishes?

In **"Song of Myself"** Whitman wrote: *"I have never seen God, nor do I know of anyone more wonderful than Me!"* In other words I hear him say: *"This is just how limited my human subjectivity is: I have never seen God, and have no experience of anyone's subjectivity except my own. I do not know of anyone more wonderful than Me!"* Whitman's **"Song of Myself"** is about a great Man loving himself truthfully in the spirit of Christ's implicit assumption. It is about the Bard of North America, a god with a small g, but faithfully shewing us nonetheless, unto the eyes of the mind, no one less than the Divine Creator, making Himself a sincere compliment, a sincere honor, in the spirit of these reflections! To love yourself as Jesus is saying you need to be an Egoist within Reason; whereas to love your neighbour like this you are called upon to be an Altruist within Reason. Whitman can be relied upon to love a stranger called his neighbor meaningfully: his self-love is Christian-perfect, a beatiful, refined, and meaningful Poem!

The Lord's teaching may be paraphrased: "*Let your self-love be perfect. You are somebody. You deserve to love yourself truthfully, without deceiving, flattering or pampering yourself, without punishing yourself irrationally, without loving and honouring God or great people with a murderer's insult unto yourself and unto others. When your self-love is as perfect as Walt Whitman's, I command you to love your neighbour as you love yourself, because your neighbour is somebody also no less than you are!"* I venture to add … **"Song of Myself"** ought to become required reading for all those poor Christian factions I allude to. They all ought to be examined in the truthfulness and sincerity of their self-love and should be penalized if their self-love is not as perfect as Jesus is assuming. **"Song of Myself"** is the only insult these poor Christians desperately require to put into their pipes and smoke, and they must not stop reading before Whitman gives them the Juice … an intense, glowing feeling of real self-worth.


*March 17th 2009 – March 3rd 2014*

## style matters …

*an essay*

IT IS no use telling ME that in a poem you care about the message only, only the truth or the falsehood, right or wrong, that you are a critic, in other words, totally insensitive to stylistic beauty, to colour, and to artistic finesse. Nor is it of any use telling ME that *"there is no such thing as a moral or immoral book: it is either well or badly written."* In a poem I look exclusively for perfect, unique fusion, totally inspired combination, of style and matter, because I am human and that is how I am made, a unique individual, displaying total fusion of body and spirit, programmed by entirely unrepeatable genes. Totally incomplete without each other, body and spirit, within humanity, complete each other. The human body is the *"artifice"*, the *"receptacle"*, of the spirit, or, in the language of criticism, the *"form"* and the *"style"* which *"clothes"*, *"sets off"* and *"displays"*, the "*message"*. This is precisely what I mean when I say that *style matters.* The body, and the spirit — likewise a part of the body *rooted* within the body, just like a tree which reaches unto Heaven but which is *rooted* within earth — belong entirely unto each other, just like the *"thought"* and the *"craft"*, and both together entirely unto God. Books which are nothing but well-written are far too carnal. Books, on the other hand, wherein the message is the only thing which matters, are nothing but disembodied spirit, ineffectual, bodiless Angels always floating higher, ***"nel blu dipinto di blu,"*** without any claim to a carnal body such as ours. I do not need them. A great poem without its unique style, its unique genetic code which can never recur, is inconceivable and extremely pallid. What follows is my attempt to describe correct balance.

Man is the mirror of the Divine Creator. Works of art are the mirror of Man as he is made, such that Man may look and perceive his own face in this mirror. Love of God is beautiful and holy. Very few people truly hate **Dios**, Who is beloved by countless millions, whether they say it or whether they suppress it. Without the critical dimension, however, no one is well-equipped for this life, though love of God may have prepared him for the next. Good parents never send little children out naked on the street just because they care for the ***"core theology"*** only. Neither do good artists do such a thing to their message. In order to show us just how well you care for your message, you must therefore always do your utmost to dress it up in a proper and appropriate style.

We must remember, always, that sincerity is an extremely artistic quality which is not Art. In regard to a point of view that God is happy with the best that any and all individuals can do, I aver that where authentic depth and real power of feeling and sentiment exist, even when the artist has scant technical skill, the feeling, and this is a phenomenon known to all real art critics, has of itself an ability to create and carve for itself, and to channel itself, into its own unique and authentic forms and rhythms, arising inherently from the depth and power of the imagination and of the sentiment. This may be described as **a triumph of LOVE** reflected in artistic success and in the teaching of the profound unity of style and content, mirroring the inexplicable unity of body and spirit. Where this profound depth and turbulence of powerful feeling is lacking in a work of art, reflecting itself in the artist's failure to create authentic form for his ideas ….. this may likewise be described as **a failure in LOVE**, and this may generate works of art which are far less pleasing to God Himself than the unique creations, inspired fusions, which I am exclusively upholding.

The time may come, and there may be a place, for great poems in the nude, in the raw, very much, perhaps, like MichaelAngelo's work on the ceiling of the Sistine Chapel, but stylistic beauty is a concept much like decency, propriety and decorum in dress, in attire. It is no use telling ME that you became an Artist to please God, thereby caring about the message only: to please ME you have to do your work well! Stylistic beauty is in itself a sincere honour. It is in itself the dignity of work well-done when ennobled by splendid craftsmanship. It is in itself a real and lasting message. It is in itself a most valid way of perceiving. It is to an artist the crown of a lifetime's achievement. And this is what incompetent critics, to whom stylistic beauty and artistic finesse are a closed book, totally fail to see.

This also, by analogy, is what pop-music is doing to you. Sexuality is your secret as it is everyone's. Pop-music is taking your secret, and through your own mouth, as you sing the words, flinging your secret far out into space and to the four winds, and I defy you, after this treatment, to close your secrets tight. Pop-music is not what I mean by real art. Real art protects you and protects all your secrets. Pop-music does not protect you in any way whatsoever. Pop-music is evil.

It has been said that, whether the music is pop or classical, or whether it is performed on classical guitar, electric guitar, or on the organ, God regards only the heart and only the soul. *"Look in thy heart and write!"*, a line by a famous Elizabethan sonneteer, is an extremely famous touchstone of advice to aspiring poets. However, whether a work of art is *"good work"* and not *"bad work",* by which I mean *"well-done", "well-crafted",* is a primary criterion of judgment as to whether it is suitable and appropriate to *"give glory to God."* Of course God regards the heart, and the soul, just as the critic beholds Housman's, an atheist, or just as Dante beheld Virgil's, a pagan. But what do we think God will tell us were we to praise Him, however truthfully, through song or writing which is nothing but *"bad work"*? Will not God Himself derive more satisfaction from being praised meaningfully through *good work* which is, stylistically as much as in spirit, a little more acceptable than incompetent *craft*?

Again, classical music tends to be well-crafted work which has stood the test of time, whereas a lot of contemporary music is often *"bad work"* which will not pass the test of time. Again, this is why critics praise an artist's craft and technique, and why trained scholars are correct to talk about style. I am also sure that a vast cross-section of trained music critics will probably agree that *classical music* represents the fine flowers of musical achievement, whereas *contemporary music* is the hotbed and the cradle where all classical music is born, and this is what it has always been. All great music, in other words, was once upon a time contemporary.

The Lord's way of perceiving is not an artist's. The Lord needs to rule multitudes of people. To Him the message matters more than the garb. This is in itself a sublime style whose hallmark is the most dignified, but deceptive simplicity. A real artist, on the other hand, and a real art critic, look for stylistic achievement, a cult of the *individual* rather than of the *flock*, or in other words the *team* or the *community*, a unique and perfect, individual fusion, an inspired combination, of style and matter. In the arts *"true"* or *"false"* do not always matter: there is no *black* and *white*, there is only *light* and *shade*, *chiaroscuro*, and *technicolor*. A sermon may be a wonderful sermon but to the art-critic may fall far short of real artistic achievement.

I aver that these two modes of perceiving, the Lord's versus all artists', are equally valid, equally appropriate in both parties, equally inappropriate were they to be switched around carelessly and capriciously, equally rich, equally interesting, equally rewarding, at the right time, in the right place. Indeed, we stand to learn a lot from each other: Christians and Artists are incomplete without each other. We urgently require to understand each other compassionately, without mudslinging, without name calling — such as calling Christians *the herd!* or Artists *the snobs and the high-brows!* Displaying what Artists call *the herd-instinct*, many Christians are only absorbing the Warmth and Love of their own Kind and huddling close for Comfort. Artists rebel against straight jacketed conformity and uniformity. Christians rebel against individual genius, the towering intellectuals, the *Seers*, what all Artists recognize implicitly as *"that one Man"*. We desperately need to learn from each other, with mutual tolerance, humility, sympathy, and respect, and to observe decorum.

When a great artist rewards you in your feelings, I agree that this is not God's Heaven, but that a great artist, within the scheme of God's plans for everyone's Salvation, in the boom and roar of the cannons, is preparing you for Heaven, the ultimate poetic intensity, by making you sensitive to immortal Beauty.


*March 22nd 2009 – March 3rd 2014*

# Part Eight:
# A little girl of long ago

*Work previously unpublished (strictly selected)*

## Printing History

**A Little Girl of Long Ago**
featuring an unpublished verse drama (c. 1979/80)
with various poems, some re-issued, 1982 - 2015
1st Edition : June 2015; re-issued : June 2018

**by Joe M. Ruggier**
with an introductory sonnet by Esther B. Cameron
photo of Joe Ruggier, by Phil Folkard
photo of Sarah Therese Ruggier, by Joe Ruggier



**MULTICULTURAL BOOKS**
Unit 114 - 6051 Azure Road, Richmond, BC, V7C 2P6
**Cell:** +604 600-8819 **email:** jrmbooks@hotmail.com
www.mbooksofbc.com



**MBooks Poetry Series #35**
1st edition : June 2015 : ISBN 978-1-897303-21-4

Reissued in 2018 as Part Eight of **Lamplighter most gracious** : Collected Poems and Selected Prose, by Joe M. Ruggier : 1972-2018.
3rd print edition of **Lamplighter most gracious** : June 2018 (expanded)
**ISBN for this (current) 3rd edition : 978-1-897303-26-9**

printed and bound by: **Lightning Source Inc., USA**
desk-top publishing: Joe M. Ruggier
approx. 125 copies in print

“Ma sedendo e mirando, interminati
spazi di là da quella, e sovrumani
silenzi, e profondissima quiete
Io nel pensier mi fingo, ove per poco
il cor non si spaura … “

*“But when I sit and gaze, endless spaces*
*I imagine beyond the hedge, and superhuman*
*silences, and quietudes most profound*
*I etch within my thoughts, where my heart*
*is all but overwhelmed ...”*

*(L’infinito, by Count Giacomo Leopardi)*

*Tulip Landscape, (downloaded from the Internet).*

## INTRODUCTION
by Joe Ruggier

**A Little Girl of Long Ago** contains previously unpublished work as well as work which is being re-issued. *Part 1* comprises a verse drama in one act, previously unpublished. *Part 2* comprises previously unpublished work, all created recently, but one poem of which is a significant improvement upon a poem previously published. *Part 3* comprises poetry that the Author wrote for women, in particular for his daughter, for his mother, for Virginia Woolf, and for Mary. Whereas poems in *Part 3* were previously published, they are now being re-issued, in one convenient location, at the request of my daughter, **Sarah Therese**, who some time ago asked me to publish again all the poetry I wrote her in one distinct collection. The result is *Part 3* of **A Little Girl of Long Ago**.

**Esther B. Cameron,** from whose hand I requested the honour of an introduction, wrote the following after having read this book:

**Dear Joe:** *I have read your book and, I may say, struggled with it. We are far apart on many matters, as you know, and speaking strictly as a poet and critic whose aesthetic was formed on classical models, there is much in your way of writing that strikes me as excessive. Yet, yours is undoubtedly an authentic poetic voice. I did not feel I could write about the book in conventional critical prose, but I did manage an unrhymed sonnet (below). I shall be glad if you find it helpful for the book, and in any case please accept it as the tribute of a friend.* **All best, Esther**

## INTRODUCTION
**HERE** read, fellow- reader, the record of a heart laid bare,
without disguise, with all its loves and all its errings,
its exile, struggle with a faith that gives not enough answers,
with mental illness, fatherhood and marriage
(that last, between the lines), with desire for fame

and need for money, but again the love
of poetry, and appreciation of friendship,
tenderness for the child, for the fellow-writer,
for the mother, friend of our frailness.
That wiser men have lived, we scarce dare say
in this time when human unsuccess is so patent;
let him who thinks he has done better consider
the human heart and its winding ways, and find
fellowship with this voice, this cry in the night.
**Esther Cameron**

**Acknowledgments**
Grateful acknowledgments for financial aid with producing this collection are owing to various clients, but in particular my loyal friends Ken Birdsall, Allan Smith Ph.D., Henry Birkett, Ross Barbour, Joe Easton, Michael Baker, Michael Hope, but above all Clif and Janet Prowse whose contribution was the most generous.

**Photo of Joe Ruggier, by Phil Folkard, 2009**

# Part 8 : A

## The Wards of Mount Carmel

*a (confessional) verse drama in one act*



*I dedicate this dramatic poem to my (gracious) pastors —*
*Mgr Anton Caruana S.J. (deceased),*
*and Fr Jim Comey, who asked whether I have any drama.*
*My play is a sincere compliment*
*to the Priest, to the Spiritual Director,*
*and to all Catholic Christians who believe*
*in the cathartic power of Confession.*

**Dramatis Personae**

**Fr Saviour** — *Abbot & chief psychiatrist of Mount Carmel*
**Fr John** — *a monk*
**Dr. Randolph Hellstrom** — *a psychiatrist on spiritual retreat, Fr Saviour's penitent*
**Polly** — *a lunatic*
**Tom** — *a lunatic*
**Vox Populi** — *a lunatic*
**Messiah** — *a lunatic*
**Professor Acadawesome** — *a lunatic*
**Linda** — *a child four years old*
**Monk's Choir**

**Scene One**
*(A chapel softly lit. The monks are singing an evening chant.)*

**Soloists**
**ACROSS** the bald and bowed and lengthening gaze of the moon
drifts a long miasma, now broadening, now blotting out,
now drawing a veil.

**Full Choir**
An ancient guilt blackmails our joy,
and lays upon us kisses deadly:
we must repent - or else we cloy -
deeply, late and sadly.

**Soloists**
Across the gentle and bowed and desolate gaze of the Crucifix
drifts a long miasma, now broadening, now blotting out,
now drawing a veil.

**Full Choir**
You will not make your sin our door,
Satan: our days of sin are ended;
you will blackmail us now no more,
like Ass or Ape appended.

*(The monks kneel in silent prayer. Some rise and leave. Some read. Some say their breviary. Father John and Saviour meet at the door. They whisper quietly.)*

**Father Saviour:**
So many regard Gregorian chant as a music to accompany the kissing of corpses and the burial of the dead, but I think

it is a music to wake the dead to life. Eavesdropping on it has always made me shudder.

**Father John:** I have always loved it.

**Fr S:** Randolph Hellstrom will arrive in a few minute's time.

**Fr J:** He was anxious over the phone. What brings him here?

**Fr S:** A solitary retreat as an excuse for meeting me.

**Fr J:** I am sure! He might have found a better place than a lunatic asylum to pray in. He misses you, doesn't he?

**Fr S:** We were the best of friends at University, where we worked, played and prayed together, nor would we have reached our academic peak without each other. Make sure the choir sings us a song for auld lang syne tonight.

**Scene Two**
*(The scene is divided in two. On one side is the reception room of the convent with fire-place, lit. On the other is the front-garden, moonlit, but plunged in shadow. Dr Hellstrom is musing alone by the garden gate.)*

**Dr Hellstrom** *{soliloquizing}:*
So here I am, in a year of doubt, it seems to me
stiffer than ever since the time that I set out
like a cramped scroll, having among other things since then

acquired the itch to reason much, the rich young man
turned sadly away: had you the knack to read a look
askance, you would have read upon his ashen face
the disease of the general economy
enshrined in a simple law: when luxuries multiply
necessities mount.

*{Pacing around.}*
Where now is the Wisdom of the School of Pain?

Nothing more plain
than this our general loss!
If you can do not join the sad refrain!

She did not, *Mantovano*!
I cannot sacrifice the happiness of three, she told me,
meaning another's, her own, and mine,
in order to secure the happiness of--meaning my own--
one alone!

Nothing more plain!

O Father, is my lovely wing for ever burnt and crippled?
Will I never my Sun attain?
Am I forever a Saint by halves?

If you can do not join the sad refrain!

To you who must, *Mantovano*,
a veiling parable will speak my pain
and tell my story.

A wife was unwilling to sleep beside her husband.
"Dear, I must be up and doing!" said she.
"Do you not love me as your husband?" said he.

"And is it by cooking my meals that you will starve me?
Right now, my dear, do sleep beside me!"

Again a husband was loathe to leave his bed in the morning.
"I love you!" he told his wife.
"And do you truly?" said she:
and is it with a kiss that you will starve me?
Right now, my dear, you must to your work as I to mine?"

It is the same, a sage once told me, with the Kingdom of Heaven.
We shall be carried like babes at the breast
and tenderly shall the groom embrace us.
We shall be sent out into the world, fortified yes,
but like sheep among wolves.
Not ours to choose the time for ecstasy.
Not ours to choose the time for descending the Mount.
Our trial lasts long as life,
but not life, nor death, save inconstancy alone,
could separate me from the lover for whom I moan.

*(Stands still for a while in silent thought. Then walks slowly to the front door and knocks. Father John enters on the other side of the stage and puts on the light on his way to the door.)*

**Dr Hellstrom:**
Not because I believe, O Lord,
but because I wish to believe.

*(Father John peeps through the spy-hole and opens the door.)*

**Fr J:** Would you be Randolph Hellstrom?

**Dr H:** Father John!

**Fr J:** Hello, Randolph! My, how your voice has changed!

**Dr H:** Perhaps I've grown up!

**Fr J:** Come in, Randolph. We do not often have visitors. Father Saviour is waiting for you in the back-garden.

**Dr H:** Well, well! After all these years, the nostalgia for a garden to chat in with the Abbot of Mount Carmel has not left me yet. Proceed.

**Exit both**

**Scene Three**
*(The back-garden. Moonlit. Suffused in shadow. Two arm-chairs, a tea-table, in one corner.)*

**Fr J:** *(calling out)* Saviour!

**Fr S:** Beside you John!

**Fr J:** Your visitor.

**Fr S:** Randolph! Since graduation I have not seen you, my old friend.

**Dr H:** I am so eager to chat, Saviour!

**Fr J:** I am pleased to have met you, Randolph.

**Dr H:** You need not leave us yet. You once taught me literature.

**Fr J:** I remember.

**Dr H:** Am I the shadow of that memory?

**Fr S:** Well, Randolph, let us all sit down and chat over a cup of tea.

**Fr J:** You were then a careful, staunch, young Catholic,
with a thick and sensuous under-lip,
and rather exaggerated essays you did write me:
tone, weary, a little depressed,
worried that problems are too much to cope with,
healthy in their touch of true serene melancholy.
A continuous effort at self-control was evident,
and you were indeed conscientious in your work,
thorough, deliberate, obstinate and stubborn,
with a precocious touch in sorting out ideas.
Your mind was restless, ego hypersensitive,
tending to influence others, a bad organizer,
rather selfish, but a practical, young economist.
Your nature was impressionable and receptive,
willing to submit to restraint and moderation,
and mark that kindly, Saviour: it is the sign
of long-suffering and of poignant disappointment.
I remember him with a soft and desolate eye,
able to weigh people and places coldly,
bluntly and to the point, belying a strong desire
to stick to essentials, sincere, reliable,
fussy, and proud, and secret, and warm-hearted.

**Dr H:** Your obedient student!

**Fr S:** John has a touch of the chameleon poet, Randolph, no?

**Dr H:** I remember him more as the virtuous philosopher.

**Fr J:** Did I not teach you Dante? And is not Dante both of these? That is the lesson he taught ME.

**Dr H:** Very interesting. I never thoroughly agreed with Keats' puckish distinction. He said, for instance, that he would rather give women a sugar-plum than his time, but then he fell in love, and changed his mind entirely. Oh sure, he was a Man, but might have been far greater. You love Dante, do you not?

**Fr J:** Very much so, once I forget and forgive him a few things. He is a supreme model of the great Christian poet, and perfection of the life adds to the greatness of the work.

**Dr H:** Ha! You are as thorough-going and amiable a didacticist as good old Dante. Is there any other lesson that he might have taught you?

**Fr J:** Certainly! He has taught me that I am myself a Divine Comedy, and except for a few in whom all is comedy and nothing is divine, he has taught me that we are all a good joke indeed, as high-serious and tender a joke as Peter sinking in the waters of Galilee for lack of faith.

**Fr S:** Yes, John. All men are 'coups de theatre', divine, unique, and unrepeatable, one and all.

**Fr J:** And although Dante's concern was the word, 'le mot juste' being the poet's crafty gift, he was in touch with the very spirit of supreme poetry, the Word made flesh and dwelling among us, the divinest coup de theatre of all, and the Word had a Mastery over Dante, and Dante had a mastery over the word.

**Dr H:** He has influenced your poetics deeply.

**Fr J:** So has Thomas A Kempis. He expressed the spirit of all true poetry when he said that he to whom the eternal Word speaketh is set at liberty from a multitude of opinions.

**Dr H:** I used to love A Kempis. Was he the instrument of my melancholy? I am afraid he was.

**Fr J:** No newfangled notions, Randolph. Original sin did that. You are no better than A Kempis, nor him any better than you.

**Dr H:** A gracious compliment!

**Fr S:** And a compliment graciously received! Do you desire to see our characters, Randolph?

**Dr H:** Lead me the way!

**Scene Four**

*(A corridor lined with padded cells. Lit softly. The madmen speak through their respective grills throughout. Except when addressing the madmen Fr Saviour and Dr Hellstrom speak quietly throughout. At the end of the corridor is the chapel. And another closed door through which the monks can be heard chatting merrily.)*

**Fr S:** The first cell is Polly's.

**Polly:** They love me, Dr!

**Dr H** *(in a subdued voice):* I know her. Is she here also?

**Polly:** They love me, doctor. Luxury.
Walls two feet deep. Verysupersoft.
I would kill myself without luxury.

**Dr H:** Poor girl! She's gone! It hurts my conscience!

**Fr S:** She was far worse!

**Dr H:** I did perceive a symptom of recovery.

**Fr S:** It will take long.

**Dr H:** I must speak to her, Saviour! Let me in.

**Fr S:** I perceive you must not.

**Dr H:** Not a word!

**Fr S:** She is unused to you behind the bars.

*(Enter Nurse with a tray of food)*
**Dr H:** Do you remember me, Polly?

**Tom:** O come in, Doctor. *(belches)* I will tell you a story.

*(Nurse opens Polly's door and enters with the food)*

**Fr S:** That'll be Tom. He only tells one story.

**Tom:** They sas a good soul sinned *(belches)* one sin at night
and died. God plunged her down in Hell. *(belches)*

**Fr S:** Did He do that to you, Tom?

**Tom:** No! He did not. *(belches)*

**Fr S:** That always calms him, Randolph.

**Vox Populi:** What God is this?

**Dr H:** How would you answer Saviour?

**Fr S:** An after life without a hell
would make a God of Love
intolerably sentimental.

**Dr H:** Yea!

**Fr S:** God is just--

**Dr H:** Indeed!

**Fr S:** And merciful!

**Dr H:** Ay. His Justice
to the adulteress
was Mercy, and His Mercy
to the Pharisees
was Justice.

*(The merry chatting of the monks increases in volume and a small child's voice is heard howling with laughter).*

**Dr H:** They are having fun, your monks.

**Fr S:** For sure! But Vox Populi is still waiting for me to reply. *(loudly)* You have a right to your opinion, Vox Populi!

**Vox Populi:** I express opinion. To express opinion you must have anything to say.

**Fr S:** Anything?

**Vox Populi:** Anything.

**Fr S:** So it is, Randolph.

**Vox Populi:** I only failed because the examiner disagreed with me.

**Dr H:** He will not disagree with me if I can help it. Well, well, Vox Populi, you are gone, you also!

**Vox Populi:** Vox Populi, vox Dei!

**Messiah:** More sanity with less madness. Crucify Him, that was Vox Populi!

**Vox Populi:** My sincere opinion, Dr! *(bows courteously)*

**Messiah:** Crucify Him, that was Vox Populi!

**Fr S:** You, or Him, Messiah?

**Messiah:** I am He!

**Fr S:** Once was enough, Messiah!

**Vox Populi:** He has a right to his opinion, Reverend Father!

*(A child's voice is again heard howling with laughter.)*

**Professor Acadawesome:** Now I have heard a madman speak of love. One! I have heard a madman speak of Hell. Two! I have heard two maddermen speak of Love and Hell together. Three! I have heard the fourth one voice opinion. Four! And I have heard the maddest called Messiah. Five! Now five is five too much and Professor will not love. Professor is no hypocrite. Humanity was never inclined to love and Professors do not love. Now give me supper for today I have spoken.

**Dr H:** More needs he baptism, Saviour!

**Fr S:** Indeed!

*(They walk towards the chapel as the curtain falls.)*

**Scene Five**
*(The chapel softly lit. One one side a closed door which leads into a room where the monks can still be heard chatting merrily. Fr Saviour and Dr Hellstrom sit on a bench at the back.)*

**Fr S:**
Randolph, what brings you here, the call of thought,
or action?

**Dr H:** A divine discontent.

**Fr S:**
Life is short. Death draws near. Eternity is long.
Never give up! Have you been writing lately?

**Dr H:** Ay! There is no better pastime to keep a wicked man quiet.

**Fr S:** With reading likewise, Randolph. I have been poring over humanity's mystical literature. Nothing like this lonesome abbey to do it in.

**Dr H:** Any discoveries.

**Fr S:** I will tell you. I have learnt a deep respect, indeed a supernatural awe, for the traditions of mankind for, although the great religions differ, the dogmas of our creed are, you may say, a tradition of secret feeling gathered into a divine manifesto. All men secretly feel a lost happiness. All possess a wry, subconscious sense of distant calamity. And all common men, I dare say, have a natural psychic attraction towards the charism of Messiahs true or false. And tell me not these are the accretions of society. For first came the individual, then society, and religion is not a subjective illusion which keeps men sane, for what sanity is that? Illusion involves reality, and the religious emotion is a historical reality as much as it is a psychological, a reality wild and immanent in the soul of man. Though he might have evolved from a thing as infinitely inferior as an amoeba, Man is neither the cause of his own existence, nor of his own human nature, and the religious emotion is objective fact. Deny it and you cease to be objective, for all true religion, dear friend, is a most objective emotion. Nor shall I ever suffer anyone to despise a man-made Heaven, for supposing it was..... Who on earth has the least little right to despise such an achievement?

**Dr H:** Very spirit-stirring, but now I'm bursting!

**Fr S:** Pour your heart out.

**Dr H:** I must tell my story!

**Fr S:** Before all else!

**Dr H:** I've just been to confession, Saviour, but as the priest absolved me, I knew that I had lost my faith, and religion means nothing, nothing of what it once meant. Now a splendour's gone out of my life, I know, and my mind stretches before me like barren fields gaping beneath the midday sun, but bless me father, for I will not rationalize, nor construct a dogma of disbelief, nor judge one single soul, nor give advice to a single client, nor marry the poor, poor girl who loves me, till I am either dead, or re-admitted into communion with all my doubts like the head of Goliath in my hand.

**Fr S:** You are not faithless, Randolph.
What have you done to lose your faith?

**Dr H:** I cannot describe a single doubt but am paralyzed by a sense of doubt about it all. And my heart is in it, Saviour! And it hurts my pride to have to admit to having lost my faith! Because I want my faith back badly! Because my heart is in it, Saviour, and though I believe no longer, at least, at least I wish so badly that my old faith be true.

**Fr S:** Know you of any obsessions that torment you,

Randolph?

**Dr H:** I have long entertained a secret feeling that as an individual I must not concede a single inch to society.

**Fr S:** Now it is well to remember that of necessity the individual preceded society but that, after all is said and done, we are still called to love.

**Dr H:** I love the least of all my clients!

**Fr S:** I suspect, Randolph, that you identify with all your cases, and strive to think, feel and fall as low as the lowest. Slander thyself no longer, friend!

**Dr H:** What makes you think so?

**Fr S:** I suspect that most poets are over-possessed by the idea of empathic experience.

**Dr H:** Are you my conscience, or my pal?

**Fr S:**
Be careful, Randolph, for you may go too far
and not come back at all.

**Dr H:** Possibly..... I begin to see why I can no longer acquiesce in absolute certainties. Another old feeling hurts me. Unless I possess the sense and sensation of faith, faith is worth nothing, for what is Heaven if it is not the feeling? and what is self-confidence but a substitute for Christian faith? And the light within me has grown dark. O what a darkness am I in!

**Fr S:** God is all to you. Though you cannot attain Him

now, do not despair that you shall ever. Neither lose faith in Him, nor let your bitterness include Him also. Be not a nihilist for you will destroy yourself. Know your worth, for nothing, nothing is more painful than the loss of good souls. The way is slow and painful, friend: the path is narrow and the track winds uphill all the way; but you must never give up. Have you confidence that His Grace will always help you?

**Dr H:** A flicker!

**Fr S:** When God demands He lends His Grace, and a good conscience is self-confidence true and enough. Now you must no longer worry about faith and vision, and unless you wish to forfeit more together with what you must now give up, you must strive to act purely out of the habit of perfection.

**Dr H:** Habit! Did you say HABIT? Why habit?

**Fr S:** I will tell you.
Man is a creature of habit, and having enough bad habits,
Randolph, God alone knows what will happen to us,
if we abandon our good habits.
Brother, switch off,
switch off that light and watch:
the darkness of God is beautiful,
oh much more beautiful than the light of man;
the fancy light that chills from the sty of contentment,
or the light in the eyes of one I have known.
Robust and tall, with fierce, Satanic curls,
I have seen him shadowing the gaze - best foot
on milestone, grasp on hip, and Spartan chin
seen profile-wise - far along the road opposed
to what Mankind, deep-down, is caught to think of.

I stopped him, crying: "Specservor,
are you as happy as you say? because I am unhappy!
Are you sure you have found happiness in vanity as you say?
Why should Mankind be then still so unhappy?
It is as you say, Mankind, selfish and vain,
nor is it Christian, but it is not happy,
and you have not told me why Mankind still is so unhappy?"
And I was struck by a bewildered anguish, and knew
I wanted to pray, but what I knew not, but knew
like the Sybil that a prayer was going to be given me.
This was the prayer that was given me.
"My God, My God, why hast Thou abandoned me?"
and the comforter was sent to comfort me.
The darkness of God is beautiful,
oh much more beautiful than the light of men.
You are not faithless, Randolph.
What have you done to lose your faith?

**Dr H:** Well put! Well asked!
What have I done?
Bless me, Father! This is my confession!
I have thought much and acted little!
I have said much and done but little!
I have understood much and loved but little!
I have brooded but not lived!
I have been vain, unchaste, a turn-coat!
I have spoken uncharitably of others and the Church!
I have changed my Master!
Pray for my need!

**Fr S:** You have seen how easy madness is, how softer than being sober.
You have asked me to set the theme for your retreat.

Truth is my theme.
Truth is stranger than fiction
for we are only used to lies and fiction
and not to Truth at all.
Stir up thy Love
for daily life and lowly drudgery,
for sanctity is an Orthodox Romance
in which you may travel to many strange isles of Love,
where the problem is how to save, not kill, the hero.
Set out! Set out!
Deeds are the proof of faith,
and anyone who loves may yet be saved,
for God is Love, and anyone who loves
believes in God: in spite of natural atheism
action may yet deliver us.
All revere Christ,
but most have but a little faith: let them
put Christ in place of idols they deny,
for no one has ever seen God.
Christ alone has ever made Him known.
And never ask me where I go.
I follow
a Voice from a hilltop crying:
"Humanity, Humanity, why do you disdain my Love?
I have not abandoned thee for ever yet!".
But you, Randolph, put on Christ and your darkness shall
flee for ever
like an evil spirit from before the face of God,
in Whose Name I do absolve you,
in the name of the Father,
and of the Son,
and of the Holy Spirit.
Watch and pray and in prayer remember me also.

**Dr H:** Dearly!

**Fr S:** Do you see all my teaching?

**Dr H** *(aside):*
Whoever you are who tempts me, I command you,
loom not so close and near as not to be seen
in a clear and agreeable perspective. *(To Fr S):*
I do not all, but I shall not contest it:
it touches me deeply. I have sought Christ
but have not found Him save in human beings
where I shunned Him.

**Fr S:** Your costliest fault.

**Dr H:** Before it work more venom
I must take it by the throat
till it uncoil around me
limply.

**Fr S:** Learn to listen.
Up, Randolph, up: Christ loves you dearly;
nor doth He seek thy ruin, but thy salvation ever.

**Dr H:** And answer me my innermost soul:
and do you want to leave you also?
Your darkest knowledge is that men love darkness,
because their deeds are wicked. You know enough
to know that, if you will, you will for ever
bear thy body on a dead nettle of despair!

**Fr S:** You are close to the head of God's Body!

**Dr H:** The light is out. Before God's light is out,
my soul, you must fix it.
Introversion haunts thee like a passion.

The more you understand,
the more you see that you shall never
understand enough of that humble, deep
and tractable Infinity you still must understand.
Oh that I were closer to His heart!
Believe thou me, my soul,
it is a deadly passion
where love is lacking: it shall drive me mad!
Thou and I, my soul, are one
as we have always been,
but only in that Body whose Life is Love,
you mug!

**Fr S:** Indeed! Think of a poem for old Paul!

**Dr H:** Look, soul, think of it this way! You're one among many, ain't you? An' you've all got bodies, hav'nt you? hands and feet and legs and arms, all part of the same body. Well we are a part of God's Body, all joined together in His Church. That's what the Church is! God's Body, God's Body on earth! And just as your eyes can't say to the rest of your body: "Oi don't want to have no more truck with you. Oi can get on OK by meself!" So none of you can break away from the rest and set up on Your own. We've got to stick together same as a man's body sticks together. Why? Because a man's body's held together by the Life inside him, that's why! And that Life ain't yours! It's God's! God give you the spark of life! It belongs to Him! Now in your body there is different parts, isn't there? The outside and inside parts, tongue and brains and inners, beside arms and legs. So the Church has all sorts of parts too, bishops and priests and parsons, teachers, choirboys, sextons, churchcleaners, besides all your mothers, nurses, doctors, businessmen, factory-workers, farm hands, all sorts! But all part of the same Body, mug! And just as your nose can't see, and the ears can't smell, so your shopkeeper can't heal the sick like a doctor, nor a parson can't drive a plough like a ploughman. A schoolteacher ain't much good in the factory, and Bishops ain't much good at gravedigging. Everybody would like to do somebody else's job, we all know that, but they can't! Don't matter what you do, save all you put your guts into it and do the best you can. A good Churchcleaner is a damn sight better than a bad bishop.

**Fr S:** An I'll tell you something else. If you could talk as clever as a lawyer, or speak as sweet as an angel, but you hav'nt no loving-kindness inside you, you're no better than an old tin-can with a hole inside it. An if you could see into the future and tell fortunes like an old gipsy tinker and if you've read all the books that was ever wrote and you knowed all the Bible by heart it wouldn't count for nothing if you haven't got loving-kindness. What do oi mean by loving-kindness? Well it ain't givin' all you got to a blind beggar, that ain't what I mean! It's givin' all you got for love. That's real loving-kindness, that sure is! An you knowed it well enough, an hoigh sanctity doth call thee, now as ever, dear friend.

**Dr H:** Pessimism must not be my passion!
*Mon Dieu, je choisis tout ce que vous voulais!*

**Fr S:** A sincere prayer.

**Dr H:** A fragment of our past, yet lovely, and yet present!
But in between: O what has come between? *(aloud)*
Whoever thou art who tempts me, I command thee,
loom not so close and near as not to be seen
in a clear and agreeable perspective!
Beloved, be the deep division
between me and this sin: snatch me from the jaws

of Hell; and save me from this Real Absence.
Let me not turn tail, O Mary, Mother of us,
whose Will is the Almighty's, I love Thee,
now as ever; and let my Spirit be
wherever you are! Bring me Communion,
Saviour. I want to eat.

**Fr S:** You require mostly
to snap the fuzzing matchsticks which stand erect
three inches from your nose, just in between
your eyes, by which Satan dizzies you, and let
the Sun unseal thy soul, serenely lost
in multitudes of others, for the Lord
to water, dress and gather, like humble flowers
that know their worth, enduring a while the devil,
a while enduring a little warped thorn in their flesh.

**Dr H:** So help me God I shall,
for I am sick of grumbling.

*(A knocking is heard on the door on the side of the chapel. Fr Saviour calls. The door opens. Enter Linda, a child four years old.)*

**Linda:** Father Taviour, Father Taviour, will you join us?

**Dr H** *(quietly):* Whose child is she?

**Fr S** *(quietly)* Our monks found her. She was lost as a kitten. An anonymous note in her frock said: "Pass her on to who wants her." I will give you Communion later, Randolph! That little child is a lot more important.

**Linda:** Is the gentleman Taddy, Father Taviour?
**Fr S:** No child! Don't sulk! You're not dying!

**Linda:** Yet! I'm dying!

**Fr S:** Little one, I as well am dying!

*(Linda rushes to Father Saviour in a sort of childish terror and Father Saviour catches her in his arms and lifts her up)*

**Linda** *(in a shaking voice):*
Is that why it is always quiet here, Father Taviour?

**Fr S:** Yes, Child! Are you afraid of quiet!

**Linda:** Will you shout at me if I call you Taddy?

**Fr S:** No, child!

**Linda:** Can I call you Taddy?

**Fr S:** Yes, child!

**Linda:** Will you take me to Taddy now?

**Fr S:** No, child!

**Linda:** Will the gentleman join us, Taddy?

**Dr H:** Gladly, child! What is your name?

**Linda:** Linda is my name. Let us go in now!

*(They walk towards the door, through which A WARM LIGHT CAN BE SEEN SPREADING. As they step on the threshhold THE UNSEEN MONKS BURST INTO SINGING.)*

May those who are not Catholics,
sighing sadly all their lives,
proud cynics, sceptics, heretics,
who never kiss their wives,
be treated on the buttocks,
be treated on the hives,
for it was but through loving,
that they were born to bluffing.

And Heaven is a Tavern
where we stop to drink together;
and Heaven is a Cavern
where blows no doubtful weather.
Zooks to the Pride of Reason!
Sweet Heaven's a high Romance,
and to put his head in Heaven
a chap gets but one chance.

So come you loyal Catholics,
sighing gaily all your lives
till Time will be Time no longer;
all you who love no antics,
remember us to your wives,
and love them all the stronger.
With love like running rhyme,
we're toasting to God's good Time.

**THE CURTAIN FALLS**

# Part 8 : B

## Selected Poems

some new; others previously published,
but improved

## To the Memory of Percy Bysshe Shelley

**A novice** sat upon the Seat of Judgment,
and arraying Shelley, that notorious atheist,
said that his next of kin, quite rightly so,
brought him to justice and to well-deserved
dishonour! "Why," he simpered thrice, "was he
an atheist?"
"The evidence indicates,"
I replied, "that Shelley was an atheist
to trap the cheers, since great Poets without
their honour may lose their souls regardless!
This, then, is what I mean that God loved Shelley,
for, as a youth, God fashioned Shelley
to be an atheist, that he may capture
the cheers and the honour, but, when he
became a great Poet, the Spirit of God
descended upon him and converted him,
well and soundly, by and within his great
and glorious verses.
A radiant sense of God
and afterlife suffused his greatest work —
a sincere honour to the One, unto
the Many, and to his beloved Keats —
which with eloquence, compassion, and persuasion
carved out a real conversion to mellower views,
though Shelley was right not to admit it: the problem
is your own, if you did not read, nor notice.
Shelley may have been crooked, but what his folk
sought was evil — to dishonour their Son in Art!
God never did such a thing, not even to
a demon! If his folk had had their way,
they'd have created precedent for worse abuses:
were they so concerned, they should have fallen on
their knees, praying all day unto the God
they did believe in …
The only issue
concerning you, obnoxious Judge, is that
he was sincere as he is within his work.
Read, then, his immortal verse, and let the poetry

arise and speak for itself! a temple of
the living God as all authentic art
shall ever be! — Truth itself! whatever
a false, top-heavy Judge may think or feel!"

*20th July — 28th November 2009*

## Swiss Army Knife

**At my** psychiatrist's, some time ago,
I displayed my expensive, deluxe
swiss army knife, saying to Clem,
my therapist …
"This is the risk you take
when you trust someone. All of us can lose our cool
and our head, but the chances are — we won't.
I have had this knife since 1997.
I bought it with my money before I went on welfare.
I never ever dreamt of using it as a weapon,
restricting its use exclusively for personal purposes.

Some time ago, on Main and Hastings,
where I was having a slice of pizza, a man
did not like the look upon my face, and I could tell
he was aching to pick a fight. He punched me.
I experienced the ghost of a temptation
to take out my knife, but I assure you
I never considered it seriously. Had I done so
it would have been tragic. Myself and my assailant
would have both been hurt, and all he was looking for
was a fight: it was serious.
I turned the other cheek
just as Jesus says, and he was gone. I seriously consider
that what Jesus says has some extremely real
practical applications …"

*10th August 2009*

## TO THE MEMORY OF MY LATE CLIENT, HARRY W. J. RAGETLI, (1923 - 2010)

**YOU WERE** a just and upright man.
You were a fellow-Catholic who took most seriously
all of your obligations towards your blood-relations
and towards your neighbour.
You were
a distinguished, extremely productive
professor of science, earning your living
convincingly from your skills in carrying out
and writing up scientific research.
All your life long
you displayed a love of books and authentic culture,
a natural gift and insight into the arts.
You discharged
towards your family all of your breadwinning obligations
conscientiously, with loving, paternal concern.
Neither
did you kid around with compassion: arguably
one of my top clients, you did not
turn me away, a poor poet at your door
selling books to make ends meet.
I am, Sir,
deeply honoured that **YOU** considered my writings
worthy of your money, and your leisure. You bought
books from me always. You gave me *gratis*
nothing but great, professional advise
whenever I asked. You supported
a few of my more expensive projects
with your well-earnt money, even though
I never paid you back. You often
contributed extra out of your kind compassion.
And on one occasion you contributed great ideas
for myself to flesh out into one of my major essays.

You have earnt, Sir,
my lifelong gratitude, which unfortunately
I can show through heartfelt prayers only,

but I know that faith and compassion such as yours
could have earnt you Heaven and only Heaven.

Faith tells us all, *"Blessed are the merciful!"* —
that you have gone to Heaven, as you so richly deserve,
or at the worst you are en route to Heaven,
detained, perhaps, for a little while only, to expiate human
frailty.
We believe you are smiling down and praying for us.
We have offered heartfelt prayers
for your speedy admitting into the joys of the Blessed,
in the glorious company of Our Risen Lord.
We are all jealous of the profound peace of your dying
moments.

May your compassion, dear Harry,
return unto you a hundredfold upon the wings of a Seraph!

*16th January 2010*

## To My Father

**Will Shakespeare** honoured God in the suppressed,
enchanted Silence, in *the lusty stealth*
*of Nature* -- the High Priest of Art inditing:
*"No Man is worthy to mention You, oh Lord!"*
Among all Saints and Artists, none made God
this peerless honour better than Shakespeare did!

Keats wrote the verse: *"Beauty is Truth, Truth Beauty!"* —
a platonic concept meaning only, God
is Beauty, God is Truth, and Beauty is Truth,
Truth Beauty, and nothing is
more beautiful than God's Truth! This cryptic verse
is how John Keats acknowledged God: the problem,
if you miss the point, is your problem only …

you have no faith, or else pay God lip-service!

You honour God, my Father, with a loud
and strident voice, dropping names, of Popes, and Saints,
and Authors, like children with a yo-yo, the perfect double
of William Shakespeare's *Polonius* … all the while
reciting what to the multitude are
prayers outworn and out of vogue!
Yet for all
of your rough edges, your old-fashioned life,
my heart is touched by the utmost delicacy
of your devotion to family in need:
shaving your dying uncle, protecting your stepmother,
flying to be beside your ailing sister,
and not least unto us all … concern
which brings to mind the Biblical account
of the Family of Nazareth —
and I honour, Dad, your family pride!
I revere
the dynamic frenzy, the sheer mental zest
with which you always conduct an argument
with me, ample evidence that *joie-de-vivre*
is not unknown to you — however noisy,
however wordy — that you care about
my input, about my intellectual gifts!

Keep your rough edges, Father, they enshroud
a heart of flesh, and your old-fashioned life
is no dishonour to a Poet bred,
like Keats, upon ideal Beauty and
Antiquity …

*10$^{th}$ May 2010*

## ELEGY FOR ROY HARRISON, MY FRIEND IN LETTERS, 1938 – 2010

**YOUR LETTERS,** Roy, display a natural gift
we shared for friendship and for dialogue.
We never quarreled, though we stood apart
many poles and many furlongs. I am certain
we could have quarreled, had we chosen, but
we got along, always. We met twice only.
I was impressed by your subdued, withdrawn
temper, shining through your work and in
your gentle Voice. You knew your mind, and though
I was a Catholic, you a far freer thinker,
neither one of us discriminated ever
against the other's principles. You always
listened! and, God bless your deep compassion,
helped me out also with timely gifts of money.
Whether I was right and you were wrong, or whether
the opposite were true, it never crossed
our minds to litigate. A mind by nature noble,
you were not ridiculous, gentle friend!
I loved you, and I ask Him I believe in
to set you apart for a favourite's treatment —
may God and just renown your portion be!
Friendship, compassion, understanding,
tolerance, sincerity, generosity,
kindness of heart by nature, and good will,
all these in you were special, gentle friend,
meriting not less than a just God's privileged Grace!

*13th September 2010*

## PRAYER, FEATURING NEW PRAISE FOR MARY

**MARY** the Beloved, Divine Mother,
Mother of God and God the Mother,
grant me, and obtain in my behalf —
of Your Own power as God the Mother,
of the power, Mary dear, of all Your prayers,
of the power of all the prayers
of all the Angels and Saints of Heaven,
of the power of God Himself,
Who is Alone, above all and topmost,
and none but God Alone is God —
all the graces, all the favours,
all the sincere compliments,
that I need most urgently and desperately,
in my body, in my soul, temporal and spiritual,
in my living and in my pocket,
right now, immediately and right away,
knowing clearly that Patience obtains all things!
*19th January 2011*

## THE FLOWER OF HUMANITY

**I CELEBRATE** the warmth of human contact,
the pity hid in the heart of Love, the smile,
exchanged with friends and strangers, which the Heart
demands we give away on principle,
such that it may come back upon the wind.
I celebrate the flower of Humanity,
at sight of whom the Song arises in me,
upon whose face the dignity of labour
shines like the love of Life and right of Reason,
the sanity of work and common people —
the waitresses and cooks in restaurants,
the shopkeepers, the bank tellers, and the typists,
the social workers, the bus drivers, the cashiers,

the secretaries, the nurses, and the doctors,
the receptionists and telephone operators,
everyone pledged to customer service,
and likewise folk I bump upon the road —
earning their living with honesty and pride,
plying their trade and harming no one. I admire
their romantic side. They only want their living,
and in return to serve me. I feel for them as
a secret lover. They never hurt me. Their smile
conveys the untold, the sincerity of which
is worth a sleepless night, and always makes
my heart beat faster, and which my heart demands,
in imperative terms, that I must return,
and must confess my secret love …

*30th July 2011*

## TO THE MEMORY OF DON PEARCE,

### MY DEVOTED READER

YOU were my devoted reader, my client from door-to-door,
to the best of my knowledge an architect.
You were a Man of Peace and very few words.
Quietude profound hung over you like a cloud,
docile, ever tranquil, ever absorbed in peaceful meditation.
You were a sensitive Man who loved the Arts.
You always bought all the books I sought to sell you,
always gave me the money I was asking,
always read the books …
You died, good old Don, and I found out,
sorrowfully, only two years after …
God wanted you safe and sound up there beside Him
for His Own purposes, such that you may appreciate the
Arts
to your heart`s content in God`s Heaven …
being an intelligent reader is a legitimate pretension!
A lump still rises in my throat whenever
I recall your memory … your genteel support for many

years,
and the peace of your passing.
As I breathe once more a prayer for your repose,
and solicit your precious prayer also,
a softening seizes my own heart again …
*15th October 2012*

## MERCY PRAYER:— A CRITICAL APPRECIATION[110]

**THE PRAYERS** we so often pray — missing,
thereby, the point of what we say, or else
the skill and craft between the lines, beneath
the words, concealed, the subtle texture, diction,
quite often expert phrasing — reveal too often,
but unto lovers only, the finest skill
which would ennoble and dignify the work
of finest craftsmen, which in famous works,
as much as in these prayers, is taken quite
for granted, overlooked, and underestimated,
but for true lovers is all there to see:
each phrase, each separate metrical contour,
each with its varying time-signature,
and different onomatopoeic timbre —
the texture, heartbeat, diction - and the music ...

*"You died, Jesus - but the source of Life*
*flowed out for souls, and the ocean of Mercy*
*opened up for the whole earth. Oh fountain of Life,*
*immeasurable Divine Mercy, cover*
*the whole earth and empty Yourself out*
*upon us. Oh blood and water which gushed forth*
*from the Heart of Jesus as a fountain of Mercy*
*for us, we trust in You. Holy God,*

[110] Originally issued in **Songs of Gentlest Reflection;** reissued in **Lamplighter most Gracious** *(Collected Poems).* Now reissued with significant improvements.

*Holy Mighty One, Holy Immortal One,*
*have Mercy upon us and on the whole earth.*
*Jesus, King of Mercy, we trust in You!* "

Penning these prayers for all the Faithful with
a low I.Q., the Lord discharges well
His duty as *Sacred Author*. His work
may all be versified with ease, and boasts
uncanny ears for rhythms of prose and verse.
Freedom is His hallmark, avant-garde
and futuristic, rhythms stirring within
contrasting rhythms, within a basic line
of five strong stresses … but no accomplished Critic
pays Jesus compliments for His achievement.
What makes the Critic think it is not Literature?
or that the Artist has a right to interpolate
artistic invention, and not the Christian?

The shifting rhythms leave
their mark through shifting *slides*, or miniature
word-pictures.

The exquisite obstruction in
the first four words precedes the melody of,
*"the source of life / flowed out for souls."*
The rhythm shifts again. We hear the Ocean
in the trochees and dactyl of, *"and the Ocean of Mercy,"*
whereas the phrase "*opened up*" conjures a sea-shell
*opening up* beneath the waves.

The second *slide*
shifts from the first the riveting rhythms of *Tsunami*:
*"Oh Fountain of Life"* evokes a Fountain, whereas
"*Immeasurable Divine Mercy*" .....
conveys the Ocean crashing upon the shore …
*"and empty yourself out upon us,"* which conjures
the image of a pot, full of boiled beetroots,
or else red roses where the beetroots were,
emptied in the kitchen sink.

The iambs which follow,
comprising the third *slide* with varying rhythm,
*"Oh blood and water which gushed forth,"* convey
the heartbeat, whereas the pirouetting swing,

the metrical medley which comes next,
*"from the heart of Jesus, as a Fountain of Mercy*
*for us, we trust in You"* — an anapaest, two iambs,
two amphibrachs, and three iambs — conjures the blood
spouting from the heart of Jesus …
                                        The concluding cadenza winds
the prayer up like lace, or like a frieze.

Thrilled by the collage of images, *slides* and rhythms,
and by the Lord's self-appreciation, We
return to this set piece, perceiving,
in the crabbed, expert twists of the phrases,
the cruel contortions of the Lord's gnarled death
upon the Cross, and in the plosives
and quiet sibilants, the silent gushing forth
of Mercy, like the gushing forth of blood,
deep within the heart and soul of the
receptive faithful who, in a real spirit
of reverence, faithfully recite these prayers,
and quietly experience the powers of Grace
which the words, although subdued, describe ...

*7th March 2001 – 24th May 2016*

## CONSIDERING DIVINITY

**GOD THE** Eternal Principle, over all,
God the Essential Verity, above all,
one Love for all Thy Creatures, sheltering all,
one Law and one Ideal, over all,
Court of Appeal above myself and Jesus
and any other god inhabiting Heaven
who hides his honour not to compromise Faith –
one God, one Truth, one common Law, one Love,
and one Ideal: there are many gods
but God is One, and He fulfills Himself
in many ways!
                              Jesus is but a god

honoured by God – to honour God and to
honour a Man: His Divinity is but
an honour, and He is but a privileged Artist!
Unto God Himself we therefore raise this heartfelt
prayer that all antagonism may cease,
that in the Sacred Heart of All God may
engender Peace and Hope and Consolation,
sincere Respect and Compliments sinsear,
kindness of Heart, good Will, and Understanding,
that God may spare us All from all anxiety –
becoming not a Man of Faith -- that God
may spread upon our Hearts and Souls the ointment
of quiet, tranquillity, and solace! Doth Jesus
possess a Sacred Heart alone?! Or can Jesus
assert Himself like God and not the Artist?!
I cannot conceive monsters more selfish. I pray
that we may All desist from governing,
and All, instead, be still and sit in place,
and know that God is God, and All in All,
but only God!

*9th – 13th August 2013*

## THE DEATH OF ANTHONY SACK

*An imaginary version of a true story*

**KNOWN** throughout all Malta as *Ninu Xkora*[111],
convicted of murder and sentenced to death,
he maintained his innocence until the end.
Circumstantial evidence was in his day
sufficient to earn a man the death-Penalty.
Poor Ninu was advised by all the Priests
to confess and to be truthful, but never to bear
false witness against himself. All the authorities
were concerned, but figured Justice must take its course.
Poor Ninu died adamant that he was innocent,
amid public shame mixed with doubt and horror.
Years later the real murderer was on his death-bed.
Terror of Divine Justice burrowing his bowels,
he crawled upon two knees towards Confession,
and the Priest told him: *"Sorry, I cannot keep
your secret – an innocent Man's Honour is at stake!"*
The Priest let out the Truth within the law-Courts.

---

[111] *Ninu*, pronounced *Neenu*, the Maltese diminutive for *Anthony*. *Xkora*, pronounced *Shkora*, the Maltese word for *Sack*. *Ninu Xkora* purports to be *a true story* that I heard being told when I was still in Malta. Some time after the 1st edition of this volume was released, it was brought to my attention, by my learned, extremely knowledgeable associate, the Maltese poet Mr George Borg, that the version of this story which I have described as *a true story* is nothing but fiction within the imagination of certain sectors of the Maltese public. Relatively *unpoetic*, the *true story* was submitted to me, photocopied out of certain Maltese publications, by Mr Borg. I was counselled that I may prefer to retain my version of this famous story, for the simple reason that it lends itself so well to poetic treatment, that I have made glorious use of it by making it poetry which is so effective. I was clearly told, however, that it is far from being the factual, historical truth, that I am required to point this matter out clearly in my book, since Ninu Xkora seems to have been, factually and historically, really and truly the murderer in question, and not the innocent Christ-like victim, executed at the gallows upon a false accusation, a trumped-up charge, as he is in the version of the story that I inherited …

Everyone saw who the real murderer was,
and where the mistake precisely lay that all
the witnesses committed. Immediately
the Maltese Courts abolished the death-Penalty
upon the grounds, not that it was unjust,
but that if a mistake is made once only,
no one can ever set it right again,
whilst the real murderer was allowed to die,
in the stench of his sin, in public shame
and in dishonour …

*11th September 2013 – 19th April 2016*

# Part 8 : C

# Poems I wrote for women:

for my daughter, for my mother,
for Virginia Woolf, and for Mary[112] …

[112] This section was compiled, and the constituent poems re-issued, at the pointed request of my daughter, Sarah Therese, who asked that I re-issue, in one convenient collection, all the poems that I wrote her ever since she was born. This section is the result. I pray that it will be found agreeable by many women even who have feminism at heart.

**DEDICATION SONNET**
*for Sarah Therese, my daughter*[113]

SWEETHEART, what brush shall frame your baby face;
a miniature of innocence and Grace?
What hand shall frame the God within your eyes?
What Art the nameless Truth which in them lies?
Do not lose your unaffected air,
as you grow up and learn to handle care!
Preserve her in her loveliest, her best;
Lord, let her not say — "Fuck!" like all the rest!
May she grow and find true Love; and find
an Editor built-in within her Mind!
May she discern true Culture; from the tart
opinion, may she be a soul apart!
Or else, if the vile world should foul her eye,
and drown her infant charm, then let her die.

29th September 1987

**FOR SARAH THERESE** tied for 1st place with 3 other poets in **THE MARK WILD MEMORIAL COMPETITION** organized by **THE RED CANDLE PRESS,** formerly of WISBECH, UK. The closing date of this contest was April 31st, 1988.

[113] Originally issued in **The Voice of the Millions;** reissued in **Lamplighter most Gracious** *(Collected Poems)*.

## WORDS[114]

*to a Child*

**DON'T ASK** me, child, I have no heart;
please, darling, don't - love hides no art.
You will find out what sorrow is,
how far aways the dreams you kiss.
I've said it once and once again,
that if you ask, I can't explain,
because that heartbreak we disown
which we don't bear all, all alone.
But put aside those jacks and queens.
You will find out what sorrow means
in your nice books, which give the sense
of words, and words, and the past tense
of all the joys which men have known,
the words we use, and sense disown.
Words have a point, your books explain,
which once you grasp, will give you pain.
Do but look up the words you write.
You will find grief in black and white.

*15th May 1982*

## TO SARAH[115]

**FAIREST** of Daughters, fabled Queen of yore,
flung from the womb and loins of Love's sweet pie,
Star of the radiant Morning, Goddess, say
from whither? to where? and when thou came, how far?
Be troubled not, dear Child, nor be afraid,
that I say Goddess, for thou art not slime,
my sensitive Plant, nor made from dirty words.

---

[114] Originally issued in **The Voice of the Millions;** reissued in **Lamplighter most Gracious** *(Collected Poems).*
[115] Originally issued in **In the Suburbs of Europe;** reissued in **Lamplighter most Gracious** *(Collected Poems).*

For Jove and Venus, the Olympians all,
false Gods were never. True as thou art true
they were, and truer, truer still, for God
it was the Honour gave, the Honour took,
and Counsellors of Job those who despised
Olympus: far worse crime was that with which
they dragged the name of God in mud and slime.
My Bible says, however, we are Gods.
I lead thee not astray, my sweetest Love.
With Honour I shall nurture my own Babe.
Thou art of Queens my Queen, my Goddess thou!
Only be thou Thyself: it is sublime
to be Thyself! Splendid and great indeed
it is to be Oneself as 'tis to be
the Lord in solitude magnificent!

Beware the venomous tooth of Parents that
the Lord do honour, but their own child despise;
their dear Soul watch over as they watch
the fickle matchlight, but their Money watch
much more. Consider, Child, how door to door
thy Father found sincerity around
Vancouver, Wisdom in quite simple folk,
though hardly higher up, and street by street,
his Soul a song of sonnets streaming hands,
his Book he sold, and money never failed,
and he could eat. Do not, I beg thee, choose
lip-service for a mate to lie beside,
who wildly wants thy darling Babe to wrench,
but thy sweet Self doth honour not, and thee
doth want to vanish. Laws of God serve with
thy Heart, with all thy Soul thy Children all;
but laws of men serve with thy lips alone.
Sublime, far-off, magnificent and proud
I want thee, smiling on the Grief of things
like marble monuments because I say so!
And thine shall be the Tears and then the Crown,
and thou shalt live the Sorrow and the Calm
of Tragedy, but Grief shall crush thee not.
Sublime, far-off, magnificent and proud
I want thee, that the herd may say how proud

thou art, and so that thou may let them say
their say.
Sleep sound in Thunder. Insult-blows
shall crush thee never. Let the Elements
arouse thee with the sweet, serene sensation
of Just Revenge and Vengeance. Fear thou Hell,
my Daughter; hold God's Revenge in holy Terror.
Not so that thou should then despise thy Body
I tell thee this: but if thou lose thy Soul,
shalt lose precisely Sex and Art. A Soul
sustains that Insult once, and only once:
that Insult drives the Soul insane. Do not
despise the Narcissism of the Masters;
their Pride hath wondrous healing Power. For Dance
and Sacred Song restoreth broken Spirits
so that the Soul may soar upon the Insult
with which Existence sends all Pretensions crashing.
Rejoice in Thunder. God is Just.
Thy Heart
thy only Guide, strive thou to be thyself
and live for that unto thyself alone.
Love nothing but what worthy is of heart-
felt Love. Great Verse, great Music, let them dwell
within thy Soul all day. Dream thou beneath
the metre's curb. Strive to refine thy Dreams,
because bad Dreams materialize no less,
and love Philosophy which sounds archaic
because 'tis timeless: not archaic, but timeless.
Let all thy Powers strive to come together
around the beauty of these things as moons,
shattered to bits by pebbles in the stream,
come all together once again. Let all
thy Powers cleave around the Truth in Jest:
Theology is a clean Joke, no more,
but learn it. Live the Good Life in all its shades
of Meaning: they are one just as thou art.
Thou shalt, perchance, read much, and many voices
disturb thee such that thou shalt then become
a wilderness of personalities. Let
them cleave together round thy heartfelt core

as if they were the Many, thou the One
and Only.
Just as God is Three in One,
both Hell and Heaven shall - the Lord and the Lord's Devil -
thy various sensibilities unite,
just as twin eyes, though two, are one in sight,
around a small, round insult, red and white!

*18th December 1990*

## QUEEN SARAH THERESE TO HER DADDY[116]

*on the day of her first Holy Communion*

**MY DADDY** is a Man like the Lord,
and God is an Artist like Shakespeare;
and My Daddy is an Artist like God,
and God is a Man like My Daddy.

**I** love My Daddy as I love God,
and I am His Queen, Her Divine Majesty
Queen Sarah Therese, because that is what My Daddy
calls Me; and I am a Queen like the Virgin Mary!

**THE** Blessed Virgin beeth God the Mother;
and I am God My Daddy's daughter ...

*2nd May 1993*

---

[116] Originally issued in **In the Suburbs of Europe;** reissued in **Lamplighter most Gracious** *(Collected Poems).*

**Sarah Therese Ruggier**
Born 3rd March 1986

## WATCH-DOGS FOR SARAH[117]

**I DREAMT** I saw two beasts draw close one night,
my daughter, and each one gently say: "Master,
let me protect your child!" Each held itself
erect – two man-like beasts I saw, shoulders
and face two men, the rest colossal dogs!
I shook their hands. "If this be Heaven-sent,"
I prayed, "protect my child, my Faerie Queene!
Beyond what I can utter, Love is blind
for Sarah Therese my Queen!" And shaking hands
with each I said to each: "I am a Man,
and what I did I did out of a need
I may not utter. The gods demanded it.
Inspiration ebbed and flowed but I made

---

[117] Originally issued in **Lady Vancouver;** reissued in **Lamplighter most Gracious** *(Collected Poems).*

Pope Caesar Art, and burnt a sacrifice
for greater needs than mine, humans for whom
Salvation lay beneath a lock and key!
With tears let me thank you, beasts of the wild:
protect my Faerie Queene! Let not the stranger
draw close with his contumely and impest her
or intrude upon the dignity of her Spirit
to abuse the awful covenant she shares
with me alone as if these were his toys!
Watch over her with eagle eyes,
Beasts whom the Lord hath sent us,
that she may sleep untroubled, blithe and chaste,
like Prospero's daughter. Trouble her not!
tell her not you lie beside her, watching,
day and night as if you her Angels were!
I pray you though, with fearsome fangs devour
dissembling suitors all. Allow not one
his villainous powers to test upon her mettle!"

Weeks later I spoke to Sarah in her ear
of my sad, unhappy temper: "I do not want
anyone but you to pray for me, my daughter!
I grow tired, beloved, aging slowly,
like the historical peasant suffering much
to make a little …
I wish for no-one's prayer but your own!

They breed all round me, the people's double faces:
the joys of youth are now unhappiness and tears!
Not so the hug you gave, not so the art-show
in those, your blessed eyes!
Angel I need thee, thy hug,
thy sweet, divinest smiles,
the art-show in thy eyes,
and no-one else's prayer!"

*3rd February 1997*

## A SONG OF GENTLEST REFLECTION[118]

**SWEET** music is not noise
but the sound and real extension of silence -
but silence may be sweeter;
and when I am dreaming let everyone step
more softly.

Whatever sublimities may be expressed,
**L'Amour** is sweeter and all sublimer,
and where Love is there are no sins:
it is not Love
which alters when it alteration finds.

Honours and people are all deceitful,
but acrimony, sanctimoniousness and despite
are of the devil
and good honour is better and far sweeter.

The eyes of little children, my beloved,
see things beyond our ken: say but half the word -
a little child will understand incredible matters
that you can't; doctors of the Church in infancy,
and better than all the visiting professors
from overseas that you or I invented.

A little child's conscience, my beloved,
is straighter than God's Gospel. Terrible indeed
it is to laugh at little children and hold them up
to ridicule against their better judgment.
Only one sin does the poor child commit,
the one with which the taunting adult
belies the children's vision,
their unpolluted conscience and their finer judgment.

Kneel down and ask a child to teach you judgment;
pray to the little ones for vision;
to dream a sweeter dream ask the children
to teach you let's pretend and make believe;
if you are sick of lies, where nothing but lies abound,
beseech the little ones to tell you a beautiful lie,

---

[118] Originally issued in **Songs of Gentlest Reflection;** reissued in **Lamplighter most Gracious** *(Collected Poems)*.

and never believe anyone else's.
Be a staunch believer
in the profound equality between great Artists
and little children: the little beastie makes
the adult swear and shed many a useless tear,
and understands love only and much sincerity;
and shall likewise understand great, private honour
when you adore it, give it one and teach it one.

*6th October 1999*

## CHILD, THE GENTLEST LOVING FAULTS ...[119]

*to a sweet thirteen*

**THE GENTLEST** loving faults are sweetest when
you send your conscience flying. Where Love is
there are no sins. Do thou but heed my thinking,
my fair little one: let no one judge thy conscience;
let no one rile thy funny bone. Despite
is of the devil; priest's acrimony a far
more wicked sin than gentlest loving fault.
Punish it with the sign of Cain. But so that
you may say I am a good philosopher,
loving though it may be, that gentlest fault,
Acrimony a far worse sin than Cause,
on Earth abstain as best you can: it's better
for Wisdom's sake; and solitude is sweeter.
Think no ill, my child, and let thy conscience be,
and come what may - be thou an altruist,
for where Love is there are no tomes nor sins:
but gentlest loving faults are far sincerer
than all the Earth's when they involve neither
another nor children born nor those unborn,
but gentlest you, and thy sweet self alone!

---

[119] Originally issued in **Songs of Gentlest Reflection;** reissued in **Lamplighter most Gracious** *(Collected Poems).*

Child, Wisdom is far sweeter than crass error,
but if you err, that error's slighter far
you err in solitude than with someone else
combined, and other lives involved: stuff Judgment!
stuff acrimony, sanctimoniousness and despite!
stuff conscience! stuff the priest-like Cain and all!
Let none disfigure little children's love,
nor children's error, nor mangle a romance:
let no one judge you, child, nor rile your conscience
with a priest's foul interest in sin alone,
or a neurotic saint's last night's hangover!
Child, cherish Divine above romantic Love
as being more romantic still. Fight for
His trust with Divinity's good secrets as being
far sweeter secrets still than the foul Earth's
indecent entertainment flung to all ears.

*9th October 1999*

## TO A CHILD[120]

**LITTLE** child, little child,
little child of long ago,
little child you are honoured
in the philosophy of Plato the great philosopher,
little girl of long ago
whom God Himself chose out of a book
just as the great Kirin did choose His women,
or just as Jesus chose His dearest mother!

Little child, little child,
blessed, divinest, sincerer child,
beware of born, grown-up deceivers
and subtlest counsellors of fraud!
Fear the revengeful, the vindictive,

---

[120] Originally issued in **Songs of Gentlest Reflection;** reissued in **Lamplighter most Gracious** *(Collected Poems).*

senior, very christian ladies and gents,
who will use beautiful honours
to revenge themselves on the souls of children!
Beware, little child, of those
who will count all your money, fleece you of money,
and give up their own money
to pillage and to murder the sweet child's vision
and your better judgment!

Little child, little child,
the art-show in your dark, sincerer eyes
is diviner than all the sights on earth
a little child will ever see!
Ah little child unfallen, go not astray:
yours is the best brain I know!
Consult your own better judgment, little child!
Be thou a life-long student of your earliest Vision!
Smell the flower of your own unpolluted conscience
before you consult deceitful priests or bibles!

Ah my false honours, little child, are better far
than the sincerity of a thousand christian faces:
devote thyself, dearest daughter, blessed Seer,
to thy own heart and earliest, tenderest love!

*29th January 2000*

## LADY APHRODITE, SWEETEST DAUGHTER[121]

**BEFORE** she was born I thought of her,
before I married a maid I softly prayed for her,
before I formed her in the womb I knew her,
and in the dark I gently called her, 'Daughter',
writing for her lines of sad but sweetest verse.

Child, I've been through hell, I have seen hell,
I suffered the second Death on your behalf —
I went to hell to bring you back upon my shoulders:

---

[121] Originally issued in **Songs of Gentlest Reflection;** reissued in **Lamplighter most Gracious** *(Collected Poems).*

daughter, I was hurt and I was lonely.

In the eternal darkness
I waited for her with profound compassion,
canadian toque and book in hand, a sad, true lover
sorrowing and hurting for the love, the hand
of a Woman, the First Lady of the Poets.

Daughter,
fear me not, be not ashamed, think no ill,
judge naught: were they not all of them
little children once upon a time?
Little One, sorrow never again.
Fear not again. Never cry again.
Woman whom I chose out of a book,
Lady Aphrodite born from the Ocean,
professor visiting *del al di lá*,
goddess reborn and reincarnate by a dogma
I myself defined ...
remember always - how cleverly you crept,
how wordlessly and how silently you stept,
out of the darkness into your father's heart,
and out of your mother's womb.

Child, what suffering I suffer'd!
With you in his arms your father was proud,
and all his ghastly wounds were healing.
Child, you were snatched out of your father's arms
with a crushing, chillingly vindictive,
studied and unspeakable cruelty!

For your dear sake, daughter, I forgive,
but kid me not, be good to me, I deserve
your pity, mercy, and your love.
I never did you harm, never did wrong by you,
nor ever thought ill of you,
and what my heart commandeth me I did.

Daughter, give me your heart.
Now that thou art growing into a Woman,
give me nothing but your hand. Nothing do I crave
but your eternal Love!

*30th March 2000*

## VIRGINIA WOOLF[122]

**WHEN YOU** wrote ***To The Lighthouse***, Virginia,
did you then, that downcast, London day,
reread ***Time Passes***, analyze, and then reanalyze
that terrible and sorrowing loneliness you felt,
surrounded as you were, my dear, by such
vindictive people,
in such petty, facetious, homely images
so well-concealed?

Did you then ask yourself, Virginia,
whether someone else was waiting
between the lines of that simple
and terrible and beautiful work of art,
someone, perhaps as lonely as you were,
perhaps the majestic Keeper
of that majestic Lighthouse
in that ghastly and terrible and magical Landscape?

Why did you not ask yourself, my dear,
whether the Artist in the Lighthouse was,
perhaps, a lot more human than yourself or me?
Do you know at all, did you ever have a clue,
Virginia, who that Majestic Artist was,
might be, or may have been,
who kept the Lighthouse and his far-flung flashlight
displayed and shone full on upon your face,
that downcast, sorrowing, terrible night,
with himself, in the shadows of that Lighthouse,
so closely hidden and so well-concealed?

Did you stop to consider, Virginia,
human though you were like him or me,
suicidal though you were like myself,
unbeliever though you were like so many,
unsuspecting though you were as a child, my dear,

---

[122] Originally issued in **Songs of Gentlest Reflection;** reissued in **Lamplighter most Gracious** *(Collected Poems)*. I consider Virginia Woolf to have been a Woman of Mary's calibre in one of Mary's past lives.

innocent and wicked though you were, Virginia,
just what a simple and terribly beautiful Art
the Artist in the Lighthouse sprang upon you,
with his far-flung flashlight on you?
just what a subtler ring of honesty and truth
and beauty your work of art possesses, perhaps,
than you ever thought it might that terrible day
on which you killed yourself, my dear?

Did you travel, Virginia,
and on your knees, maybe, say thank you
to that majestic Keeper, and kiss his feet,
the great Artist in the Lighthouse
with his far-flung flashlight on you,
and himself in the shadows so well-concealed?

Did you ask yourself, Virginia,
just who on earth was he, that majestic Keeper
that on your feelings wrought such magic?
or did you then merely publish
that simple yet terribly beautiful book
which made you famous,
with an uncalled for feminist curse, perhaps,
on a man such as your friend the majestic Keeper
in the shadows of that Lighthouse,
with his ghastly flashlight,
the flashlight of that great Artist in the Lighthouse?

You should have simply asked yourself, my dear,
whether someone else was waiting there,
perhaps as lonely, perhaps as sorrowful as you were,
perhaps with a heart himself, which your heart only
craved as his own, or whether your heart
told you things your mind did not understand,
and never left me to moan and to mourn,
a few thousand miles away, as I always cry
for a personal lover, a personal friend,
a favourite book, and a personal loss,
your sad, bitter, unconsoled, and lonely end,
with nothing, perhaps, in your dying ears,
nothing perhaps but a voice which hopeless eyewash,
revengeful mockery, and shameless effrontery

may have seemed to you and me? tragic heroine?
tragic romantic idol by a book-lover well beloved?

And who knows, my dear,
if anything wiser would have occurred
to my dull mind and me
in a dilemma just as painful and just as terrible?

*2nd April 2000*

## MARY[123]

**AH MARY**, divinest Witch[124] in Christendom,
divine, blessed Mother, Woman-God,
alone of all Your Sex resplendent, Woman
Whom God the Messiah, from pre-existence, chose,
between the lines, out of a beautiful book,
for His most intimate friend in time, and made
You Alone His Mother, high, divine Priestess
of Messianic Culture ... did You likewise, Mary,
choose your own Son out of a beautiful Book?
Did You likewise, perhaps, pre-exist, a Maid,
as Wordsworth wrote, whom there were none to praise,
and very few to love, in hidden, forgotten
lives, maybe many lives, but honoured by Plato
the Visionaire, in his Philosophy only?
Were You, perhaps, divinest, blessed Mother,
in previous, hidden existence, introduced
to Your Own Divine, future Son, as to Your Lover,
at a top-secret dance, the dance of God,
of Time, Eternity, and of the Hours?

---

[123] Originally issued in **Songs of Gentlest Reflection;** reissued in **Lamplighter most Gracious** *(Collected Poems)*.

[124] The term "Witch", in my own language of the heart, is no more a term of disparagement than the word "Fake" was a term of disparagement in my poem, **Eucharist**. It is intended exclusively as a term of affection and endearment just as a beautiful poet may be called a sorcerer, an enchanter, a bewitcher, or a magician ...

Mary, Woman-Priest of the re-incarnate God,
marriages such as Yours are made in Heaven,
and such-like Lovers are all chosen out
of beautiful Books! Those there be, divinest Mary,
who do not honour You because You are
not God, but many a critic honours the man
he pleases, and many a reader talks of Dante,
the divine Poet, or the divine Artist
Michael Angelo, and many a Poet loved You,
and many an Artist, and many a wise, old Sage,
and many a Man adores You, Mary, though
he may not boast that he is Yours -- so what?
and many a Child, and many a beating Heart!
Gods of the new Religion salute You, Mary,
divine, blessed Mother, Woman-God,
divinest Witch in Christendom .....
The Peace of God be with You, Mary, the starriest
Calm of Art, as of the reddest rose in June!
And sweet, gentlest reflection be my portion
in return for the Poet's softest speculations!
Let Sarah Therese, my dear daughter, speak ...
Helena of my own Book, unique, only Child
of my own Culture .....

*22nd May 2000*

## DIVINEST MARY[125]

**DIVINEST** Mary
Who took care of the Christ-child
when He crept and hid His greatness there,
beneath a Woman's heart,
just as the child in your womb, I say,
just as the child in Elizabeth's,

---

[125] Originally issued in **Songs of Gentlest Reflection;** reissued in **Lamplighter most Gracious** *(Collected Poems)*.

at Your glad greeting leapt for joy,
and Your spirits both rejoiced,
your's and Elizabeth's .....
and just as likewise the child in ours,
as much as in your womb, or in Elizabeth's,
are our Hope, all the Hope
we shall ever be given,
the Promise of a bright new Day .....
divinest Mary
give me children!

I hate You not.
I wish You no ill nor harm.
Mary heed me not
if I was ever provoked to swear.
Mary heed me not
if I bitch and loathe myself
for bitching, and then a Woman-God like You.
Slap me hard once, but forgive me.
Mary, I am ill, far too ill of the thought
of such loathsome things.
I adore You, Mary,
as a Man adores a Maiden
made all of gold and sunlight.
I am spotted compared to You.

Be it done with me
according to Thy Word, divinest Mary.
Not the Word, I say,
of an extremely great supernatural God,
above all and topmost --
which always made me feel
so very little, Mary,
so cuttingly discouraged,
so cruelly bruised beneath His heel:
but the Word of a Woman-God,
which makes my heart
leap and rejoice like Yours
when the child rejoiced
beneath Your heart and beneath Elizabeth's!

Just a verse, divinest Mary,

made of naught but breath between us,
made of naught but of my love and Yours.
If I publish it, divine blessed Maid -
as is the vogue with poets -
be not taunted,
be not insulted,
and if You say, tear it,
I'll tear it, Mary;
but ever I shall retain untarnished,
fleshed out and etched in the heart's red blood,
the memory of my sweet golden love
for eternal youthful You.

*31st July 2000*

## POETRY IS ..... [126]

*to my Mother*

**LIKE** cooking, like darning clothes, poetry is
a loving skill, a stitch in time, like all
good deeds - a nobility in the blood, much like
the genes themselves, fruit of the womb prepared
at conception, with lifelong labours purchased.
Gifts of the Spirit, knowledge of Art - together
with negative ability - are both
required theological virtues,
the Arts being a viable vocation for
the millions, who have naught besides.  It's bad,
it's wrong to say that poems make nothing happen:
like grains of mustard seed, great poems are acts
of Faith - Faith in oneself, as much as in
a mightier Spirit capable of moving mountains;
prayers for and upon the Soul of Man.
Itself by Man created, Dante called it

[126] Originally issued in **Songs of Gentlest Reflection;** reissued in **Lamplighter most Gracious** *(Collected Poems).*

*'the grandchild of God'*: great Art created jobs,
and employment for masses upon masses
of worthy people. It is the '*Caus Causarum*'
of what one may call the most momentous event
of all, the silent, interior conversions, the changes
of heart, of dreary, habitual thought, which with
a change in Art, like change of scene, brighten
upon this Earth the light of common day,
and which God only knows, and only He
can keep thereof the records, documents,
and profoundly historical chronicles.

*2nd October 2000*

## SAINT MARY CHRISTIAN[127]

*an elegy for my mother, Marie Ruggier*
*7th February 1925 – 29th April 2008*

**SAINT** Mary Christian made her family one prophecy only:
*"You will seek me and will not find me!"* And was wont
to say: *"the Heart forecasts and foretells upon intuition!"*

I was hungry. My Mother gave me to eat.
I was thirsty. My Mother gave me to drink.
I was naked. My Mother clothed me.
I was bedridden. Mother watched and prayed beside me.

All in all a simple soul, Mother was
most capable, and most clever at what she did well.
She was everywhere, she did everything:
the heartbeat of our family. Every day
she cooked three meals from scratch, proof of her love,
for father and all seven of us: her cooking was,
in its own right, a unique, genuine cuisine —
the proudest thing in her devoted life.

---

[127] Originally issued in **Lamplighter most Gracious** *(Collected Poems)*.

She did the laundry, washed dishes, knitted wool,
(and scarves with the colors of our favourite soccer club),
sewed our clothes, helped us all, with father, with our
schoolwork,
and often read my writings. We took her quite for granted,
but
we loved her all—except when she yelled, and then
we would all hate her for what she elegantly described
as *"behooving sin"*!
Her frugality was a work
of exquisite art: nothing was wasted,
all scraps of food consumed, and the leftovers
went to the birds … With father, she economized
fractions of cents, supporting all seven of us
on pennies—not a lifestyle
that I could ever grow accustomed to;
but excellent for publishing poetry …

Feminists will look askance at her lifestyle, arguing that
the quality of her life could have been better: one ignores
a movement such as Feminism at one's own peril;
but Mum and Dad would say that Love
is the only quality of life there is; and Salvation
the only sincere honour!
Though she cared for the Arts,
Mother did not know better: to adjust her vision
to feminist viewpoints called for a contradiction
to everything she knew, everything she learnt,
and was conditioned to be, since early childhood,
by her own parents and upbringing;
a major readjustment which could have
positively unhinged and unsettled her.

Mum and Dad
were happy, a Man and a Woman, permanently in love,
always getting along: their Marriage was a sacred Memory
of a traditional Past; with no guarantee
that modern marriages are happier!

The Mother who, with untold self-denial,
bore us, bred us, fed us, clothed us, educated us,
and every day said prayers with us … is in her grave:

but her spirit of prayer knew no bottom,
Mass and her Rosary being her favorite charms—
her frugal way of maximizing fractions of idle Time!
Laying up treasure for herself in Heaven,
she lives on in the fragrance of her prayers!

May the Divine Will be fulfilled
in her Life and in her passing!
May the Saints she loved immerse her
in God's bottomless Mercy;
invoking upon her holy Soul
the infinite blessings of Divine Mercy!
And may Saint Mary Christian
still pray for all of us below …

*1st May 2008*

### A SEQUENCE OF SIX POEMS IN FREE FORM

## Poem 6: upon Vancouver's pavements green ...

**IF I COLLAPSE** and fall down dead upon the pavement,
if I drop down dead right here like a cone falling from a
tree,
will You be there to greet me, with Proserpin gathering
flowers
beside You, in the classic-laid rose garden? upon the gold
brocade? Will Mary the Beloved be there likewise?
Will You be there to meet me? to kiss me upon my cheek
the kiss
of merciful Love? to grab by the stem this sensitive Plant
which is withered, and to snap it tight once more,
to snap it proud and right? to slip into my dead grasp
my ticket and my wages? my cheque for my next
twenty-years' tuition? and my certified copy
of the word-processor designed by God for me?
Will You be there to help me recoup my losses? to tell me--

be it done with you according to your Faith?
according to the great Hope inside you,
in the shadow of which you lived?

... will anyone I know
carry me away upon a Shield?
*17th April 2001*

## A LITTLE GIRL OF LONG AGO[128]

*notes for a new Religion presented as a Poem ...*

**Prose Abstract**

**Baudelaire's version** of pacts with Satan conceals wicked humor directed against the hypocrisy of Society. The critics let him get away with it because it is both humorous and candid. *The Devil is far more sensitive than human beings, to the Arts and to the insult he suffers: it is equally true that he is converting. You do not have a right to snap with an insult as you please not even a poor devil. You are not an Angel so privileged.*

The only purpose of this Author's version of a pact with a devil is Salvation. His intentions are not as tendentious as Baudelaire's. All he is asking is to be judged with an open mind and allowed to get away with it as the critics allow Baudelaire.

The core tenet of New Religion is the Redemption and Salvation of the damned through Reincarnation. Despite its emphasis upon the universal virtue of Compassion,

--[128] First issued in *Lady Vancouver, 9 poems by Joe Ruggier, (1997),* **A little girl of long ago** was re-issued in *Lamplighter most Gracious, collected poems and selected prose, (1972-2009)*, in the original length of 2 pages, now expanded to 7. It was re-issued also in the 7-page version in **Pope Caesar's Wake**, my book of *letters to Pope Woytyla.*

New Religion is not Christianity: Christianity does not acknowledge Reincarnation, not even as a Purgatory, nor does Christianity encourage making Artists — the reward promised by new Religion unto all who practice the Mercy of saving lost Souls in this manner.

Yet New Religion is a sister Religion to Christianity. It gathers together and absorbs what is best in all the Religions of the World, Buddhism, Hinduism, Confucianism, even Islam, Judaism, other Systems, as well as Plato's Faith in Reincarnation, bridging the gap between Christianity and all other Religions.

New Religion is neither Christianity nor a spoke in the wheel of Christianity. It is not an antagonist, engaged in a power struggle, but a fine tuning, a competitor as a competitor should be. Christianity and new Religion may be practiced together as long as one makes the required leap of Faith that *Reincarnation* is but another way of saying *Purgatory*: in this instance another chance, a trial, a test, and truly a Purgatory, with a real chance to regain Paradise, for the lost; a golden opportunity to set right all the bad things you did in a past life, especially if you lost your dear Soul, as long as you repent of all the mistakes of your past existence!

Countless folk in modern society boast three University degrees and more in poetic effects, feelings and sentiments. Let them but practice the Mercy of saving poor devils in the manner in which I am teaching it … God Himself will give them solid academic credentials in Mercy and Compassion as well as bless them forever with His Own Love, Mercy and Salvation in such a way that they shall themselves never again become lost souls in need of the dogma of Reincarnation!

It is the Author's prayer that New Religion will teach all people to contemplate eternal damnation with profound Compassion, without losing their cool and their nerve.

**The Poem**

**A Wise** Man sat upon the Seat of Honour
in ancient China, and said unto His Daughter:
"I love you much, Beloved, heed what I say!
Know that before your birth I knew about thee,
that you have lived before and I have read
your work which in your last existence flourished,
and I, thy Padre, loved your terrible beauty,
the divinity concealed in your sorrowing spirit.
Knew also of your tragic end and how,
as a good Man sayeth to me, you went
down to the shades below, which made me weep,
My Love, tears that I would weep had my
own little child been lost. Heed what I say!
A little child thou art but you can read,
and when this book which earnt me fame I wrote
to celebrate my marriage vow, I said
these words to thee alone with all my heart,
though you forgotten were. In your spiritual
ear I whispered aery verse the lines
of which concealed my grief and secret love
and with my verse I tempted thee and made
with thee a pact that you my daughter shall
become and may one day rejoice as you
deserve, Thou beautiful, tragic, troubled spirit —
the only poor devil I ever made a pact with —
and never said unto a single soul
a single word within my bosom buried!
Know then, my little one, you're old and wise
enough to be your mother's Blessed Mother!
Let no one then teach you, my troubled Queen,
facts of your life which with my faltering verse
I have said unto you far better than
your teachers can.
........................ From years before Thy birth
I felt for Thy misfortune sorrow intense
and painful, flesh torn from My flesh, without
relief from pain. I ask of Thee a favour:
feel for Thyself the pity and the sorrow
that I felt for Thee. Admire the beauty of

such overpowering, tragic pathos —
but save Thy dear Soul: Salvation is
egoism as God wanteth, Damnation not.
Love and untold riches shall be Thy portion
for bearing with **Me** the most cruel insult.
I am reborn just as Thou art. Kirin's
Incarnation is Kirin's Reincarnation.
He and His Mother chose each other just
like Me and Thee. I was choked and knowing not
how best to say it! I am poor as Lazarus,
but Thy reward is the Honour of Thy dreams —
a gift of beautiful imagination
to bring Thee Joy in Solitude, whenever
Thy Honour shall flash upon Thy inward eye —
and being a Genius at school, as Padre was.
The time shall come when I shall make Thee rich:
for suffering with **Me** the cruel insult
You deserve the Jackpot!
Beloved Daughter, know
that I have chosen Thee out of a Book
just as the great Kirin did choose His Mother,
two poor devils who could not be consoled
without each other! Were they not all of them
little children once upon a time?
no guile? nor malice in their eyes? misled
by the World? by untold temptations scatter'd?
by fast ones led away to endless ruin?
Thy brows with roses red forever crown'd,
I declare herewith the Reincarnation of
poor souls in need a dogma of the Faith
which with My Sacred Heart inscribe on Thine,
high, divine Priestess of future Culture,
around Whose Honour all the Creeds of Earth
have been united in one common effort
to win Mercy for all Mankind, though lost
throughout the Centuries — born again Christians
as Buddhists teach and Hindus, and the great
Confucius, through a dogma of Rebirth
as majestic as of Resurrection!

God loves dearly the faithful of old Religion
who live Its mourning and mortification
without making anyone insults too great to bear.
They did to Me, and I deserve truer Religion.
True Religion is pregnant with new Religion,
and new Religion calls all Mankind to Mercy —
save a fiend to win Thyself God's Mercy!
Unless We have Compassion on the damned
nobody shall, and We may still be lost
and in despairing need for such a Miracle,
and no one heed Our hoarse, despairing cry,
and no one have Compassion on Us either.
To save Thy Soul save a poor devil, such as
Thou art; Thou art not Angel so privileged!
God may still abolish Hell forever. Instead
He may establish the Reincarnation of
poor souls in need as the alternative,
postpone the Judgment through a Faith like Plato's,
and charge, perhaps, the bill for many lives,
demanding pact and truth of countless lovers —
just one more way of saying: **"Purgatory!"**
To say once more that **God is not a sadist!**

What do some Humans think they are? — to feel
so privileged, though they be not, as to make
some others demons just because their Padre,
because He loves them, gives them second birth,
because He wishes them a second chance?
Do not fear, gentle Daughter, I boast
a history just like Thine, and I accept
the Judgment with Thee in writing. Repent of all
the faults of Thy past Life. Real Glory
lieth in freedom from the cycle of
Rebirth. Pray for Salvation only. Pray
for Resurrection. Rebirth is but a Purgatory,
which God allows the worthy for real reasons only!

Only the wicked do not acknowledge Hell:
we must, if Truth, affirm its Truth! Rebirth
is but a viable alternative
for all poor Souls who need rehabilitation:

God is not a sadist! We all implore Him
to consider this well-made suggestion … that all
may be allowed to earn Salvation, proving
to God Himself how merciful they are!

No living Man or Woman is owned by Demons.
Let all Mankind take turns, with works of Art,
and with their Love, to save poor souls in need,
and save them well, one fiend at a time!
Old Faith and New vaunt equal power to save you:
God respects entirely your freedom to Choose!
*Call it Thy own pro-choice Philosophy —*
*You have a right to choose the Child You bear,*
*but You must love and cure Her as I did,*
*or 'twill be worse twice over for that poor Devil!*
*Prescribe Your wish to God Himself in prayer,*
*allowing God to offer You the Choice!*

Be good to Thy poor devil. Devils care
for works of Art. They shall prove sensitive
to Thy creations, concerned as these should be
with the harsh blow They suffer. Help Them bear
Their insult with a well-intended honour,
to save their face and show them that You care —
and Thy reward shall be Salvation, Thine Own
and all You love, for all of Whom Thou shalt
win Mercy. Thou shalt become a beautiful
Artist, as Thy recompense for boasting heartfelt
Mercy, and shalt be paid with money made
of silver, gold, jewels and precious stones!

I have no evidence but intimations.
Throughout My sixty years, since early childhood,
My recollections brought Me but one Story.
I was a Poet in My native tongue,
most minor, though I took pride I was the first
to grace with verse My language. All My life
My Aunt encouraged Me, and I believed her
because I loved her — Conchita was her name.
But I lay dying and I told My Aunt:
*"Surely You will give Me the honour, when*
*I'm gone, just as You did in Life!"* She said:

*"Do you not know how musical, how complex*
*the foreigner's Art all is? What theories It*
*conceals between the lines? How can I give*
*the Honour to a Poet such as You?*
*John Anthony? You are too small for words!"* It was
the Gospel Truth: John Anthony was most minor —
but all she did was to revenge herself
and stoke Me in My dying minute! She should
have left Me up to God — Who doth not hate Me!
I did not die well and I lost My Soul,
galled and bedevilled in My dying Hour,
and told the Gospel Truth with wrong intent,
but still recall Kirin, gently talking
to Me in Hell: *"You suffered a gross injustice,*
*John Anthony, and I shall give Thee birth again.*
*I shall make Thee a Poet famous with*
*the foreigner, writing in another tongue —*
*a chance to save Thy Face and make the point*
*that Thou art capable, not as Auntie said!*
*protecting Thee from false compliments like hers!*
*Beware the Falsehood of parading as*
*great Artist be Thou not the real thing!"*

Though I was born again, incarnate just
like God, though but a poor, defenceless Babe,
My memories all fled and wiped out clear,
by Recollection of past Life deserted …
the Priests laughed up their sleeves at Me, saying:
*"There is no other God but God, nor any*
*other true Religion except for Ours,*
*which states Reincarnation is not true,*
*and therefore We baptize this Child a fool,*
*and in top secrecy murdering his daemon,*
*and hold him up to scorn with aftertime*
*for claiming Reincarnation as his door to Fame!"*

**Figlia,** Kirin's Secret and His Beata Madre's
hath blossomed in Our Heart like a blossoming Flower.
My Cause and Thine is just as any Priest's:
a Man and a Woman deserve truer Religion –
their true Religion is bust who with true Religion

can only bust us! Scoundrels who, neither Saints
nor Artists, neither here nor there, still love
to dominate and lay it down as if
they were Church Doctors — but their skull is thick
and heart not tender: their true Religion alone
is beyond criticism, and any other
enjoys no sense in which it is true also!

**Figlia**, I was healing — with Thee against
My Heart, but Thou wert snatched out of My arms!
**Figlia**, a Woman has no right to fight
the Man who loves Her for their mutual Honour:
either You love Your Man sincerely, and He
shall honour You, or You may be sent packing
where Kirin Himself in Your past Life did send You!

**Figlia**, the pact We made was crystal clear:
Thy Padre went to Hell to bring Thee back
upon His shoulders, on condition only
that Thou wilt save Thy Soul. He doth not wish
to go to Hell for Thee again. Salvation
is in good taste, but not Damnation. If
Thou wilt not save Thy Soul, We shall both lose
the argument, a pact with Satan gone sour
and not Our way, and Thou shalt but incur
Thy sorrowing, heartbroken Father's deadly Wrath!

Know also, Thou tragic, sorrowing, troubled Spirit,
discussing facts of life is then for Thee
forbidden fruit, for in such trivial truths
much lying is and all things seem, and many
little ones like Thee have gone astray
by fast ones lost and slain, and been denied
the beautiful Sun, the terrible *claire de la Lune*,
and starlight shedding balm on secret Love,
by trivial truth incullionated. Forget it then,
My Beautiful! Touch not forbidden fruit!
Be happy with what you know and seek no more
save for the useful skills you learn at school;
and keep thy word same as thy Father did!
The eyes of little children, my Beloved:
the art-show there is all I wish to see –

Lady Aphrodite born from the Ocean;
professor visiting *del al di là*!

Drink of the good Honour which I have given,
My little one, whom I have given fame
for ever for the effect We both produced!
We were but two poor demons, but are not
the Bastard's property, to snap in two
with insults as He pleases, though He was never
Angel so privileged! True though it may be
I was a poor devil, confounded in My thoughts,
I prayed with You and felt Compassion, and prayed
for Your Salvation: I was never ever
the real Satan! You are such a poor devil —
with a straight face, lecteur, which God Himself
gives All, that They may not be caught as long
as They admit! If anyone feels the need
to take revenge, let him pray to Saint Michael,
Whose privilege it is! Thy Padre wishes only
to give Thee Honour like the Queen of Heaven's,
unique and unrepeatable with God's Secret,
like Hers, but different from Hers. *Strew on her*
*roses, roses, and never a spray of yew!*
Woman I chose out of a Book: *"salve*
*alla Regina vestita con il Sole!"*
Thee and Thy **Padre** shall dine at Journey's End
with Kirin and with His **Madre**, with a just revengaunce
upon the prime foundation of Heaven and Hell.

*26th February 1997 – 8th May 2018*

# Part Nine:
# Biography, Reviews, & Index

## Biography of Author

**BORN** in Malta on 26 July 1956, **JOE RUGGIER** immigrated to Canada on 28 December 1981. At the Royal University of Malta he graduated, in 1977, with first class Honours in English. In Malta, he worked as a Teacher and Private Tutor of English Language and Literature. In Malta also, he published extensively, both in the Maltese papers, as well as publications relating to his career as a teacher in schools in Malta. He has published poetry in Maltese; a paper about Malta in the ***JOURNAL OF MALTESE STUDIES***; as well as a book about Malta first released in 1991, viz.: ***IN THE SUBURBS OF EUROPE***. In Canada he obtained the Publishing Certificate from Simon Fraser University.

**MR. RUGGIER** is primarily a poet and literary critic. He has been published significantly in poetry magazines in Britain and has also published in ***MALTESE FORUM,*** a Toronto-based magazine for Maltese immigrants to Canada edited by the late **C. CARUANA.** Published by Pierpont Press, ***THE VOICE OF THE MILLIONS,*** his Selected Poems, appeared in Wisconsin in 1988, and since then the book has run into a 3rd Edition. The 6th, definitive Edition of ***OUT OF BLUE NOTHING*** - his cycle of 24 Shakespearean sonnets which first came out in 1985 and which previously ran into a 5th Edition as a book in its own right - is now featured as Part Four of ***THIS ETERNAL HUBBUB***. The first five editions of ***OUT OF BLUE NOTHING*** have been sold out and this book has attained national bestseller status for a Canadian book of poetry. ***REGRETS HOPES REGARDS AND PRAYERS ...*** , ***LADY VANCOUVER, A RICHER BLESSING, SONGS OF GENTLEST REFLECTION, POPE CAESAR'S WAKE, THIRTY SONNETS, A LITTLE GIRL OF LONG***

***AGO,*** and this volume of ***COLLECTED POEMS,*** are his most recent publications in North America.

**MR. RUGGIER** belongs to an international circle of poets and editors who have committed themselves to reforming the prevailing literary climate by bringing about a Traditionalist Revival in writing. In this regard, **RUGGIER** manages his own small Press, **MULTICULTURAL BOOKS,** and is the Managing Editor and 100% Owner of his own poetry magazine, ***THE ECLECTIC MUSE,*** which he publishes and edits in his spare time with the valued, voluntary assistance of diverse associates. Business qualifications: full-time author and publisher; professional editing, ghost-writing and secretarial skills; desk-top publishing operator; qualified word-processing operator (VVI); qualified typist (Malta); diploma in Publishing (SFU).

**MR. RUGGIER** is also the Author of various private collections of belles-lettres exchanged with British and North American Authors. Released in Minnesota in 1985 by influential friends of Rex Hudson, **RUGGIER**'s book - ***INTELLIGIBLE MYSTERY*** - which deals with the poetry of **REX HUDSON,** a Pulitzer and Nobel Prize Nominee from Minnesota who passed away in August 1996 - was his first major critical work.

**JOE RUGGIER** presently resides in Richmond, British Columbia. His daughter Sarah Therese was born in 1986. She is now a qualified, professionally employed French teacher, has obtained a Masters Degree from UBC, and presently resides in North Vancouver with her mother.

## Other Books by the same Author

Intelligible Mystery (1985)
Out of Blue Nothing (1985)
The Voice of the Millions (1988)
In the Suburbs of Europe (1991)
This Eternal Hubbub (1995, 2004)
regrets hopes regards and prayers ... (1996)
Lady Vancouver (1997)
A Richer Blessing (1999)
Songs of Gentlest Reflection (2003)
Pope Caesar's Wake (2005, 2010, 2013, 2018)
Thirty-One Sonnets (2009)
Lamplighter most Gracious (2009, 2018)
A Little Girl of Long Ago (2015)

## Translations

The Poetry of George Borg —
Translated from the Maltese by Joe Ruggier (2000)

## Cassettes

Moods for Lovers (Cassette) (1993)

## CD-ROMs

MBOOKS on CD-ROM [electronic resource] ...

## Edited by Joe Ruggier

The Eclectic Muse, A Poetry Journal
Volumes 1-23, 33 issues, 1989-2017

**LAMPLIGHTER MOST GRACIOUS:** ***Collected Poems and Selected Prose**, 1972-2009 by Joe M Ruggier* With an author's preface. **MBOOKS OF BC**, ISBN: 978-1-897303-07-8 revised printing July 2009. xxiv + 546 pp. $50.00.

— reviewed by Esther B. Cameron Ph.D. (Madison, WI)

**AS THE** back cover already confesses, this book is not quite a collected works, as it omits the poetry and prose published in This Eternal Hubbub (2004). This, however, is mainly a prose collection; its poetic component consists mainly of the sonnet sequence *Out of Blue Nothing* and the long poem *The Dark Side of the Deity*. Thus, *Lamplighter Most Gracious* contains the bulk of Joe Ruggier's verse, as well as much prose.

It is a beautifully-titled work, and there is much that is beautiful in it. Among contemporary poets, Joe Ruggier is one of those most faithful to the tradition of Western poetry. Not only does he frequently use rhyme and meter, and wield blank verse especially in a way that is often very musical, but he has somehow escaped the mandate of flat affect that has trammeled the Anglo-Saxon muse since Auden.

This must be partly due to the fact that Ruggier has not subscribed to the prevailing atheism of the contemporary literary elite. He is a Catholic, though a problematic one; his work is informed by the belief that humans were created in the Divine image with immortal souls, and therefore what happens to us matters terribly. He feels a bond as artist with the Creator. Concerning the slow movement of Beethoven's Ninth Symphony, he writes: "The music, I have always felt, describes the divine beauty of the human spirit created in God's image and likeness." This feeling is, I believe, the fundamental feeling of Western poetry. It was for long deeply rooted in Western consciousness, and could take seemingly-secular forms, as in Millay's "that man was a special creature, no commodity, and improper to be sold." "Post-modernism," which seems finally to have exorcised that faith, still produces "poems"; but they are like bodies without souls.

The freshness of feeling in Ruggier's best work may be attributable to the fact that he comes to the Western world from the isle of Malta, an outlying province of Western culture that was slow to feel the recent decline. In the section entitled "In the Suburbs of Europe," Ruggier writes that though his first words were Maltese, his schooling was in English. There he gained a solid grounding in the Western classics. "In the Suburbs of Europe," first published separately in 1991, contains an essay on Maltese culture and translations of some recent Maltese poets, most notably Dun Karm Psaila's "A Visit to Jesus."

A few lines from that poem:

> It was the Season
> When vines undress and to the lord yield up
> The very last bunches, and the pleasant breeze
> Carries the yellow leaves and a thick low pallor
> Of cloud strains heaven and the very first drizzle
> Of rain begins in due season…

The poem beautifully evokes the landscape of the island and the deserted chapel where the poet, haunted by longing for his deceased mother, receives consolation. Ruggier's comparison of the poem to Wordsworth is, I think, apt. His translation creates for us an environment where nature was still close and traditional faith was strong. Years after making this translation, Ruggier would recreate something of this atmosphere in his elegy for his own mother, "Saint Mary Christian."

A number of poems are printed in the original Maltese as well as in translation, allowing the reader to glimpse a fascinating language whose core is Semitic while much of its vocabulary is European. Here, a future edition could do with a key to Maltese pronunciation, which appears to be as idiosyncratic as Welsh.

Early in the 1980's, as a young man, Ruggier came with his family to Vancouver and there experienced culture shock, as reflected in his poem "Vancouver":

> Clad smart as print, and trendy, thoughts derailed
> by the rush-hour, souls are racked and nailed
> downtown, drawn tight upon the humming wires

-- a wonderful evocation of the city's effect on the *nerves* of an unaccustomed subject. The poem concludes:

> Withdrawn upon Grouse Mountain, you will find
> how lost you are; and love-sick, tear-blind –
> far from the dreadful din, the nuclear tone –
> how terrified, how unconsoled, and how alone!

That phrase "nuclear tone" recurs; and this reviewer remembers Ruggier speaking, in a phone conversation, of "the terrible nuclear boom of the twentieth century." In May 1985 Ruggier wrote one of his finest poems, "Chrysanthemums for Coffined Eternity," an all-stops-pulled-out howl for the dead of Hiroshima and for the fate of humanity in general. Perhaps it could only have been written by someone not accustomed from the cradle to the "nuclear tone." There is also the villanelle "Warmongers" ("WARMONGERS! Sport, or suicidal rage? ... Prehistoric monsters in this day and age") which hits the nail on the head. To one who has learned to mistrust some uses of the word "peace," it is still good to see the appalling nature of war reflected with uncorrupted feeling and without connection to dubious political agendas.)

Ruggier attended Vancouver University but did not graduate; in 1985 founded his own press, Multicultural Books, which has published his own poetry and that of many others. He also founded *The Eclectic Muse,* which remains one of the few venues for traditional poetry in the English-speaking world. Much of Ruggier's work concerns his personal struggle as a poet outside the various establishments that either make no place for poetry (e.g., one gathers, the Church) or absorb only to defuse it (the universities). He feels himself to be floundering in the gap that opened up in the twentieth century between an etiolated "elite" culture, and a "pop" culture from which spiritual and aesthetic values have been expunged. A number of poems describe a career of selling his work door to door, which is evidently not an easy way to earn a living, or part of one. A wry commentary on this way of life is afforded by "15 Poems of Place," which describes the various dwellings the poet has lived in since coming to Vancouver. In "Lord Joe of the Rood" (addressed "to the arts councils") he justly describes himself as "a war-poet though/ he never went to war."

A fair warning: should any reader out there chance to be a purist of any kind, such a person would need to read this book with patience and charity, for it contains excesses. There are passages of truculent self-praise, of intemperate language; there is some profanity; there is occasional bathos; there are forms that are not completely realized, as though the poet had been comforted by the presence of free verse into relaxing the severity of classical form. But here the poet can point a long-established tradition of skeltonics and dithyrambic poetry, which besides the eponymous John

Skelton includes Christopher Smart, the late Blake, and Whitman. Ruggier's excesses are by and large those of a poet who cannot adopt a "cool" disguise, and who has brought himself to the verge of hoarseness by speaking in a just cause – the cause of a poetry informed by a vision of the Divine Image. The glimpses of such which Ruggier has given the world are well worth the patience, and the price.

reviewed by Esther B. Cameron Ph.D.
*Madison, WI*[129]

**LAMPLIGHTER MOST GRACIOUS**
© Joe Ruggier, ISBN 978-1-897303-14-6, 2nd Edition
Publisher: **MBooks of BC**

— **reviewed by Candice James.**
**Poet Laureate, New Westminster, BC**[130]

**JOE RUGGIER**, a brilliant writer with a unique style, whets our literary appetite with this offering of extremely credible poetry and prose as he presents his erudite offerings to us in **"Lamplighter Most Gracious"**. In this collection of his complete poetical works and selected prose spanning a myriad of years [excluding bestselling poetry published in **"This Eternal Hubbub"**], he takes us down memory lane to wander the pathways of his childhood, replete with impressions of childish fantasies filled with pain and glory, then brings us blatantly back to

[129] The Eclectic Muse, Volume 15, Christmas 2009, *pp. 23-25.*
[130] The Eclectic Muse, Volume 17, Christmas 2011, *p 43*

his present day status as an ‘aging’ man’s struggle with the agony and ecstasy of merely living.

Joe stands tall for human rights in his poems and spills his spirituality through his pen onto the pages in a gentle yet raging parade. He has a penchant for describing the inner workings and slow destruction of the aging process as he stalks the slow moving footsteps of old age. He guides us through a plethora of emotions, running the full gamut from elation to sorrow, as he paints vivid, life-like portraits of those who breathe no more.

He allows us a quick furtive glimpse into the tender, empathetic side of his heart before he yanks us back into the acrid underbelly of society and his cynical darker side, and then throws us head first into the caustic world of where the living has no rhyme or reason to the timbre of man’s melody. Nobody can touch the darkest side of dark as easily and with such grace and surrender while brandishing the sword of heroism and bravado, as the Dark Knight, Joe Ruggier. He allows us to witness him being led into temptation, lingering there in fevered sweat, and then managing to extricate himself for a brief moment, knowing full well the darkness will never cease its quest to envelop him completely.

The raw saw edged rage running rampant through some of his offerings in this book chills and curdles the blood as it flows through our veins. Oh to have lived in woe begotten times long ago that are painted so adeptly with the brush of Joe’s words. It would have been unbearable as evidenced by his poems bearing violent witness to the atrocities inflicted upon the young, the defenseless and the imprisoned innocent, horrendously led like lambs to their slaughter by the world’s charismatic madmen. The pain oozes out; every pen stroke dripping the stench of brutality onto the pages. Joe Ruggier is a master classicist at work, spinning our minds on the axis of abhorrence.

This book is filled with brilliant, historical, lyrical and totally engrossing prose and poesy. Ah yes, **"Lamplighter Most Gracious"** is a stellar work of literature packing a heavyweight punch that rips and shreds the frills and disguises covering mankind's follies; literature that engages a gunslinger's swift bullets to waken the dead and cause the moribund mannequins, the walking dead to open their sleep riddled eyes, take up arms, head for the dance hall of discovery and be the best part of the day of reckoning's showdown of truth. Joe Ruggier will be there, wielding his words of wisdom, brandishing his sword of truth!

This book is a must have for the eclectic mind and the collector's library. It is an eye-opener and a thoroughly worthwhile journey through the pages.

***ABOUT THE REVIEWER:***

**CANDICE JAMES**, Poet Laureate – City of New Westminster, BC; A full member of the prestigious "League of Canadian Poets"; member of Federation of British Columbia Writers; author of three poetry books: "A Split In The Water © 1979 *Fiddlehead Poetry Books*"; "Inner Heart – A Journey © 2010 *Silver Bow Publishing*"; "Bridges And Clouds © 2011 *Silver Bow Publishing*" "Midnight Embers – a Book of Sonnets ©2012 *Libros Libertad Publishing*".

**A RICHER BLESSING:** *Poetry & Prose by Joe Ruggier*
ISBN 0-9681948-3-4. 1st Ed: July 1999; **MBooks of BC**

**reviewed by Virginia Tobin**

HAVING HAD no further experience in writing reviews than having read a few, and having taken a philosophy of literature class for my college major, I am honored that Joe Ruggier has opened himself to my critique of his recent work. Published in July of last year, it is at once a credo, a professional apologetic, a poetic potpourri, and a personal expose.

As a fellow believer, although not of the Catholic tradition, I was delighted to open my gift volume at random to the essay entitled, "The Devotion of Catholics to the Sacred Heart of Jesus." After years of sleeping under a tapestry on my bedroom wall of Jesus and the Sacred Heart, a gift from my also non-Catholic father, I at last discovered the particular significance of this universal Catholic symbol. As a poet, I enjoyed Joe's explanation of the symbolism of its major elements. His conclusion: "The Sacred Heart, the Holy Eucharist, and Love are one and the same thing and our acutest problems, personal and social, stem from a lack of love." Practical suggestions challenged me to apply my faith more specifically to daily life.

One can't read far in Joe's published work without noticing his passion for a revival of neoclassical poetry. In his essay, "A Personal Affair", reprinted in part from THE ECLECTIC MUSE **2:1, Christmas 1990**, Joe tersely quotes T S Eliot: "for the poet who wants to do a good job, there is no such thing as **free verse**." This demand that would-be poets first pay their dues by mastering the classical forms was like a breath of fresh air to me when I first read **The Muse**, after having found not a resonant chord among my college fellow-poets. However, Joe doesn't stop at a theoretical exposition of his philosophy of poetry, but describes subjectively how the creative muse strikes him, and how his books are born. Like many a writer before him, he confides, he drinks wine or beer while his ideas converge. Perhaps as a suggestion of this source of inspiration, a row of wine decanters in a window decorate the front cover of the book. Going beyond a description of the creative process, Joe opens the door to his editorial office, and shares his philosophy and his personal history as a publisher.

Poetically, the volume is rich with examples of the classical, lyrical style Joe promotes. It sings with lines like, "Give me serenity and clear sight: / ... Give me to feel the real Master's might .." in a study on contrasts entitled "Clutter." Among the wide range of themes is environmental degradation: "Earth's bowels are burnt aloud above our head, / ... The seas now lose their spell; we inhale dirt" ("Our Deserted Oceans"). The solution? Not one popularly advanced, but well worth considering. Theology and passionate conviction notwithstanding, in the poem, "Shall it Be Sex or Art?" Joe transparently shares his personal struggle between what he believes and how he behaves: "My blood boils endlessly; I am not chaste."

Joe's wrestlings bring to mind the Biblical Jacob, who, while struggling all night with an unnamed assailant, declared, "I will not let you go unless you bless me." Joe's devotion to Christ, as well as to his art, war with the very human yearnings common to our race. The fruits of his struggles are boldly and generously shared in "A Richer Blessing."

**Virginia Tobin**
*Japan - First N.A. Rights*
*569 words*

## Joe Ruggier, Author and Publisher – an Appreciation by Dr. Philip J. W. Higson President of the Baudelaire Society

JOE M. RUGGIER has earned the respect of other literary figures as an original poet, as a commentator on the aspirations and limitations of humanity, as a critical theorist & companion of other authors, & as a sensitive editor & publisher of their work. He brought great energy and professionalism to the rhyme-revival movement, to which he and his stable of authors are committed. I rejoice to note that this movement can draw added confidence from a revived interest in the deeper mysteries of the earth, such as the eternal and ubiquitous Divine Proportion / Golden Section, which (some of us believe) played an essential role in the birth of the sonnet form. But Joe does not allow his relish for the music in formal poetry to prevent him from appreciating and even publishing other kinds. The either-or mentality is disastrously limiting, no matter to what party the limiters belong; and Joe's mind remains fearlessly open to eclectic enrichment -- that adjective figuring significantly in the title of his poetry journal. Similarly, he has decided not to reject the most up-to-date ways of presenting his and his fellow authors' work to the public. In this world one must at best take on the difficult balancing-act of defending one's lyrical and spiritual autonomy and yet communicating the resulting leaven to others - especially to those who in a world of escalating technical sophistication have (as Baudelaire feared) let their spiritual faculty atrophy. There are some who, elated by the power which modern technology confers, disdainfully dismiss their own humanity and that of others in their cultivation of slick 'communication skills'. Those to whom the inner messages of heart and soul are of supreme importance must fight back against these subtle enemies. I am only guessing, but perhaps it is in this spirit of counter-attack and damage-limitation that Joe Ruggier -- one of the heroic solitaries of present times -- has decided to release no less than nineteen books, twelve of them his own, on Compact Disk so as to maximize their accessibility. I am sure that the results will be worth having, and as he embarks on his new venture I wish this gallant and lyrical spirit well. **P. J. W. H.**

**A RICHER BLESSING:** *Poetry & Prose by Joe Ruggier*
ISBN 0-9681948-3-4. 1st Ed: July 1999; **MBooks of BC**

**reviewed by Tim Lander**

**TWO** things you can say about Joe Ruggier: He will not be popular, his poetry will never be fashionable. If he had a good editor and a conscientous publisher, his book would never have appeared. It is the sort of book that could only have been published by a self publisher. And I am so glad he pubished it.

He says he is a traditionalist, a romantic, but he is more. His ostensibly religious work is full of quirky humour and accidental self revelation as well as very real spiritual and psychological suffering. He quite accurately says that it is poetry that saved him from insanity.

He is an immigrant from Malta, coming to Canada as a 25 year old man. He learnt his English from the Poets at the University of Malta, and this schooling is strong in his work, but his work has a freshness and immediacy, the feeling, the struggle, the suffering are real, there is no sentimentality, though there is perhaps an obsessive personality, but the personality of Joe Ruggier comes over very strongly through poems which start out as fairly standard devotional pieces. His is a poetry of energetic tumbled symbolism, a poetry that leads where it wants to go, a religious poetry filled with anger at the injustices of the world, not a religious poetry that your church going Christian would be likely to accept.

He says: *"It is far better*
*To lead a wholesome life in wild persuasions*
*Than be a wicked Catholic."* -- **The Rule**

And again: *"The Saint will cast*
*A shred of cloth or bone in metal for you;*
*The Poet lays bare his soul. Which is more precious?"*
-- **The Reliquary**

He is a self publishing poet who has made his living and supported his family selling his books door to door. His commitment to his way of life comes through in this passage:

*"Saints*
*Are Saints; they are not fools, they care, but if*
*You care to read me, do not disturb my atoms!*
*Judging of poems you judge of Souls: beware!*
*Are you unworthy?"* -- **The Reliquary**

**Tim Lander**
**Vancouver**

## Index of First Lines

CPSIA information can be obtained
at www.ICGtesting.com
Printed in the USA
LVHW05*2150210618
580945LV00001B/1/P

9 781897 303269